TE DUE

Atlas of the Textural Patterns of Granites,
Gneisses and Associated Rock Types

ATLAS OF THE
TEXTURAL PATTERNS OF GRANITES, GNEISSES AND ASSOCIATED ROCK TYPES

S.S. AUGUSTITHIS

Professor of Mineralogy, Petrography, Geology
National Technical University of Athens
Athens, Greece

Elsevier Scientific Publishing Company
Amsterdam · London · New York 1973

ELSEVIER SCIENTIFIC PUBLISHING COMPANY
335 JAN VAN GALENSTRAAT
P.O. BOX 330, AMSTERDAM, THE NETHERLANDS

AMERICAN ELSEVIER PUBLISHING COMPANY, INC.
52 VANDERBILT AVENUE
NEW YORK, NEW YORK 10017

Library of Congress Card Number: 71-179995

ISBN 0-444-40977-7

With 687 illustrations and 4 tables

Printed in The Netherlands

In Memory of my Father
Panagiotis G. Augustides

Preface

In the present state of the development of the geosciences, it is widely believed that only exact analytical "quantitative" data contribute to the advancement of the science.

In contrast, it is believed that the concept of comparative anatomy and histology of biological sciences is equally useful in the geosciences for the understanding of the textural patterns and their genesis in rocks.

The origin of granites has been a controversial subject for centuries. During the last few decades, a number of books (e.g. Drescher-Kaden, F. K., 1948: *Die Feldspar-Quarz-Reaktionsgefüge der Granite und Gneise*; Drescher-Kaden, F. K., 1969: *Granitprobleme*; Mehnert, K. R., 1968: *Migmatites;* Raguin, E., 1965: *Geology of Granite*; Read, H. H., 1957: *The Granite Controversy*; Sederholm, J. J., 1967: *Migmatites*; Marmo, V., 1971: *Granite Petrology and the Granite Problem*) have been published on this subject discussing the historical development of thoughts and presenting interpretations. However, with the exception of the two books by F. K. Drescher-Kaden, most of the others contain very few new observations on granitic textures.

It is believed that, for the understanding of the granite problem, it is essential first to present a picture of the textural patterns of these rocks and then to attempt to interpret these textures on the basis of the concept of comparative anatomy. The present volume is an Atlas of the most common textural patterns of granitic rocks, and their genetic significance.

S. S. Augustithis

Contents

Chapter 1 | The granite problem and the importance of granitic textures

In the last two centuries, mainly two contradictory [1] theories (magma and granitisation of sediments) with their many variants, have been proposed to explain the origin of the granitic rocks.

The importance of granites was realised early in the course of the development of the geological science and, in turn, the prevailing theories on the origin of the granites have exercised an influential role in the shaping of geological thinking in general. It is, therefore, not surprising that granites have been the subject of a vast number of publications (Hutton, 1788, 1795; Lyell, 1830, 1833, 1838, 1875; Green, 1882; Bowen, 1928; Eskola, 1932a; Backlund, 1938b; Kropotkin, 1940; Niggli, 1942; Reinhard, 1943; Read, 1943/44; Holmes, 1945, Backlund, 1946; Reynolds, 1947d; Bowen, 1947; Goodspeed, 1948a; Drescher-Kaden, 1948; Raguin, 1948/49; Daly, 1949; Misch, 1949a; Perrin and Roubault 1949; Erdmannsdörffer, 1950; Read, 1951; Backlund, 1953; Perrin, 1954; Eskola, 1955; Tuttle, 1955; Tyrell, 1955; Perrin, 1956; Read, 1957; Raguin, 1957; Mehnert, 1959; Walton, 1960; Marmo, 1968; Mehnert, 1968; Drescher-Kaden, 1969; Marmo, 1971) which treat this subject exclusively; and still a greater number of publications make reference to granites in connection with other petrological problems.

Periodically, the literature on the granites has been reviewed and certain explanations have been emphasized over others. (This has been necessary as a result of new information and facts as well as due to the appearance of new explanations or the "reformulation" of old theories.) However, the development of our thinking has not been a simple or harmonic process; often bitterness and polemics have governed the judgement of opposite views.

Whereas the views of the magmatists and transformists have predominated the controversy, a third group has emerged, prepared to make concessions, and accepting evidence from both sides without rejecting either of the two completely; as a result, we often hear the expression "there are granites and granites" introduced by Read (1948):

"Once this (granitisation) has been admitted, we shall realise that rocks with granitic characters have been formed in more than one way — there are granites and granites; some granitic rocks are of igneous origin, others arise by granitisation. We have to examine, however, the possibility of all kinds of granitic rocks, igneous or not, being the consequence of one cause and marking stages in one unified process."

Furthermore, the intrusive character of some granites and particularly their metamorphic aureole have been strong arguments put forward by magmatists, mainly by Rosenbusch (1877), in support of a melt origin (magmatic origin).

In contrast, and with equal right, it has been argued by transformists that transitions from paragneisses to granites and other assimilation evidences signify an ultrametamorphic origin, i.e., transformation of sediments.

Partly as an attempt to harmonise "somehow contradictory evidence" and partly because of the common association of granites with orogenic belts where material mobilisation is more or less acceptable, a convergence of these two opposed views has been formulated in a range of anatectic explanations whereby sediments, under temperature and pressure increase give rise to a melt or by ultrametamorphism give rise to granites (Sederholm, 1907, 1910, 1913 a,b,c, 1923, 1926, 1932, 1934, 1967; Goldschmidt, 1920; Drescher-Kaden, 1926; Quirke, 1927; Eskola, 1933, Wegmann, 1935b; Drescher-Kaden, 1936; Scheumann, 1936, 1937; Erdmannsdörffer, 1939; Koch, 1939; Hoenes, 1940; Drescher-Kaden, 1940; Erdmannsdörffer, 1941a; Drescher-Kaden, 1942; Smulikowski, 1948; Harry, 1951; Hirota, 1952; Kizaki, 1953; Kranck and Oja, 1960; Augustithis, 1960; Barth and Sørensen, 1961; Issamuchamedow, 1961; Scheumann, 1962; Mehnert, 1962; Wenk, 1962; Steuhl, 1962; Härme, 1962; Fourmarier and Anthonioz, 1963; Emmons, 1964; Von Platen, 1965; King, 1965; Härme, 1965, 1966; Dietrich, 1967; Winkler, 1967; Mehnert, 1968). Other anatectic views permit a significant role to juvenile magma.

Sederholm (1907) introduced the term "migmatites" and the concept of palingenesis of magma by the melting of sediments.

Particularly the argument that there are "granites and granites" suggests that every case should be judged on its own merits. Nevertheless, a unifying principle, common to all granites, is the presence of identical textural patterns.

On a tectonic-structural and geochronological basis, often "new intrusive" granites are recognised and the trend is to consider these bodies as true magmatic intrusions (e.g., the Nigerian younger granites). In contradistinction, granitic rocks exhibiting evidence of granitisation (transgression to metasediments and assimilation phenomena) are considered to be of ultrametamorphic origin. However, the distinction between granitised and magmatic granites, on this basis, is no more than arbitrary and no definite textural criteria have been recognised in support of this division.

Recently, a geochemical approach has been introduced based on the ratio of trace elements as a criterion to distinguish between granitised metasediments and "true magmatic granites," which, if such a difference really exists, might render useful information and, in conjunction with other structural and petrological evidence, could in cases be applicable. However, it will be difficult to distinguish between an anatectic granitic intrusion and granitisation of sediments without passing through a melt phase. In both cases initial sedimentogenic materials have been mobilised and differences in the ratios of trace elements would not signify fundamental differences in material derivation. Nevertheless, it is hoped that this geochemical approach to differentiate between juvenile magmatic and granitised products can be used.

Differences in the ratios of trace elements have been successfully applied to distinguish between terrestrial and extra-terrestrial materials, e.g. volcanic glasses from tektites (corresponding moon and earth rocks – Apollo 11. Conference, Houston, Texas, 1970); however, in this case, we are dealing with material of different initial stock, i.e., a case of extrapolation, whereas in contrast, distinguishing between granites of different origin is a case of intrapolation and this will be difficult.

In addition to the possibility of differences in the derivation of material, the granitic rocks exhibit compositional variations which are beyond the limits of the definition of a granite: "a granite is a deep-seated igneous (or eruptive) rock composed of quartz, alkali-feldspar and ferro-magnesian minerals such as biotite, amphibole or pyroxene, in grains sufficiently large to be distinguished by the naked eye, and possessing a texture produced by the crystals as a whole interfering with one another's free development." Whereas the definition of the "ideal granite" may fit a handspecimen, very often it does not apply to a granitic complex which shows great variations in composition including "foreign" structures and textures. Strictly speaking, chemical-composition limits can hardly be applied since transitions from granites to more basic phases (even amphibolites) are common. In addition to the granitic marginal phases rich in "xenoliths", basic portions as integral parts of granitic complexes are not uncommon.[1]

Considering the 'mode' to distinguish between "granitised and magmatic granites", the present aim is to illustrate, describe and interpret the common textures and textural patterns in granites of "supposed diverse origin" and to compare these textures and patterns with those of paragneisses and metasediments. Furthermore, a comparison of well-established metablastic growths in metamorphics with the endoblastic growths in granites is included; it shows that the endoblastic growths are not deuteric (secondary) but of primary building importance in the transformation of initial sediments or metasediments to granitic rocks.

In contrast to the views that the granitic textures are the result of deuteric post-crystallisation mobilisations and reactions (i.e., secondary effects produced after the consolidation of the granitic magma), a careful study of textural patterns of granitic rocks reveals the stage-by-stage changes and processes responsible for the transformation of metasediments to granitoids and granites. The textures of the granitic rocks reveal the true history of the rock formation.

It should be pointed out that the endoblastic growths are in reality metablastic, i.e., metamorphic traits, and are recognisable also in granites which show an intrusive character and which are free from subsequent influences of metamorphism. The interpretation of endoblastesis as a metasomatic trait (i.e., endoblastesis = metablastesis) in granites, is supported by detailed textural evidence.

---

[1] These material inhomogeneities in granitic complexes are believed by magmatists to be either more basic differentiates or xenoliths in the process of assimilation by the engulfing granitic magma. In contrast, the transformists regard these as portions or parts of more basic metasediments left as relics in the process of granitisation.

Chapter 2 | Granitisation: A process of the geological cycle

"Granites in their composition and texture Hutton considers that they cannot be in the original state of (their) creation, since nature would be considered as having operated in an infinite diversity of ways, without that order and wisdom which we find in all her works; for here would be change without a principle, and variety without a purpose." (loc. cit., p.313)

H. H. Read *(The Granite Controversy, 1957, p.51.)*

The configuration of the earth's crust and, to a great extent, the building up of its outer part, is the result of the geological cycle. The beginning of the geological cycle can be considered the formation of the atmosphere, the operation of which on the initial "star crust" resulted in the initiation of the geological cycle.

The operation of external agents through the process of rock weathering and erosion resulted in the denudation of land masses. Further, the so-made-available material entered into another physical environment and passed into the stage of aggredation. Sedimentation, diagenetic processes and subsequent endogenetic movements formed new land masses (also volcanism).

This cycle of processes, namely destruction and reconstruction of land masses, is the fundamental idea of the concept of the geological cycle. In contrast though to the outlined cycle of processes, the rock masses, products of aggredation, often are subject to further changes by the operation of endogenetic causes in a geotectonic environment of orogenic belts. Whereas weathering can be considered as the breaking down of minerals, metamorphism is the opposite process.

In the case of weathering minerals which are unstable under atmospheric conditions, mainly minerals formed under conditions of higher temperature and pressure are susceptible to mineral disintegration processes, with the result that minerals stable under atmospheric conditions are produced. In contrast, metamorphism is the building up of minerals stable under conditions of higher temperature or pressure — physical conditions which are prevailing in the realm of metamorphism. To the development of our knowledge on metamorphism and metamorphic rocks the following contributions have been of importance: Lyell (1830, 1833, 1838, 1875); Becke (1904); Grubenmann (1910); Daly (1917); Cloos (1922); Goldschmidt (1922); Becke (1923); Tilley (1924); Harker (1932); Eskola (1932b); Reinhard (1935); Erdmannsdörffer (1936); Fyfe et al. (1958); Palm (1960); Winkler and Von Platen (1957, 1960, 1961); Winkler (1965); Den Tex (1965).

The metamorphism of sediments can be seen as a progressive process which, ultinately, through the process of ultrametamorphism and rheomorphism, could reach anatexis and palingenesis.

Granitisation has been defined by MacGregor and Wilson (1939, p.194) as follows: "We define granitisation widely as the process by which solid rocks are converted to rocks of granitic character. This includes all such processes as palingenesis, syntexis, transfusion, permeation, metasomatism, migmatisation, injection, assimilation and contamination, as used by various authors but rarely with well-defined meanings."

In addition to the classical contributions on the subject by Erdmannsdörffer, Drescher-Kaden, Read, Wegmann, Backlund (reference to their work is made in relevant sections of the present atlas), a great number of publications exists dealing with granitisation in general or describing specific cases e.g., Reynolds (1943, 1946); Erdmannsdörffer (1948); Eskola (1948); Read (1948); Misch (1949, a, b, c); Eskola (1950); Chao (1951); Ramberg (1952); Rösler (1953); Härme (1958, 1959); Engel and Engel (1960); Gavelin (1960); Drescher-Kaden (1961a).

Within the realm of ultrametamorphism is the granitisation of sediments. The transition of sediments to paragneisses (metasediments) through "migmatisation" and ultimately to granites, represents progressive processes in accordance with the classical views of transformists.

The stage-by-stage change of initial sediments to paragneisses and migmatites and ultimately to granites, can be attributed to internal static mobilisation processes such as recrystallisation and blastesis, and to material mobilisation which represents metamorphic-metasomatic processes and as such belongs to the realm of metamorphism which is a stage in the geological cycle.

In contrast to these granitised metasediments, granites with true intrusive character and field relations exist. Detailed textural studies reveal metamorphic traits in granitic bodies showing an intrusive character comparable and commensurable to that observed in granites formed by ultrametamorphism of sediments.

3

The question arises how can we explain the simultaneous existence of metamorphic traits and intrusive character exhibited by the same granitic body and how far can we accept a granitisation (in the sense of Read[1]) origin for granites indicating intrusive character? In what physical state was the granitic material at the time of its intrusion?

---

[1] Granitisation means the process by which solid rocks are converted to rocks of granitic character without passing through a magmatic stage.

Chapter 3 | Granite: An earthy rock

Due to chemical differentiation, a layering of the earth has taken place representing compositional differences and having different geophysical properties. The initial earth crust would theoretically be a product of such a differentiation.

On experimental evidence, fractional crystallisation is considered to be a mechanism of chemical differentiation, which, in turn, can explain the differentiation of rock types. The Bowen-Niggli concept of petrographic provinces is based on chemical differentiation of a cooling melt. The differentiation trend of a cooling magma, i.e., ultrabasic → basic → intermediate → acid could theoretically explain certain acid rock types. However, the extensive granitisation of the basements and the granitic intrusions associated with orogenic belts contradict a magmatic differentiation, due to the absence of proportional basic material associated with granites. Perhaps the Bowen-Niggli concept fits more the volcanic petrographic provinces where rock types could be explained by the principle of chemical differentiation, e.g. the olivine and tholeiitic basaltic differentiation trends. Read (1957, p.81) states: "Whilst the amount of the visible acid volcanic rocks like rhyolite appears to be of the right order to be derived by crystallisation - differentiation from the visible basalts, the gigantic volume of granitic rocks is, in my opinion, an unsurmountable objec-

tion to this theory. After all, what has to be explained is what is seen in the crust, not what is seen in 'the bottom of a little crucible'."

It is too early to conclude on the petrography and composition of the moon's crust; nevertheless, the results of the Apollo 11 exploration (Kushiro et al., 1970) showed that acid differentiates, in a phase of mesostasis and representing 10% in proportion can be present in basic lunar igneous rocks. Micrographic intergrowths, feldspar/quartz (see Fig. 366) also support the possibility of acid volcanic rocks on the lunar crust. However, it should be emphasised that acid volcanics (i.e., rhyolites) are not the effusive equivalent of granites. Despite comparable chemical composition, the granitic textures reveal a metamorphic-metasomatic origin which, in turn, indicates products of the geological cycle, i.e., the granite is an earthy rock.

An important geotectonic environment of ultrametamorphism and of granite formation is in the root zone of geosynclines. This, in turn, explains the association of granitic rocks and orogenic belts. The extensive occurrences of granitic rocks in the shield areas (basements) is again in accordance with the association of granitic rocks with the orogenic belts since the basements are built up of successive orogenic belts.

Chapter 4 | Crystalloblastesis

"A mineral separating from an igneous magma grows, like a crystal of salt suspended in its saturated solution, by the tranquil addition of a layer upon layer under more restraint than is implied in viscocity and surface tension. In metamorphism there is no such freedom. The growing crystal must make a place for itself against a solid resistance, and is to be conceived as forcibly thrusting its way outward from its starting point. In consequence of the constraint so imposed, metamorphosed rocks of all kinds come to have a particular structure, or class of structures, for which we adopt Becke's term crystalloblastic, connoting the idea of spouting or shooting (βλαστανω)."

Alfred Harker (*Metamorphism*, 1950.)

Igneous petrography considers a crystal growth to be the result of a physico-chemical state of equilibrium between the crystal and its surrounding melt. In a comparable way, metamorphic petrology considers a crystalloblastic growth to be in a state of physico-chemical equilibrium with the rock in which it has been formed. A crystalloblastic growth is the result of the metamorphic and metasomatic reactions and processes within a rock. However, in contrast to classical metamorphism which regards a blastic growth as the result of a state of equilibrium of the crystalloblast and the bulk of the rock, a crystalloblast should be seen as a topometasomatic growth (topomorph) in the sense that it is formed at a locus within the rock as a result of restricted local reactions of the mobilised material and its "micro-environment" surrounding the crystalloblast.

A crystalloblast is a growth not necessarily in a physico-chemical equilibrium with the bulk of metamorphosed rock, but the reaction product of the mobilised material (metasomatically supplied by diffusion and intergranular transportation) and of the material within the locus and its immediate surroundings, i.e., a crystalloblast is an individual.

In a sense, crystalloblastesis is a static process, i.e., a crystallisation in a solid environment under pressure without necessitating the operation of dynamic influences (stresses).

However, crystalloblastesis (parablastesis) also can be the result of tectonic influences, in the sense that it is a recrystallisation (breaking down of the lattice and neocrystallisation) under tectonic influences. As a result of

parablastic growth, fine quartz grains by recrystallisation and blastesis build up "superindividuals". As locii of crystalloblastic growths under dynamic metamorphism could act the intersection of planes due to straining.

Perhaps the most representative case of crystalloblastesis under tectonic influences is the S-garnet crystalloblasts, where an S-shaped distortion of the garnet crystalloblast and of the included ground-mass can be observed.

So far considering crystalloblastesis, we have seen it as a static crystal-growth process and as the result of dynamic metamorphism. However, crystalloblastesis is more a "textural term" designating a phenomenology of crystal growth "where the growing crystal must make a place for itself against solid resistance" and as such is recognisable in rocks of diverse origin (Augustithis, 1959/60).

Whereas crystalloblastesis is to be conceived as forcibly thrusting its way outward from its starting point — and most of the crystalloblastic textural patterns conform with this concept and picture — observations reveal crystalloblastic growth where the growth has taken place by coagulation of colloids or metacolloids "imbibed" into pre-existing ground-mass, thus simultaneously indicating a colloform structure and exhibiting crystalloblastic characteristics, e.g. enclosing, corroding and pushing autocathartically pre-existing ground-mass components. Most characteristic crystalloblasts, blasto-colloform in nature, are described by Drescher-Kaden (1969) and Augustithis (see Chapter 12).

Chapter 5 | Tecoblastesis

In contrast to the typical crystalloblasts described in metamorphics and in granitised sediments, crystalloblastic (tecoblastic) textural patterns are observed in volcanics, i.e., feldspar tecoblasts in a basaltic groundmass. Observations by the author (Augustithis, 1960; 1964c), have shown a phenomenology of the feldspar phenocrysts that has no harmony with the generally accepted views.

Detailed microscopic observations have revealed plagioclase phenocrysts assimilating and digesting components belonging to a pre-existing crystallisation phase. Examples have been described showing a tecoblastic nature for these feldspars; that is, the plagioclase has corroded and assimilated pre-exisiting pyroxene phenocrysts and ground-mass components. The assimilation of the ground-mass can be followed in all its transitions from unaffected minerals (grains) to pigment-rests. However in this case, there is no great time difference in the crystallisation of ground-mass components and the crystalloblasts, in contrast to the case of the crystalloblasts in metamorphics. Nevertheless, the space-genetic relations of the crystalloblast in metamorphics and of the tecoblasts in the volcanics are comparable and commensurable, and indicate that tecoblastesis is a process that belongs to the last phase of the consolidation of a basaltic melt.

The phenomenology of plagioclase tecoblasts: assimilation of pre-existing pyroxenes by later tecoblastic plagioclases

A type of tecoblastic (post-pyroxene) plagioclase is illustrated in Fig. 1 and 2. As a result of the force of crystallisation of its growth, it has penetrated the pre-existing pyroxene, probably along a primary crack. The plagioclase shows evidence of pyroxene assimilation, which influences the zonal composition of the tecoblast.

The An-content varies in different parts of the plagioclase (Fig. 1 and 2) which are recognised as Zones I–IV. The An-content of these different zones is as follows:

Zone IV	34%	An.
Zone III	31–32%	An.
Zone II	44%	An.
Zone I	38–39%	An.

Zones IV and III are independent of the presence of the pyroxene. In contrast, Zone II is as wide as the pyroxene; this zone shows the greatest An-content, which is due to the assimilation of the pyroxene by the tecoblastic feldspar; pigment rests of the pyroxene are present. Zone I has a lower An-content than Zone II, but higher than Zones III and IV. It is probable that the plagioclase has grown in the direction from Zone IV to Zone I.

During the assimilation of pyroxene by the tecoblast, isotropisation of the pyroxene has occurred. Final products of "assimilation" are isotropic pigment-rests, representing elements which could not be assimilated by the plagioclase lattice.

Another interesting case of pyroxene being partly assimilated by a tecoblast is observed in Fig. 3. Here again, the pyroxene shows all the phenomenology of assimilation; rests of pyroxene and pigment-like bodies are present in the plagioclase part which is a product of the mesosomatic reaction of the two phases.

Assimilation and digestion of the ground-mass by the later tecoblastic plagioclase

In volcanic rocks often the ground-mass is penetrating or "infiltrating" into the pre-existing phenocrysts. As a result of the later association of the ground-mass components with the phenocrysts, it frequently appears as though ground-mass has been included by the phenocrysts. Such inclusions of ground-mass components have often been explained as liquid drops of the magma enclosed by the crystallising phenocrysts; the liquid drops, in turn having crystallised and produced components identical to the ground-mass. The above explanations are in accordance with the idea that the phenocrysts have crystallised first, and it is frequently the case that they show all the appearance of magmatic corrosion.

However, observations of plagioclase phenocrysts of lower An-content than the ground-mass and indicating all phenomena of having assimilated pre-existing mineral phases, have been described by Augustithis (1959/60, 1964c).

Fig. 4 and 5 show most interesting examples of plagioclase tecoblasts enclosing ground-mass components. Small pyroxene and ground-mass feldspars are enclosed in a later formed plagioclase tecoblast. The ground-mass mineral components are equally distributed in a frame of plagioclase. The amount and the extent to which the ground-mass can be enclosed, assimilated or "autocathartically" (by self-cleaning processes) pushed along lines or margins of the host plagioclase can vary.

Often, as a result of composition differences, the ground-mass components in the host feldspar are surrounded by reaction margins. Such reactions and a type of zoning surrounding the inclusions are seen as being due to the degree of assimilation of the ground-mass by the building-up of the later feldspar tecoblast.

Fig. 6 shows a great amount of ground-mass mineral components enclosed by a feldspar tecoblast. Differences in the plagioclase (interference colours) represent reactions of the building-up of the feldspar with the pre-existing ground-mass components. Similarly, Fig. 7 shows ground-mass components surrounded by a tecoblast feldspar with a marked zoning due to differences in composition.

The cases so far described have shown ground-mass components distributed in the plagioclase tecoblast. However, additional observations show that pockets of ground-mass can also exist in the tecoblast. Fig. 8 shows an example of such a pocket with, nearby, and also enclosed in the tecoblast, corroded and partly assimilated ground-mass components. Due to the assimilation of the ground-mass, pigment rests are present in the feldspar. The corrosion and assimilation of the ground-mass components enclosed in the tecoblast can vary from grain to grain: often idiomorphic ground-mass components, with little or no corrosion appearances, are enclosed. More often, however, the mineral components of the ground-mass enclosed in the tecoblast can show all the appearances of corrosion and assimilation. Fig. 9 shows ground-mass components in a plagioclase tecoblast where, although the ground-mass is to a great extent unaffected, it also contains mineral components clearly corroded and reduced to the form and appearance of pigments. It is of interest to mention that the pigments, as seen in the detailed photomicrograph of Fig. 10, follow the cleavage direction of the plagioclase tecoblast. It is assumed in this case that the ground-mass components have been corroded and assimilated by the tecoblast: within the complex processes of pigment production, pigment rests representing elements that could not be assimilated or incorporated in the lattice of the plagioclase partly show evidence of assimilation and partly are pushed or confined along the cleavage of the tecoblast. Within the same tecoblast, as seen in Fig. 8

and 9, mineral components of the ground-mass can be unaffected with an obvious crystalline outline, while the adjacent ground-mass components can be affected and reduced to a pigment form.

Indeed, the phenomenology of tecoblasts can show most convincing examples of ground-mass mineral components assimilated and greatly corroded by the later-formed feldspar. Fig. 11 shows a large tecoblast full of inclusions of ground-mass, and the series of figures from 12 to 14, gives more detailed information on the form and corrosion of these components. In Fig. 12 rounded and corroded ground-mass components are shown enclosed in this tecoblast and also, in contrast, the mineral components of the ground-mass exterior to the tecoblast are seen to be larger and more crystalline in form. The ground-mass enclosed in the tecoblast is corroded and reduced to pigment size, as is shown in a detailed view in Fig. 14. Fig. 15 shows that pyroxenes of the ground-mass can also show corrosion appearances as well as the pigment rests.

The corrosion of the ground-mass can, in turn, result in differences in the anorthite content of the tecoblast part immediately surrounding the ground-mass inclusion or its rest-relics, respectively. In addition to Fig. 6 which clearly shows differences in the plagioclase parts surrounding the enclosed ground-mass, further observations in Fig. 16 and 17 show that variations in the composition of the tecoblast feldspar exist, depending on the reaction of the ground-mass with the feldspar. In Fig. 17, the arrow shows the initial ground-mass mineral components, enclosed in the tecoblast and reduced to pigment rests, surrounded by a reaction zone of the feldspar.

Additional observations showing an interrelation between pigment distribution and composition of the tecoblast are seen in Fig. 18. Here, pigment rests of assimilated ground-mass are distributed in a zonal manner within the tecoblast, and a zone of the tecoblast free of pigment rests is also distinguishable. Such a process of self-cleaning from inclusions is known as "auto-katharese" (autocatharsis).

Despite the fact that the series of observations introduced show to an extent the post-ground-mass age of the tecoblast, in cases the relationship of the tecoblast with the ground-mass is still difficult to explain and uncertain. For example, Fig. 19 shows ground-mass extending into a tecoblast. (This observation can be regarded as dubious, since it could be argued that it is a part of the ground-mass partly enclosed by the later tecoblast but still retaining its connection with the ground-mass outside the tecoblast.)

The composition of the tecoblastic phenocrysts

Universal stage determinations by the author (Augustithis, 1959/60) have shown a composition difference between the ground-mass plagioclase and that of the phenocrysts. In contrast to the usual statement that the plagioclase phenocrysts are richer in anorthite and older than the ground-mass components, the tecoblasts described are younger than the ground-mass, and their composition shows an anorthite content lower than the ground-mass (pre-pyroxene) feldspars (Fig. 20).

The tecoblasts often show reverse zoning and they resemble the blastic plagioclases in metamorphogenic gneisses. Frequently, the tecoblasts show local variation in the anorthite content of the patches or zones building up these crystals. Fig. 21A, B shows a tecoblast with zones of variable An-content:

Zone I	25%	An.
Zone II	15%	An.
Zone III	24%	An.
Zone IV	25–27%	An.

It is interesting to note that the central Zone I is richer in An-content than Zone II. Pigmentrests of assimilation are present in Zone I. Also noteworthy is the fact that Zone III is richer in An-content than Zone II, thus showing a type of reversed zoning. This example shows too that the An-content also depends on the extent of assimilation, as shown by the presence of assimilation rests in Zone I.

The photomicrographs of Fig. 16 and 17 show local differences actually conditioned by differences in the An-content, which in turn depend on the reaction of enclosed ground-mass components with the surrounding tecoblast.

Comparison between tecoblastesis and the processes of plagioclase pseudomorphism after augite

Analogous to the tecoblastic phenomenology is the plagioclase pseudomorphism after augite introduced by Pieruccini (1961). Further, the pseudomorphic transformations take place by hydration processes in tuffs, whereas the tecoblastic growths have been observed in effusives (lavas, often with cellular structures), and have taken place within the consolidation period of the melt. Pieruccini (1961) shows in a series of original illustrations the transformation of augite into plagioclase whereby the crystal form, or outline, and the typical cleavage of the augite, is taken over by the "neogenic" plagioclase. Also, additional observations showing relics of augite as well as details of gradual transformation of plagioclase after augite (through a phase of synisotropisation), have been given extensive treatment by Pieruccini. This transformation is seen as an example of the process of "grado-separation".

In a comparison of the tecoblastic growths with the pseudomorphic transformations, it should be emphasised that, whereas the former are blastoid growths, the latter are replacements. It must be noted that, despite the differences between these processes of tecoblastic assimilation and pseudomorphism, isotropisation of the affected pyroxene is observed as a phase. As shown in Fig. 1 and 2 and in their description, in Zone II of the plagioclase tecoblast enclosed pigments indicate the phenomenology of isotropisation.

Chapter 6 | Endoblastesis: Crystalloblastic growths in granites

The crystalloblastic textures have been divided into metablastic (metamorphic textures) and endoblastic (magmatic). In accordance with this concept, the endoblastic textures in granites have been considered to be magmatogenic. In contrast, Drescher-Kaden (1948, 1969), Erdmannsdörffer (1950) and Augustithis (1962b) have shown that the endoblastic textures in granites and granitic rocks are in reality metablastic (metamorphic-metasomatic in origin).

The recognition of the granitic endoblastic textures as metamorphic is indicated in the following quotation of Erdmannsdörffer (1950): "Newer studies by Erdmannsdörffer and Drescher-Kaden have shown that in granitic granular rocks of different compositions (granite, granodiorite, quartz monzonite and in potassium rich rather than the potassium poor ones) structures appear that are definitely crystalloblastic, i.e., having metamorphic character, although the . . . crystallisation sequence . . . geological disposition, transgressive contacts, inclusions apophyses, marginal facies, etc. clearly indicate an intrusive character in spite of the fact that the whole complex had undergone no tectonic deformation and therefore no alteration to metamorphic rock."

However, it is the systematic study of the granitic textures by F. K. Drescher-Kaden (1948, 1969) in his two classical books that the endoblastic textures of the granitic rocks are shown to be metablastic. The present atlas of the granitic textural patterns provides numerous observations in support of a metamorphic origin. Also in support of a metasomatic-metamorphic origin for the endoblastic textures of granites is the discovery of microfossils in granitic plagioclases by Termier and Termier (1970).

The crystalloblastic intergrowths, the synantetic reactions (myrmekitisation), symplectic intergrowths and in general all the recrystallisation textures have been considered by orthodox petrography to be deuteric textures (formed in a post-consolidation phase of the granitic magma). However, it is difficult to explain as deuteric textures (post-consolidation phenomena) the microfossils in granitic plagioclases found by Termier, the micrographic quartz–feldspar intergrowths found in the pebbles of granitised conglomerate, the rounded and regrown zircon grains in granites (indicating different cycles of granitisation), and all the "xenoliths" and sedimentogenic relics often abundant in granitised sediments as well as the transitions, metasediments to granites.

Deuteric structures can occur in granitic rocks due to tectonic influences, i.e., micromylonitisation of granites. In such cases, a gneissic appearance is due to tectonics (Fourmarier, 1959; Guitard, 1963) and should not be confused with the foliation and relics of sedimentogenic structures which are often exhibited in gneisses and in incompletely granitised sediments.

In contrast to the deuteric textures, the crystalloblastic growths and the synantetic and symplectic reactions and textures are protogenic, indicating rock-building processes and structures of first genetic importance in the transformation of sediments into granitic rocks under granitisation.

Different periods and sequences of protogenic growths (i.e., sequences of blastic growths) may occur in granitic rocks in accordance with the evolutionary history of the transformation of sediments to granite.

Chapter 7 | The relation of the crystalloblastic growths to their environment

Synthetic mineralogy has succeeded in the formation of large crystal growths in sand by solutions "imbibing" into the intergranular space. The continuity of the crystal lattice and form are maintained despite the great proportion of the volume of the inclusions to the volume of the crystal. Comparable crystal formations can take place in metamorphism where a crystalloblast includes, corrodes, assimilates and pushes aside the pre-existing ground-mass which is the immediate environment in which a crystalloblast grows.

In the case of classical metamorphism, porphyroblasts (large crystalloblasts) can be formed with a poikiloblastic or "sieve" structure, in which case the crystal of one mineral encloses numerous smaller crystals of another. Poikiloblastic growths in granites are very common and very important in the formation of the rock; depending on the nature of blastic growths K-feldspar, plagioclase, quartz, hornblende and even biotite poikiloblastic crystalloblasts have been determined.

A crystalloblast can be formed in situ by recrystallisation "under static processes" of pre-blastic components of the same mineral kind, in which case the derivation of the substance is the locus of its formation (topomorph).

More often a crystalloblast is a growth which involves transportation of the substance out of which it crystallises. Metasomatism takes place in the locus of its formation. In the case where the supply is derived from the immediate environment of the crystallisation locus, the crystalloblast is topometasomatically formed. However, often crystalloblastic growths involve large scale transportation and metasomatism of material. (The transportation and supply of material is dicussed in Chapter 16.)

In the cases of metasomatic and topometasomatic growths, agglutination of the material takes place (collision and unification of small globules of supplied material) which results in a crystalloblastic growth.

In crystalloblastic growths, complex reaction processes and replacements take place between the supplied material and the pre-existing mineral components at the locus of the crystalloblastic growths. Often crystalloblastesis results in the assimilation and digestion of the pre-blastic components. Observations reveal all transition stages from intact to completely assimilated pre-blastic mineral components as inclusions in crystalloblasts. The phenomenology of this process is most complex and each individual case depends on the sum total of reactions that take place between the existing crystal phases and the crystalloblasts.

The assimilation and the reaction products will depend on the "aggressiveness" of the crystalloblast-forming solutions to the pre-existing grains. The extent and nature of the reactions and assimilations will in turn influence the composition of the crystalloblasts. Topodifferences in the composition of the crystalloblast to some extent depend on these reactions and assimilations (also on differences in the nature and periodicity of the supplied crystalloblastic material).

A large series of observations is introduced (see Chapter 11) to show examples of textural relations and reactions that take place between crystalloblastic growths and the pre-blastic components.

Theoretically, the assimilation of pre-blastic components by a blastic growth will depend on the extent and whether their chemical constituents could be accommodated in the lattice of the crystalloblast. Elements which cannot be incorporated in the crystalloblast lattice are left over as unassimilated rests or pigments. In addition to these crystallochemical reactions, often a crystalloblast tends to clear itself from inclusions by "autocatharsis" either by pushing them at its periphery or confining them along certain crystallographic directions within the crystalloblasts.

Harker (1950) in his classical book *"Metamorphism"* describes autocatharsis as follows: "Growing crystals endeavour to clear themselves by expelling foreign inclusions of any kind, but their power to do so depends upon their inherent force of crystallisation... An instructive case is that in which a growing crystal has been able to brush aside foreign material, but not completely to eject it; the result being that grains of inclusions remain caught in the crystal along certain directions in which the force was least effective. The chiastolite variety of andalusite is a familiar example ..."

Most often ground-mass components are irregularly distributed within the crystalloblasts. In cases, though, the inclusion of ground-mass components (e.g., myrmekitised plagioclases and corroded biotites) in granitic K-feldspar crystalloblasts follows exactly the 001, 010,

110 face of the host (see Fig. 45). Also, often corroded plagioclases and biotites follow a zonal distribution in the orthoclase crystalloblasts. In such cases the ground-mass components are incorporated in the K-feldspar host during the different periods of zonal growth of the crystalloblast.

Chapter 8 | The shape of the granitic crystalloblasts

The crystalline form of granitic mineral components (that of the crystalloblasts) – in comparison to the classical studies of metamorphics – also depends on the crystallisation force of the individual crystal components which determines the interference of one crystal growth with its neighbours. Quoting Harker's metamorphism, one can clearly see the principles on which the classical studies of metamorphism explain metamorphic textures and crystal shapes: "Despite mutual accommodation, crystals starting from neighbouring points and thrusting out, each from its own centre, necessarily come into competition in a struggle for space, or more accurately for shape. In a completely reconstituted rock the shape of each crystal has been determined by its encounters with its immediate neighbours. That is, the shape of a crystalline form depends on the crystallisation force or, more correctly, on the crystalloblastic force."

The force of crystallisation ("Kristallizationskraft") is defined by Becke as a vectorial property of growing crystals depending on crystallographic direction and being specific to the mineral species.

The granitic rocks, however, vary from completely reconstituted to types where sedimentogenic components or early metamorphic – representing the palaeosoma or pre-blastic components – co-exist with later blastic growths. Therefore, the shape of the crystalloblasts will depend on the influence of the blastic growths among themselves and on the interference, degree of assimilation and influence (resistance) exercised by the pre-blastic components on the later blastic growths.

A large number of observations are introduced illustrating the relation of the granitic crystalloblasts to the palaeosoma (see Fig. 45, 46, 49, 63, 67).

In contradistinction to the xenomorphic and idiomorphic crystals of the magmatogenic petrography in metamorphic–metasomatic rocks, depending on the crystalloblastic force and supply of material, we recognise xenoblastic and idioblastic crystal growths.

Whereas in magmatogenic petrography the textural patterns depend on the order of crystallisation which, in turn, depends on the liquidus–solidus equillibrium of the cooling melt, in rocks products of progressive metamorphism–metasomatism (e.g., gneisses, granites, etc.) will depend on the nature, extent and sequence of blastic growths as well as on the metamorphic and metasomatic reactions involved. In completely reconstituted metamorphics under simultaneous crystalloblastesis of the mineral components, the mutual boundaries of the growing crystals will be determined, depending on the crystallisation force (crystalloblastic force).

Based on Becke and Grubenmann, Harker (1950) recognised the following crystalloblastic series:

In argillaceous and arenaceous rocks

Rutile, pleonaste;
Garnet, sillimanite, tourmaline;
Magnetite and ilmenite, andalusite;
Muscovite, biotite, chlorite;
Plagioclase and quartz, cordierite;
Orthoclase and microcline.

In calcareous and igneous rocks

Sphene, spinel minerals, pyrites;
Wollastonite, lime-garnet, apatite;
Magnetite and pyrrhotite, zoisite and epidote;
Forsterite and chondrodite, hypersthene and diopside, chalybite and dolomite;
Scapolite, albite, muscovite, biotite and phlogopite;
Tremolite, idocrase and calcite;
Plagioclase, quartz, orthoclase and microcline.

Considering the main components of granitic rocks: feldspar, quartz, and mica, it can be seen that they stand low in the crystalloblastic series. However, observations (Fig. 22) show feldspar crystalloblasts due to crystallisation force pushing aside and dislodging pre-existing mineral components in the vicinity of their immediate environment of growth.

Chapter 9 | Blastic sequence in granitic rocks

"The usual kind of classification of the igneous rocks given in the textbooks is excellent for the arrangement of rock-specimens in cabinets, but I feel that a genetic classification would introduce divisional planes which would appear as dark chasms on the neat chart of the textbooks."

H. H. Read *(The Granite Controversy, 1957)*

Whereas idioblastic and granoblastic growths (simultaneous blastesis of equal grained components) are observed in granitic rocks, the textural pattern depends more on the sequence of events. The blastic sequence is to be determined in each individual granitic rock on the basis of the textural behaviour and relations of the mineral components as these will be revealed by exact microscopic observations. Mineral boundaries, synantetic reactions, symplectic intergrowths, replacements, corrosion effects and textures due to infiltration could be considered as helpful criteria for suggesting the order of events in granitic rocks. The order of events (crystallisation of blastic phases) is variable and independent of the classification of granitic rocks into gneisses, microgranites, granites, granodiorites, migmatites, etc.

Rocks apparently different (like gneiss and granite) can differ only in the extent of their blastic growths. In fact granites and gneisses having the same blastic sequence have been studied by the author (Augustithis, 1962b) in the Precambrian basement of the East African shield. In contrast, blastic processes of a different nature can give rise to the same rock type (thus granites showing different blastic sequence may exist). The recognition of "an order of events" – the history of a rock – is more important than the classification into gneissic, migmatitic or granitic types.

The pegmatites (pegmatoids), aplitic and leucocratic discordant vein type bodies, associated with gneisses and granites but not confined to them, also show blastic sequence. Initial pre-blastic mineral components belonging to the palaeosoma (sedimentogenic mineral components) present in granitic and gneissic rocks are less important in pegmatites (where the blastic growths attain megablastic dimensions) which are considered to be exudation products of granitised material along tectonic planes or fissures.

Textural studies in granitic rocks reveal that the blastic processes can vary from simple (monoblastic types) to complex multiblastic types. In the monoblastic types in a sedimentogenic or early metamorphic texture (representing the palaeosorna) only a blastic growth has occurred. In contrast, a series of blastic growths or multiple blastic growths can take place concurrently; indicating that progressive changes and building phases occurred in the formation of these rocks.

Considering the existence of pre-blastic components (palaeosoma) and of the multiple blastic growths which represent the neosoma and indeed, considering that a great time difference of formation can exist between these two phases as well as the fact that the multiple blastic growths can take place in a great time span, it can be seen that the time necessary for the formation of granitic material can differ from the time necessary for the cooling of a granitic melt (consolidation of magma) which will be a single event (orthomagmatic, pegmatitic, pneumatolytic and hydrothermal phases of the magmatists).

Considering the structural-geological age of a granitic intrusion, i.e., the transversive behaviour of an intruding granitic body, in respect to the age of the country rocks into which the "younger body" has been emplaced and moreover taking into consideration the age determinations (geochronologically) of mineral components of the same body; often, paradoxically, a great difference of time – in terms of millions of years – between the two has been determined.

The geochronological determinations on granitic rocks are mainly based on age determinations of biotites, zircons, etc. which are components of the palaeosoma (i.e., belong to the pre-blastic phase). It is therefore not surprising that the age of emplacement – intrusion – of a granitic body differs from the age determined for some of its components. The age of a granitic intrusion does not necessarily coincide with the age of formation of its mineral constituents (see Chapters 18 and 24).

In support of this statement, is the great variation in

millions of years of the age of zircons in granites (see Chapter 18) indicating a greater time-span for the formation of the granitic components than what would be acceptable on the basis of the magmatists' views who regard the formation of the granitic components as products of crystallisation in the orthomagmatic phase. This is incompatible with the above-mentioned geochronological data.

Chapter 10 | "Xenoliths" (Relic structures in granites)

"After musing upon what I have seen myself or heard from others about the granite regions in Fennoscandia and abroad, I think I dare express the theory that banding in granites resulting from the alignment of dark materials is in most cases, if not always, where it cannot be interpreted as stress schistosity, a result of resorption of schistose igneous or sedimentary rocks. Furthermore the spottiness in granites may depend, in most cases, on the presence of incompletely resorbed fragments."

J. J. Sederholm (1967)

The understanding of the origin of "xenoliths" (foreign rocks) in granitic rocks is of fundamental importance for the understanding of the origin of the granites themselves (Salomon-Calvi, 1891, 1908/1910; Milch and Riegner, 1910; Erdmannsdörffer, 1912; Drescher-Kaden and Storz, 1929; Holmes, 1936; Goodspeed, 1948b; Drescher-Kaden, 1961b; Wimmenauer, 1963; Gyr and Gansser, 1964; Gansser and Gyr, 1964).

Early magmatogenic interpretations considered biotite-rich nodules (biotite-rich xenoliths) as products of early magmatic crystallisation. However, magmatists regard banded xenoliths as engulfed and metamorphosed sedimentogenic country rocks, enclosed by the intrusive granitic magma. The magmatists, in order to explain the granitic space problem, have proposed the "stoping" hypothesis, namely that accommodation of the granitic intrusion would be provided partly by engulfment and partial assimilation of the country rocks by the granitic magma.

As Mayo (1941, p. 1069) has remarked for certain Californian masses, "it is not easy to imagine much downward stoping where highly viscous masses moved upward", and he clinches this valuation of stoping by recording the "fact that throughout the area, with a few local exceptions, the internal structures of granitic and metamorphic rocks alike are conformable parts of the regional pattern". The abundance of the xenoliths in granitic rocks is indeed variable. At the marginal phase of intrusive granitic bodies, often there is a greater abundance of xenoliths. However, there can be other factors than marginal incorporation that govern the abundance of these relic bodies in granites, e.g. the extent of assimilation by the granite.

In contrast to these views, transformists regard the "xenoliths" as relics of the transmutation (transformation) of the initial rocks to granite. In this connection, it should be noted that the xenoliths are regarded not as

foreign bodies but as representing a phase of the material or part of the material that has been transformed into granite.

Gneissic xenoliths in gneiss-granites provide evidence of the transformation of metasediments to granitic rocks; often the foliation of the enclosed gneiss corresponds to the traces of foliation in the gneiss-granite which, incidently, can show folding corresponding to the initial folds of the metasediments. Here again the xenoliths can be regarded as portions of the initial rock rather free of K-feldspar blastesis (Fig. 23).

Under the process of granitisation, it is the extent of feldspar blastesis that determines the extent of transformation; parts of the initial rocks, free from feldspar-blasts, remain as relic (i.e., xenoliths). Extensive feldspar blastesis results in the homogeneous granitic types free of xenoliths, however, the initial rock phase is represented by the palaeosoma (pre-blastic mineral components) which is interspersed within and between the feldspar blasts and the later formed quartz (see Chapter 18).

In contrast to the xenoliths relatively free from K-feldspar blastesis, field observations show xenoliths in granites with K-feldspar crystalloblasts forming patches and following planes of the "schistosity" (i.e., the feldspar-forming solutions followed directions of greater penetrability within the xenolith). Also in this case the feldspar crystalloblasts are topometasomatically formed and correspond to double inclusions (Fig. 24).

Very often xenoliths show a different degree of preservation within the granitic mass. Whereas parts of the initial sedimentogenic phase due to pronounced K-feldspar blastesis within the relic phase show an appearance of advanced assimilation, adjacent xenoliths with corroded outline show a high degree of preservation (Fig. 25).

In addition to the variation of the composition of the xenoliths their phenomenology, structural behaviour, distribution and abundance within the granitic bodies is of great petrogenetic significance. Field observations from the Bergeller Granite "assimilation zone" show a greater proportion of xenolith material to the granite (Fig. 26). Comparable is the case of parts of the Lagriev Granite; observations show that the granitisation follows the greater penetrability directions along the foliation of the gneiss (Fig. 27).

Drescher-Kaden and Storz (1929) have determined in the Bergeller granitic massif a structural correspondence between the direction of elongation of the xenoliths and the structural behaviour of the surrounding country rocks, i.e. schistosity, thus deducing an in situ granitisation whereby initial structural features of the pre-granitic phase have been preserved after granitisation.

In contrast, often granitic apophyses intrusive in marbles include biotite-hornblende-rich xenoliths. This structural behaviour clearly shows a transportation of the xenolith from its initial position of origin along with the granitic apophysis which has intruded into the marbles (Fig. 28).

Very often the abundance and distribution of xenoliths within the granites is problematic and difficult to explain. Observations from the Adamello massif show a part of the granite very rich in "xenoliths" sharply in contact with a portion of the same granite almost free of xenoliths. The margin between the xenolith-rich and xenolith-free parts of the granite is linear sharp and strangely follows a zig-zag line. No explanation could be provided for such a distribution of the xenoliths (Fig. 29).

In contrast to the "xenolithic bodies" with corroded and assimilated outlines, vein-shaped hornblendite xenoliths following tectonic fissures within the granites are in cases observed (Fig. 30 and 31). These bodies are regarded by magmatists as being basic magmatic differentiates. Field observation shows hornblendite veins transversing along tectonic fissures of the Seriphos Granite, Greece. Often a wedging-out of these bodies within the granitic mass has taken place. The incorporation within the granite of these bodies must have taken place under pressure and tectonic influences (perhaps in a plastic state). Incidently, it should be noted that hornblende-schists occur as country rocks adjacent to the Seriphos Granite.

Whereas magmatic interpretations regard xenoliths as rests of magmatic corrosion and assimilation of the enclosed country rocks, it is logical to expect that a reconstitution due to thermal metamorphism had taken place. However, phyllite xenoliths are abundant in the Mt. Blanc massif (as exposed in the new Mt. Blanc tun-

nel), indicating non-thermal reconstitution or metamorphism into hornblende-schists as would be expected due to thermal influence (see Chapter 23).

Commensurably "sandstone" nodules enclosed in granitic bodies show no evidence of "recrystallisation" (reconstitution), (Fig. 32). In addition, marble "xenoliths" enclosed in granitic apophyses in Seriphos, Greece, show no contact metasomatism of epidote–garnet formation. Most often, however, biotite schists, hornblende schists and gneisses occur as granite xenoliths which represent rather a pre-granitic or contemporaneous metamorphic phase.

Often biotite-hornblende gneisses representing a pre-granitic metamorphic phase are imbibed by feldspar-forming solutions, resulting in the granitisation of these rocks, the relics of which are biotite-hornblende xenoliths in the granitised masses (Fig. 33).

A number of selected examples are presented so as to show the diversity of the phenomenology and nature of these relic bodies in granitic rocks. In addition to phyllite, schist and gneisses, other rocks of diverse origin and composition can be present in granitic rocks as "xenoliths". The relic structures in granitic rocks primarily depend on the initial nature of the pre-granitic rocks which have been granitised, or on the nature and structure of foreign bodies engulfed or included in the material granitised. In general, fine-grained rocks and structures tend to disappear under granitisation more readily than coarse-grained. The diffusion rate, which depends on the compactness and grain size of the initial rock, determines to a certain extent the degree of preservation of the relic structures. As a corollary to the above-mentioned prerequisites for the preservation of relic textures, conglomerates render most elucidating examples.

Granitisation of quartzitic conglomerates

Buri-Rashitcha, Ethiopia

The metamorphosed conglomerate from Buri-Rashitcha consists of quarzitic pebbles showing different degrees of metamorphism and assimilation and a gneissic matrix. However, microscopic studies reveal textures which are definitely typically granitic in nature; the micrographic quartz–feldspar intergrowths are recognised as such textures. The observation that granophyric intergrowths occur in pebbles showing only partial "resorption" but still retaining the initial quartzitic nature, indicates that these textures are produced during the metamorphism of the conglomerate.

The metamorphosed conglomerate from Buri-Rashitcha is an example of a sedimentary rock which has been partly granitised. In contrast to anatexis or any partial melting, this rock remained in a "solid state" during the metamorphism. Infiltration of solutions, remobilisation of material and topometasomatic processes, effective and dependent on the increased solubility in intergranular spaces, are considered responsible for the granophyric and blastogenic growths observed. Megascopically (Fig. 34) the conglomerate consists of quartzitic pebbles showing different degrees of resistance and alteration in a metamorphosed matrix of biotite, neocrystallised quartz and feldspar. Both in hand-specimen and microscopically, many of the pebbles are unaffected and have their rounded surfaces as boundaries (Fig. 34). Fig. 35 shows a general microscopic view of an unaffected quartzitic pebble and of the surrounding "matrix". The pebble contains fine laths of muscovite, biotite, small zircons and apatites, but consists essentially of interlocking quartz grains exhibiting a typical quartzitic mosaic texture. A veinlet of neocrystallised quartz extends from the matrix into the pebble (Fig. 36), however, to a limited extent, solutions have also infiltrated into the unaffected pebbles; some K-feldspar formation has also taken place in the pebbles.

In contrast to the unaffected pebbles, others maintaining their initial quartzitic nature but showing simultaneously a variable degree of alteration and metamorphism are recognisable (Fig. 34). Particularly under microscopic examination these pebbles show initial quartzitic structures (i.e., interlocking quartz grains idential to those of the unaffected pebbles) and, at the same time, exhibit new textures and growths which have been produced during the metamorphism and granitisation of the conglomerate.

All transition stages and phases are observed, from the interlocking quartzitic textures to the new-formed micrographic quartz–K-feldspar intergrowths, whereby the feldspars are topometasomatically formed. Fig. 37 shows a detailed view of a part of a pebble with recrystallised and mobilised quartz grains in a background-mass of metasomatically formed K-feldspar. The texture of the quartz grains exhibited is a transition phase between the interlocking mosaic texture typical of the quartzites and the micrographic texture. Despite the fact that the matrix is greatly metamorphosed and has attained a gneissic appearance and, furthermore, despite the extensive alteration of some of the pebbles, the rock maintained its sedimentogenic appearance and most probably has not passed through an anatectic phase. The fact that unaffected and altered pebbles exist in proximity to each other and that many of the pebbles maintained their initial quartzitic nature supports the view that the rock remained in a solid state during its metamorphism. However, the metasomatic influences were most probably brought about by the agency of hot-water ("hydrothermal") solutions, the solubility and transportability of which were greatly increased in intergranular spaces.

Malga Macceso, Italy

Salomon-Calvi (1891) and Drescher-Kaden (1969) have described "xenoliths" in a tonalite from Malga Macesso, Val di Salarno, Italy, which represent an initial phase of conglomerate in the Werfener Formation. Due to resorption and incorporation of the conglomerates under granitisation, basic xenoliths have been formed as relic structures in the granodioritic tonalite (Fig. 38).

Most impressive examples of ultrabasic xenoliths in granite are described by Drescher-Kaden (1969) and other authors. Drescher-Kaden regards the olivinefels "sphaeroids" of Val Bondasca to be fragments of an olivinefels mylonite engulfed and partly corroded by a fine-grained granite. Corrosion and reaction phenomena between the olivinefels sphaeroids and the granitic rock are also described. These are true xenolithic bodies (foreign bodies) and cannot be regarded as relics of an initial phase in the granite's transformation (Fig. 39).

Another example of relic structures due to "resorption" and granitisation of conglomerates is provided by the sphaeroidal granites. Diffusion, material mobilisation and exchange as well as "Sammelkristallization" might have played an important role in these transformation processes.

Relic structures of initial limestones engulfed in granites or representing an initial layer in the granitised material are rare, nevertheless evidence does support their existence. In granitic contacts with marbles, or where granitic apophyses have protruded into the marble, cases of calcareous xenoliths without epidote-garnet contacts have been observed (Fig. 40).

In contrast, initial limestones included in the Harrar Granite (Ethiopia) show reaction-resorption and contact phenomena. As a result of the reaction between the limestone and the granitised material in the neighbourhood of the xenoliths, plagioclases along with recrystallised calcite and epidote have been formed in predominantly K-feldspar granite.

Micro-fossils in granitic rock

Perhaps the most impressive relic texture so far described in granitic rocks is the existence of micro-fossils in granitic plagioclases (Termier and Termier,

1970). The following are some quotations from their recently presented paper: "Une plaque mince taillée dans cette dernière roche montre: structure grenue (non orientée), quartz granitique, plagioclases souvent poecilitiques, andésine à 45% d'An., feldspaths zonés (à extinction roulante du centre à la périphérie), microcline, micropegmatite, pyroxène intermédiaire entre diopside et augite (strictement incolore, polarisation atteignant le violet de la fin du premier ordre, allongement positif, maclé h_1 de deux individus, extinctions jusqu' à 48° et même 50°), souvent poecilitique, amphibole incolore, poecilitique et maclée, apatite sphène.

Précisons bien qu'il s'agit d'une roche très cristalline dont les éléments (ni roulés ni juxtaposés et non réunis par un ciment) ne sont pas détritiques: il ne s'agit pas d'une arkose mais d'un granite.

... La substance constituant l'élément squelettique observé est de la silice. Or le réseau que nous venons de décrire est de type échinodermique. On sait que le test des Echinodermes actuels et fossiles (jusqu'à présent décrits) est toujours constitué par de la calcite ou de l'aragonite *(Holothuries)*. Nous avancerons donc l'hypothèse que l'object que nous décrivons a subi une silicification ayant conservé molécule à molécule la texture d'un édifice échinodermique. Une telle finesse de substitution ne nous est pas connue dans les épigénies diagénétiques qui conservent la forme générale des fossiles mais dont le grain de recristallisation détruit la majeure partie de la texture histologique. On peut penser que cette silicification a été d'ordre métasomatique et qu'elle s'est produite avant que la calcite de l'organisme ait pu recristalliser.

... Si nous nous référons à des squelettes actuels d'Echinodermes, l'élément en cours d'étude se présente comme une écaille très menue, ce qui est compatible avec celles qui incrustent les épidermes ou même recouvrent d'une fine mosaïque les plaques marginales des *Carpoïdes cincta* ou de Stromatocystioïdes comme *Eikosacystis*. Ces citations ne sont pas limitatives et ne sont mentionnées ici que pour choisir des exemples dans le Cambrien.

... Or, *Cidaris* est un type archaïque d'oursin (rapporté aux Périschoéchinoïdes, groupe surtout paléozoïque).

... Les conditions exceptionnelles de conservation de cette écaille échinodermique nous permettent d'apporter un élément positif à la connaissance de l'évolution de la texture des Echinodermes, puisqu'il s'agit, selon toute vraisemblance, d'un Echinoderme cambrien.

... Comment expliquer la rencontre extraordinaire d'un débris échinodermique dans un granite? Ainsi que nous l'avons déjà dit à maintes reprises, le granite du Tichka est en grande partie métasomatique, et certains de ses aspects font même penser aux granites stratoïdes de Madagascar.

... La présence d'un fossile dans le granite pose sous un jour nouveau le problème de la genèse de cette roche fondamentale."

Chapter 11 | Blastic growths in granitic rocks: "Blastesis"

One of the key points regarding the origin of granitic rocks is the origin and crystallisation of the feldspars. In particular, the K-feldspar crystallisation, since in acid granitic rocks, this is the most important mineral phase. The controversy over granite actually is a controversy regarding the origin and formation of K-feldspars.

According to magmatists, it is a crystallisation phase dependent on the physicochemical reactions of a cooling melt (magma) which will determine the crystallisation sequence of the mineral components of a granite (e.g., Niggli and Beger, 1923; Eskola, 1932a; Bowen and Tuttle, 1950; Barth, 1962b).

In contrast, transformists regard the K-feldspar as a crystalloblastic growth and they point out a parallelism between crystalloblastic formation of K-feldspar in gneisses and a similar formation in granites. The significance, origin and derivation of material which resulted in K-feldspar blastic growths is extensively discussed in the following publications: Mügge (1917); Drescher-Kaden (1927); Mehnert (1940); Erdmannsdörffer (1950); Exner (1951); Von Gaertner (1951); Neuerburg (1957); Robertson (1959); Augustithis (1959/60, 1962b); Andreatta (1961); Jones (1961); Stone and Austin (1961); Langerfeldt (1961); Roubault (1962); Dimroth (1963); Savolahti (1963); Filatova (1964). However, of particular importance have been the contributions of Drescher-Kaden (1948, 1969).

Depending on the extent of K-feldspar blastesis, the initial foliation of gneisses tends to disappear — with intense K-feldspar blastesis — and a homogeneity results. A comparison of the textural patterns of K-felspar blasts in gneisses with textural patterns of K-feldspar in granites shows that they are identical, i.e., in both cases the K-feldspar is a crystalloblastic growth.

The phenomenology of K-feldspar blasts

Fig. 41 shows a K-feldspar megablast in a gneiss-granite from Melca-Guba, Borona, Ethiopia. The K-feldspar blastesis due to crystalloblastic force has pushed aside the components of the ground-mass or has partly enclosed them.

A convincing example in support of the crystalloblastic nature of K-feldspar in granites is the identical textural pattern exhibited by the K-feldspars of the granite and the "double inclusion" in granitic xenoliths. The double inclusions are infiltrations of solution in the xenolith thus giving rise to a crystalloblast in the sedimentogenic xenolith (Fig. 42, Naxos double inclusion).

Very often the K-feldspars in a granite show a parallel orientation which has been interpreted by magmatists as a fluidal texture. However, the crystalloblastic nature of these orientated K-feldspars is supported by textural studies (commensurable and comparable textural patterns as K-feldspar crystalloblasts in gneisses). The parallel orientation of crystalloblasts is due to a direction of greater penetrability of K-feldspar-forming solution within its crystallisation environment (Fig. 43).

In contrast to the crystalloblast where the crystalline form depends on the crystallisation force of the growth, K-feldspar crystalloblasts as "superindividuals" can be formed intergranularly between granitic quartz. The K-feldspar forming solutions have taken advantage of the intergranular space between the quartz grains (Fig. 44).

The crystalloblastic nature of the granitic K-feldspars is indicated by its relation to pre-blastic components (palaeosoma) and by its synantetic reaction with pre-blastic growths. Fig. 45 shows a K-feldspar megablast which has "incorporated" pre-blastic plagioclases, and biotites (component of the palaeosoma) which are partly corroded and resorbed by the later K-feldspar growth. The pre-blastic relics are distributed within the K-feldspar megablast, following well-defined crystallographic directions within the crystalloblast (see Chapter 7). In contrast, a K-feldspar crystalloblast shows pre-blastic components (indicating corrosion and resorption) following the zonal structure of the K-feldspar (Fig. 46 and 47). In the same K-feldspar crystalloblast the textural behaviour of the pre-blastic components may vary from components following the zonal growths of the K-feldspars to components in random distribution within the crystalloblast (Fig. 48).

In contrast, the pre-blastic component may be at random orientation within the K-feldspar blast. As shown in Fig. 49, abundant pre-blastic components are partly "resorbed" by the crystalloblast. The crystalloblast's outline is defined by its relation to the pre-blastic components. In addition to orthoclase, microcline crystalloblasts show a comparable behaviour to pre-blastic components. A great portion of the material that gave rise to the crystalloblast "originated" from resorption and recrystallisation of the palaeosoma in situ. Similarly, Fig. 50 shows a microcline crystalloblast enclosing and assimilating recrystallised components of the matrix of the granitised conglomerate of Buri-Rashitcha, Adolla, Ethiopia. The shape of a crystalloblast is dependent on its crystallisation force which, in turn, determines the crystalloblastic series. Additional factors determining the shape of a crystalloblast are the synantetic reactions which take place between the pre-existing mineral phases and the later crystalloblast.

Fig. 51 shows a K-feldspar crystalloblast in contact with plagioclase. A reaction zone is formed as the plagioclase is affected by the later orthoclase crystalloblasts. Such reaction margins are discussed in Chapter 13. In contrast to these reaction margins devoid of myrmekitic quartz, myrmekitisation is exhibited in these reaction zones of a pre-existing plagioclase in contact with a later K-feldspar crystallisation.

The outline of the crystalloblast depends on the reaction-resorption and replacement of the pre-K-feldspar minerals. Fig. 52 shows K-feldspar blasts invading and replacing a zoned plagioclase. The replacement and corrosion affected the outer zone of the plagioclase and partly followed it. These synantetic intergrowths indicate a later crystalloblastic origin for the K-feldspar.

Again in support of a later K-feldspar crystallisation is the corrosion and reaction margin shown by pre-K-feldspar plagioclase. In the reaction zone, reversing of the twinning is indicated (Fig. 53). It should be mentioned that such synantetic reaction margins of plagioclase are often myrmekitised, as is indicated in a series of illustrations (see Chapter 13).

The synantetic reaction of a pre-existing biotite and a later K-feldspar blast often shows replacement and assimilation of the mica by the feldpar. Fig. 54 and 55 show biotite corroded and replaced by K-feldspar, opaque minerals, apatites. Small sillimanites originally associated with the biotite are left as relics in the K-feldspar, as it has replaced the biotite. Often the K-feldspar tends to assimilate the relics of the replacement, or autocathartically (self-cleaning processes) tends to push the non-assimilated relics at the outer part of the K-feldspar blast.

In cases, as a result of replacement and assimilation of the biotite, a reaction margin is produced in the K-feldspar itself (Fig. 56 and 57). Here again corrosion and replacement of the mica has taken place by the later K-feldspar which has resulted in the taking over of opaque minerals form the biotite as relics of replacement. The replacement of biotites by K-feldspar may result in crystalloblasts "tourbid" with relics of replacement. Biotite parts incompletely assimilated together with accessory relics (originally associated with the biotite) are included and dispersed within the K-feldspar crystalloblast. Replacement of biotite may proceed following the cleavage of the mica. The K-feldspar – biotite boundary depends on the corrosion and replacement processes involved (Fig. 58). Apatites initially associated with the biotite are partly freed from their association with the mica and are partly engulfed by the K-feldspar. Accessories often occur in K-feldspar representing relics of replacement. The textures involved are described in Chapter 18.

The synantetic reactions of K-feldspar with biotite often result in corrosion and replacement processes of the mica by the feldspar. Reaction margins with myrmekitic quartz are formed as a result of K-feldspar blastesis in contact with a pre-existing biotite. Biotite corrosion and replacement by K-feldspar crystalloblasts are shown in Fig. 59 and 60.

As a corollary to the synantetic reaction described where replacement and corrosion were shown, Fig. 61 shows a hornblende in contact with a K-feldspar blast, which has replaced the hornblende along its cleavage.

Plagioclase blastesis

Comparable to K-feldspar is the plagioclase blastesis. Metasomatic or topometasomatic mobilisation of Ca–Na has resulted in a plagioclase blastic phase which can co-exist with a K-feldspar blastesis. Comparative studies of the Naxos migmatite and granite by Augustithis (1959/60) have shown a predominance of the plagioclase phase in the migmatite as compared to K-feldspar blastesis in the granite. It has been suggested that a Ca-rich environment of the pre-granitised sediments was the cause of the predominance of plagioclase blastesis in the migmatite. Marble bands associated with the migmatites are considered as supporting evidence of a Ca-rich environment. The synantetic reaction involved between marble "xenoliths" and the granitised surroundings often resulted in plagioclase formation within the granite.

The formation of plagioclase blastesis under granitisation depends on the initial composition of the sedimentogenic material under granitisation and on metasomatic and topometasomatic mobilisations. Plagioclase blastesis can be a part of the blastic sequence in the transformation of sediments to granitised rocks.

The textural patterns of the plagioclase blastesis reveal a phenomenology comparable and commensurable to blastic patterns of K-feldspar. Fig. 62 shows a plagioclase crystalloblast which at its marginal phase has enclosed quartz and corroded biotite. Often the enclosed pre-blastic components either tend to be assimilated or pushed to the margins by the crystalloblastesis. Similarly, a zoned plagioclase crystalloblast encloses partly assimilated quartz at its outer zones (Fig. 63). The zoning of the crystalloblast could depend on variations of the composition of the crystalloblast forming solutions and on the assimilation-reaction processes involved. Fig. 64 shows a plagioclase crystalloblast from the Naxos migmatite; pre-blastic quartz (of the palaeosoma) is enclosed and partly assimilated. Two plagioclase generations are distinguished: (*1*) plagioclase of the palaeosoma (pre-blastic) enclosed and myrmekitised by a K-feldspar blast and (*2*) the plagioclase crystalloblast in contact with the K-feldspar blast. It should be noted that the crystalloblast is later than the K-feldspar, thus explaining the absence of myrmekitisation from the plagioclase crystalloblast. Depending on the blastic sequence (whether the plagioclase is older than the K-feldspar) myrmekitisation of the plagioclase can take place.

Accessory components and biotite may be enclosed by plagioclase blast. Fig. 65 shows a plagioclase crystalloblast with apatites, biotite and sillimanite (?) in a central zone of the plagioclase. Simultaneously, the plagioclase, due to autocatharsis and its crystallisation force has pushed aside and corroded biotites at its outer margins. The crystalloblastic growth resulted in the concentration of pre-blastic accessories in its central zone and simultaneously cleared itself and pushed its pre-blastic "surroundings".

In contrast to the plagioclase crystalloblasts that have cleared themselves due to autocathartic processes, often the crystalloblasts are "turbid" with ground-mass components (pre-blastic) which are interspersed within the crystalloblast. Fig. 66 shows a plagioclase crystalloblast with amphiboles and micas (components of the ground-mass) enclosed and partly assimilated by the later feldspar. As the plagioclase surrounds an amphibole rest, a reaction margin is shown in the plagioclase in contact with the amphibole. Similarly, Fig. 67 shows the rests of the ground-mass interspersed within the plagioclase crystalloblast. The growth of feldspar was partly due to the assimilation in situ of the pre-blastic components and partly to solution infiltrations in the intergranular of the ground-mass. In comparison to the mafic component, i.e., the constituents of ground-mass outside the plagioclase crystalloblast, the ground-mass components enclosed by the plagioclase show a "reduction" in size due to corrosion and assimilation by the crystalloblastesis.

The plagioclase crystalloblastesis is often a post-biotite growth. Fig. 68 shows a plagioclase crystalloblast that has enclosed a biotite fragment and has simultaneously pushed the biotite autocathartically at its margins. Blastogenic force (due to crystallisation force) and autocatharsis have played an important role. It should be noted that the biotite enclosed in the crystalloblast has the same orientation as the biotite outside the feldspar.

The crystalloblastic plagioclase growths can cause, due to blastogenic force, "deformation" of the components of their "environment" of growth. Fig. 69 shows a plagioclase crystalloblast in contact with a biotite. The plagioclase has pushed aside the mica and has caused an undulating extinction due to the deformation produced by the blastogenic force of the plagioclase. During plagioclase blastesis often reaction with the pre-blastic biotite takes place. Plagioclase extends into the mica cleavage and, in turn, its outer composition is influenced as a result of the synantetic reactions involved (Fig. 70). The plagioclase blastesis often shows unmistakable replacement phenomenology. Fig. 71 shows biotite in contact with a later plagioclase crystalloblast replaced, corroded and partly engulfed.

In contrast to the synantetic reaction and replacement phenomena, often plagioclase crystalloblasts have corroded, replaced and partly "assimilated" biotite included in the plagioclase (Fig. 72 and 73). In cases, biotite fragments are included in blastic plagioclase arranged parallel to the polysynthetic twin lamellae and showing no reaction or corrosion appearance (Fig. 74). In contradistinction, other blastic plagioclases include biotites and hornblendes parallel and at an angle to twinning, and in these cases the mica is corroded and shows a reaction margin (Fig. 75).

The process of biotite corrosion and replacement by plagioclase may result in most complex textural patterns. Fig. 76 shows biotite infiltrated and replaced by a plagioclase crystalloblast along directions of cleavage. The plagioclase crystalloblast in cases may show biotite laths perfectly orientated within the plagioclase. Fig. 77 shows biotite laths parallel and perpendicular to the plagioclase twinning. In addition to biotite, hornblendes are often enclosed, corroded and affected by a later plagioclase crystalloblast. Fig. 78 shows twinned hornblende with an apatite enclosed by blastic plagioclase. Similarly, Fig. 79 shows hornblende corroded by a later plagioclase crystalloblast. The plagioclase blast has enclosed and corroded a "first-generation" plagioclase, i.e., the plagioclase is older than the crystalloblast.

Plagioclase blastesis may result in corrosion and replacement of the pre-blastic components included, however, idiomorphic pre-blastic components without corrosion and reaction phenomenology may be enclosed in plagioclase blasts. Fig. 80 shows idiomorphic hornblende, apatites and corroded quartz enclosed by a plagioclase crystalloblast.

The nature of plagioclase crystalloblastic inclusions can vary. In addition to the pre-blastic components described and to the orientated biotite laths (Fig. 77), orthoclase may be enclosed by later plagioclases (Fig. 81 and 82). It should be noted that we have a case of pre-existing K-feldspar surrounded by a later plagioclase. Such relations have been regarded as necessary for the myrmekite formation by Becke, however, in the present example no myrmekitisation of the later plagioclase has taken place (see discussion on myrmekitisation, Chapter 13).

A rather dubious case is presented by the bands of interlocking quartz with micaceous minerals included in plagioclase crystalloblasts parallel to the twinning lamellae. Most probably they represent quartzitic relics in a later plagioclase blastesis (Fig. 83).

Comparable to the orientated laths of biotite in plagioclase crystalloblasts (Fig. 77), are the sillimanite (?) needles perfectly orientated within the plagioclase crystalloblast (Fig. 84). In both cases, however, the orientated mineral phases do not represent exsolved phases due to the lack of miscible phases between these two minerals. There is no miscible system of plagioclase–biotite or plagioclase–sillimanite. They could be either intracrystalline penetration or orientations within blastic processes somehow comparable to plagioclases in K-feldspar crystalloblasts (Fig. 45).

Hornblende blastesis

In contrast to the accepted sequence of the crystallisation of granitic rocks but, however, in harmony with the concept of blastic growths, hornblende crystalloblasts — with textural patterns comparable and commensurable to classical blastic growths — are observed in granitic rocks. Topometasomatic processes — internal remobilisation of material — are considered to be mainly responsible for this amphibole blastesis. In addition to basic xenoliths, remobilised and recrystallised sedimentogenic material also attributes to the formation of amphiboles attaining a true crystalloblastic character in granitic rocks and showing a textural pattern in accordance with blastic phenomenology.

Fig. 85 shows a twinned hornblende blast enclosing, corroding and assimilating pre-blastic components (palaeosoma) consisting of quartz, feldspar, apatites, and ore-minerals. The pre-blastic inclusions are rather restricted in the central zone of the crystalloblast due to autocathartic processes. The outer zone of the hornblende is almost inclusion-free. Fig. 86 shows in detail the pre-blastic component of the central zone of the hornblende crystalloblast.

Comparable to K-feldspar blastesis, whereby pre-blastic plagioclases are following either well-defined crystallographic directions within the crystalloblast or its zoning, are hornblende blasts with pre-blastic plagioclase corroded, assimilated and arranged parallel to the crystalloblastic zoning (Fig. 87 and 88). Also comparable to K-feldspar crystalloblasts which develop by the concentration of topometasomatic materials within the intergranular and by partly incorporating the pre-blastic components, hornblende crystalloblasts enclosing quartz and feldspars develop in the intergranular spaces (Fig. 89). Similarly, Fig. 90 shows a hornblende crystalloblast enclosing and corroding quartzes of different size. Rounded quartz grains of the pre-blastic (palaeosoma) are only partly engulfed by the hornblende blast.

In the more basic granitic rock types (e.g., granodiorites), hornblende blastesis is often associated with plagioclases either as a component of the palaeosoma or representing an early blastic phase. Fig. 91 shows a hornblende megablast enclosing and partly assimilating plagioclases. The hornblende blast partly engulfs the plagioclases that are outside giving the impression of a blastic superindividual following the intergranular of the pre-blastic palaeosoma but nevertheless enclosing components of it. Similarly a hornblende crystalloblast with extensions occupying the intergranular spaces between the pre-blastic plagioclases is shown in Fig. 92.

Plagioclases with rounded outlines clearly showing a corrosion by the later hornblende crystalloblast are shown in Fig. 93 and 94. In Fig. 93 the enclosed plagioclase is partly replaced by quartz which is pre-hornblende, since both the plagioclase and the quartz that has replaced it have been equally subjected to corrosion by the hornblende crystalloblast. In some cases, the hornblende crystalloblast is xenomorphic showing an outline clearly being the product of reactions with its environment. Nevertheless its blastic behaviour is demonstrated by the corrosion, replacement and partial assimilation of pre-hornblende plagioclases (Fig. 95).

Hornblende blasts often are intergranular between plagioclases and quartz. The plagioclases may show outlines which are the result of corrosion between the pre-existing phases and the blastic hornblende (Fig. 96). A veinlet of quartz–hornblende occupying the intergranular space between differently orientated K-feldspars (Fig. 97) is in support of the later hornblende mobilisation.

Blastic quartz

A study of textural patterns in granite rocks reveals that the quartz may represent different generations of diverse origin. Initially, sedimentogenic or early metamorphic quartz is an important constituent of the palaeosoma associated with plagioclases, micas and the accessories. In contradistinction to the pre-blastic sedimentogenic quartz (as a result of synantetic reaction of an existing mineral and a later blastic growth) worm like myrmekitic bodies are formed, e.g., myrmekitisation of plagioclases, biotite, muscovite, epidote, etc.

However, quartz blasts comparable and commensurable to the crystalloblastic formation of other minerals exist in granitic rocks. This quartz is low in the crystalloblastic sequence and usually xenomorph. Regrowths of quartz in optical continuation with rounded clastic grains can take place under low temperatures, i.e., under diagenetic conditions. Fig. 98 and 99 show rounded clastic quartz with overgrowths of diagenetic quartz. The mosaic quartz of quartzites is the result of recrystallisation under tectonic influence.

In granitisation, in addition to the synantetic quartz infiltrations and the graphic replacement growths, blastic quartz is usually formed in the intergranular space and encloses pre-quartz grains. Fig. 100 shows a quartz blastesis which partly encloses marginal plagioclases. The quartz blast has been formed in the intergranular space and, due to autocathartic processes, has pushed aside and corroded the adjacent pre-quartz grains.

In contrast to the intergranular quartz blasts, quartz megablasts (Fig. 101 and 102) show an internal zonal arrangement of assimilated and corroded pre-quartz components (i.e., of the palaeosoma), represented by pre-blastic quartz, mica and plagioclases. The interzonal arrangement of the non-assimilated relics of "first generation" quartz, plagioclases and micas, is due to autocathartic processes within the quartz crystalloblast. Often the assimilation-rests within a quartz crystalloblast are in the periphery of the quartz or are randomly interspersed within the quartz blast (Fig. 103 and 104). Sometimes later crystallised quartz causes a reaction-margin on pre-existing biotites, which are corroded and invaded along the cleavage by penetrations of quartz-forming solutions, producing a synantetic reaction-margin in the biotite which is shown as a decoloration (Fig. 105). Later quartz may form a margin and surround plagioclases which are corroded and show a reaction-margin as they are affected by the quartz (Fig. 106).

A textural pattern of different generations of quartz is shown in Fig. 107. An idiomorphic six-sided quartz is enclosed in a plagioclase. A later quartz grain extends into the plagioclases replacing the felspar and the six-sided quartz.

Biotite blastesis

In granitic rocks, biotite represents an early phase of crystallisation. Biotite laths often represent a pre-blastic phase of crystallisation often corroded, enclosed and assimilated by later blastic feldspar and quartz (see Fig. 108). Nevertheless, textural patterns of biotites comparable with classical crystalloblastic growths have been observed, although a blastic biotite phase is dubious and rather rare.

In the sequence of blastic growth, biotite blastesis is pre-K-feldspar in formation. Nevertheless accessory components (e.g., apatites and zircons) may represent the pre-blastic phase which are enclosed and accommodated as relics parallel to zoning. Fig. 109 shows a biotite crystalloblast with random accessory apatite and zircon in the mica. The contact of the biotite with an adjacent K-feldspar shows corrosion, and myrmekitic quartz is formed in the mica. In contrast, Fig. 110 shows apatites following a zonal distribution within the biotite crystalloblast. The biotite shows margins that have exploited the intergranular between pre-existing mineral grains. Similarly, Fig. 111 shows apatites with their elongation-axes arranged parallel to the zonal structure of the biotite.

Not only the accessory minerals occur as "orientated" inclusions in the biotite. Fig. 112 shows plagioclases partly corroded and following zones within the biotite crystalloblast.

The biotite crystalloblasts often are in contact with feldspar showing a corroded outline. The biotite is zoned and encloses corroded relics of pre-biotite minerals.

A dubious textural pattern of biotite with amphibole "augen" structure is shown in Fig. 113. It is uncertain whether the amphiboles are pre-biotitic in age. (It could perhaps be that the amphibole augen structures represent a later tectonically introduced phase.)

As has been discussed under biotite myrmekitisation, biotites may exhibit reaction margins in contact with K-feldspar. Comparable synantetic reaction margins are shown as the biotites interact among themselves (Fig. 114).

Chapter 12 | Colloform blastoids in granitic rocks

Colloidal "quartz"

The silica gels, due to a molecular dispersed system, are easily reversible from gel to sol and consequently the tendency of transformation to crystalline would be the ultimate stable phase.

Silica gels in rocks of diverse origin tend ultimately to be transformed into cryptocrystalline, microcrystalline and crystalline aggregates in which the initial gel structure could only partially be preserved as "colloform" relics. In order to understand the change of gel structures to crystalline, a brief general consideration of the colloid condition is advanced. The condition is characterised by the occurrence of the dissolved substances within certain limits ($1-200\mu$). With an increase in size of the particles between $100-500$ μ there is a transition of the solution to a suspension. In general, in dispersed systems, the following grades are recognised: coarsely dispersed, colloidally dispersed and molecularly dispersed. Thus the formation of a colloidal solution for the coarsely dispersed systems is effected by dispersion, whereas for the molecularly dispersed substances existing in true solution it is effected by condensation.

To explain a gel structure which has changed into a crystalline structure, a rearrangement of the atoms must be assumed. This can take place more in the state of a sol than in that of a gel, therefore the property of reversibility of gel to sol is important. The colloid conditions from which gel silica is formed are believed to originate rather from condensation than from dispersion, moreover, such systems have the property of reversibility. Consequently, the alteration of gel into sol will result in the formation of true solutions in which rearrangement of the atoms can take place and a crystalline structure can be produced. It must be emphasised, however, that the reversibility of gel to sol is often incomplete and gradual, and the formation of true solutions can be local and restricted, so that the change of gel silica into quartz can take place and yet the initial gel features can be maintained. The tendency of transformation from gel to crystalline is discussed by Augustithis (1967b).

A series of photomicrographs illustrates the transformation of silica gel to quartz. Fig. 115 shows a "veinlet"

of chalcedony with quartz grains in the central part. Relic gel-structures are preserved simultaneously in several quartz grains. Both the chalcedony and the quartz have been formed from colloidal solutions with subsequent crystallisation to quartz.

Arrows (a) in Fig. 115 and 116 show a quartz individual with relic gel structure simultaneously exhibiting a texture resembling crystal zoning. In this particular case it is difficult to differentiate between gel-relics and zonal growth. It is perhaps possible that the central part of the grain has grown as a crystal nucleus (a crystalline outline is shown). However, in the outer part of the same quartz, relic gel-structures are present (Fig. 116, arrow b). Similarly, Fig. 117 shows structures in quartz grains which, despite a geometrical outline, might represent an original gel-structure. Additional observations (Fig. 118, arrow a) show relic gel-structures traversing different quartz individuals. (The gel structure is a relic of a colloform phase and is preserved in the individual quartz grains after the transformation of silica-gel to quartz.) Fig. 118 (arrow b) also shows a relic ring gel-structure in one of the quartz grains. It is interesting to note that the relic gel-structure simulates zonal growth (Fig. 118, arrow c).

The transformation from a gel-phase to a crystal is difficult to understand. It has been proposed by the author (Augustithis, 1964d) that the transformation of gel to crystalline uraninite involves an intermediate solution phase which facilitates the rearrangement of the atoms from an amorphous state to a crystal lattice. Whether a gel-phase can change to a crystal without an intermediate solution phase is difficult to answer. Levicki (1955) has shown that silica gel can change to quartz, leaving the original gel-structure preserved as gaseous inclusions in the crystal. Commensurably, Fig. 119 shows original colloform textures preserved as relics in quartz aggregates, whereby the quartz individuals show different extinction positions. Additional evidence for the original silica gel-phase are the minute limonitic granules often preserved in the quartz. The limonite pigments show an overall arrangement which indicates colloform structures (Fig. 120). The limonitic granules were interspersed with silica gel, however, with the subsequent crystallisation of the silica gel into quartz, the original pattern of the limonitic granules is preserved. Fig. 121 shows limonitic pigment-bands in quartz grains actually consisting of limonite granules originally interspersed in the silica gel. The original pattern of the pigment bands has been preserved after the change of the silica gel to quartz.

Colloform or colloform relics textures are rare in granitic rocks, nevertheless, such structures have been observed by Drescher-Kaden (1969). Present observations (Fig. 122) reveal a veinlet of microcrystalline to fine crystalline quartz (a colloidal infilling) partly resorbed in later quartz. The transition from cryptocrystalline to microcrystalline quartz from the margin of the veinlet to the centre is comparable to the transition of chalcedony to fine quartz in colloform silica infillings. Similarly, Fig. 123 shows a veinlet transversing quartz and feldspar, consisting marginally of chalcedony and transgressions into fine quartz towards the centre. The transition from microcrystalline to fine quartz is in support of colloidal infillings which have attained by transition a microcrystalline to crystalline state.

Such indirect evidence of colloform quartz in granitic rocks is also shown in Fig. 124 and 125. A band consisting of larger quartz grains transverses a mass of fine quartz and mafic grains. Within the quartz band are fine lines of granules (pigments), inclusions indicating an original colloform structure. Often lines of fine granules (pigments) transverse the boundaries of differently orientated quartz (Fig. 126). In comparison to Fig. 124, these lines of pigments could be interpreted as relics of an original colloidal formation of silica which has been transformed to crystalline quartz. However, the pigment granules maintained their original distribution (i.e., as lines within the colloform structure) after the transformation of colloform silicate to quartz.

Colloidal structures in plagioclases

In contrast to the gel-silica and the colloform relic structure in crystalline quartz, colloform structures in feldspar are more uncertain and they can only be inferred on the basis of the textural patterns of their zonal growth. In contrast to the hydrothermal nature of silica gels, zonal growths in feldspars simulating colloform structures are observed in plagioclases of diverse origin. Fig. 127, 128, 129, and 130 show fine zonal growth of plagioclases from basalts of Debra-Sina, Ethiopia. Augustithis (1963) has determined on an optical basis (universal stage determinations) an oscillatory nature, and has pointed out the similarity of the textural pattern exhibited by colloform structures. Fig. 127 shows fine oscillatory zoning of plagioclase phenocrysts simulating a gel-

structure, and where the zoning is transversed by the polysynthetic twinning a "parket"-structure is produced. Similarly, Fig. 128 and 129 show colloform-like zoning of plagioclase phenocryst which simultaneously exhibits polysynthetic twinning. Furthermore, a pocket of ground-mass components acts as a nucleus which is surrounded by plagioclase exhibiting oscillatory zoning and which simulates colloform structure (Fig. 128).

Despite the resemblance of the oscillatory zoning to colloform structure, it has been formed under "dynamic" conditions, i.e., the growth of feldspar has taken place in a moving melt as pointed out by Augustithis (1963). In the case of the Debra-Sina plagioclases, however, the oscillatory zoning is caused by variations in the chemical compositions of the melt. The crystallisation of the plagioclase phenocrysts took place in a dynamic, rather than a static system and was mobile in the sense that the plagioclase phenocrysts were in motion within the melt thus coming into contact with portions of the melt having different compositions. The material building up the phenocrysts was supplied in stages, the crystallisation of the material supplied in each stage resulting in an An-rich zone followed by an An-poor zone. However, since the feldspars were in motion and thereby coming in contact with portions of melt varying in composition, an oscillatory zoning could result.

In contrast, the zonal growth of granitic plagioclases is formed under static conditions and is comparable and commensurable to colloform growth under hydrothermal conditions. As has been pointed out regarding the transformation of colloform silica to crystalline, the crystalline form is the ultimate stable form and the tendency will be for the transformation of colloform structures → to crystalline. The relative scarcity both of colloform structures and of their relics in granitic rocks is conditioned by the readiness of transformation of gel → to crystalline phase.

The zonal growth of granitic plagioclases often shows colloform structural patterns. Fig. 131 shows a plagioclase megablast with the zonal growth representing stages of growth and resembling colloform zones of formation. Components of the ground-mass are enclosed in the plagioclase megablast. The growth of the colloform blast has taken place under static conditions. It should be pointed out that the zonal growth is transversed by later-formed twinning which is subsequently developed to the zonal growth. (The zonal growth represents the stage-by-stage development of the colloform phase.) The twinning is developed during the transformation of the colloform to the crystalline phase.

As microscopic observations reveal, the zonal growth is continued through the twinned individual. The continuation of the colloform zones across the twins of feldspars is comparable and commensurable to the continuation of colloform relic structures across differently orientated quartz (Fig. 118), formed at the transformation of gel-silica to quartz crystal grains. In both cases the colloform zoning was the initial phase and due to transformation of colloform to crystalline, the zoning of the initial phase has been preserved in the crystalline. Similarly, the zonal growths in the megaphenocrysts of Debra-Sina (Fig. 129) represent the first phase and twinning is due to crystallisation.

In contrast, other megablasts indicate a zonal structure following exact geometrical shapes and representing crystal zonal growths. Fig. 132 shows granitic plagioclase with crystal zonal growth and with a corroded biotite incorporated parallel to the crystal zoning. The outer zonal growth attains a colloform structure. The change of character of crystal zonal growth to colloform has also been observed in quartz individuals (Fig. 116), which shows a crystalline centre surrounded by colloform outer-zonal growths.

Plagioclase megablast may show crystal-growth zones with biotites incorporated parallel to the zoning and locally topo-colloform structures are formed. The relation crystalline—zonal growth and collomorph may show topo-variations within a crystal (Fig. 133). As is illustrated in Fig. 117, quartz, colloform in nature, may show crystalline zoning. In the case of the feldspar crystalloblast, comparable crystalline zoning may be collomorph in nature. Fig. 134 shows a plagioclase crystalloblast, enclosing pre-blastic components, with collomorph zoning (zonal growth attains collomorph appearance) and simultaneously exhibiting twinning. Whereas the twinning is well-defined in certain parts of the crystal, when the twinning transverses the outer margin of the plagioclase with colloform-zonal structure, the polysynthetic twin lamellae are "diffuse" in their "delimitation". The fact that the polysynthetic twinning transversing the colloform zonal growth is "diffused" supports the explanation that colloform zonal growth proceeded the polysynthetic twinning which, in this case, "due to the colloform nature of the plagioclase" has not attained its full development (well-defined individuals). This represents an intermediate phase from colloform to crystalline, whereby polysynthetic twinning is fully developed.

In contradistinction, plagioclase megablast (Fig. 135) including marginally ground-mass components of the pre-blastic phase (palaeosoma), shows fine zonal growths transversed by polysynthetic twinning, and in this case the polysynthetic twinning has developed after the zonal growth. The plagioclase crystalloblast shows a reaction margin in contact with the ground-mass components.

In the case of normal crystalloblastesis, the crystal growth started from a "locus" of crystallisation and, due to crystalloblastic force, pushed or assimilated the pre-blastic components which comprise the environment in which the crystalloblast grows. As is indicated in Fig. 45 and 46 biotites and plagioclase could be zonally incorporated along crystallographic directions. In contrast, in the case of gel-crystalloblasts, colloidal solutions "due to coagulation resulted in a colloform structure which partly incorporated the pre-blastic palaeosoma", and at the subsequent transformation from colloform to crystalline (development of polysynthetic twinning) the crystalline character has been attained. Fig. 136 shows a collomorph plagioclase crystalloblast partly surrounding pre-blastic plagioclase and including a zircon which is orientated parallel to the crystalloblast's zoning. The pre-blastic zircon is incorporated by the later crystalloblast. Polysynthetic twinning is developed transversing the collomorph zoning. Similarly, the plagioclase crystalloblast (Fig. 137) shows a central part with colloform structure surrounded by a "diffuse" zoning which includes a lath of biotite. The outline of the crystalloblast depends on its reaction with its environment (i.e., the outline is not idioblastic).

Very often the plagioclase crystalloblast exhibit complex zonal structure. Fig. 138 shows zonal development in plagioclase crystalloblasts with resorption intervening between the zoning of the plagioclase. Certain zones of growth indicate collomorph structure. Crystal-zoning, gel-zonal growth and resorptions were fluctuating phases under colloform—blastogenic condition of plagioclase formation.

Additional observations (Fig. 139) show zoned plagioclase crystalloblasts with an "unconformity" in the zoning representing an intervening phase of resorption between the two phases of zoning (which are distinguished by an "unconformity" of zonal layering). Similarly, Fig. 140 shows a plagioclase crystalloblast with two phases of zoning separated by a phase of "uncomformity" in the running of zonal layers — probably indicating in this case a resorption phase. Pre-blastic plagioclase is incorporated parallel to the outer plagioclase zoning of the crystalloblast.

The variation and complexity of the zonal growths is illustrated by a series of photomicrographs. Fig. 141 shows a central part of a plagioclase which, at its margin, shows "diffuse" colloform zonal growth which, in turn, changes character and transgresses into well-defined crystalline zoning following crystal faces of the plagioclase crystalloblast. An "unconformity" is marked between the colloform and outer crystalline layering of the zonal growths. Often broad, well-defined crystal zonal growths indicate within themselves complex fine zoning attaining colloform character. Whereas the broad zones exhibit a crystalline outline, the "interzonal"-zoning represents a phase of coagulation (Fig. 142) and consists of complex gel-like structures. In some cases, as pointed out, local disturbances may occur in the fine crystalline zoning resulting in complex-colloform-zonal patterns. Fig. 143 shows fine zonal growths of plagioclase. Parallel to these fine zones is a feldspatic grain (partly resorbed) which acts as a centre of colloform-zonal patterns. The entire zonal system is transversed by polysynthetic twinning which indicates the transformation from colloform to crystalline state.

Chapter 13 | Symplectic — synantetic intergrowths

The symplectic–synantetic intergrowths and their genetic significance

Plagioclases associated with K-feldspar often show quartz worm-like bodies in intergrowth with their plagioclase host. These textures are referred to as myrmekites. The symplectic quartz–plagioclase myrmekitic textures have been for a long time a subject of controversy. Becke (1908), Sederholm (1916), Christa (1928), Paraskevopoulos (1953), Carman and Tuttle (1963) consider a post-K-feldspar crystallisation of the plagioclase as a pre-requisite for their formation.

In contrast, Michel-Levy (1874), Erdmannsdörffer (1941b, 1946), Drescher-Kaden (1942, 1948, 1969) and Augustithis (1959/60, 1962b) have argued a post-plagioclase crystallisation for the K-feldspar. Some other workers have attempted to explain myrmekites as eutectic or as unmixing products due to deformation effects, e.g., Sarma and Raja (1958, 1959), Shelley (1963, 1970). In the present atlas the wide spectrum of the myrmekitic phenomenology is discussed and new observations are introduced.

The explanation according to Becke (1908) that the myrmekitic textures are the result of the reactions of a pre-existing K-feldspar and a later crystallised plagioclase, is in contradiction to microscopic observations. Fig. 144 and 145 show an orthoclase "double-inclusion" (K-feldspar megablast topometasomatically formed by infiltration of solutions into a granitic xenolith) enclosing, corroding the xenolithic mineral components and causing marginal myrmekitisation to the pre-existing plagioclases. In general, mineral contacts are dubious regarding age-interpretations, however, in this case we have a demonstrably later K-feldspar and the corrosion outlines of the plagioclases can be attributed to the effects of the later orthoclase. Comparable is the phenomenology when K-feldspar megablasts of the granite come in contact with the margins of the xenolithic components and in this case pre-existing plagioclases of the xenolith are corroded and myrmekitised by the later K-feldspar (Fig. 146, 147 and 148). A series of selected microscopic evidence demonstrates the corrosion phenomenology of myrmekitised plagioclases by K-feldspar. Fig. 149 shows plagioclase corroded by K-feldspar and partly myrme-

kitised. Myrmekitisation occurs only in a restricted part of the plagioclases. It is difficult to explain the lack of myrmekitisation in other parts of the plagioclase margins.

The contact of a later K-feldspar with a corroded plagioclase is not necessarily accompanied by myrmekitisation of the latter. Fig. 150 shows K-feldspar in contact with plagioclase (corroded but not myrmekitised) and, paradoxically, the same K-feldspar is in contact with corroded biotites which show quartz myrmekitic intergrowths. In other comparable instances, myrmekitisation of both biotite and plagioclase has taken place (Fig. 151).

Most convincing evidence of plagioclase (myrmekitised) corrosion by later K-feldspar is deduced by textural comparisons. Fig. 152 shows U- and Y-shaped myrmekitic quartz bodies in plagioclase which is in contact with K-feldspar. Fig. 153 similarly shows V-shaped myrmekitic quartz body, however, the K-feldspar has corroded and replaced the greatest portion of the plagioclase part between the V-shaped myrmekitic quartz body. Evidence of further replacement and corrosion of plagioclase parts is illustrated in Fig. 154 where the entire part of the plagioclase (which was existing) between the V-shaped myrmekitic quartz has been replaced. In addition, often due to plagioclase corrosion and replacement, K-feldspar protuberances extend into the myrmekitised plagioclase partly freeing the myrmekitic quartz (Fig. 155).

Other evidence of myrmekitised-plagioclase corrosion by K-feldspar is furnished by the textural behaviour of the quartz myrmekitic bodies themselves. Due to corrosion of the already myrmekitised plagioclase, quartz bodies are partly freed from their initial association with the plagioclase and "protrude" into the K-feldspar. Furthermore, the K-feldspar replacement took advantage of certain plagioclase lamellae. Similarly, Fig. 156 and 157 show quartz bodies partly or entirely enclosed in the K-feldspar, and in this case the myrmekitic quartz bodies were freed from their association with the plagioclase due to the latter's corrosion. A characteristic case of quartz myrmekitic body entirely freed from the plagioclase and now in the K-feldspar is indicated in Fig. 158.

Often the corrosion of myrmekitised plagioclase by

K-feldspar infiltrating into and replacing the plagioclase results in the typical "rounded" contours between these two mineral phases (Fig. 159). Similarly, corrosion of the myrmekitised plagioclase has taken place in the case illustrated in Fig. 160, where in addition, a plagioclase "cross-lamella" is partly preserved as relic structure in the K-feldspar. In many cases the plagioclase replacement has taken place by K-feldspar "infiltration" taking advantage of margins between differently orientated plagioclases (Fig. 161). A detailed photomicrograph shows intergranular K-feldspar corroding and replacing the plagioclases. Typical corrosion appearances and partial freeing of myrmekitic quartz is again illustrated (Fig. 162).

Most convincing evidence of the myrmekitised plagioclase corrosion by K-feldspar is provided by the corrosion appearances of the myrmekitic quartz bodies themselves. Fig. 163 shows myrmekitised plagioclase with corrosion (rounded outlines) against K-feldspar; also the myrmekitic quartz body has fallen subject to the corrosion and shows a concave margin to the K-feldspar. In addition relics of myrmekitic quartz are now in the K-feldspar (Fig. 163). Additional evidence of myrmekitic quartz corrosion is shown in Fig. 164. In this case a "myrmekitic" quartz body acts as a delimiting margin to the corrosion of the myrmekite (plagioclase with quartz worm-like intergrowths) by the K-feldspar.

A special case of interest showing the corrosion and replacement of the myrmekitised plagioclase by the K-feldspar is shown in Fig. 165. A protruding K-feldspar apophysis in the myrmekitised plagioclase replaces the latter; a myrmekitic quartz fine body is preserved in the K-feldspar.

The phenomenology of myrmekitic-symplectic intergrowths

The phenomenology of myrmekitic intergrowths is very complex and in cases dubious, nevertheless an attempt is made to present a general picture of the textural behaviour of the myrmekitic quartz in their host plagioclases.

The complexity and extent of myrmekitisation can vary greatly from a few myrmekitic quartz bodies to extreme cases where broad margins of the plagioclase or the greater portion of the host feldspar is extensively myrmekitised (Fig. 166). Fig. 167 and 168 show marginal myrmekitisation of a plagioclase in contact with K-feldspar whereby fine quartz myrmekitic canals extend from the contact K-feldspar–plagioclase into the latter, perpendicular to the plagioclase twinning. Several fine myrmekitic quartz-canals unite to form a myrmekitic body.

A replacement of the plagioclase by the myrmekitic quartz "infiltrations" has taken place as is evidenced by the outline of the myrmekitic quartz. Small indentations are indicated corresponding to twin-lamellae of the plagioclase. Also, differences in the interference colours of the myrmekitic quartz corresponding to the initial plagioclase twin lamellae are shown. Other microscopic observations which support a later crystallisation of the quartz bodies in the myrmekitic intergrowth with the plagioclase are shown in Fig. 169 and 170.

The plagioclase twinning of the pre-existing host has exercised a control on the form of the later myrmekitic quartz (an arrow, Fig. 170, shows that a plagioclase twin lamella has influenced the shape of a myrmekitic quartz body). In other cases, however, myrmekitic quartz bodies have crossed the twin lamellae. Nevertheless, the plagioclase twin lamella has in cases acted as a barrier which prevented the further penetration of quartz.

Myrmekitic quartz bodies often include "relics" of fine plagioclase twinning (arrow "a" in Fig. 171 and 172) clearly indicating a replacement of the pre-existing plagioclase by the quartz-forming solutions.

Whereas often the myrmekitic quartz crosses the plagioclase twinning, myrmekitic quartz bodies following either plagioclase lamellae or interlamellar spaces are observed (Fig. 173). In other instances myrmekitic quartz bodies extend into the plagioclase and attain a parallelism within the plagioclase host which corresponds to possible interlamellar spaces (Fig. 174). In such cases, the controlling factor determining the shape and orientation of the quartz myrmekitic bodies has been the "directions" of maximum penetrability within the plagioclase host. However, directions of greatest penetrability are not exclusively interlamellar spaces but depend also on "lattice spaces" of the host plagioclase.

Most characteristically orientated quartz-myrmekitic bodies in the plagioclase host are indicated in Fig. 175. Elongated myrmekitic quartz bodies (rhabdites) are orientated perpendicular to the margins of the host plagioclase (arrow a in Fig. 175 shows myrmekitic rhabdites perpendicular to one another). Both the shape and the orientation direction of these myrmekitic quartz bodies depend on penetrability directions within the host plagioclase. Similarly, Fig. 176 illustrates myrmekitic quartz bodies with two prevailing directions of orientation, the one being perpendicular to the other corresponding parallel and perpendicular to the twinning of the plagioclase host.

In contrast to the Y- and U-shaped or complex branching-form, rhabdite myrmekitic bodies are common and show often a tendency of parallel orientation, again controlled by directions of penetrability within the host (Fig. 177).

Furthermore, observations reveal that the form of myrmekitic quartz may depend on direction of penetrability of the plagioclase host. Fig. 178 shows myrmekitic quartz partly following the plagioclase twinning and also extending perpendicularly to its host, probably following another direction of penetrability perpendicular to the twin lamellae.

The size of the myrmekitic quartz can greatly vary. Fine myrmekitic quartz may represent infiltrations following a different penetrability direction within the host than the more coarse myrmekitic quartz (Fig. 179). Cases are described "Reaktionsgefüge" by Drescher-Kaden (1948) where the coarse grain myrmekitic quartz encloses fine myrmekitic quartz bodies, thus suggesting distinct "episodes" (generations?) of myrmekitisation (Fig. 180).

Comparable to the myrmekitic worm-like quartz bodies, is the myrmekitoid quartz. Fig. 181 shows K-feldspar in contact with corroded and affected plagioclase. Fine quartz canals extend from the reaction margin of the plagioclase inwards uniting to form a "myrmekitoid" quartz body; this textural behaviour of the myrmekitoid quartz is commensurable to the case described in Fig. 168. Myrmekitoids of variable form are illustrated in Fig. 182.

Fig. 183 shows quartz outside the plagioclase with a worm-like myrmekitic extension which attains a myrmekitic form and character inside the plagioclase. Such textural patterns support an "independent" quartz formation, an extension of which by infiltration and replacement gives rise to myrmekitic intergrowth. Similarly, quartz grains in contact with plagioclase send off extensions penetrating the feldspar and attaining myrmekitoid character (Fig. 184).

Ring-like myrmekitoid bodies may exist in plagioclase (Fig. 185 and 186) in textural association with biotite included in the feldspar. Fig. 186 indicates, the myrmekitic quartz "curved" around a part of the biotite. The form and size of myrmekitoid bodies is often "unorthodox" and difficult to explain. Fig. 187 shows a quartz myrmekitoid, ovoidal in shape, associated with fine myrmekitic quartz.

The phenomenology of plagioclase reaction-zones and myrmekitisation

In addition to the corrosion outlines of myrmekitised plagioclases in contact with the later K-feldspar, the reaction margins of myrmekitised plagioclases are of petrogenetic significance in support of a later K-feldspar

crystallisation. Nevertheless, in contradiction to the myrmekite formation where a pre-existing plagioclase (generation I) is surrounded by later K-feldspar, cases are described by Drescher-Kaden ("Reaktionsgefüge" 1948 p. 84) where a later blastic plagioclase (generation II), post-K-feldspar in age, is showing a reaction margin myrmekite (type II). A comparable case is presented in Fig. 188 and 189.

Whereas, in general, myrmekitisation is associated with marginal reaction-phenomena of the plagioclases, detailed microscopic observations show divergences from this rather oversimplified textural relation. Fig. 190 shows twinned plagioclase in contact with K-feldspar and the plagioclase margin perpendicular to the feldspar shows a fringe of reaction with myrmekitisation. No obvious reversing of the twinning is observed in the reaction margin. Fig. 191 and 192 show that within a reaction margin, later myrmekitisation can be restricted in only certain parts of it. In contrast, plagioclase reaction margins with K-feldspar may be free of myrmekitic quartz. Paradoxically, a quartz myrmekitic growth may extend, in a case following a plagioclase lamella, into the unaffected plagioclase immediately after the reaction margin (Fig. 193). In some cases, the myrmekitic quartz bodies are restricted to a relatively narrow "zone" within a broad reaction margin immediately at its contact with the unaffected plagioclase (Fig. 194 and 195).

Very often "corona" type myrmekitised margins of plagioclase exist (Fig. 196) and clearly demonstrate the relation between myrmekitisation of plagioclase and K-feldspar association. A corollary to these "corona" types of myrmekite is the "epiphysis" of myrmekite to zoned plagioclases (Fig. 197). In contrast to the broad reaction margins described, a post-myrmekitic-quartz thin reaction fringe can be present. Fig. 198 shows a myrmekitised plagioclase with a myrmekitic quartz body "protruding" due to differential resistance to corrosion of the plagioclase by the K-feldspar; the reaction margin is a post-corrosion formation. However, myrmekitisation of plagioclase in contact with K-feldspar can also take place without observed marginal reaction phenomena (Fig. 199). Sometimes myrmekitisation is observed restricted to the outer "zone" of a zoned plagioclase (Fig. 200). It is dubious whether the outer plagioclase zone is the result of contact reaction with the K-feldspar or whether it represents a crystal zonal growth in the outer zone of which myrmekitisation has taken place.

In general, as microscopic observations indicate, the reaction margin (and the associated myrmekitisation) is due to a "synantetic" reaction between a pre-existing plagioclase and a later K-feldspar. Nevertheless, cases exist where reaction margins of plagioclase to K-feldspar

are myrmekitised, whereas contacts of the same plagioclase in contact with another plagioclase show reaction
margins free of myrmekitic quartz (Fig. 201). Furthermore, considering the reaction margin of plagioclase
with K-feldspar, often myrmekitisation has been observed to be associated with this synantetic zone. In contrast, observation shows myrmekitised plagioclases with
abundant myrmekitic quartz in the centre and myrmekitic quartz-free marginal parts (Fig. 202). Also a plagioclase reaction margin may be relatively poor in myrmekitic quartz as compared to the central parts of the
plagioclase (Fig. 203). Fig. 204 is in support of the
explanation that myrmekitisation can be restricted to
the outer zone of an already zoned plagioclase. It should
be noticed that the quartz-myrmekitic bodies took
advantage of a greater interzonal penetrability of the
plagioclase. However, often myrmekitisation of plagioclase is restricted to a reaction margin of the plagioclase with the K-feldspar. Reversing of the plagioclase twinning is indicated in this reaction margin (Fig. 205, 206
and 207). In cases, the myrmekitised plagioclase (with
myrmekitic quartz restricted in the reaction margin)
shows a reversing and "displacement" of reaction margin
twin lamellae (Fig. 208)

*The "infiltration" phenomenology of myrmekitic and
myrmekitoid quartz bodies*

In contrast to the quartz myrmekitic bodies in plagioclases associated with K-feldspar, myrmekitic or myrmekitoid quartz bodies may exist independent of the
association K-feldspar–plagioclase. Fig. 209 shows a plagioclase with a crack, perpendicular to which fine myrmekitic quartz bodies have penetrated into the plagioclase. Interleptonic (between fine spaces) penetration of
solution is considered to be the cause of this type of
myrmekite. The absence of K-feldspar in this textural
pattern should be noted. Most characteristic symplectic
intergrowths, myrmekitic-like in appearance, may be
produced as a result of intracrystalline penetration of
solutions. Myrmekitic-like intergrowths of an undeter-
mined nature are observed in pyroxene phenocrysts of
an olivine basalt (Fig. 210 and 211). It should be noted
that the forms attained, by intracrystalline penetration,
resemble symplectic myrmekitic intergrowths.

Impressive infiltration myrmekitoid textures are
shown in Fig. 212 and 213. Twinned plagioclase has
been "infiltrated" by a quartz-forming solution resulting
in the formation of myrmekitic-like bodies partly following the twinning and partly delimited by twin planes.
Similarly, Fig. 214 shows quartz marginal to plagioclase

with protuberances extending into the feldspar replacing
the plagioclase and attaining quartz myrmekitoid form.

Most indicative infiltration and replacement quartz
myrmekitic intergrowths are exhibited where a muscovite lamella is partly enclosed by a plagioclase. Quartz-
forming solutions have infiltrated taking advantage of
the interleptonic spaces between plagioclase and muscovite and have partly replaced both mineral phases, resulting in a myrmekitoid textural pattern. The quartz-
forming solutions have partly followed the twinning
planes and interleptonic spaces of the plagioclase
(Fig. 214, 215 and 216). Additional interleptonic myrmekitic quartz formation has taken place between differently orientated parts of plagioclase (Fig. 217 and
218). The quartz-forming solutions have taken advantage
of the interleptonic spaces in addition to normal replace-
ment-infiltration myrmekitic quartz. In Fig. 218 a sillimanite needle is partly taken over by the myrmekitic
quartz replacement.

Additional evidence in support of an "infiltration" of
the myrmekitic quartz-forming solutions is provided by
the relation of myrmekitic bodies, or parts of them, with
the intergranular-interleptonic spaces between different
minerals. Fig. 219 shows a U-shaped myrmekitic quartz
body with one of its limbs following intergranular space
as defined by the contact of two differently orientated
plagioclases.

Another observation indicating the influence in the
shape of the myrmekitic bodies exercised by the host's
penetrability is shown in Fig. 220. A myrmekitic quartz
body extends from the plagioclase to its contact with a
biotite, partly following the contact but not extending
into the mica. The cleavage orientation of the mica was
not favourable for the prolongation of the myrmekitic
quartz body as well into the biotite.

A corollary to the quartz infiltration explanation is
the myrmekitisation of biotite independent of K-feldspar contact reactions (Fig. 221). The quartz myrmekitisation has taken advantage of the biotite-cleavage as a
direction of greater penetrability. Similarly, myrmekitisation of biotite in contact with later formed K-feldspar
is shown in Fig. 222 and 223 and in these cases the
quartz formation has taken advantage of the biotite-
cleavage which is a direction of greater penetrability.

According to Becke's explanation, the myrmekitic
quartz–plagioclase intergrowths have been explained as
the result of the reaction of pre-existing K-feldspar with
later plagioclase. However, microscopic observations of
myrmekitic intergrowths reveal a phenomenology contrary and fundamentally different to Becke's views.
Fig. 151 shows K-feldspar in contact with plagioclase
and biotite. Myrmekitisation of the plagioclase and bio-

tite has taken place as a result of the synantetic reactions of plagioclase and K-feldspar as well as biotite and K-feldspar. In contrast to the "explanation" whereby the reaction plagioclase–K-feldspar has taken place, as shown in Fig. 151 also myrmekitisation has taken place in the biotite which is an older mineral than the K-feldspar.

In order to explain the myrmekitisation of plagioclase and biotite simultaneously in contact with the same K-feldspar, an explanation of myrmekitic quartz-formation independent of the reaction plagioclase–K-feldspar and allowing for sufficient theoretical freedom in order to explain also the myrmekitic quartz in the biotite, is necessary. As such, a hypothesis is proposed whereby intracrystalline infiltration and replacement of quartz-forming solution is possibly – but not necessarily – a forerunner phase of K-feldspar crystallisation.

In support of this explanation are:

(1) The corrosion of an already myrmekitised plagioclase by later K-feldspar whereby myrmekitic quartz is set free from its association with plagioclase and is protruding as resistant relics in K-feldspar. On the basis of these observations it can be seen that, to a great extent, the quartz myrmekitisation as a phase preceded the corrosion of the plagioclase by the K-feldspar since myrmekitic quartz has itself been partly a victim of these corrosions.

(2) The relation of myrmekitic quartz to penetrability directions within the plagioclases (Fig. 173).

(3) Additional evidence of an independent forerunner phase of the myrmekitic quartz-forming solutions is provided by Fig. 151 where in addition to the plagioclase, biotite – a mineral phase independent of the reaction K-feldpar–plagioclase – as well has been infiltrated and myrmekitised by the quartz-forming solutions.

Further evidence of myrmekitic or myrmekitoid quartz in intergrowth with both plagioclase and biotite is indicated in Fig. 224 and 225. The myrmekitic quartz-forming solutions have infiltrated irrespectively into both mineral phases, and as shown in Fig. 225 (arrow *a*) myrmekitoid quartz bodies transverse the contact of both biotite and plagioclase.

More common are the textural patterns of biotite corroded by later K-feldspar, (Fig. 226). Here again myrmekitic quartz is in intergrowth with the mica and most probably represents a pre-corrosion phase. In contrast, though, myrmekitic quartz-forming solutions have infiltrated both the biotite and the associated K-feldspar, clearly representing a later infiltration: metasomatic replacement which attained a myrmekitic form and character (Fig. 227 and 228).

Myrmekitisation of biotite can take place as reaction contacts of pre-existing biotite with later quartz (Fig. 229). The quartz myrmekitic bodies represent infiltration and are related to the later quartz crystallisation. A special case of myrmekitised plagioclase grain entirely enclosed in quartz is shown in Fig. 230. However, in this case the quartz is a recrystallisation phase and is independent of the myrmekitised plagioclase, which represents an already myrmekitised component of the palaeosoma that happens to be surrounded and enclosed by the blastic quartz.

In addition to myrmekitic quartz in intergrowth with biotite, also muscovite shows myrmekites. Fig. 231 shows muscovite and plagioclase in contact with later K-feldspar. As a result of the synantetic reaction between an existing muscovite and a later K-feldspar, a reaction margin is produced in the mica in which myrmekitic quartz intergrowths are present. The same K-feldspar is in contact with plagioclase which is also myrmekitised (Fig. 232 and 233). (These textural patterns are comparable and commensurable to those illustrated in Fig 151.) Here again the Becke-hypothesis that myrmekitisation is the result of a reaction of a pre-existing K-feldspar and a later plagioclase is in contradiction to microscopic observation. The evidence supports the explanation that myrmekitic quartz bodies are infiltrations that have "penetrated" into the host minerals.

Comparable to the marginal myrmekitisation of the plagioclase, is the marginal myrmekitisation of muscovites as illustrated in Fig. 234. The quartz myrmekitic "infiltrations" have exploited directions of penetrability perpendicular to the host margins and interzonally. The shape and size of myrmekitic quartz in intergrowth with muscovite shows variation. Fig. 231 shows fine marginal myrmekitic quartz attaining a myrmekitoid character within the same muscovite host.

The association of K-feldspar with myrmekites is not a necessary pre-requisite. Intergrowths of myrmekitoid quartz in plagioclase show continuation with external quartz, the myrmekitic quartz being infiltrations and extensions of the external quartz. Fig. 235 shows "sievelike" structure of quartz composed of scale-like quartz individuals differently orientated and in contact with plagioclase. Detailed photomicrographs (Fig. 236 and 237), show extensions of the quartz sieve-structure into the plagioclase attaining myrmekitoid character.

In contrast to a "synantetic" reaction of plagioclase with later quartz, infiltration of quartz-forming solutions is responsible for these types of "myrmekites". Additional evidence, indicating an independence of the myrmekite formation as a result of the synantetic reaction of K-feldspar and plagioclase, is shown in Fig. 238 where a plagioclase is in contact with a muscovite. The plagioclase shows a myrmekitised reaction margin with the mica.

Further evidence of myrmekitic quartz as infiltration intergrowths is provided by the association of myrmekitised epidote in contact with K-feldspar (Fig. 239).

The myrmekites so far considered, represent symplectic textures in granites, gneisses and granitic rocks in general. In contrast, myrmekitic-type intergrowths exist in rocks of diverge petrogenetical origin. Fig. 240 shows myrmekitic quartz in plagioclase – clastic components in coarse grained marbles. Rounded (due to transportation) clastic plagioclases are infiltrated by worm-like quartz infiltrations. The clastic plagioclase is surrounded by recrystallised calcite. The myrmekitic quartz represents a topometasomatic mobilisation of silica and infiltration into the feldspar under metamorphism.

Despite a different petrogenetic origin, textures of comparable synantetic intergrowths are shown in an olivine bomb in a basalt (Fig. 241 and 242). Due to a magmatic reaction, corroded reaction margins are formed in bronzite due to infiltration and magmatic corrosion of the pyroxenes by the basaltic melt. The infiltration of solutions has caused a reaction margin in which intracrystalline penetrability has played a role. Similarly, due to magmatic corrosion and infiltration, a decoloration margin has been formed in a chromspinel with magmatic infiltration attaining myrmekitoid appearance (Fig. 243). A comparable decoloration margin and comparable infiltrations and mobilisation of serpentine due to serpentisation in chromites has resulted in myrmekitic serpentine in chromites (Fig. 244 and 245).

Chapter 14 | Graphic quartz—K-feldspar intergrowths

The graphic quartz–K-feldspar intergrowths have been explained as eutectic simultaneous crystallisations. In addition, several laws have been proposed as governing the crystallographic relationship of these simultaneous crystallisations, e.g., Fersman's "law" (there is a parallel orientation of the prismatic edges of the feldspares to the edge between two adjacent rhombohedral faces of the quartzes). A number of workers besides Fersman (1915), independent of explanations of origin, have recognised regularity in crystal orientation and have introduced a number of rules and "laws", (e.g., Rose, 1837; Breithaupt, 1839; Von Rath, 1870; Woitschach, 1881; Sabersky, 1891; Högbom, 1899; Vallerant, 1902; Christa, 1927).

In contrast to these views, Broegger (1886, 1890), Mügge (1903), Hintze (1904), Nordenskjöld (1910), Drescher-Kaden (1948), and Augustithis (1962a, b), believe that there is no "law" of geometrical space relation of feldspar and quartz in the case of graphic intergrowths. Further, a study of the quartz proportions in different types of graphic quartz–feldspar intergrowths by Erdmannsdörffer (1924) shows a variation in the quartz volume between 15–60% and points out that this variation is not in accordance with an eutectic crystallisation where more constant proportions would be expected.

James Hutton, in his *Theory of the Earth* (1795), was the first to point out a later crystallisation of the quartz in graphic granites. In contrast to the eutectic explanations (e.g., Vogt, 1928, 1931; Wahl, 1929; Johansen, 1923; Nockolds, 1947), a number of workers have explained the graphic intergrowths as products of metasomatic replacements and intracrystalline penetration of solutions (e.g., Schaller, 1926, 1927; Wahlstrom, 1939a, b; Drescher-Kaden, 1948; Schädel, 1961; Augustithis, 1962a, b, 1964a, 1966; Schloemer, 1962).

In contrast to the definite crystallographic relationships and to the eutectic crystallisation of graphic quartz–K-feldspar, a study of the phenomenology of these textures reveals metasomatic replacements and recrystallisation processes. Furthermore, a study of commensurable and comparable textures in rocks and systems of diverse origin and genesis, reveals that graphic quartz–feldspar intergrowths can originate under diverse petrogenetic conditions. Fig. 246 shows metasomatic and infiltration processes in pegmatoid (handspecimen). Replacement of K-feldspar has taken place by the infiltration of quartz-forming solution. Corrosion outlines and K-feldspar rests as well as the infiltration-character of the "graphic quartz" are in support of metasomatic replacements.

A most interesting case is observed where a pegmatoid (representing an exudation phase, mainly of K-feldspar) is transversed by a later quartz vein of 1–2 m thick. The quartz in contact with the pegmatoid extends into the latter by infiltration and replacement and attains graphic quartz form and character in the microcline of the pegmatoid (Fig. 247). Microscopic observations of the contact of quartz vein with the K-feldspar phase of the pegmatoid similarly show extension of the vein quartz attaining graphic quartz form and character (Fig. 248 and 249). In addition, Fig. 250 again shows vein quartz attaining graphic-like form in the K-feldspar of the pegmatoid and indicating undulating extinction due to strain.

The infiltration-replacement origin of graphic quartz in K-feldspar is indicated by its relation to the cleavage of orthoclase. Fig. 251 and 252 show graphic quartz with parts of it following the cleavage interleptonic spaces of the host feldspar. Further evidence of "infiltration" and replacement is provided by the relation of graphic quartz to the intergranular of K-feldspars (Fig. 253 and 254). Also the contacts of graphic quartz with the K-feldspar support an infiltration of the quartz-forming solutions. Small quartz indentations protrude in the K-feldspar (Fig. 255, 256, 257, and 258). Additional evidence of a post-K-feldspar crystallisation for the quartz is illustrated by graphic quartz extensions in veinlets of fine quartz in the K-feldspar (Fig. 259). In cases, partial resorption of the fine quartz of the veinlet has taken place by the graphic quartz (Fig. 260 and 261).

The distribution and behaviour of graphic quartz in the K-feldspar shows great variations. In contrast to crystallographically orientated intergrowths, often the distribution of graphic quartz in the K-feldspar depends on the zonal growths of the host K-feldspar. Fig. 262 shows a central K-feldspar part free of quartz, delimited by rather well-developed crystal faces and surrounded by an outer K-feldspar zone similarly orientated, with graphic quartz intergrowths. The graphic quartz has exploited the interzonal spaces and from there radiates into the outer zone. Often there is a reaction zone between the K-feldspar free of quartz and the outer K-feldspar zone with graphic quartz intergrowths (Fig. 263). As the detailed photomicrograph (Fig. 264) indicates, there is a relation between the reaction zone and the shape and distribution of the graphic quartz. The fact that such reaction zones are related to the graphic quartz presence and form and, furthermore, the presence of the quartz-free K-feldspar, supports that quartz infiltration "impregnated" only the outer K-feldspar zones, causing a reaction margin within the central K-feldspar zone. A comparable phenomenology is indicated in Fig. 265.

According to the eutectic hypothesis (simultaneous crystallisation of quartz and K-feldspar) the graphic quartz should be restricted within the K-feldspar phase. On the contrary, microscopic observations indicate a wider range of possibilities of graphic quartz intergrowths. Fig. 266, 267, 268 and 269 show plagioclases surrounded by K-feldspar. Graphic quartz is in intergrowth with K-feldspar, however, infiltration, replacement and extensions of the graphic quartz are shown also to exist with the plagioclase. In particular, Fig. 268 shows plagioclases surrounded by K-feldspar. Graphic quartz is in intergrowth with an outer zone of the orthoclase and extensions of the quartz continue in the inner K-feldspar zone forming a ring around the included plagioclases and partly invading them. The quartz crystallisation has taken advantage of the intergranular spaces (margin of plagioclases with the K-feldspar).

On the basis of microscopic observation, it can be seen that graphic quartz can be in intergrowth simultaneously with K-feldspar and plagioclase. Fig. 270 shows zoned plagioclase surrounded by K-feldspar. Graphic quartz is in intergrowth with K-feldspar and individual grains of graphic quartz transverse the margin K-feldspar–plagioclase. Quartz in graphic intergrowth also occurs in the outer plagioclase zone. The relation of graphic quartz to plagioclase enclosed in K-feldspar is variable. Fig. 271 shows plagioclase surrounded by K-feldspar in intergrowth with graphic quartz. Graphic quartz grains follow the margin K-feldspar–plagioclase and partly protrude into the latter, however, they do not extend into the plagioclase but only partly protrude into the reaction zone of the plagioclase.

Another case illustrating graphic quartz in intergrowth with albitic plagioclase is shown in Fig. 272. Similarly Fig. 273 shows graphic quartz in intergrowth with the plagioclase. A reaction margin is indicated at the contact of the plagioclase portion with graphic quartz and the plagioclase portion free from quartz. The reaction margin of the plagioclase (reversing of zoning) is most probably caused by the reactions involved due to the infiltration of quartz-forming solutions.

The phenomenology of graphic quartz–K-feldspar intergrowths

Fig. 274 shows the behaviour of graphic quartz to the K-feldspar host twinning. Graphic quartz is shown with "reversed" orientation in the twinned K-feldspar, most probably different directions of penetrability existed in the twins. Most impressive textural patterns of graphic quartz with K-feldspar are indicated in Fig. 275, 276, 277 and 278. The orientation of the graphic quartz depends on the penetrability direction of the single or twinned host individual. The crystal-penetrability is crystallographically orientated, as is shown in the case of the twinned individuals (Fig. 276). It should be noted that the proportion of graphic quartz to K-feldspar is very high.

The form and distribution of graphic quartz in the K-feldspar host can also greatly vary. Fig. 279 shows allotriomorphic graphic quartz; the degree of idiomorphism of graphic quartz can show all degrees of gradation. Idiomorphic graphic quartz is shown in Fig. 280, and Fig. 281 shows micrographic idiomorphic quartz.

In contrast to the idiomorphic and subidiomorphic oriented quartz, is the rounded quartz associated with an outer zone of a K-feldspar. The common orientation of quartz individuals is in support of their graphic nature (Fig. 282).

The shape of the graphic quartz may depend on biotite laths included in the K-feldspar. Biotite laths act as a controlling factor in the development of a granophyric individual. Fig. 283 and 284 show a biotite lath perpendicular to the direction of penetrability followed by the quartz-forming solutions.

Microscopic observations of graphic quartz often reveal that a single individual is in reality composed of subindividuals (Fig. 285 and 286). In addition, graphic quartz may show undulating extinction due to "recrystallisation" under strain.

The morphology of granophyric quartz can be variable indeed: granophyric quartz, fine worm-like intergrowths with K-feldspar have been often observed and have been confused with myrmekitic quartz. A series of observations, however, reveal the contradistinction between myrmekitisation and graphic quartz. Fine worm-like granophyric quartz may follow the penetrability direction in the host-K-feldspar as well as the margins of perthite (Fig. 287). Often the granophyric quartz, or parts of it, attain "idiomorphic" forms and thus reveal their granophyric nature. The morphology of these granophyric bodies is illustrated in Fig. 288, 289 and 290. Fig. 290 shows that the granophyric quartz worm-like bodies are a phase independent of myrmekitic quartz formation, which in contradistinction, is a synantetic reaction phenomenon. In this photomicrograph, (Fig. 290), a myrmekitised plagioclase is also illustrated and it can be seen that the myrmekitic intergrowths are independent of the symplectic granophyric (worm-like) intergrowths in the K-feldspar.

In contradistinction to the rounded micrographic intergrowth in the outer zone of the K-feldspar host (Fig. 282), is the globular in form graphic quartz (Fig. 291) representing metasomatic replacements of perthitised K-feldspar, relics of which are interglobular (Fig. 292). Graphic quartz in intergrowth with microcline and showing rounded outlines is shown in Fig. 293.

In contrast to the explanation that the graphic quartz is an eutectic crystallisation simultaneously with K-feldspar, microscopic observations reveal a wider range of graphic intergrowths of mineral phases that are contrary to eutectic crystallisation, e.g., graphic quartz in intergrowth with hornblende, graphic quartz in intergrowth with myrmekitised plagioclase, graphic quartz in association with quartz, and graphic quartz in intergrowth with micas. These ranges of possibilities clearly support a non-eutectic origin. In comparison to the infiltration-replacement phenomenology of the graphic quartz–K-feldspar, also in these cases commensurable textural patterns are observed suggesting infiltration and replacements.

Fig. 294 shows infiltration of quartz along the cleavage direction of hornblende. No graphic character is attained by this quartz. In contrast, Fig. 295 shows hornblende in intergrowth with graphic quartz. The graphic quartz-forming solutions have exploited the contact of hornblende and its adjacent plagioclase. Fig. 296 shows graphic quartz following the intergranular space of K-feldspar grains as well as those of K-feldspar–hornblende. Graphic quartz intergrowths result as the quartz (solutions) infiltrates into the outer zone of the hornblende.

Textural patterns of hornblende, in association with graphic quartz and in intergrowth with K-feldspar are shown in Fig. 297 and 298. The graphic quartz may occupy intergranular spaces between the hornblende or may be in graphic intergrowth with it. In this case, a later quartz has infiltrated into the hornblende with which it is now in graphic intergrowth. Additional evi-

dence of the infiltration, replacement nature of granophyric quartz in intergrowth with both K-feldspar and hornblende is indicated in Fig. 299. Granophyric quartz in intergrowth with K-feldspar transverses the boundary K-feldspar and hornblende and maintains its granophyric character in the amphibole.

It is indeed difficult to visualise an eutectic and simultaneous crystallisation of hornblende, quartz and K-feldspar. The textural patterns rather suggest the following interpretation: the hornblende crystallised first, this was followed by K-feldspar, and the graphic quartz is a later phase that has infiltrated into both. It should be noted that accessory apatites (Fig. 299) representing a first phase of crystallisation, are present partly in the hornblende and partly in the K-feldspar. The graphic quartz-forming solutions have exploited the intergranular spaces between the apatites.

Additional evidence of the non-eutectic origin of the graphic quartz–K-feldspar intergrowths is provided by the textural patterns shown in Fig. 300, 301, and 302. Graphic quartz in intergrowth with K-feldspar transverses the contacts and extends into myrmekitised plagioclases included in the K-feldspar.

The textural patterns of graphic quartz in intergrowth with K-feldspar and myrmekitised plagioclase should be interpreted as follows: pre-K-feldspar plagioclases are surrounded by or come into contact with later blastic K-feldspar and as a result of the synantetic reaction – or as a forerunner phase – myrmekitisation of the plagioclase has taken place. As a later phase, graphic quartz-forming solutions by infiltration and replacement resulted in graphic quartz growths into the K-feldspar and transversing the boundary K-feldspar–plagioclase. It should be noted that the myrmekite (worm-like bodies in plagioclase) are also transversed by the later graphic quartz as can be seen in Fig. 300, 301, and 302. An interesting textural pattern, whereby granophyric quartz is in intergrowth with K-feldspar and with a different generation of quartz, is observed in Fig. 303. It shows granophyric quartz in intergrowth with both, K-feldspar and a different generation of quartz. It is dubious whether this quartz is a pre-graphic phase or a post-graphic quartz replacing the K-feldspar and freeing the granophyric quartz which in turn has been enclosed.

The infiltration origin of graphic quartz is nevertheless indicated by its association with K-feldspar and by sending protuberances into an adjacent biotite. Fig. 304 shows graphic quartz in intergrowth with K-feldspar and with an extension into the biotite following the cleavage of the mica. Comparable textures are shown in Fig. 305 where granophyric quartz in intergrowth with K-feldspar transverses the boundary K-feldspar and enclosed biotite, and extends into the latter maintaining its granophyric character. Further evidence of the replacement and infiltration origin of the granophyric quartz is shown in Fig. 306. Granophyric quartz in intergrowth with K-feldspar extends into an adjacent biotite, infiltrating and replacing the mica and maintaining its granophyric character.

The quartz infiltration into biotite can be of two generations. Fig. 307 shows biotite with reaction margins in contact with K-feldspar. Myrmekitic quartz exists in the biotite reaction margin as a synantetic intergrowth. In addition, infiltration of quartz independent of the reaction margin can take place, resulting in graphic-like patterns.

Most complex textural associations of graphic quartz–K-feldspar–muscovite are shown in Fig. 308, 309 and 310. Fig. 308 shows the general pattern of the complex intergrowth. It can be seen that the graphic quartz (in graphic intergrowth with K-feldspar) has infiltrated and replaced the muscovite as well. Fig. 309 and 310 show details of graphic quartz in the muscovite. The quartz, in addition to the infiltration into muscovite and replacement along its cleavage, also corroded parts of the microcline associated with the mica. Other complex textural patterns of graphic quartz in intergrowth with muscovite and K-feldspar (or plagioclase) are shown in Fig. 311 and 312. Fig. 311 shows K-feldspar in intergrowth with muscovite attaining graphic form. It is probable that the graphic muscovite intergrowths in the K-feldspar might represent a replacement relic of the mica by the K-feldspar. Graphic quartz is shown in the muscovite and also forms a fringe around the graphic-like muscovite associated with the K-feldspar. The graphic quartz has infiltrated into the intergranular space between the muscovite-rests of corrosion (graphic muscovite) and the K-feldspar. So the infiltration occurred later than the corrosion of the mica by the K-feldspar. Comparable complex intergrowth patterns are shown in Fig. 312. Graphic quartz is present in plagioclase. Also muscovite is present in the feldspar. The muscovite in the plagioclase is infiltrated and replaced by quartz which protudes as well into the twin lamellae of the plagioclase. The quartz attains a graphic-like form.

Far more simplified infiltration and replacement textures are shown in Fig. 313 and 314. Fig. 313 shows K-feldspar in contact with muscovite. Quartz infiltrations in the K-feldspar extend into the muscovite as replacements. Similarly in biotite associated with hornblende, quartz infiltrations attain a "graphic"-like form and have taken advantage of the biotite cleavage (Fig. 314).

Graphic-like quartz infiltration-replacement can take place at low temperatures and at a late phase of the granite formation. "Graphic" quartz extends into a K-feldspar which is chloritised. The quartz extends into the feldspar as well as into the chlorite (Fig. 315).

In contradistinction to the graphic quartz intergrowth with feldspar, mica and hornblende, a series of observations reveal that in addition to quartz other minerals can show graphic intergrowth forms. Fig. 316 shows graphic quartz in K-feldspar and also in the same K-feldspar hornblende graphic intergrowths co-exist. The graphic hornblende in intergrowth with the K-feldspar represents a system that cannot be physicochemically explained as eutectic crystallisation. Comparable graphic-like hornblende intergrowths with K-feldspar are illustrated in Fig. 317. It should be noted that the hornblendes form a ramified and anastomosing system of infiltrations and replacements and have followed the contact of K-feldspar with a plagioclase. Similarly a system of amphiboles, vein-like in form, have infiltrated into the K-feldspar (Fig. 318). In both cases, a topometasomatic infiltration of amphiboles has taken place simulating graphic-like forms.

In the pegmatites from Ruggles Mine, graphic-like uraninite is in intergrowth with microcline (Fig. 319 and 320). The uraninite graphic forms are skeleton growths and represent a later crystallisation in the K-feldspar. An eutectic system of uraninite–K-feldspar is not physicochemically thinkable.

A graphic-like intergrowth of an "unidentified" mineral occurs in plagioclase representing rather an infiltration textural pattern (Fig. 321). Another case of graphic intergrowths which contradicts an eutectic crystallisation is the graphic-like tourmaline intergrowths with perthitised K-feldspar (Fig. 322 and 323). (The perthitic bodies partly follow the contacts of tourmaline with K-feldspar.) Physicochemically, the crystallisation of the tourmaline cannot form an eutectic system with the K-feldspar.

Graphic-like sericite(?) and graphic quartz occur in K-feldspar and such textural patterns support a replacement rather than simultaneous crystallisations under eutectic crystallisations (Fig. 324).

Pseudographic intergrowths of worm-like relics of muscovite and quartz may exist (Fig. 325). As Fig. 326 and 327 show, such textures are formed by replacement of the mica by the quartz, the worm-like intergrowths representing relics of muscovite or assimilation "shadows" in the quartz. Fig. 327 clearly indicates that quartz has taken advantage of the cleavage of the mica. In contrast to the graphic-like intergrowths due to infiltration and replacement, graphic intergrowth can also occur

GRAPHIC QUARTZ–K-FELDSPAR INTERGROWTHS

under volcanic (magmatic) crystallisation processes. Fig. 328 and 329 show bronzite and olivine (olivine and bronzite nodules in basalts) associated with graphic spinels.

The textural relation of graphic quartz to perthites

The textural relationship of graphic quartz to perthites in the K-feldspar with which quartz is in intergrowth is variable. Microscopic observations show later graphic quartz transversing bands of perthites (Fig. 330). In support of a later age of the graphic quartz, relics of microcline and perthite are in a process of replacement by later graphic quartz (Fig. 331). In contrast, other microscopic observations reveal a later perthitisation than the graphic quartz formation in the K-feldspar (Fig. 332, 333, 334 and 335).

On the basis of the textural pattern introduced in this volume, the post K-feldspar age of the graphic quartz has been illustrated, and similarly a post-K-feldspar age of the perthites is demonstrated on the basis of microscopic observations (see Chapter 15). Since both phases (i.e., graphic quartz and perthites) are metasomatic infiltrations and replacements, the order of events will depend on the changeable sequence of these topometasomatic replacements in the host K-feldspar.

Fig. 332 shows graphic quartz partly sheathed by later perthite; due to "corrosion" an indentation margin of the graphic quartz and relics parts in the perthite, indicate a later age for the perthitisation in this case.

The series of photomicrographs (Fig. 333, 334, 335 and 336) show graphic quartz in perthitised K-feldspar. Fine fringes of perthite partly follow the contact margin of graphic quartz to K-feldspar indicating a later perthitisation. However, if such detailed evidence of post graphic quartz perthite (intergranular between the graphic quartz and the K-feldspar) is missing, the age relation of graphic quartz and perthites is dubious (i.e., it could as well be the graphic quartz transversing the perthite bands – such a case is shown in Fig. 330). Very rarely transition phases are observed (Fig. 337), where a graphic quartz protuberance in the K-feldspar transgresses into perthite bands as continuations of the quartz protuberance. However, the same graphic quartz-individual shows well-defined outlines (see arrow b in Fig. 337).

In cases, the relation of graphic quartz and perthitisation is complex and dubious in its interpretation. A series of observations (Fig. 338, 339 and 340), show graphic quartz with undulating extinction containing "shadow lines" which most probably represent resorption of perthites. They are particularly indicated in Fig. 339. However, it should be pointed out that there is

no coincidence of direction between the perthitisation of the K-feldspar and the "shadows" of resorption. Furthermore, as Fig. 340 shows, the perthites of the K-feldspar form a fringe following the intergranular space of the graphic quartz and the K-feldspar.

Fig. 341 shows graphic quartz in intergrowth with plagioclase and, due to the reaction involved, as the quartz-forming solutions have infiltrated into the plagioclase, a reaction margin with a reversing of the twinning is formed in the plagioclase. The presence of biotite has influenced the form of the graphic quartz.

Graphic quartz may form a network structure in a K-feldspar host. The quartz-forming solutions have followed directions of greater permeability (i.e., cleavage, intergranular spaces) within the K-feldspar. A plagioclase associated with the K-feldspar is surrounded by the graphic quartz which took advantage of a greater penetrability of the intergranular spaces between plagioclase and K-feldspar (Fig. 342). Comparable textural patterns of graphic quartz, following cleavage and intergranular spaces of plagioclases, are illustrated in Fig. 343.

Graphic quartz due to infiltration and replacement may be restricted by the twinning of the host feldspar. As a result of the reactions involved, when the later graphic quartz-forming solutions come in contact with an already existing plagioclase, a reaction margin is formed in the feldspar. Such reaction phenomena would be absent if the graphic quartz and plagioclase were simultaneously eutectic crystallisations (Fig. 344). In cases, the form of the graphic quartz in intergrowth with feldspars is influenced by the presence of biotites. Fig. 345 and 346 show a biotite lath ("restricted" in shape between two graphic quartz).

The significance of skeleton graphic quartz textural patterns and their metasomatic relation to microcline

The graphic quartz intergrowth in K-feldspar represents an intermediate phase (a skeleton crystallisation) to the fully idiomorphic quartz crystal growths, where all crystal faces are developed. Microscopic observations (Fig. 347, 348, 349 and 350) show all transition stages from graphic quartz skeletons to fully developed idiomorphic forms (six-sided in cross-section). It should be noted that the extent of replacement determines the extent of idiomorphism. However, it should also be noted that the cross-section of an idiomorphic quartz is not an equilateral-hexagonal figure. The distorted form of the hexagonal figure rather supports a replacement origin of the quartz. Under replacement, the crystallisation force of the quartz is not involved in the growth. Fig. 349 shows a skeleton graphic quartz outline and is compared to the hexagonal form which would have been attained if the quartz was fully developed. As the graphic quartz tends to attain idiomorphic form the enclosed microclines and perthites in the central part of the quartz would tend to be replaced by the graphic quartz.

Micrographic quartz due to recrystallisation of quartzitic quartz

In the polymictic conglomerate of Buri Rashitcha, quartzitic pebbles and the matrix have been subjected to granitisation. The transformation of the matrix produced granoblastic textures with microcline microblasts (see Chapter 11, Fig. 50). The extent of transformation of the quartzitic pebbles depended to a great extent on their compactness. However, infiltration of solutions and topometasomatic mobilisations have taken place in the quartzitic pebbles as well. As a result of K-feldspar blastesis (topometasomatic) in quartzitic pebbles and due to recrystallisation and mobilisation of the quartz, all phases of transition are observed of quartzitic quartz grains "inbibed" with K-feldspar blastesis (Fig. 351), to recrystallisation and reorientation of the quartzitic quartz to form graphic quartz in association with K-feldsparblast in parts of the quartzitic pebbles of the Buri Rashitcha Conglomerate.

The phenomenology of recrystallisation and remobilisation from quartzitic to graphic quartz and the intermediate phases involved are illustrated in a series of figures (Fig. 351, 352, 353, 354, 355, 356) and their descriptions. It should be noted that the micaceous laths present in all the phases of the transformation from quartzitic to granophyric intergrowths are supporting evidence for this transformation.

Graphic quartz intergrowths due to corrosion and mobilisation of quartz in contact with K-feldspars

In addition to the infiltration-replacement and recrystallisation growths of graphic quartz in intergrowth with feldspar, microscopic observations reveal that graphic quartz can be formed due to simultaneous corrosion and mobilisation of quartz in contact with K-feldspar. Fig. 357 shows quartz with rounded outlines due to corrosion in contact with K-feldspar and simultaneously having extensions which attain a graphic quartz character in the K-feldspar. It is dubious whether these graphic-like textures represent relics of quartz or "remobilisations". In contrast to Fig. 357, other observations reveal quartz invaded by K-feldspar with graphic textures

resulting, due to the replacement of the quartz by the feldspar (Fig. 358 and 359).

The co-existence of corrosion boundaries and infiltration-mobilisations attaining graphic form in one and the same quartz individual indicates the complexity of the processes concurrently taking place.

Infiltration of quartz "droplets"

The phenomenology of quartz "infiltrations" is very extensive and variable, as has been discussed in Chapters 13 and 14. A corollary to the so-far discussed quartz "infiltrations" are the quartz "droplets" infiltrations in a wide range of minerals. Fig. 360 shows droplets of quartz following trends of greater penetrability in a quartz host. Similarly, droplets of quartz may infiltrate a plagioclase in cases transversing twin lamellae (Fig. 361). It should be noted that most of the quartz droplets have the same orientation and most probably belong to the same phase of solution infiltration. Comparable fine quartz droplets may exist in K-feldspar following a line which corresponds to a direction of greater penetrability in the K-feldspar. Grains of coarser quartz of comparable origin also co-exist (Fig. 362).

Granophyric quartz–feldspar intergrowths in aegirine rhyolite

In support of the diversity of the petrogenetic conditions under which granophyric intergrowths can be formed, are the micrographic quartz–feldspar intergrowths present as phenocrysts in aegirine rhyolites, Kuni, Asba-Tafari-Chercher, Ethiopia (Fig. 363, 364 and 365). The fact that these quartz–feldspar intergrowths are in textural intergrowth with aegirine and the textural patterns as a whole, is in contrast with the xenocryst-interpretation (xenocrysts are picked up crystals from rock formation transversed by the volcanic melt; in this particular case picked up from granite). The textural intergrowth of this graphic intergrowth with aegirine (which is abundant in the ground-mass of the rhyolite) is in support of the interpretation that these intergrowths represent a crystallisation phase of the rhyolite.

Furthermore, it should be pointed out that, despite their volcanic origin, these intergrowths are not eutectic crystallisations since, due to their phenocrystalline nature, they belong to the early crystallisation of the rhyolitic melt whereas, theoretically, the eutectic crystallisation would take place in the concluding consolidation phase of a melt.

Quartz–feldspar graphic intergrowths in volcanics from the Tranquillity Sea

In the preceeding chapter, we discussed graphic quartz–feldspar intergrowths of diverse petrogenetic origin. It has been seen also that graphic intergrowths cannot be restricted under the physicochemical condition of eutectic crystallisation.

In contrast to the phenomenology of graphic quartz formed by solution following interleptonic spaces and the cases where replacements have been shown, graphic quartz in intergrowth with feldspars with comparable textural patterns can be the result of crystallisation of melts as is shown by the phenocrysts (graphic quartz in intergrowth with feldspar shown in rhyolite), but more convincingly illustrated by graphic quartz–feldspar intergrowths in moon volcanics where a rather dry system (water free) has been involved. Weill et al. (1970a, b) have shown quartz–feldspar graphic intergrowths in igneous lunar samples.

Fig. 366 shows graphic quartz in intergrowth with K-feldspar. The graphic quartz-forms are restricted in the outer margin of the K-feldspar; a quartz-free central part of feldspar is indicated. The contact between quartz-free feldspar and graphic quartz containing feldspar, follows defined crystallographic faces. (Fig. 367 shows a scanning microprobe picture of the distribution of graphic quartz in intergrowth with the feldspar.)

Quartz–feldspar–muscovite symplectic tectonites

Most complex symplectic textures whereby recrystallisation replacement and tectonic influences have played a role, are illustrated in Fig. 368, 369, 370 and 371.

Fig. 368 shows a quartz–feldspar–muscovite symplectic textural pattern, which simultaneously behaves optically as a tectonite (microtectonic unit). A sieve intergrowth pattern of recrystallised quartz, whereby feldspar replacement has taken place and indicating a bending of the tectonite, also is illustrated in this photomicrograph.

Detailed observations of the complex symplectic intergrowth (Fig. 369) shows muscovite in K-feldspar (also plagioclase is present). Late phase crystallisation of quartz occurs partly as an independent growth and partly intergranularly between the muscovite. Often corrosion and replacement of the muscovite by the quartz has taken place. Fig. 370 shows "sieve" intergrowth of recrystallised quartz texturally associated with quartz–feldspar symplectic intergrowth. Similarly Fig. 371 shows quartz–feldspar symplectic intergrowths with the crystal grains attaining idiomorphic forms. These textural patterns are most dubious and difficult to interpret, however, recrystallisation and tectonic influences must have played a role.

Chapter 15 | The phenomenology of perthites

Perthitic textures, general

According to orthodox views, the perthitic textures are ex-solutions in K-feldspars. The following publications are in support of the unmixing theory: Niggli and Beger (1923), Andersen (1928), Spencer (1937), Bowen and Tuttle (1950), Köhler (1948), Laves (1951), Mackenzie and Smith (1955), Yoder et al. (1957), Michot (1961), Ramberg (1962), Barth (1962a), Laves and Soldatos (1963).

In contrast, Mäkinen (1913) has described perthites extending into plagioclases included in K-feldspars. However, it is mainly the work of Drescher-Kaden (1948, 1969) and Augustithis (1959/60, 1962b, 1964b) that has demonstrated a post-K-feldspar metasomatic origin of perthitic bodies. Also, in contradistinction to the ex-solution explanation, Nickel (1953) and Augustithis (1964b) have described perthitisation due to resorption and mobilisation of pre-K-feldspar plagioclases included in orthoclases and microcline.

In the present chapter, perthitic textural patterns are introduced which are incompatible with the ex-solution hypothesis. Furthermore, in order to avoid misunderstandings caused by the diversity of the perthitic nomenclature and, in particular, to avoid the erroneous criticism that the perthites described are cleavelandites (with random orientation), a series of photomicrographs is included which shows orientated flame, flake and vein perthites to be clearly of intracrystalline replacement, i.e. of metasomatic origin.

Perthites and their relation to K-feldspar zoning

In zoned K-feldspar, often the perthitic intergrowths follow interzonal spaces or are restricted to certain zones of the host. Infiltration of perthite-forming solutions and metasomatic replacements along directions of greater penetrability in the K-feldspar are considered to be the cause of the zonal distribution of perthites in the K-feldspar host.

The unmixing theory is in contradiction to interzonal perthites which transgress into diffused and anastomosing perthitoid bodies in K-feldspar (Fig. 372). On the other hand, fine perthites are restricted to certain of the K-feldspar zones, indicating a greater penetrability and susceptibility of the infiltration and replacement by some of the zones of the K-feldspar (Fig. 373). In contrast to the zonal perthites, metasomatic perthites may transverse K-feldspar zones and are independent of the host zoning (Fig. 374).

The penetrability and replacement of K-feldspar by perthite-forming solutions does not necessarily follow defined crystallographic directions but rather is conditioned by topo-crystalline conditions (lattice deformation, interzonal spaces, cleavage, twinning planes) of the host K-feldspar.

Fig. 375 shows zoned K-feldspars with perthite veinlets transversing the zones and having extensions interzonal in character. In addition, perthite-rich and perthite-free zones of K-feldspar are indicated. Topo-crystalline conditions would determine the penetrability of replacement and infiltration of the perthite-forming solutions in the K-feldspar host.

Fig. 376 shows fine linear perthite, and transversing perthitic veinlets in the central part of a K-feldspar. In contradistinction, the peripheral part of the K-feldspar is free from perthites. It should be noted that a perthite-free halo is surrounding the transversing perthitic veinlets. Despite a metasomatic origin, this textural pattern simulates textural patterns of ilmenite with haematite ex-solutions, where haematite-free margins exist.

In contrast to the well defined zonal perthites or interzonal perthitic bodies, Fig. 377 shows perthitic bodies following curved planes within the K-feldspar host. Also a ring perthite-structure is present. It is possible that the perthite-forming solutions infiltrated into strained curved planes of the host K-feldspar. In contradistinction to the well-defined zones of perthite, diffused zones or patches of perthite replacement in K-feldspar may also exist (Fig. 378). These represent small agglutinations of metasomatic replacement of K-feldspar by perthite.

Comparable to the diffused perthitic bodies, interzonal fine perthitic bodies "dot-like in form", following zones of the K-feldspar may exist (Fig. 379). These dot-perthitic bodies in this case are agglutinations of replacements.

Perthites following the cleavage of the host-K-feldspar

In contrast to the zoned perthites, infiltration and replacement can take place along the cleavage of the host K-feldspars. As in the case of graphic quartz following the cleavage direction of the host K-feldspar, similarly perthite-forming solutions have infiltrated into the K-feldspar host following the interleptonic spaces of the cleavage of K-feldspar. Fig. 380 shows irregular fine veinlets of perthite transversing the cleavage of the K-feldspar and often extending along and occupying interleptonic spaces as defined by the cleavage of the host. It is clear that the perthite-forming solutions have infiltrated into the host along directions of greater penetrability as provided by the cleavage. Similarly, Fig. 381 shows fine perthitic veinlets transversing the cleavage and twinning of the K-feldspar and sending extensions following the interleptonic spaces provided by the cleavage of the host K-feldspar.

The relation of perthite–cleavage can be seen as a direction of greater penetrability of the K-feldspar host to the perthite infiltrating solutions, however, metasomatic replacement can take place at the sides of the interleptonic planes (side walls) as defined by the cleavage. Fig. 382 shows ganglion-like perthitic bodies formed by replacement of the walls of the cleavage planes. Additional observations showing cleavage perthites are in Fig. 383 and 384. As shown in Fig. 384, irregular metasomatic anastomosing perthitic veinlets terminate in cleavage-perthites which follow in a linear way the cleavages of the host. Replacement of K-feldspar along the cleavage directions has also taken place. Fig. 385 shows linear perthites and cracks filled with perthite. The perthite-forming solutions have infiltrated and replaced the K-feldspar along interleptonic spaces provided by cracks and cleavage.

Another type of cleavage perthite is illustrated in Fig. 386. The metasomatic perthite replacements form flake-like bodies along the cleavage but not filling the interleptonic spaces, i.e., perthitic flakes situated along the cleavage of the host. Due to the metasomatic replacement, a reaction margin surrounds the flake perthitic bodies.

In contrast to infiltration perthites, replacement perthites which follow the cleavage of the K-feldspar due to metasomatic replacements can be delimited by cleavage directions, i.e., the flake perthites formed, have cleavage boundaries as margins (Fig. 387).

Post-tectonic and fissure perthites

In addition to the penetrability direction provided by interzonal spaces and cleavage direction, tectonic fractures, fissures and strained planes within the K-feldspar host may form directions of greatest penetrability.

The association of perthites along penetrability direction, such as tectonic cracks, fissures or quartz veinlets, is caused after the crystallisation of the host K-feldspar, and supports a later formation of these perthites. This is in contradiction to the unmixing hypothesis which would require a simultaneous crystallisation of the host K-feldspars and the perthitic plagioclase.

Fig. 388 shows microfissures in K-feldspar with flame perthitic bodies starting from the fissures and extending into the K-feldspar perpendicularly to the cracks. This textural pattern indicates an unmistakable relation between the fissures and the perthitisation. Some perthitic bodies actually follow the microfissures, however, the majority of the flame perthitic bodies extend into the K-feldspar having the microfissure as a starting point perpendicular to it. Similarly Figs. 389 and 390 show a microfissure set (the fissure systems follow approximately 3 directions) occupied by post-microfissure perthitic infiltrations. The fissure system has acted at directions of greater penetrability along which the later perthite-forming solutions have infiltrated. The perthites are following a microtectonic fissure pattern and are therefore post-tectonic in origin.

Comparable are the perthitic bodies which occupy – and are associated with – the "block-displacement patterns" observed in microcline. Fig. 391 and 392 show cross-twinned microcline with "block" dislocation and microfissures, the interleptonic spaces produced as a result of block dislocation and the interleptonic spaces of the cracks have acted as "paths" of greater penetrability within the K-feldspar host along which the perthite-forming solutions have penetrated.

In contradistinction to these clearly post-tectonic perthites, Fig. 393 and 394 show perthitic bodies associated with or following strain planes within the K-feldspar. Particularly Fig. 393 shows a distinct relation between perthitisation and strained direction (anomalies in the extinction position of the host K-feldspar). It is dubious whether these types of perthites are post or synkinematic (i.e., perthitisation simultaneous to strain). The explanation of unmixing under synkinematic conditions seems improbable, since often strained directions in K-feldspar are not accompanied by perthitisation. It is possible that in these cases as well, the perthitisation is actually post-kinematic, that is the perthite-forming solutions have infiltrated into the K-feldspar host along directions of greater penetrability provided by the planes of strain.

Comparable to the perthites associated with the

microfissures, are perthitic bodies related or following small veinlets in the K-feldspar. Fig. 395 and 396 show a veinlet of quartz in microcline and perthitic bodies transversing the quartz veinlet and partly following it; perthitic extensions follow the quartz veinlet. This textural pattern illustrates a post-veinlet age for the perthitic bodies. Similarly a perthitoid occupies a part of a quartz veinlet (Fig. 397), however, the perthitoid attains a vein-like form within the K-feldspar. Additional observations of flame perthites interrelated with a quartz veinlet in K-feldspar are shown in Fig. 398 and 399. In both cases the flame perthites start from the quartz-veinlet and extend perpendicularly into the K-feldspar. These observations are comparable to the cases where the flame perthitic bodies are related to microfissures and, in this case, the perthite-forming solutions used the quartz veinlet (or the intergranular boundaries of quartz to K-feldspar) as the direction of greatest penetrability for the perthite-forming solutions.

Comparable textural patterns of flame perthites are shown in association with a later amphibole veinlet in K-feldspar. Fig. 400 shows an amphibole (hornblende?) veinlet intruding a twinned K-feldspar. Flame perthitic bodies start from the veinlet and extend perpendicularly into the K-feldspar. Also perthitic bodies follow the margin amphibole—K-feldspar and attain flame perthitic character in the latter. Also, in this case, the perthitic-forming solutions have taken advantage of the intergranular hornblende-K-feldspar and are post-K-feldspar in age.

Pre-tectonic perthitisation

In contrast to post-tectonic perthitisation, described perthitic types are observed exhibiting tectonic influences. Fig. 401 shows "elongated augen"-shaped perthitic bodies in K-feldspar. The lens shaped perthitic body (Augen-perthite) is a tectonically "mobilised" body within the K-feldspar. Similarly, Fig. 402 shows a strained perthite with boundaries conditioned by tectonic influences in the K-feldspar. Additional evidence of a pre-tectonic perthite is shown in Fig. 403 illustrating perthite with an undulating extinction due to strain.

The relation of perthitisation to twinning

The perthite-forming solutions, in addition to the topocrystalline conditions of penetrability such as interzonal planes cleavage, and microfissures, also infiltrated into the host taking advantage of an intracrystalline direction of penetrability, such as the twin-planes of the host would be. Fig. 404 shows a twinned K-feldspar with

perthite crossing the twinned plane, other perthites, however when they reach the twin-plane run parallel to it. The perthitic-forming solutions have followed the penetrability direction provided by the twinning plane of the K-feldspar. As can be seen, however, the twin-plane is not an "impenetrable" barrier since perthites cross the boundaries of twinned individuals.

A most characteristic pattern of vein and flame perthites following directions of the cross-twinning of microcline is illustrated in Fig. 405 and 406. The infiltration and replacement advanced following the penetrability directions provided by the cross twinning of the microcline. Commensurable is the behaviour of metasomatic-replacement perthites as illustrated in Fig. 407. Perthitisation tends to follow the cross-twinned lamellae of the microcline; in contradistinction to the flame-perthites in Fig. 405 and 406. In this case we have diffused perthites. Another example of perthitisation related to intracrystalline, topocrystalline penetrability is shown in Fig. 408. The perthitisation follows a lamellar structure of the host K-feldspar. In all the described cases, the perthite-forming solutions followed directions of crystal penetrability of the host K-feldspar which correspond to inter-twinning planes, but are not restricted to them.

In contrast, the metasomatic perthitisation may transverse the crystal boundaries and extend into another K-feldspar differently orientated (Fig. 409 and 410). The perthitic bodies, besides transversing the crystal boundaries, follow the boundary between the two differently orientated K-feldspar individuals. The perthitic bodies also form a ring surrounding enclosed quartz whereby the perthite-forming solutions have exploited the intergranular between quartz and feldspar. Additional evidence of the metasomatic infiltration origin of the perthites is the relatively high proportion of the perthites to the K-feldspar host. The variation in the amount of perthites is more in harmony with the metasomatic infiltration explanation for the perthitic bodies.

In contradistinction to the perthitic vein bodies transversing the twinning planes of differently orientated K-feldspar individuals, Fig. 411 shows metasomatic replacement of twinned K-feldspar by plagioclase extending from the margin and crossing the twinning plane. As a result of the replacement, a great portion of the original K-feldspar has changed into plagioclase. In contrast to the unmixing hypothesis, intergranular plagioclase often sends extensions into adjacent K-feldspars which attain perthitic character. Fig. 412 and 413 show intergranular plagioclase with protuberances infiltrating and replacing and adjacent K-feldspar. The intracrystalline plagioclase attains flame perthitic form and character.

The textural patterns support a metasomatic origin for these flame perthitic bodies and thus contradict an unmixing hypothesis, i.e., simultaneous crystallisation of the two feldspar phases. Additional observations in support of a metasomatic replacement origin of flame perthitic bodies are shown in Fig. 414. Marginal plagioclase infiltrates into the K-feldspar attaining a flame perthitic form and character. The flame-perthites are not equally distributed throughout the K-feldspar (as it would be if unmixing had taken place) but tend to "concentrate" within the K-feldspar following directions of greater penetrability.

Often intergranular perthite between two differently orientated K-feldspars, sends extensions attaining perthitic flame form and character into both the K-feldspar hosts (Fig. 415). Clearly the intergranular perthite and its extensions are due to infiltration of perthite-forming solutions following the intergranular and, by intracrystalline infiltration and replacement they attain perthitic form and character. The solution-infiltrations took advantage of the greater penetrability as provided by the intergranular spaces.

Undeniable K-feldspar replacement by metasomatic plagioclase starting from the marginal phase and extending into the K-feldspar is shown in Fig. 416 and 417. The extent of K-feldspar replacement by the later metasomatic plagioclase may vary as can be seen comparing Fig. 416 to Fig. 417.

Perthitic bodies intergranular between two differently orientated perthitised K-feldspars indicate a metasomatic infiltration, in which case the perthite-forming solutions have infiltrated and followed the direction of greater penetrability as provided by the contact of the two K-feldspars (Fig. 418). Comparable metasomatic replacement can take place where intergranular perthite between K-feldspar and quartz sends extensions into the K-feldspar which, by infiltration and replacement, attain a perthitoid form and character. Fig. 419 shows intergranular plagioclase between quartz and microcline with protuberances attaining perthitoid character, i.e., bodies having a perthitic appearance due to infiltration and metasomatic replacements. Parts of quartz are enclosed in the intergranular perthitic body. Similarly, Fig. 420 shows intergranular plagioclase between quartz and K-feldspar sending an extension into the latter and attaining flame perthitic form and character.

In both cases, the metasomatic perthite-forming solutions have infiltrated into the intergranular and have taken advantage of the greater penetrability provided. Due to metasomatic replacement and infiltration into the K-feldspar, the perthitoid and perthitic bodies have been formed. Such observations contradict the unmix-

ing hypothesis which would require a simultaneous crystallisation of K-feldspar and perthite (ex-solutions). The metasomatic and replacement character of marginal plagioclase between quartz and K-feldspar which has extensions attaining a perthitoid form and character by infiltration and replacement in the K-feldspar, is further supported by extensions of the plagioclase as well into the adjacent quartz which has been infiltrated and replaced by the plagioclase.

As a corollary to the metasomatic origin of intergranular plagioclases with perthitoid extensions, Fig. 421 shows intergranular plagioclase (between K-feldspar and quartz) with protuberances of the plagioclase extending and replacing both the adjacent mineral grains, i.e., the intergranular perthitoid mass extends and replaces the quartz as well.

In contrast to the perthitic and perthitoid form of plagioclases in K-feldspar, transgressions of perthitoids into plagioclase flame bodies is shown in Fig. 422. The band perthites also attain the form of a fine intergranular film following the boundary of K-feldspar with the adjacent quartz. The transgression of perthitoids to flame plagioclase and the intergranular perthitic film both support a metasomatic replacement origin of these perthitic bodies. Similarly, irregular perthitoid veinlets, often branching and anastomosing, form an intergranular "band" layer which follows the intergranular space between K-feldspar and an adjacent quartz (Fig. 423). Also, in this case, the metasomatic replacements have taken advantage of the greatest penetrability as provided by the intergranular spaces. In addition to metasomatic replacement there are perthites which are extensions of intergranular plagioclases between two different K-feldspars or between K-feldspar and quartz. Fig. 424 shows a microcline which is marginally replaced by albitic plagioclase; replacement protuberances of which attain perthitoid form.

Often plagioclase adjacent to K-feldspar sends perthitoid extensions into the latter which follow strained planes within the host K-feldspar. Fig. 425 shows plagioclase with protuberances following curved planes within the K-feldspar. The perthitoid followed the directions of greater penetrability which were formed by straining.

Perthites extending beyond the K-feldspar into other mineral phases (e.g., plagioclase, quartz, biotite, tourmaline)

The observations so far have established a relation between topocrystalline penetrability and infiltration replacement of perthitic bodies, i.e., the perthite-forming solution followed intergranular spaces, tectonic planes, cleavage, etc. However, in all the cases described, the perthites were in textural association with the K-feldspar. In contrast, perthites may extend beyond the boundaries of K-feldspar and occur in intergrowth with other mineral phases. These textural patterns support an infiltration of the perthite-forming solution into mineral phases with which the perthites have no physico-chemical relationship, i.e., the perthites cannot be exsolved products by unmixing. Fig. 426 shows a plagioclase enclosed in perthitised K-feldspar, and the perthite-forming solutions extend from the K-feldspar into the plagioclase as well. Similarly flame perthites extend into a plagioclase enclosed in K-feldspar and simultaneously partly surround a corroded margin of it. The flame perthite-forming solutions also have extended into the plagioclase, (Fig. 427).

Additional observations supporting an infiltration origin of the perthites are shown in Fig. 428 and 429. Perthitic veinlets penetrate through a plagioclase enclosed by the K-feldspar. The perthite-forming solutions have penetrated through the K-feldspar and the pre-K-feldspar enclosed plagioclase. In cases, perthites protrude and extend into adjacent plagioclases which have been previously corroded by the later K-feldspar. In Fig. 430 the perthitisation occurred after the synantetic reaction of plagioclase and K-feldspar and transversed the boundaries of the two feldspars.

Another case illustrating different and independent generations of plagioclases in a granite is Fig. 431. Pre-K-feldspar plagioclases are enclosed in metasomatically formed perthites which have been formed by solutions replacing the microcline host.

Detailed observations of quartz in K-feldspar show fine perthitic margins surrounding the quartz crystal grain. The perthite-forming solutions exploited the interleptonic spaces, i.e., the intergranular between quartz and K-feldspar, and have extended from the intergranular into the K-feldspar attaining flame perthitic character (Fig. 432). Similarly, a perthite margin surrounding a quartz grain enclosed in K-feldspar extends and protrudes into the enclosed quartz (Fig. 433). The intergranular nature of the perthitic margin and the perthitic extension in the K-feldspar suggests that the perthite-forming solutions followed by infiltration the interleptonic intergranular spaces which were topo-crystalline directions of greater penetrability; furthermore, the association of perthite with quartz in this case as well is contrary to the unmixing hypothesis. Additional evidence for a metasomatic origin of the perthites is shown in Fig. 434. A perthitic ring surrounds a quartz grain enclosed in the K-feldspar. Also perthitic diffused veinlets transverse the boundary of two differently orientated K-feldspars.

The perthites are not restricted in their association with feldspars and perthitic extensions may protrude into adjacent minerals. Fig. 435 shows perthitised K-feldspar in contact with biotite. Diffused perthitic veinlets in the K-feldspar extend marginally and follow the contact K-feldspar–biotite, extensions of the perthite follow the cleavage direction of the biotite and protrude into the mica. The perthite-forming solution infiltrated by replacement into the K-feldspar and continued into the interleptonic spaces provided by the cleavage of the biotite. These textural patterns contradict the unmixing hypothesis for the origin of the perthitic bodies.

Most interesting is the behaviour of perthite to idioblastic sphene. Fig. 436 shows perthites following the intergranular boundaries of the K-feldspar host to the idioblastic sphene. In contradistinction, Fig. 437 shows idioblastic sphene transversing perthitic bands. In the case of Fig. 436 the perthitisation is post-sphene in age and the perthite-forming solutions took advantage of the intergranular interleptonic spaces between the sphene and the K-feldspar.

In addition to perthites extending into an adjacent biotite, Fig. 438 shows tourmaline in perthitised K-feldspar, also perthitic veinlets in the K-feldspar transverse the tourmaline. A reaction has taken place between tourmaline and perthitic infiltrations. Both, textural patterns shown (i.e., vein-form perthites) and the immiscible physico-chemical relations of tourmaline to perthitic plagioclase, suggest an infiltration and vein-form character for the vein perthites in the tourmaline, which are the continuations of the vein perthites in the K-feldspar.

"Interpenetration perthitic margins" of adjacent K-feldspars

Often marginal perthites of differently orientated K-feldspar interpenetrate with one another or, as indicated in Fig. 439, the perthitic phase of the one extends into the marginal perthite of the adjacent K-feldspar. In contrast to the case exhibited in Fig. 439, Fig. 440 shows a marginal perthite of K-feldspar (in the extinction position) in interpenetration intergrowth with the perthites of the adjacent K-feldspar. It is interesting to note that the interpenetration extension of the marginal perthite protrudes into the adjacent K-feldspar as well. Such symplectic perthitic intergrowth clearly indicates contact-reaction between the crystal phases formed and contradict an unmixing hypothesis. Comparable are interpenetration textures where marginal plagioclase is interpenetrated by perthitic extension of an adjacent

K-feldspar (Fig. 441). The marginal plagioclase in contact with the infiltrated perthite shows corrosion outlines (concave outlines).

Metasomatic flake perthites with margins of lamellar (vein) perthite partly enclose quartz and plagioclase grains in the K-feldspar and partly extend into the intergranular space between the marginal quartz grains. Also perthitic lamellae extend into an adjacent K-feldspar differently orientated (Fig. 442).

The interpenetration of perthites of two differently orientated K-feldspars, (the interpenetration of two marginal perthitic phases), as well as the transition of perthitic bodies into marginal plagioclase are in support of infiltration, metasomatic and synantetic reactions of different phases of feldspar formation.

Flame perthites

In addition to the phenomenology of flame perthites discussed and illustrated in Fig. 388, 398, 413 and 415, whereby evidence of infiltration and replacement has been put forward as a corollary, a series of additional observations is presented. Fig. 443 shows a quartz grain included in K-feldspar in which a marginal perthite partly following the intergranular between quartz and plagioclase extends into the microcline attaining a flame perthitic form and character. Similarly, flame perthitic bodies following the intergranular between enclosed mica and enclosed quartz by K-feldspar extend into the microcline attaining a flame perthitic form and character (Fig. 444). Also, in this case, the flame perthites are products of solutions which have exploited intergranular spaces between existing mineral grains.

Another type of flame-perthite transgressing into linear perthitic type is illustrated in Fig. 445. The flame-perthitoid partly surrounds enclosed quartz grains in the K-feldspar. The flame perthitic bodies are metasomatic infiltrations and replacements and they attain a linear form due to the infiltration of solutions along the penetrability directions of the K-feldspar.

As a corollary to the textural pattern illustrated in Fig. 446, flame perthite extending from the margins of mafic minerals (amphibole) into the K-feldspar encloses small mafic grain. This flame perthite is a metasomatic infiltration taking advantage of the intergranular mafic K-feldspar and enclosing unassimilated mafic relics. The metasomatic origin of flame perthites is supported by the transgression of irregular flake-perthites into protuberances and extensions which attain a flame perthitic form and character (Fig. 447).

In cases, irregular lens-shaped flame perthitic bodies follow a penetrability direction within the K-feldspar and by collision of several individual "aggregates", ganglia or flake-like bodies are formed (Fig. 448). Such "aggregates" depend rather on the penetrability direction of the host K-feldspar and are not the products of unmixing. Fig. 449 shows flame perthitic bodies parallel orientated following "shadows" (due to anomalies in the extinction position within the K-feldspar host) of the K-feldspar which correspond to topocrystalline anomalies within the orthoclase. Also, in this case, the perthite-forming solutions have infiltrated along directions of greater penetrability of the K-feldspar. In contrast to the individual flame-perthitic bodies, perthites of this type may exist as extensions of branching and anastomosing perthitic veinlets. Fig. 450 shows perthitic veins changing into a ganglio-perthite and an extension of the plexus attains a flame perthitic character. The transition and gradation support a metasomatic origin for these textural patterns. As relics of metasomatic replacement, relics of microcline are observed in the ganglio-perthitic bodies.

As a corollary to the metasomatic origin of flame perthitic types, Fig. 451 shows plagioclase, replacing K-feldspar, extensions of which attain flame perthitic character. All transitions of the replacement and infiltration processes are indicated. Later infiltration of quartz veinlets is also associated with the metasomatic plagioclase and its perthitoid extensions, suggesting the complexity of the processes.

In contradistinction to typical flame perthitic bodies, often flame perthites follow, or are related to, boundaries and corroded outlines of plagioclases enclosed by K-feldspar. Fig. 452 shows K-feldspar partly enclosing a pre-existing plagioclase which has been corroded and myrmekitised as a result of the synantetic reaction with the K-feldspar. Flame perthitic bodies follow the margin of corroded plagioclase and extend into the K-feldspar. These perthitic bodies must have been formed after the corrosion of the plagioclase by the K-feldspar. Similarly, flame perthitic bodies surround quartz myrmekites freed from their initial association with the plagioclase and now lying in the K-feldspar (due to corrosion and replacement of the myrmekitised plagioclase by the K-feldspar). The perthite formation has enclosed the quartz myrmekitic relics in the K-feldspar indicating that perthitisation has taken place after the plagioclase corrosion and replacement (Fig. 453).

A most convincing flame perthite formation after the synantetic reaction K-feldspar–plagioclase is shown in Fig. 454. Flame perthitic bodies extend into and occupy the concave corroded outline of the plagioclase. This textural pattern may be interpreted as follows: a pre-K-feldspar plagioclase has been corroded by the later orthoclase; flame perthitic bodies following partly the intergranular plagioclase and K-feldspar and extending into the plagioclase's corroded furrows have been formed after corrosion of the plagioclase by the K-feldspar. It is possible that the corrosion of the plagioclase was simultaneous with the K-feldspar formation, thus the postcorrosion perthite formation could imply a post K-feldspar perthitisation.

Flake perthites

The shape and form of perthitic bodies varies greatly, as studies of this phenomenology have revealed. The variation in form is a function of the topocrystalline conditions within the host which acts as a controlling factor on the shaping of the perthites and on the extent of topometasomatic infiltrations and solutions. In the observations so far, we have observed a 2-dimensional behaviour of the perthitic bodies under study. One should not forget that the perthites are 3-dimensional bodies and not surfaces. The so-called "flake" perthites are 3-dimensional bodies and one could imagine, by extrapolation on the basis of the two-dimensions, that comparable or commensurable would be the phenomenology of the third dimension. It should be remembered that the flake perthites are 3-dimensional bodies and that the spindle and linear perthites as well as the veins have a third dimension only to be extrapolated on the basis of the two dimensions observed. Thus other parameters are equally important for their understanding, such as volume.

Before the infiltration and replacement hypothesis could be acceptable, the question of space problem should be accounted for. The statement, that infiltration and replacement extends into portions of weakness of the host lattice is not providing a satisfactory answer. The accommodation of perthitic bodies that would require up to 50% of the volume of the host, still is an open question. The assimilation and incorporation of the one phase by the later, leaves unsolved the problem of elements that could not be accounted for in the replacing phase. Comparable problems are discussed in cases of feldspar substitution by later calcite.

A possible explanation is, that the solution (dissolved) of the host phase may have proceeded as a forerunner phase to replacement. The mobilisation of material should, in this case, be accounted for. In the complex process of solution mobilisation and replacement, there is a lot of room to imagine a solution of one phase to be the source of topometasomatic mobilisation for the formation of another new "blastesis" elsewhere concurrently with the replacement processes.

In the case of perthitisation to the extent of 50% of the volume of a K-feldspar, the dissolved K-feldspar that originally occupied the space (volume) of the present perthites has topometasomatically resulted in K-feldspar blastesis elsewhere within the mobilisation and diffusion capacity of the solutions. Fig. 455 shows a K-feldspar metasomatically replaced and infiltrated by flake and vein perthites simultaneously. The relatively great proportion of the perthite to the host K-feldspar is incompatible with an unmixing hypothesis. Also in support of a metasomatic explanation is the plexus of branching and anastomosing veinlets. Similarly, Fig. 456 shows flake perthites sending anastomosing and branching perthitic veinlets. The irregular margin of the flake perthites and their irregular extension are in this case also in support of a metasomatic origin. Within such perthitisation processes, when a biotite enclosed in the K-feldspar is in turn surrounded and corroded by the later perthitisation, within the reaction margin of the biotite, quartz myrmekites may be formed (Fig. 457).

Flake perthitic bodies may be present in two different twin individuals sending anastomosing vein-like extensions which extend across the twin plane and act as a connecting "channel" between the two flake perthites present in the different twins (Fig. 458). It appears that the flake perthites and their branches form a plexus extending throughout the perthitised K-feldspar.

Flake perthites may be distributed throughout the K-feldspar host. Often, as is shown in the case in Fig. 459, there seems to be a common orientation of the polysynthetic twinning of flake individuals, suggesting that the metasomatic infiltrations have followed a pattern of penetrability within the host, whereby the crystallisation of the solution resulted in flake perthites having approximately a common orientation or behaviour of orientation.

Perthites as a phase of multiple metasomatic infiltrations

One could see the perthite metasomatism in perspective with the multiple metasomatic infiltrations which can take place in the same K-feldspar host. In cases, intergrowth and textural association may exist between the different infiltrations. Fig. 460 shows a K-feldspar in which multiple metasomatic infiltrations are present. In addition to vein-type perthite, also mica (muscovite or even biotite) may be in vein-form mobilisation within the same K-feldspar and texturally in intergrowth with the perthite. As a third phase a branching and anastomosing quartz veinlet, is again in textural association with the perthite. In this case the multiple infiltrations follow a common direction of penetrability within the host.

If one attempts to explain the perthitic veinlets in terms of unmixing, due to these textural associations one would be expected to account similarly for the mica and quartz veinlets. It is not possible to expect such diverse mineral phases to be ex-solved products of one and the same K-feldspar.

A rather simple case of multiple infiltrations is shown in Fig. 461. Metasomatic diffused perthite is partly in textural intergrowth with metasomatic infiltrations of quartz. In such a case, the quartz infiltration is later than the perthite since it has equally penetrated both feldspars. Another case of repeated infiltration and metasomatic replacements is illustrated in Fig. 462 and 463. Branching and anastomosing veinlets of perthite, attaining ganglia form, are infiltrated and replaced by later quartz, with the intergrowth within the perthite assuming a pseudo-myrmekitic form and character. As Fig. 463 shows, metasomatic quartz is sending protuberances into the perthite, which attain myrmekitic quartz form and character. These textural patterns, where perthitic plagioclase shows a "pseudomyrmekitisation", are in contrast to the synantetic reaction types of myrmekitisation whereby a pre-K-feldspar plagioclase is corroded and myrmekitised (quartz formation as a forerunner phase of K-feldspar blastesis) as a result of the complex reactions involved when later K-feldspar reacts with a pre-existing plagioclase. In the case of the pseudomyrmekitisation, we have a quartzification of the perthitic plagioclase independent of the relation of perthitic plagioclase and K-feldspar. In contrast, the textural patterns are to be understood on the basis of multiple infiltration-replacement processes.

Pseudoperthites–remobilisation perthites

Plagioclases due to corrosion by later K-feldspar, have "extension-relics" that attain a pseudoperthitoid form with the K-feldspar, (Fig. 464). In contrast to these pseudoperthites, perthitic textures may result when pre-K-feldspar plagioclase (the plagioclase may belong to the palaeosoma) is remobilised and sends "Schnuren", string-like extensions perthitoid in form, within the later K-feldspar blastesis.

The phenomenology of such remobilisation perthites is illustrated and discussed in Fig. 465 and 466 and their description.

Vein perthites with reaction margins

In contradistinction to the unmixing hypothesis and as a corollary to the remobilisation perthites, vein perthites may show reaction margins with the K-feldspar.

As Fig. 467 shows, these reaction margins are restricted to the perthite and could represent a synantetic reaction between remobilised perthite and later formed K-feldspar. It is hardly to be expected that such reaction contacts would be formed on an ex-solution phase which has been formed by unmixing from the host.

Perthitised K-feldspar in intergrowth with plagioclase

Very difficult and dubious is the intergrowth of perthitised K-feldspar and plagioclase shown in Fig. 468 and 469. Two contradictory explanations can be proposed:

(a) The plagioclase is a later metasomatic phase, and by replacement engulfs, encloses and infiltrates into the perthitised K-feldspar. The fact that perthitised K-feldspar is enclosed by the plagioclase shows that plagioclase formation has taken place after perthitisation of the K-feldspar. The extension of perthite into the plagioclase (Fig. 468) represents engulfed relics of replacement by the plagioclase.

(b) The K-feldspar has infiltrated into the plagioclase enclosing parts of the plagioclase due to replacement, and the perthitisation is a later phase invading also the plagioclase (see Fig. 468).

Antiperthites

Comparable but reciprocal to the perthites, are the antiperthites which were considered to be exsolutions of K-feldspar in plagioclases. However, on the basis of the textural patterns exhibited, the antiperthites are infiltration and replacement bodies which were formed from solutions taking advantage of topocrystalline conditions of greater penetrability. Fig. 470 shows antiperthites replacing the plagioclase and following the twinning of the host. These antiperthitic bodies have been formed by infiltration of solutions which have exploited the greater plagioclase penetrability along the twinning. In addition, it can be seen that an antiperthitic body extended into a mica contained in the plagioclase. This textural pattern is comparable and commensurable to the perthitic bodies following topocrystalline directions of greater penetrability within the K-feldspar host, e.g. cleavage.

Similarly, as in the case of marginal perthitisation, whereby perthitic plagioclase from intergranular extended into the K-feldspar and attained perthitic forms and character, marginal K-feldspar by replacement and infiltration attains antiperthitic character in the plagioclase (Fig. 471).

Comparable to perthitic veinlets which branch and anastomose within the K-feldspar host, antiperthitic veinlets branching and anastomosing are present in plagioclases (Fig. 472 and 473).

The textural patterns indicate in this case as well replacement of the plagioclase and infiltration of antiperthite-forming solutions. These textural patterns are incompatible to an unmixing hypothesis for the antiperthite formation. Furthermore, antiperthitic flake bodies of microcline are shown in plagioclase and in this case the antiperthitisation is due to replacement and infiltration of solution (Fig. 474). Similarly, small antiperthitic flakes may be interspersed within twinned plagioclase (Fig. 475).

In cases, flake antiperthites metasomatically formed partly surround some existing inclusion in the plagioclase. Fig. 476 shows antiperthitic flakes partly surrounding accessory apatite. Other antiperthitic bodies form a fringe partly surrounding a quartz. The antiperthite-forming solutions have exploited the intergranular space between the quartz and plagioclase. Such textural patterns support an infiltration replacement for these flake antiperthites.

Metasomatic antiperthite in K-feldspar attains flake form and includes relics of non-replaced orthoclase which follow a zonal distribution within the plagioclase. Simultaneously the antiperthitic flake sends protuberances into K-feldspar which attain flame-like form (Fig. 477).

Most convincing textural patterns of metasomatic post-plagioclase microcline antiperthites are shown in Fig. 478. The antiperthite (i.e., later K-feldspar) in contact with a pre-existing plagioclase resulted in quartz myrmekitic formation as a result of the synantetic reactions of older plagioclase and younger K-feldspar. Comparable textural patterns, whereby the antiperthite formation resulted in corrosion and myrmekitisation of portions of the plagioclase host, are shown in Fig. 479. Here again, the antiperthitisation is in synantetic reaction with a pre-existing plagioclase.

Plagioclase transversed by plagioclase veinlets

In contradistinction to the vein antiperthites, plagioclases may be transversed by later plagioclase veinlets which, in comparison to the host plagioclase, may show a reversing of the twinning. Such "recrystallisation" or infiltration veinlets indicate the complexity of "solution" infiltration patterns within feldspars (Fig. 480 and 481).

The significance of the perthite problem

In contrast to orthodox views which consider the perthite exsolution phase at the temperature range $\sim$ 500–600°C, the present studies on the phenomenology

of perthites show textural patterns within the range $\sim$ 200–300°C, which support a metasomatic origin for these structures. These as well as comparable textural patterns are not exceptions or deviations from the normal. Studies of thin-sections of more than 500 "granites" of worldwide distribution, show that infiltration, replacement and metasomatic perthitic patterns are rather the typical rule.

In contrast to the orthodox view that the perthites represent an exsolution phase at relatively high temperatures which are assumed to have prevailed during the crystallisation of the Na/K-feldspars from the granitic melt, the phenomenology of the introduced perthitic patterns contradicts an exsolution hypothesis.

The perthitic intergrowths show texturally a far more complex picture to conform to the simplistic ideal picture of exsolution lamellae in a parent crystal. The textural evidence introduced shows a wide spectrum of perthitic patterns. The typical (ideal) perthitic patterns are a common variant of the possibility of textural pattern variations. The patterns suggest an infiltration mobilisation origin for the perthite-forming solutions whereby intracrystalline penetrability along crystal directions of weakness played a controlling role. The infiltration of perthite-forming solutions is along cracks, crystal-cleavages and all possible "channels" of greater "Wegsamkeit" as would be provided at the margin and contacts of minerals associated with the host K-feldspar.

Observations on a wide range of minerals indicate that the perthites are more common than the reciprocal textural pattern, namely the antiperthites. Whereas both are products of solution infiltration, the difference in the abundance of these two phases is worthwhile considering and has a genetic implication.

The K-feldspar blastesis is a predominant phase in gneisses and granites; the post-K-feldspar plagioclase-forming solutions follow the crystal "Wegsamkeit" in the K-feldspar host and perthitic patterns are thus "reproduced". In contrast, when a pre-K-feldspar-plagioclase phase is enclosed and engulfed by the later formed K-feldspar-blast, this pre-K-feldspar phase is mobilised giving rise to "remobilised" perthitic patterns (pseudoperthites).

In the majority of cases, the perthites are explained as products of infiltration of plagioclase-forming solutions in a recipient K-feldspar blast as a host. It is interesting that the less common in abundance plagioclase blastesis is the recipient of the antiperthite-forming solutions. The perthite and antiperthite-forming solutions are a later solution phase of either a K-feldspar or plagioclase blastesis respectively.

The infiltration of plagioclase (perthite) into a K-feldspar involves solution penetrability along directions of weakness or cracks of the host K-feldspar. Also a replacement of the host by the infiltrating solutions is probable. In very few cases, the vein perthite bodies show reaction margins with the host K-feldspar. This observation reveals that the perthites are more or less an intergrowth of two particular mineral phases. However, present observations (Fig. 427, 429, 433 and 435) show that the feldspar-forming solution can infiltrate into neighbouring mineral phases as well.

The infiltration of solutions represents open-space filling, like minute veinlets, which can transverse any mineral boundaries. In contrast, there are also metasomatic infiltration phases taking advantage of the directions of "Wegsamkeit" (penetrability) and are associated with metasomatic replacement of the feldspar, i.e., intracrystalline penetrations.

Chapter 16 | Diffusion and its significance in granitisation

In the transformation of sedimentary and metasedimentary masses to gneisses and granites and towards the understanding of metasomatic processes in general, of utmost importance is the transportation and mobilisation of materials. In general, the rock material should not be considered as being in a static state, i.e., once formed, it is fixed and not subject to internal and external mobilisation. The formation of blastic growth, the synantetic reaction and the mobilisation, replacement and recrystallisation processes require, as a pre-requisite, a mechanism of transportation.

Metamorphism and metasomatism are widely accepted processes which would be senseless without a mechanism of substance transportation and, indeed, in rock transformation the transportation mechanism nowadays widely accepted is diffusion.

In the biological sciences, diffusion is a mechanism which long before (the geosciences) has been accepted and studied in great detail. In contrast, in the geosciences there has been a reluctance to accept diffusion as a mechanism to explain a great deal of the transportation and mobilisations in rocks. Particularly, Harker (1932, p. 18, 19, 75, 203, 204, 300) considered diffusion to be so slow a process that the limit of effective diffusion would be a small fraction of an inch. Similarly, Niggli (Grubenmann and Niggli, 1924, p. 451) limited the action of diffusion in crystalline silicates to the boundary faces of the grains. Moreover, Perrin and Roubault (1939, p. 18) considered the intergranular transportation due to diffusion as virtually impossible on the grounds that temperature must be uniform in the short distances involved.

As a counterproposal, Perrin and Roubault (1937, 1939) and Bugge (1946) proposed that diffusion may take place either along the grain surfaces or through the crystal lattice, and they proposed as a mechanism for a great amount of substances, mobilisation diffusion in the solid state. The following publications discuss diffusion in solid state and its significance as well as limitations as a petrogenetic process: Adams (1930), Eskola (1934), Jost (1937), Goldsmith, (1952), Drescher-Kaden and Böttcher (1955), Wenden (1957). In this connection, I would like to quote Read (1957, p. 236): "There are plenty of proofs of solid diffusion in metallurgy and in mineralogy. We need only to instance the homogenisation of perthitic feldspars at high temperatures and the sericitisation of feldspars or the experience of cement manufacture. Some of the metallurgical examples are concerned with single crystals and conclusions drawn from them are not strictly valid for the multigranular aggregates of natural rocks, where surface processes are not automatically excluded."

In contrast to the views delimiting the importance of intergranular diffusion and transportation by solutions in the realm of metamorphism, metasomatism and "plutonic" metamorphism (granitisation processes in general), Wegmann (1935a, b), and Wegmann and Kranck (1931) have emphasised its importance. Similarly, Eskola (1932b, 1934) has proposed intergranular diffusion as a mechanism for metamorphic differentiation. But it is the work of Drescher-Kaden (1948, 1969) that has shown that the granitic textures: blastesis, graphic undergrowth, perthites, myrmekites, etc., are "hydrogenic" the result of solution infiltrations, reactions, and mobilisation of material in solution either intergranularly or intracrystalline. A basic pre-requisite for intergranular diffusion is the presence of solutions and the solubility of substances in a "hydrogenic" solution; also of fundamental importance is the state of the substances in solution (whether atoms or ions). Among others, Pieruccini (1955) has emphasised the importance of fossil water in granitisation. In addition Drescher-Kaden (1961c, 1962) on the basis of chemical analyses of granites, points out "the importance of H_2O and its role in diffusion and metasomatic processes". The significance of "hydrothermal", i.e., hydrogenic solutions in metamorphism, metasomatism and granitisation in general is discussed in the following publications: Erdmansdörffer (1943), Kennedy (1944), Pieruccini (1955), Mosebach (1955), Yoder (1955), Pieruccini (1960), Drescher-Kaden (1961c), Drescher-Kaden and Heller (1961), Drescher-Kaden (1962), Erhart (1963), Weill and Fyfe (1964), Harder and Flehmig (1967).

Furthermore, Drescher-Kaden (1961c, 1962) has pointed to an increase of solubility in intergranular conditions as compared with the solubility of solutions in open space. Also dependent on the increased solubility and diffusion of substances in intergranular spaces, is the transportation and mobilisation of materials. Considering that for each blastic and metasomatic growth transportation of materials is necessary, one can understand the importance of mobilisation of substances by diffusion. In general, the topometasomatic growths, e.g., blastic K-feldspar in xenoliths (double-inclusion), blastic feldspar, graphic intergrowths, perthites and myrmekites (see Chapters 11, 13, 14 and 15) are dependent on intergranular and intracrystalline diffusion of solutions. As has been pointed out already, the increase of solubility in the intergranular and the great time-span over which granitisation can take place, enables us to see diffusion as an effective mechanism of material mobilisation, a concept necessary for understanding metamorphism and metasomatism.

A relatively low temperature (200°–400°C) but an increased pressure would further increase the solubility in the intergranular and would render intergranular and intracrystalline diffusion an effective mechanism of material transportation in the realm of granitisation.

Other evidence of diffusion is found in the basic fronts and the contact metasomatic phenomena, which are interrelated with granitic intrusions. The basic-front hypothesis of Wegmann (1953b) and Reynolds (1947a) is primarily based on diffusion of solutions (or emanations) under granitisation. Similarly, in the present work, the Mg—Fe metasomatic contacts of granitic intrusions and the skarn bodies are considered to be due to diffusion of Mg—Fe solution out of the granitic intrusion as a results of the granitisation of amphibolites (of an amphibolitic pre-granitic phase including K-feldspar blastesis) and due to the gradoseparation of amphiboles liberating the Mg—Fe solutions which diffused out of the granite (see Chapter 23). Here again, diffusion has played a predominant role.

Another line of evidence of diffusion of solutions and solution fronts is provided by the study of stylolitic structures in limestones, marbles and rhyolites. The solution fronts migrate through a solid rock under atmospheric temperatures. Particularly, Golding and Conolly (1962) have shown microstylolitic structures transversing quartz grains of a rhyolite, thus pointing to intergranular and intracrystalline diffusion of solutions. Another instance of solution fronts at surface temperature whereby intergranular and intracrystalline diffusion has taken place, is described by Augustithis and Ottemann (1966): "At Dangago (about 10—15 km from Dire-Dawa, on the way to Harrar) concentric diffusion rings (Fig. 482) and sphaeroidal weathering forms have been developed on outcrops of microgranitic rock types. The diffusion-ring patterns vary in size from a few centi-

metres to forms having a maximum diameter of about 2—3 m. Also, the width and number of the iron precipitation zones vary. In some cases structures are formed consisting of only a few limonite precipitation rings; however, in other cases, more than twenty of such rings have been counted. The width of the zones is also variable.

... Mineralogical and X-ray fluorescence spectrochemical comparisons have been made between the diffusion rings rich in limonite, and the alternating leached zones. In addition to iron, other elements have migrated; in fact an exchange of elements has occurred between the zones.

... Despite the fact that microscopic observations have failed to show any noticeable difference in the main mineral constituents which comprise the brown and the whitish zones (with the exception of intense limonite precipitation in the first-mentioned zone), X-ray fluorescence spectroanalyses and comparisons reveal noteworthy differences in the proportions of the elements present in these two zones. Materials representing the "white" and "brown" zones of the diffusion ring structures have been separated and finely powdered prior to examination by X-ray fluorescence spectroscopy. Care has been taken that adjacent "white" and "brown" zones (actually representing the leached and its counterpart enriched in Fe zones) were analysed, so that a comparison of their chemical composition and a study of the elements migration was possible. The following comparative values are obtained by taking the intensities of the elements in "white" as a unit ($Ti = Ca = K = Si = 1$): $Ti = 1$; $Ca = 1.6$; $K = 0.9$; $Si = 0.8$; $Al = 0.6$ (Dangago "brown"). The calcium has increased in the "brown" zone $1.6\times$, whereas in contrast the contents of K, Si and Al have decreased in this zone. In the brown zone the concentration of Fe and Ca increased whereas the concentrations of Zr, Y, Rb, Al, Si and K relatively decreased."

The significance of intracrystalline diffusion and the symplectic intergrowths of granitic rocks.

The significance of intracrystalline diffusion[1] has been argued and in particular Mehnert (1968, p. 96) delimits the effectiveness of intracrystalline diffusion as a mechanism of granitisation: "In all these experiments the intracrystalline diffusion coefficient was determined as being of the order of 10^{-8}—10^{-12} cm^2/sec at the tem-

---

[1] In contradistinction to diffusion in solid state, intracrystalline diffusion is considered to be the diffusion of solutions through the crystalline lattice, along the direction of crystal disorder.

peratures investigated. Assuming a reaction time of 1 million years, which is a reasonable time interval for geological processes, a diffusion distance of the order of a few centimeters to a few meters is obtained. This calculation, however, is purely formal, because it is hardly likely the concentration gradient would remain constant over such a long period of time. But even then it is too small as a possible explanation of extensive metasomatic processes like granitisation, etc. It can thus be concluded that the values obtained experimentally for lattice diffusion rule out the latter as an explanation of migrations of geological importance."

In contrast, experimental work by Gerlach and Heller (1966), Schloemer (1962) and microscopic observations by Drescher-Kaden and Augustithis, indicate that in addition to the significance of intergranular diffusion (as an effective mechanism of transportation and granitisation), intracrystalline diffusion has played a significant role in granitisation and particularly in the genesis of symplectic intergrowths, e.g., myrmekitic, graphic, perthitic intergrowths (see Chapters 13, 14 and 15). In this connection, a synopsis is introduced of experimental evidence of intracrystalline diffusion and its significance to petrogenesis. In 1924 Friedel (see Gerlach and Heller, 1966) succeeded in producing secondary liquid inclusions in an alum crystal. Similarly, Lemmlejn (1929) succeeded in producing secondary liquid solutions in a number of minerals, e.g., NaCl crystals. With a sharp blade he cleaved the crystal to the extent where he obtained interference colour effects along a fine crack (i.e., the width of the crack was in the order of light wavelength). Subsequently, he filled this crack with a water solution containing NaCl and in a short time he observed inclusions of liquid with regular outlines in the crystal which showed no connection with the crystal face, i.e., intracrystalline infiltration of solutions had taken place.

In addition, the experimental result of Gerlach and Heller (1966) have supplied information regarding the direction of the path of liquid diffusion in NaCl which is considered to be between 2.83 Å and 3,800 Å: "Da es nahe lag, bei künstlich aus Schmelzfluss erzeugten Steinsalzkristallen ein Material zu erhalten, das wesentlich frei von Gitterfehlern war, wurden NaCl-Kristalle, die von der Firma Leitz hergestellt und als optisch einwandfrei, das heisst, frei von Spaltrissen etc., bezeichnet worden waren, dem gleichen Versuch unterworfen. Diese Kristalle zeigten jedoch genau die gleichen Einschlussformen in der gleichen Häufigkeit, wie die "Real-Kristalle". Es scheint demnach, dass auch im künstlichen Material die gleichen Fehlerstellen vorhanden sind, wie im natürlichen (Fig. 483). Der Gitterabstand des NaCl-Gitters (Würfelebenen) beträgt 2.83 Å, die Lichtwellenlänge 3,800 Å

(blau); das bedeutet, die Dimensionen der Einwanderungswegen müssen zwischen diesen beiden Werten liegen."

In contradistinction to the above-mentioned experimental results obtained mainly from salt crystals, Schloemer (1962) succeeded in the formation of graphic-like quartz bodies in K-feldspar. Graphic or granophyric structures have been produced experimentally by hydrothermal-metasomatic processes where quartz has infiltrated (by intracrystalline diffusion) into K-feldspar. The quartz metasomatic infiltrations into the K-feldspar were achieved at a temperature of $400°$ C and at a pressure of 1,000 atm in the presence of H_2O with the experiments lasting 18 and 30 days. The structures so formed, according to Schloemer, correspond to and resemble the granophyric and graphic intergrowths described by Drescher-Kaden (1948), where the quartz is later than the K-feldspar.

It should be mentioned that the graphic and granophyric intergrowths described in the present work (the graphic intergrowths in the "plutonics") resemble – and their genetic interpretation is in accordance with – the results of experiments on the infiltration of quartz-forming hydrothermal solutions into an existing feldspar.

As a corollary to these experimental results of silicate diffusion, microscopic observations reveal intracrystalline infiltrations into pyroxene phenocrysts (actually olivine bombs) of ground-mass, i.e., ground-mass melt has infiltrated by intracrystalline diffusion into an already crystallised pyroxene. The diffusion path has followed irregular directions of crystal penetrability. It should be mentioned that the intracrystalline textures produced by diffusion of solution or melts attain myrmekitic-like intergrowths (Fig. 484). Similarly, infiltration solution paths due to diffusion of solutions along directions of greater crystalline penetrability show again myrmekitoid textural patterns (Fig. 210 and 211). These patterns are comparable to liquid inclusions synthetically produced by Gerlach and Heller (1966), (Fig. 483). Additional microscopic observations (Fig. 485) show a basaltic pyroxene phenocryst partly surrounded by an alteration front (due to reaction with the melt of the groundmass). The alteration front (margin) shows "solution front extensions" advancing into the unaltered pyroxene. Also, in this case, intracrystalline diffusion of melts has taken place.

From the above considerations, it can be seen that diffusion is an effective process (mechanism) of transportation of material and that it plays an important role in metamorphism, metasomatism and granitisation. Whereas diffusion in a solid state might be restricted to a special mechanism, e.g., sericitisation of feldspars, intergranular diffusion (pore-liquid diffusion) is considered to be the most effective mechanism (process) of material mobilisation.

According to Mehnert (1968) the relative effectiveness of intergranular and intercrystalline diffusion is as follows: "According to the experiments it can safely be assumed that the coefficient of intracrystalline diffusion within the H_2O-bearing "intergranular film" exceeds that of intracrystalline diffusion by a factor of the order of 10^6. This corresponds, if extrapolated to a geological time of 1 million years, to a diffusion distance of the order of 100 m—1 km."

In the realm of metamorphism and in particular under granitisation, both intergranular and intracrystalline diffusion are effective and of importance. The two processes may occur concurrently, i.e., the intergranular diffusion would explain migration of material on a large scale and over large distances, while in contradistinction, intracrystalline diffusion would explain all replacement and infiltration textural patterns, such as synantetic myrmekitic intergrowths, symplectic graphic intergrowths, etc.

Chapter 17 | The rapakivi structures

"I would brutally recall once again that similar rapakivi ovoids (to those in the rapakivi granite) occur isolated in the country rocks – an occurrence everybody admits. Are we to believe that the complicated physico-chemical controls operate also in the country-rock environment in exactly the same way as they did in the consolidating magma?"

H. H. Read (*The Granite Controversy*, 1957, p.138).

Of particular interest are the so-called rapakivi textures (structures), (rapakivi granite in Finnish = rotten rock). Among others, Sederholm (1967, pp. 174–179) has studied these structures and abstracts are quoted here from his original work:

"The rapakivi of Buckholm and the neighbouring small islands near the Vȧtskär pilot station is very typical. It is a coarsely porphyritic granite, showing phenocrysts of a dark brownish-red potash feldspar with an ovoid form, coated by rims of green plagioclase and surrounded by a granitic mass of rather coarse texture in which crystals of gray quartz are conspicuous. The length of the feldspar ovoids is commonly 4–6 cm, though it may occasionally reach 10 cm (4 inches); their breadth is about 2/3 of their length. The plagioclase is an oligoclase with about 25% An. It forms macroscopically visible borders around the orthoclase with a thickness of 3–4 mm, and sometimes also several concentric inner zones due to a repetition of the same causes. The outer oligoclase border does not always possess as regular an ovoid form as the core of potash feldspar, but often shows a tendency to the development of crystal surfaces."

"On microscopical examination the potash feldspar reveals itself as either microcline or orthoclase, the latter being more common. The substance of this potash feldspar is very impure: it is intergrown with oligoclase in irregularly interspersed patches, and also contains quartz in so great a quantity that the microcline may often be regarded as a kind of skeleton crystal. The quartz fills interstices in the feldspar whose forms are determined by the feldspar's crystallisation. The walls of these interstices are sometimes cased with a feldspar which is more transparent than the main crystal and seems to have a different composition. Micropegmatite also occasionally occurs as a filling of these interstices. Small biotite crystals are likewise included in the feldspar ovoids."

"The crystal form of the orthoclase in granitic rocks shows the predominant surfaces (010), (110), (001), (101), (201), (021) and (111), and is in itself very nearly ovoidal. It is only necessary for the sharpness of the angles and corners to become attenuated, to give the thicker feldspar crystals nearly the form of an ovoid, slightly deformed by being protracted along the axes a and c. On close inspection we find too that the ovoidal form of the phenocrysts of rapakivi is not always quite regular, but that an indication of the crystal form of orthoclase is often visible. The surfaces (010) and (110) are often especially well marked, when the outlines of the crystals are partly rectilinear."

"The author regards the ovoids as imperfect crystals whose impurity accounts for the defective development of their crystal forms.

If the oval form were due to corrosion, we should expect to find crystals showing the usual Carlsbad twinning which had been afterwards rounded, when the boundary between the twins might occasionally intersect the longer diameter of the ovoids. But when twinning occurs, the ovoid is always divided into a number of sectors which radiate from the centre. Obviously in each of these sectors layer has been deposited upon layer during the whole growth of the crystal."

"There are signs which seem to indicate that the feldspars have crystallised within a partly solid rock."

The rapakivi structures have been explained by a number of workers (e.g., Holmquist, 1901; Harker, 1909; Eskola, 1928; Popoff, 1928, Von Eckermann, 1937, 1938; Stewart, 1959; Savolahti, 1962) as the result of complex magmatic crystallisations. In addition to diverse mechanisms of magmatic operations (crystallisation diagrams, i.e., solidus–liquidus equillibria) proposed as an explanation for the formation of these textures in granites, it is more difficult to explain (on the basis of magmatic consolidations) rapakivi structures occurring in xenoliths enclosed in rapakivi granites and the rapakivi structures found in the country rocks.

A very vigorous controversy has taken place between magmatist Von Eckermann (1937, 1938) and transformist Backlund (1938a, b, c); however, this controversy has changed into a controversy on the origin of granites. In support of the transformist's point-of-view and based on the concepts of metamorphic-metasomatic textural pattern in gneisses and granites, it is attempted here to mention the textural criteria which, in the author's opinion, support a blastogenic origin of the rapakivi structures.

(1) The rapakivi structures in granites and, particularly, the cases of those in xenoliths, are turbid crystals with inclusion of quartz, biotites and other feldspars. The behaviour of K-feldspar to inclusions is that of a crystalloblast. The case of rapakivi structures in xenoliths is comparable to the behaviour of K-feldspar "double-inclusions" to the xenolithic component included (i.e., the inclusions of the rapakivi ovoids in xenoliths are enclosed and engulfed xenolithic components as is the case with the inclusions of the double-inclusion crystalloblasts).

(2) Despite the fact that Sederholm considers the rapakivi growths to be due to "diffusion of magmatic origin", his description fits more a crystalloblastic interpretation than a magmatic one.

(a) Sederholm regards the ovoids as "imperfect crystals whose impurities account for the defective development of their crystal forms". This interpretation is in harmony with crystalloblastic force of K-feldspars and the "fact that crystalloblast" may show poikiloblastic patterns. Often ground-mass components plagioclases may follow a zonal arrangement in the "ovoidal" crystalloblasts (Fig. 48).

(b) The existence of K-feldspar ovoids free of plagioclase margin as well as the fact that ovoids may occur with a mantle of plagioclase and, furthermore, the fact that plagioclase "zones" may be included in K-feldspar – also a repetition of K-feldspar and plagioclase crystallisations may exist – could be interpreted on the basis of blastic phases, i.e., K-feldspar crystalloblast followed by plagioclase blastic margins.

In this connection it should be pointed out that Read (1957) describing the plagioclase margin surrounding the K-feldspar, points out the following: "The mantled ovoids show a polysomatic ring of oligoclase, allotriomorphic against the internal potash feldspar and idiomorphic outside."

The fact that rapakivi structures often consist of repeated zones of K-feldspar and polysomatic plagioclase, and moreover the fact that such structures may exist as double inclusion (supply of material by intergranular diffusion), supports a metamorphic–metasomatic origin whereby different blastic periods represent a different supply of solutions topometasomatically.

(3) Additional evidence of the blastic origin of the ovoid K-feldspars is the presence and inclusion in them of myrmekitised plagioclases. The myrmekitisation should be seen as a result of synantetic reactions of a plagioclase and a later formed K-feldspar crystalloblast (see Chapter 13).

(4) The perthitisation of the K-feldspar ovoids is in this case the result of metasomatic processes due to intracrystalline diffusion of albite-forming solutions. The evidence provided in Chapter 15 for a metasomatic infiltration origin of the perthites is equally valid for the perthitisation in the rapakivi K-feldspar ovoids. These intracrystalline diffusion textures indicate that metasomatic processes occurred in the sequence of processes that resulted in the formation of the rapakivi crystalloblasts.

(5) Additional evidence of the metasomatic processes in rapakivi structures is provided by the graphic and micrographic intergrowths (Fig. 252). Infiltration of granophyric quartz along the cleavage of the K-feldspar crystalloblasts as well as granophyric quartz extending along twin lamellae or forming a ring around enclosed plagioclases (Fig. 268) are in support of a metasomatic origin of the micrographic quartz in the rapakivi structures.

Chapter 18 | The accessory minerals in granites and their genetic significance

The accessory minerals are considered by magmatists to represent early crystallisation products in the ortho-magmatic phase of the granitic melt consolidation. Their textural association with biotites and amphiboles by which usually zircons and apatites are surrounded, was attributed to a pre-biotite crystallisation from the granitic melt. Particularly Moorhouse (1956), Wyllie et al. (1962) and Kraus (1963) consider the accessory zircons in granites to be magmatogenic in origin, i.e., crystallisation products of consolidating melts. Rounded forms were attributed to magmatic corrosion.

In contrast to these explanations, a study of the phenomenology of accessory minerals in granites reveals textural patterns which are in support of a sedimentogenic origin. Wyatt (1954), Poldervaart (1955, 1956), Bader (1961), Hoppe (1962a, b, c, 1963, 1964, 1966), Augustithis (1967a) and Drescher-Kaden (1969) support a sedimentogenic or an early metamorphic origin of the accessory zircons in granitic rocks. Furthermore, re-growths and neo-crystallisations of the accessories have taken place during the geological history (i.e., sequence of formation) of the granitic rocks.

Fig. 486 shows a large accessory zircon consisting of two zircon generations. The central zircon (generation I) is rounded and corroded and is overgrown by zircon (generation II). An interzonal quartz grain is between the two zircons. Similarly Fig. 487 shows a small zircon (generation I) rounded, corroded and included in a larger zircon (generation II) which is again rounded. Additional observations reveal that zircon-grains (generation I) may be surrounded by an overgrowth of zircon (generation II) with a well-developed crystalline form. Further evidence of two generations of zircon formation are shown in Fig. 488 and 489. In both cases, a nucleus (central grain) of zircon is surrounded by an overgrowth of zircon (generation II). In cases, the overgrowth of zircon around a rounded and corroded zircon generation I may take the form of several zones, the outer of which attains an eucrystalline form (Fig. 490).

In all the described examples rounded and corroded zircons are surrounded by an overgrowth of a second generation of zircon formation. Such textural patterns, namely a corroded central zircon and a later overgrowth, are dubious. Two contradictory explanations could be

provided, namely the central rounded zircons represent first crystallisation which was subsequently corroded by magmatic corrosion, and the overgrowth represents a second generation within the same orthomagmatic phase of crystallisation.

In contrast to this magmatic interpretation, transformists consider the first generation zircon as representing a sedimentogenic phase, i.e., the zircon is subjected to rounding due to transportation in the erosion cycle, and the overgrowths as representing a later generation under the influences and conditions of granitisation.

In contrast to the rounded and corroded central zircon, corrosion effect due to synantetic reaction can be exhibited. Fig. 491 shows a zircon crystal with corrosion effects and simultaneously shows an overgrowth in different parts of the same crystal individual. As a corollary to reaction and corrosion effects, Fig. 492 shows a zoned zircon corroded by a later ore mineral (magnetite). In both cases, the zircon corrosion was the result of contact mineral reactions and cannot be compared to the roundening due to transportation under erosion.

In addition to the zircon-inclusion in zircons of a second generation, apatites can be enclosed and corroded by a later zircon growth (Fig. 493). In other cases, the zircon forms an overgrowth or partially surrounds an apatite (Fig. 494). In both bases the zircon growth is later than the apatite.

Similarly zircon may include ore-minerals (Fig. 495) or, ore-minerals (iron oxides) may occupy an interzonal position within a zircon. Fig. 496 shows an opaque mineral (iron oxide? magnetite) in a zone of a zircon and simultaneously it forms a margin surrounding the zircon. Fig. 497 shows a zircon with a corroded and rounded outline enclosing a magnetite. An overgrowth of the rounded zircon attains eucrystalline form. The zircon overgrowth, however, is not continued over the magnetite. It is possible that, for the formation of a zircon overgrowth, an already existing nucleus of zircon is necessary.

In contrast to the corroded zircons or to the partly corroded forms, Fig. 498 shows a partly corroded fine zoned zircon, i.e., the corrosion outline cuts across the zoning. Idiomorphic (blastic) zircons also exist. Fig. 499 and 500 show an idiomorphic zircon in biotite. Included in the zircon are parts of the biotite, the cleavage of which corresponds to the cleavage of the biotite outside the zircon. The zircon is a blastic growth and due to its crystallisation force it has attained an idiomorphic shape. The zircon blastesis is in contradistinction to the explanation that the zircon is invariably an earlier crystallisation than the mica. Fig. 501 shows a zircon in biotite sending irregular protuberances and partly engulfing biotite. Such textural patterns are in support of a later zircon formation blastically in the biotite. Often interpenetrations of zircon are observed in biotite suggesting a blastic intergrowth of the two individuals, (Fig. 502).

The textural patterns of apatite in granitic rocks, despite similarities with those of the zircons, show a fundamental difference. Whereas the zircon (generation I) shows a rounded outline due to corrosion under transportation, this being evidence that the zircons are of sedimentogenic derivation in the granites, the apatites tend to show a tendency of idiomorphism. However, compared to the zircons comparable and commensurable patterns are indicated by the apatites. Fig. 503 shows an idiomorphic apatite which encloses a smaller apatite of first generation (in contrast to the first generation zircons which usually show rounded shapes, the apatites of generation I are idiomorphic.)

Similarly, Figs. 504 and 505 show an apatite partly enclosed i hornblende and partly in feldspar. The portion in th hornblende shows corrosion and encloses a small apat te whereas, in contrast, the apatite in the feldspar shows an overgrowth margin. In addition to the inclusions of apatite (generation I), zircons are often included; Fig. 506 shows a zircon partly enclosed by apatite. Similarly Fig. 507 shows a zircon enclosed in a zoned apatite which attains idiomorphic form. In both cases, the apatite crystallisation is later than the zircon. As is the case of zircon (generation II) and idioblastic zircons in biotites (Fig. 500), blastogenic apatites in biotites also exist. Fig. 508 and 509 show blastic apatite enclosing corroded and partly assimilated portions of the mica. In contrast to zircons which are resistant to synantetic reactions, the apatites often show reaction-corrosion margins as a result of reactions and replacements by post apatite-growths.

In contrast to the blastic apatite, in the majority of cases, the apatite is an early crystallisation in the granites. Fig. 510 shows an apatite enclosed in a myrmekitised plagioclase. Corrosion and a reaction margin is formed due to the later plagioclase effects. The same apatite individual is in contact with a microcline (which has caused a synantetic reaction margin on the plagioclase); as the apatite is in contact with the microcline, it shows a corrosion outline that clearly depends on the influence exercised by the later K-feldspar. Comparable is the corrosion of apatite by later quartz. Fig. 511 shows zoned apatite corroded and invaded by later quartz which, from intergranular, attains infiltration character along cracks of the apatite. Corrosion and small scale replacement of the apatite by the later quartz has taken place. Another case of apatite corrosion by later quartz is shown in Fig. 512. An idiomorphic apatite is associated with plagioclase and biotite. A later quartz replaces the plagioclase and similarly has caused reactions and replacement on the apatite. In addition, corrosion of apatite has taken place by blastic hornblende in which apatites are included. Fig. 513 shows an apatite corroded and replaced by hornblende. The initial outline of the apatite is shown in the hornblende.

Apatites are often associated with biotites. In the case of blastic biotite, apatite inclusions may be accommodated along interzonal spaces of the mica. Corrosion and replacement of apatite by the biotite are comparable to the effects of blastic amphiboles on the apatite. Fig. 514 shows apatites in a marginal "zone" of the biotite blast. Detailed observations reveal replacement of the apatites. Fig. 515 shows an apatite replaced by biotite, only a central part of the apatite has resisted the replacement. The initial outline of the apatite can be traced in the biotite. In addition to the replacement phenomenology of apatites by biotite, often apatites enclosed by biotite show corrosion outlines (Fig. 516 and 517). Fig. 516 shows an apatite in biotite and K-feldspar, the portion of the apatite in the biotite is corroded by the mica. In contrast, the position of the apatite in the K-feldspar shows an overgrowth zone. It is difficult to account for the simultaneous corrosion and overgrowth of the same apatite individual.

In contrast to the small apatite crystal grains which belong to the palaeosoma or are early blastic growths within the granitisation process, apatite "superindividuals" also exist. Fig. 518 shows an apatite superindividual between the margins of biotite and quartz. However, the boundaries of the apatite to the mica are difficult to explain since, despite the intergranular position of the apatite, corrosion appearances and biotite protruding in the apatite are simultaneously exhibited. Similarly, an apatite "superindividual" extends across feldspars and biotites (Fig. 519); particularly the position of the apatite associated with the biotite shows extensive replacement and corrosion. Apatite "superindividuals" are often corroded and replaced by feldspar and quartz, again indicating an early apatite blastesis. Fig. 520 shows an apatite megablast corroded by plagioclase which also extends into the apatite. Similarly, quartz infiltration extends into the apatite along the crack.

The accessory sphene often shows a blastogenic character. Fig. 521 shows a zircon enclosed in an idioblastic sphene. Idioblastic sphene may be formed later than the blastogenic hornblende in granitic rock. Fig. 522 and 523 show blastic twinned hornblende with apatite inclusions, surrounded by idioblastic later sphene. The sphene also includes quartz either in association with the hornblende or as an isolated inclusion in the sphene blast. Contrary, a case of blastic sphene surrounded by blastic hornblende is shown in Fig. 524. The blastic sequence of sphene depends on topometasomatic conditions and does not follow in all cases the same order of events.

Ore minerals are often accessory components in granitic rocks. The textural patterns discussed have shown iron ores included and rounded in zircons and also forming interzonal phases in zoned zircons. The relation of ore minerals (mainly magnetite) to the accessories is further discussed in Fig. 495 and 496. Fig. 525 shows rounded quartz as an inclusion of a biotite and in turn containing corroded ore-mineral grain.

The accessory minerals as components of a pre-granitic paragneissic phase

Textural studies by Augustithis (1967a) have shown that the accessory minerals of the Melca-Guba Granite, Ethiopia, belong to a pre-granitic paragneissic phase and are incorporated in the granite by the transformation paragneiss → granite. Present microscopic observations reveal that the accessory minerals in the Melca-Guba Granite represent components of a pre-granitic paragneissic phase, relics of which are partly incorporated in the granite as pre-blastic minerals and partly represented as sedimentogenic xenoliths in the granite. The present state of the Melca-Guba Granite is the result of a series of changes, i.e., it is the product of complex and multiple processes of metamorphism and metasomatism.

In contrast to the orthodox magmatogenic hypothesis which considers granitic rocks as the product of solidification of intrusive magma, present studies reveal that this granite is the product of a paragneissic phase which has been subjected to further changes whereby blastic growths have played a predominant role. Evidence of the pre-granitic paragneissic phase are the abundant xenoliths — bodies of sedimentogenic material enclosed in the granite — and nodules of similar bodies and the individual pre-blastic components engulfed and contained in the blastic phase of the granite. The degree of dispersion of the paragneissic phase throughout the granite is considered to have been conditioned and brought about as follows:

The pre-granitic paragneissic phase has been subjected

to tectonic influences; parallel to the dynamic influences, blastic growths — mainly K-feldspar blastesis — occurred as a result of metasomatic and topometasomatic mobilisations whereby increased solubility in intercapillary spaces, diffusion and intergranular mobilisation of materials played a predominant role.

The size of the xenoliths in the Melca-Guba Granite varies from small bodies to bodies of 1–2 m width and several meters in length. Microscopic observations show quartz and feldspars (mainly sericitised albitic plagioclase and orthoclase) together with biotite laths; the texture is that of an initially sedimentogenic rock which, due to metamorphism, has changed into a paragneiss. A series of observations shows that zircon, sphene, apatite, and ore minerals occur as components of the xenoliths. Fig. 526 and 527 show idiomorphic or sub-idiomorphic zircons and apatites associated with quartz, feldspars and biotite of the xenoliths. Similarly, Fig. 528 shows apatite, sphene, ore minerals and zircons present. Fig. 529 and 530 show apatites both as idiomorphic crystals and as inclusions in the biotites of the xenoliths. It is thus clear that the apatites are components grown during the transformation of the sedimentogenic components into the paragneiss. Similarly, zircons are observed as inclusions in biotites. These observations exclude the possibility that these accessory minerals are components introduced into the xenoliths from the granite or its melt.

The contact of the xenoliths with the granite is interpreted here as being the contact between the paragneissic relics and the granitised mass. Fig. 146 and 147 show contacts of the xenolithic components with the granite, i.e., with K-feldspar crystalloblast thereof. The plagioclase of the xenoliths is corroded and myrmekitised by the orthoclase crystalloblasts of the granite. Fig. 531 illustrates plagioclases of the xenolith corroded and myrmekitised by the granitic K-feldspar; also, an apatite is partly surrounded and taken over by an orthoclase crystalloblast of the granite (Fig. 531 and 532). Additional observations (Fig. 533) show a K-feldspar crystalloblast of the granite in contact with myrmekitised plagioclases of the "xenoliths" and also enclosing quartz and apatite components of the latter.

As already mentioned, the Melca-Guba Granite is the product of paragneisses which were transformed into granite due to blastic and recrystallisation processes. Remnants of the original paragneiss are present in the granite, either as pre-blastic minerals or as obvious rests, i.e., xenoliths. Mineral components identical to those of the "xenoliths" are present — as a dispersed phase — in the granite and are, in turn, corroded and partly assimilated by its later crystalloblasts. Fig. 534 shows a nodule consisting of plagioclase (generation I), quartz (generation I), orthoclase, microcline, biotite and accessory minerals between K-feldspar crystalloblasts.

A series of illustrations is introduced showing the behaviour of the pre-blastic components, e.g., zircon, apatite, etc. in the Melca-Guba Granite. Fig. 535 shows zircon, apatite and biotite (components identical to the accessory minerals of the "xenoliths") enclosed in neo-crystallised quartz (generation II) of the granite. Fig. 536 shows quartz (generation I) and apatite engulfed and surrounded by newly crystallised quartz (generation II); the apatites are partly corroded by the later growths. Fig. 537 shows biotite, orthoclase and zircon adjacent to a later crystallised quartz (generation II); the biotites show corroded outlines and a portion is enclosed by the quartz (see arrow marked "Bi" in Fig. 537); a zircon is also entirely enclosed in the recrystallised quartz (see arrow marked "Zr" in Fig. 537). The biotites, zircon and orthoclase are pre-blastic components and belong to the pre-granitic paragneissic phase. As a corollary to Fig. 537, Fig. 538 shows apatites associated with biotite enclosed by a later blastic quartz. The accessory apatites were originally associated with the biotite which has been "invaded" by the quartz. The biotite associated with the accessories was originally a part of the larger biotite grain.

Additional observations (Fig. 539) show a blastic K-feldspar of the granite enclosing apatite and zircon as well as being in contact with quartz (generation I). Again, in this case, the zircon and apatite have been taken over by blastic minerals of the granite from pre-blastic components occurring as nodules in it. Similar observations (Fig. 540) show a blastic plagioclase of the Melca-Guba Granite in contact with the pre-blastic components: quartz (generation I), biotites, etc. The apatite enclosed in the plagioclase crystalloblast has a margin of quartz remnant, which is probably a part of a quartz grain (generation I) initially associated with the apatite. In this connection it should be mentioned that, due to blastic growths, the feldspars and quartz of generation I are more readily assimilated than the apatites and zircons, which resist assimilation to a greater extent.

The significance of the textural patterns of the accessories in granitic rocks

On the basis of the phenomenology exhibited in this Chapter, the following textural patterns can be established:

(1) Textural patterns of zircons

(a) Rounded and corroded zircons representing zircons (generation I).

(b) Overgrowths of zircon (generation II) on nuclei of zircon (generation I) or other accessory. The overgrowths form zones which attain idiomorphism and represent growth within the granite's formation processes.

(c) Limited corrosion phenomena due to synantetic reaction of crystallised zircon and later blastic growths.

(d) Post-biotite blastic zircon growths in biotites.

(2) Textural patterns of apatites

(a) The apatites tend to be idioblastic. In contrast to the corroded and rounded zircon (generation I), the corresponding apatites (generation I) are idiomorphic or found to be so.

(b) The corrosion and replacement phenomenology exhibited depends on the synantetic reaction of crystallised apatite and later formed blastic growth of feldspars, hornblende, biotites and quartz.

(c) Regrowths of apatites. Enclosing first generation apatite or zircons, the apatite attains an idiomorphic character (generation II).

(d) Blastic apatites. The regrowth type could be considered to be a blastesis; blastic apatites in biotite.

(3) Textural patterns of sphene

Sphene tends to be idioblastic post-hornblende and pre-hornblende; sphene idioblasts have been observed. Also post-zircon sphene blast are shown.

In addition to these textural patterns, it has been shown by Augustithis (1967a) that the accessory minerals: zircon, apatite, sphene, iron ores and associated biotite as well as pre-blastic quartz (generation I) and plagioclase of the palaeosoma, represent relics of a pre-granitic paragneiss, and are engulfed and incorporated by the blastic feldspar growth of the Melca-Guba Granite.

Studies on zircon by Hoppe (1962b) and Drescher-Kaden (1969) from the Bergeller and Adamello massifs have shown that rounded and corroded zircons are sedimentogenic in origin and that the granitic massifs are products of granitisation of sedimentogenic material. Corollaries to the above hypotheses are geochronological studies on granitic rocks by Coppens et al. (1965) which show a great variation in age for the zircons in a "granite". A method developed in the Centre de Recherches Radiogéologiques, Nancy, permits to obtain in excellent conditions the age of zircons taken one by one, by the ratio $^{207}Pb/^{206}Pb$. This method has been applied to the zircons from the granite of La Clarté-Ploumanac'h in Britanny. The ages measured are comprised between 32 and 1,316 m.y.; these values can be considered as characterising the distinct periods of formation.

Since the consolidation of a granitic melt and the orthomagmatic crystallisation phase could not have been of 'such a duration, it is to be concluded that zircons different in age and derivation exist in the same granite, i.e., sedimentogenic zircons and new zircons formed within the transformation and granitisation (granite formation). These geochronological determinations are in harmony with the textural patterns established; namely: *(1)* rounded and corroded zircon (generation I) of sedimentary derivation and *(2)* a new zircon crystallisation as overgrowths or blastogenic within the granitisation processes.

From the textural patterns established, it can be concluded that the zircon accessories are of great petrogenetic significance, since they can be pre-granitic sedimentogenic in origin and they definitely form a strong argument in support of a transformation origin of the granitic rocks. The sedimentogenic derivation of the zircons (generation I) is in harmony with the chemical and attrition resistance of zircon and thus could survive — as a resistant sedimentogenic relic — the transformation processes.

Chapter 19 | Tectonic influences on granitic rocks

Tectonic influences on granitic rocks and the tectonic behaviour of the granitic components

Quartz veins in granodioritic rocks, when subjected to compression, are deformed. Fig. 541 shows quartz with strain effect simulating a pattern produced by the non-distortion planes of the theoretical strain ellipsoid (Fig. 568) whereby the theoretical non-distortion planes correspond to the two intersecting planes of non-distortion in Fig. 541.

In contradistinction to the "strain-ellipsoid" effect, strained quartz veinlets in granodiorites may show a "banded undulating texture". The tectonic deformation produced a pseudo banding and simultaneously a pre-phase of mylonitisation is reached, as indicated by the fracturing of the middle undulating band of Fig. 542.

Due to tectonic deformation, undulating quartz is produced due to recrystallisation under tectonic influence. As shown in Fig. 543, two intersecting planes of deformation are produced which correspond to the non-distortion planes of the theoretical strain ellipsoid. One of the distortion planes is a marked plane of mylonitisation (fracturing) of quartz. Fig. 544 shows in detail the deformation planes (see also Fig. 543) which are simultaneously planes of quartz fracturing (micro-mylonitisation). At a high state of deformation, the quartz is extensively micro-mylonitised as indicated in Fig. 545. The transitions from undulating quartz to micro-mylonitised quartz are evidence that the interlocking small quartz grains are formed by micro-mylonitisation. Quartz veins in granitic rocks may be micro-mylonitised to such an extent that an interlocking "pseudo quartzitic" texture may result. Fig. 546 shows a pseudo mosaic texture of vein quartz produced by tectonic deformation. Also a shearing tectonic plane is indicated.

In contradistinction to micro-mylonitisation, often quartz reacts to tectonic deformation by recrystallisation, or plastic deformation. As a result of the plastic deformation of a crystal lattice, "compensation or rearrangement" occurs which may result in changes in its shape or physical character. Studies by Berman (1938), Bailey et al. (1958), Paulitsch and Ambs (1963) showed that the optical undulation, the transposition of quartz optical axes, follows crystallographically defined posi-

tions, i.e., the transposition of axes occurs in the zone [m:c] and only in some cases in the zone [a:c]. In addition, Ramsauer (1941) and Paulitsch and Ambs (1963) suggested that the plane of axes transposition is parallel to the "Gefüges Symmetrieebene" (Tectonic Plane of Symmetry) [a:c]; thus pointing out a relation between lattice changes in a crystal and the direction of external stresses. Thus, the transposition of the quartz axes influenced by external stresses is considered to be the result of lattice rearrangement or compensation due to plastic yielding.

Often in strained quartz the undulation attains complex patterns. Fig. 547 shows an x-shaped undulation anomaly in strained quartz which may correspond to two deformation directions intersecting at an angle, i.e., an x-shaped undulation pattern could correspond to the non-distortion planes of the theoretical strain ellipsoid. Of particular interest regarding the deformation effects on quartz and on the mineral components of rocks in general are the following publications: Sander (1930, 1948, 1950), Drescher-Kaden (1932), Schmidt (1934), Drescher-Kaden (1954), Paulitsch (1966), Guyot and Paulitsch (1967).

Due to tectonic deformation and recrystallisation out of the fine granitic ground-mass, quartz superindividuals may be formed, i.e., recrystallisation of fine quartz into a large individual under tectonic deformation (Fig. 548). The quartz superindividual is characterised by undulating extinction and is "interlocking" to finer recrystallised quartz.

Plastic deformation of quartz

Augustithis (1965) has discussed cases of plastic deformation of quartz. Fig. 549 shows paracrystalline quartz squeezed between plagioclase and biotite, ground-mass quartz grains subjected to strain have been permanently deformed. Two alternative suggestions are put forward:

(1) Pre-existing quartz grains of the granitic ground-mass are subject to strain, compressed between biotite and plagioclase. As a consequence, the quartz lattice breaks down, i.e., the quartz changes into a liquid and, subsequently, recrystallisation of the quartz occurs, as-

suming a form conditioned by the continued compressional force.

(2) Pre-existing quartz grains of the granitic groundmass are subjected to compression. The yielding of the quartz individuals takes place by plastic flow, i.e., solid flow.

The fact that the quartz individuals show anomalous extinction supports the explanation that a solid phase has been strained, rather than the idea that a quartz crystallising out of a liquid will show influences of strain. According to this interpretation, the plastic deformation of the quartz is the result of lattice readjustment or compensation to strain rather than complete breaking down of the lattice (i.e., a transformation of a crystal to liquid phase). Similarly Fig. 550 shows plastically deformed quartz squeezed between plagioclase and microcline. Additional observation reveal plastically mobilised quartz showing undulating extinction invading fractures of a tectonically affected plagioclase (Fig. 551). The undulating extinction of the quartz and the fact that the plagioclase fissures are due to tectonic influence supports plastic flow of the quartz under tectonic influences. Similarly, Fig. 552 shows fracturing of the plagioclase and plastic flow of quartz along the tectonically fractured plagioclase (bending of the lamellae and fissuring are simultaneously exhibited). A certain amount of plagioclase replacement (corrosion) has probably also taken place. The quartz exhibits the typical influences of tectonic effects (undulating extinction). A very convincing case of plastically squeezed quartz is shown in Fig. 553. Bent and fractured plagioclase is invaded by plastically mobilised quartz attaining a wedge form.

The plastic behaviour of quartz in relation to feldspar can attain forms that simulate a "diapiric penetration". Fig. 554 shows plastically deformed and recrystallised quartz of the ground-mass bulging into the weak parts of an adjacent K-feldspar. A rather more advanced phase of quartz penetrating diapirically into K-feldspar is shown in Fig. 555 where quartz, due to plastic deformation, is pushed into K-feldspar. The quartz is recrystallised and eventually a wedge-shaped body is penetrating into the feldspar. Similarly Fig. 556 shows recrystallised and plastically mobilised quartz penetrating into a reaction canal of a plagioclase. The relation of mobilised quartz to the reaction canal is dubious.

Plastic deformation. Plastic deformation can be defined as a permanent change of the shape of a body (De Sitter, 1956) which does not involve discontinuity (rupture). Recent theories on the strength of materials suggest that, when solids are subjected to great strain, yielding can take place in the form of "plastic flow" (i.e., the material behaves as a visco-elastic body): Plastic deformations in crystals involve irreversible changes which originate at the points of greatest elastic tensions (Smekal, 1938).

In contrast to the plastic deformation of quartz where a plastic flow has taken place, bending of micas can take place due to tectonic deformation (Fig. 557 and 558). In both cases, bending of the biotite can be understood in terms of lattice deformation. The phyllosilicate (sheet arrangement of the tetrahedra) permits readjustments of plastic deformation, as would be the bending of the micas. In addition, undulation of the extinction of biotite may result under tectonic influences. Fig. 559 and 560 show planes of microdisplacement and undulating extinction of tectonically influenced biotite. These figures (559 and 560) correspond to a different position of orientation of the microscope stage.

Also, due to tectonic influences, a deformation wedge may be formed in biotites (Fig. 561 and 562). The textural pattern resembles a pattern due to plastic deformation under shock waves. However, in the present case, the wedge deformation patterns are due to compressional forces. As in the case of shock deformation, included (accessory minerals) apatites have not been deformed (bent). The difference in the deformation behaviour of biotite and apatite under the same tectonic influences is to be attributed to their different lattice patterns. In contrast to the apatite, the biotite shows a greater plasticity due to the sheet arrangement of its tetrahedra.

Micaceous minerals can be pulled out in the form of "tails", "Schnuren", due to tectonic deformation. Such effects are again due to plastic deformation under tectonic influences (Fig. 563 and 564). As shown in Fig. 564 the mica is bulged, folded and pulled out along the direction of tectonic deformation within deformed quartz and feldspar. In some cases, the "Schnuren" are string-like, and tectonically pulled out biotite may resolve into minute bodies following a continuation with string biotite. As shown in Fig. 565, the string-like biotite in the quartz resolves into minute "globular bodies". Similar minute globular bodies are present in the K-feldspar and, in this case, represent resolved biotite.

In contrast to these banded plastic deformations of biotite, micro-folds of banded gneiss, consisting mainly of quartz and biotite (some zircon accessories also might be present), show that the micro-folding has taken place without plastic deformation of the biotite (no bending of biotite is observed). As Fig. 566 shows, the biotite laths are re-oriented with deformed quartz (recrystallised and showing bending, i.e., plastic yielding). Similarly, laths of biotite are arranged in a zig-zag way (Fig.

567) resulting in a "type of isoclinical folding" consisting of biotite laths which on the whole are not plastically deformed. In both cases of micro-folding in gneisses, the tectonic deformation of the rock resulted in a re-orientation and rearrangement of the micas rather than in the plastic deformation of the micaceous components.

Plastic mobilisations along the non-distortion planes of the theoretical strain ellipsoid

As has been discussed, it can be seen that the main granitic components: feldspar, quartz and micas, may exhibit a variable deformation phenomenology due to tectonic influences. Complex tectonic patterns may be observed in granitic rocks. The relation of plastic mobilisation of muscovite and quartz along the non-distortion planes of the theoretical strain ellipsoid has been discussed by Augustithis (1965). Such selected examples and additional observations are introduced to show the phenomenology of plastc flow and tectonic deformation in granitic rocks (tectonically an isotropic system).

The relation of the strain ellipsoid to the stress is given as follows: the two vertical planes each of which contains the normal to a circular section of the stress ellipsoid (strain ellipsoid), meet at an angle which is internally and externally bisected by the maximum P.H.S. (= principal horizontal stress – Means, 1963) and minimum horizontal stress directions (Fig. 568). In particular, as stated by Hills (1953), (actually a simplification of the above relations): "It is found that the angle that is bisected by the axis of least strain (which corresponds with the axis of maximum stress in irrotational strain) is acute for brittle substances and obtuse for ductile substances." The granitic rocks behave as brittle-mechanically isotropic bodies, i.e., the acute angle formed by the intersection of the non-distortion planes is bisected by the axis of maximum stress. Fig. 569 and 570 show the relation of the non-distortion planes (micro-faults and micro-cracks occupied by "pushed-in" muscovite) and the direction of the principal stress *EF*; also, *GH* shows the direction of the maximum strain.

The relation of a fissure system in granitic rocks occupied by plastically mobilised muscovite to the theoretical strain ellipsoid is shown in Fig. 569. The arrangement of the micro-fissure in the K-feldspar corresponds to the non-distortion planes of the theoretical strain ellipsoid (indicated in the attached diagram and shown by *AB* and *CD*). Also, the direction of compression is indicated by *FF*. Since K-feldspar is a brittle substance, the bisectrix of the acute angle corresponds to the maximum strain (see description). As is seen in the same figure (Fig. 569), a micro-displacement has taken place of the

muscovite lamella which is in the extinction position. In addition, a fine margin of quartz has been plastically mobilised in the fissure gap between the mica and the K-feldspar (Fig. 569). Evidence that the fine quartz fringe is a plastically mobilised phase is shown in Fig. 571 and 572. Fig. 572 shows muscovite partly sheathed by plastically mobilised quartz. The quartz sheath consists of plastically mobilised protuberances of a tectonically affected quartz which shows undulating extinction. Similarly, Fig. 571 shows muscovite plastically mobilised in a K-feldspar micro-fissure. As the mica enters into the quartz, a plastically mobilised quartz protuberance partly extends between the mica and K-feldspar. On the basis of the evidence of plastically mobilised quartz protuberances (Fig. 571 and 572), the fine quartz film between the mica and feldspar (Fig. 569) is also a plastically mobilised quartz that has been mobilised along the micro-fissure system. An additional series of photomicrographs illustrates the phenomenology of plastically mobilised muscovite and quartz along the micro-fissure system. Fig. 573 and 574 show muscovite plastically occupying a micro-fissure system that corresponds to the non-distortion planes of the theoretical strain ellipsoid. As shown especially in Fig. 574, a portion of the muscovite is folded and creased like a creased sheet of paper when subjected to oppositely directed forces. Particularly these detailed observations to the effect that, pushed into the fissures, muscovite is creased, are undeniable evidence of the plastic deformation of muscovite and its (tectonic) plastic implacement within the micro-fissure. Similarly, Fig. 575 shows muscovite occupying micro-fissures and a portion of it again shows a creasing texture due to the fact that the muscovite was pushed plastically into the fissure system. Comparable to Fig. 569, Fig. 576 shows plastically mobilised muscovite and quartz occupying micro-fissures. It can be seen that one micro-fissure terminates within the K-feldspar and, in this case, plastically mobilised quartz partly sheaths the muscovite. In contrast, Fig. 577 shows muscovite following micro-fissures and the boundary of two differently orientated K-feldspars. The same mica individual, by bending and branching, follows fissures of different directions (and in this case, the micro-fissure follows the non-distortion direction of the theoretical strain ellipsoid).

The textural behaviour of tectonically mobilised muscovite and its relation to K-feldspar and quartz

In cases, the tectonically mobilised muscovites occupy micro-fissures due to micro-faulting (Fig. 578). Similarly, muscovite follows a zig-zag micro-fissure and shows a small-scale displacement of the mica (Fig. 579). Also, as a result of tectonic influences, anomalous extinction due to straining is shown in the K-feldspar in which muscovite is tectonically pushed. Furthermore, the relationship of micro-crack and muscovite tectonically mobilised is shown in Fig. 580. Micro-fissures in the K-feldspar extend into the adjacent quartz. The muscovite occupies the K-feldspar fissure and partly extends into its continuation in the quartz. However, one of the muscovite lamellae terminates at the point where the micro-crack transverses the boundary K-feldspar–quartz. Similarly (Fig. 581), tectonically mobilised muscovite occupies a micro-fissure in K-feldspar, however, the muscovite is not extending into continuation of the micro-fissure when the latter transverses the boundary of the K-feldspar and an adjacent quartz. The continuation of the micro-fissure can be followed in the quartz where eventually it fades out. Additional observations show a micro-fissure transversing K-feldspar and quartz included in the orthoclase. A tectonically mobilised muscovite occupies the micro-fissure in the K-feldspar but, as the micro-crack transverses the quartz grain, the mica thins out (Fig. 582).

As is shown in Fig. 580, 581 and 583, there is a difference in the behaviour of micro-fissures transversing K-feldspar and quartz. The feldspar under tectonic conditions behaves as a brittle substance where a micro-fissure is an open interleptonic space; in contrast quartz, due to its great plasticity, heals (i.e., a micro-fissure tends to close, due to the more plastic behaviour of the quartz). Due to this differential behaviour under tectonic influence, one can understand the presence and absence of muscovite respectively in the different parts of a micro-fissure.

A most interesting observation of the plastic behaviour of quartz is shown in Fig. 584. A muscovite is tectonically ruptured and one fragment has been pushed through a quartz individual. As the muscovite fragment has been pushed through the quartz, an anomalous extinction shadow marks the path that was followed by the mica into the quartz. It should be noted that the two mica fragments and the shadow in the quartz are in continuation. What seems of interest is the fact that a muscovite fragment was allowed to be pushed through a solid quartz. The fact that the anomalous extinction path (extinction shadow) is noticeable in the quartz, is evidence of its solid state. Such a phenomenon could be explained by assuming a plastic property of the quartz at the time the muscovite was pushed through it. Probably, due to tectonic influence, a local increase in temperature could perhaps result in the increase in plasticity along the lines of stress.

Tectonic influences on muscovite lamellae tectonically pushed into micro-fissures and micro-faults

The muscovite lamellae tectonically mobilised in micro-fissures, show deformation effects themselves. Fig. 585 shows muscovite which is tectonically pushed into a K-feldspar micro-fissure and exhibits undulation and fragmentation of the mica. Similarly, Fig. 586 shows muscovite occupying micro-fissures in K-feldspar. A muscovite lamella (plate) is split into fine muscovitic lamellae. Another case of muscovite bulging which is accompanied by lamellae separation is shown in Fig. 587. Muscovite occupies micro-fissures transversing feldspars and quartz, the bulging of the muscovite lamella is restricted to the part of the fissure transversing the quartz. The difference in the behaviour of the same muscovite lamellae and the bulging of it in the quartz is attributed to the relatively greater plasticity of the quartz as compared to the K-feldspar, i.e., due to the brittle nature of the K-feldspar, the fissure maintained its walls when transversing the orthoclase. Apparently this was not the case in the quartz. Sometimes muscovite lamellae separating from the main muscovite mass may be attributed to other factors than tectonic deformation (Fig. 588).

Tectonic mobilisation of muscovite and simultaneous mobilisation of quartz. Complex textural patterns due to concurrent plastic behaviour of quartz and muscovite

The concurrent tectonic mobilisation of muscovite and quartz has already been mentioned and discussed in Fig. 582 and its description. As a corollary to it, Fig. 589 shows muscovite occupying micro-fissures in K-feldspar and simultaneously showing deformation effects, such as splitting apart of lamellae into fibre structure. Mobilised along the same micro-fissure system also is quartz which partly sheaths and partly encloses the mobilised muscovite. This is a complex tectonic pattern of plastically mobilised crystal phases (i.e., quartz and muscovite) along tectonic disturbances of a more brittle phase such as the K-feldspar.

Additional microscopic observations showing plastic mobilisation concurrently of quartz and mica are shown in Fig. 582, 590 and 591. Fig. 582 shows muscovite lamellae occupying micro-fissures in K-feldspar and some of the muscovite lamellae transverse the boundary of K-feldspar to an adjacent quartz. The same quartz individual sends plastically mobilised protuberances into other micro-fissures occupied by muscovite. Thus, it can be seen that, in the same quartz individual, muscovite is tectonically pushed in, and simultaneously other parts of the quartz send mobilised extensions into micro-fissures occupied by the mica. In contrast, plastically mobilised quartz sends protuberances into micro-fissures in the surrounding K-feldspar occupied by mobilised muscovite while a prolongation of micro-fissure transversing the quartz is not occupied by mica (Fig. 590). Similarly, deformed quartz sends extensions (plastically) into micro-fissures of K-feldspar occupied by muscovite. The plastic mobilisation of quartz along fissures is to be understood as plastic flows along directions of weakness of its immediate environment.

Tectonic deformation of feldspar

On the whole, feldspars behave as brittle substances in comparison to the more plastic muscovite and quartz. Nevertheless, plastic deformation of feldspars is often observed. Fig. 592 shows twinned plagioclase with undulating extinction which is in reality a plastic deformation, comparable and commensurable to undulating extinction in quartz, muscovite, and biotite. However, in this case no noticeable bending of the polysynthetic twinning accompanies the undulating extinction.

In contradistinction, bending of plagioclase polysynthetic twinning is evident in the case of plastic deformation of the feldspar indicated in Fig. 593 and 594. As is illustrated in Fig. 553, bending (plastic deformation) preceded fracturing. The polysynthetic twinning shows a bending prior to fracturing (into which the more plastic quartz has been pushed). These observations are in accordance with the fact that, when the limit of elasticity is surpassed, rupture takes place. In contrast, fracturing of feldspar in terms of micro-faults may take place without noticeable bending. Fig. 595 shows fracturing of microcline (i.e., micro-faulting). Also, the fracturing of K-feldspar whereby the microfissure system corresponds to the non-distortion planes of the strain ellipsoid has been illustrated, whereby the yielding was rather that of a brittle substance. (However, in this case the strain ellipsoid implies a certain amount of plastic deformation inherent to the concept of the strain ellipsoid.)

In contrast to the plastic mobilisation of quartz along micro-fissures (Fig. 551), quartz may be introduced and may replace the feldspar along the direction of tectonic weakness. Fig. 596 shows quartz extending into plagioclase and replacing the feldspar along the direction of weakness.

Brittle and plastic mineral phases

In garnet-pegmatites, a tectonically affected brittle garnet has been fractured and, into the fracture, plastic

quartz and mica have been tectonically mobilised (Fig. 597 and 598).

The "Augen" textures originate as a result of the brittle and plastic behaviour of mineral phases in granitic rocks whereby a brittle feldspar phase is in an environment of plastically mobilised quartz or micas. Fig. 599 shows a K-feldspar augen texture surrounded by plastically mobilised (recrystallised) quartz in a plane of shearing within a granitic ground-mass. Similarly, Fig. 600 shows a plagioclase augen structure partly "engulfed" by a tectonically mobilised biotite string in a general background of recrystallised quartz. In contradistinction to the "augen" structure, due to the different brittle–plastic behaviour of the feldspar and quartz in granitic rocks, plastically mobilised quartz often invades cracks and tectonic fissures of feldspars.

In addition to the plastic behaviour of recrystallised quartz squeezed between feldspars or feldspars and biotite, recrystallised quartz may show intense (fracturing) micro-mylonite formation along shearing planes. Fig. 601 shows two intersecting planes of micro-mylonitisation. Here again, a relation to the strain ellipsoid could be inferred. The micro-mylonitisation planes correspond to the non-distortion planes of the theoretical strain ellipsoid. A detail of the micro-mylonitisation shows a fine brecciation of the quartz and a string-like plastic mobilisation of micaceous minerals (Fig. 602).

In quartz–gold–tourmaline veins with chlorite, in granodiorites, under tectonic influence, recrystallisation and fracturing of the quartz may take place. Fig. 603 shows undulating quartz, tectonically fractured at the marginal parts, with chlorite mobilisations along fractured planes. Micro-displacements and micro-faults often are observed in tectonically affected granites (Fig. 604, 605 and 606).

Theoretical considerations on the plastic properties of micas, quartz and feldspars and their crystal structure

In a consideration of the elastic and plastic properties of minerals, crystal composition and structure, i.e., the arrangement and nature of the atoms or group of atoms within a crystal, are important.

Examples of micas with different properties of elasticity and plasticity

Crystallochemical considerations of the mica group based on the work of Machatschki (1953) show that, in these sheet silicates, the elastic and plastic properties decrease with the increase of substitution of Si by Al in the tetrahedra-nets and the subsequent introduction of additional cations. The following examples are quoted from Machatschki, showing that by increasing the substitution of Si by Al, the crystal structure becomes progressively less elastic, from pyrophyllite to margarite:

(1) Pyrophyllite: $\frac{2}{\infty}(OH)_2 Al_2 {}^{[6]}(Si_4 O_{10})$

The formula is electrostatically balanced and the double sheet units are held together by van der Waals' forces. There is no substitution of Si by Al in the tetrahedra nets. The mineral is easily subjected to layer dislocation ("Schichtverschiebung") and deformation.

(2) Muscovite: $\frac{2}{\infty}K^{[12]}(OH)_2 Al_2 {}^{[6]}(Si_3 Al O_{10})$

Considering the formula of muscovite, there is some substitution of Si by Al in the tetrahedra nets (a quarter of the Si is substituted by Al); as a consequence, there is $K^{[12]}$ between the double sheet units. The muscovite is characterised by a "facility" of layer dislocation parallel to (001) and furthermore the mineral shows elastic and plastic properties.

(3) Biotite:
$\frac{2}{\infty}K^{[12]}(OH, F)_2 (Mg, Fe, Mn, Al, Ti)^{[6]}_{2-3}(Si_3 Al O_{10})$

Due to the variation in the composition of the biotite group, there is a variation in its properties. The elasticity of the cleavage fragment is often reduced owing to the substitution of Si by Al in the tetrahedra nets and to the introduction of additional cations in the lattice.

(4) Margarite: $\frac{2}{\infty}Ca^{[12]}(OH)_2 Al_2 {}^{[6]}(Si_2 Al O_{10})$

Additional evidence of the reduction of elasticity with more substitution of Si by Al in the tetrahedra is provided by a consideration of the composition and crystal structure of margarite. In margarite ("Sprödglimmer"), the elasticity is reduced due to the extensive replacement of Si by Al (half of the Si is substituted by Al) and due to the presence of Ca cations in the lattice.

It can be concluded that the elasticity and plasticity of the mica depend upon the extent of substitution of Si by Al in the tetrahedra-nets. As this substitution is greater in some of the sheet silicates, the elastic and plastic properties decrease. (Depending upon this substitution, the presence of additional cations is determined in the lattice, which in turn influences the plastic and elastic properties of the minerals.) This is obvious from a comparison between the composition, crystal structure and physical properties of pyrophyllite and margarite.

A comparison of the elastic and plastic properties of quartz and feldspar on the basis of their crystal structure.

Microscopic observations reveal that, under similar tectonic conditions, quartz is more plastic than albitic plagioclase. Fig. 551 shows fractured plagioclase with quartz squeezed into and occupying the feldspar cracks. It is interesting that under the same tectonic conditions, the quartz and feldspar behave differently; that is, the one yields by plastic deformation and the other by fracturing. A comparison and consideration of the crystal structure and composition of quartz and feldspars reveals the following:

(1) In both cases the structural pattern of the lattice is a three-dimensional "Gerüst" (framework).

(2) The Si atom of the tetrahedra is surrounded by four shared O atoms, i.e., electrostatically, the lattice framework is balanced and the formula is SiO_2.

(3) Depending upon the substitution of Si by Al in the tetrahedra-nets, as is the case with the feldspars, there is an excess of negative charges balanced by cations occupying spaces of the lattice framework.

(4) In the quartz there is no such substitution, i.e., Al is not substituting Si in the tetrahedra-nets.

(5) In the plagioclase feldspars substitution of Si by Al takes place in the tetrahedra-net. Considering the end-members of the plagioclase series, the crystallochemical formulae are as follows:
albite: $\frac{3}{\infty}Na^{[6]}(Si_3 Al O_8)$;
anorthite: $\frac{3}{\infty}Ca^{[6]}(Si_2 Al_2 O_8)$.
It is obvious that substitution of Si by Al and the introduction of cations of Na and Ca respectively takes place.

By comparing the lattice framework structure where there is no substitution of Si by Al, i.e., in the case of quartz, with the lattice framework structure of the plagioclase (anorthite) where as much as half of the Si atoms are substituted by Al in the tetrahedra-nets, it can be seen that a reduction in the elasticity and plasticity takes place with the increase of Si substitution and with the introduction of additional cations to balance the chemical formula; commensurable with this was the case of pyrophyllite and margarite.

Chapter 20 | Late-phase metasomatic and alteration processes in granitic rocks

Alteration processes in granitic rocks

The alteration of granitic rocks can be considered as a low temperature transformation whereby pronounced mineralogical changes occur. The breaking down and alteration of feldspar due to hydrothermal processes or due to weathering is the most significant mineralogical change which results in the alteration and weathering of granitic rocks.

Both feldspar phases (K-feldspar and Na-rich plagioclases) are susceptible to alteration changes. The breaking down of feldspar is outlined by Machatschki (1953) as follows: "K-feldspar ($\frac{2}{\infty}$K, $AlSi_3O_8$) due to hydrothermal solutions or due to weathering, by loosing the K and partly the Si changes or partly changes into kaolinite: $\frac{2}{\infty}(OH)_4 Al_2 {}^{[6]}(Si_2 O_5)$. Another common alteration of feldspars is into sericite: $\frac{2}{\infty}K^{[1\ 2]}(OH)_2 Al_2 {}^{[6]}(Si_8 AlO_{10})$, or other micaceous aggregates.

Fig. 607 shows plagioclases enclosed in a K-feldspar megablast. Alteration processes resulting in sericitisation have taken place in both feldspars, however, the plagioclases are more altered due to their susceptibility to alteration. This is a typical case of feldspar alteration, in fact the tendency is for the plagioclases to be altered the most. Similarly, Fig. 608 shows plagioclases sericitised with the micaceous individuals orientated within one of the plagioclases. Well-developed laths of sericite following the feldspar twinning, or at an angle to it, have been formed. In contrast, the K-feldspar is free of alteration. Additional observations indicating the preferential alteration of the plagioclases are shown in Fig. 609. Plagioclases and K-feldspars are enclosed in later formed quartz. Sericitisation and alteration of variable extent is only indicated by the plagioclases; in contrast, the K-feldspars are free of alteration (no sericitisation is observed). The alteration of the plagioclases has taken place by "hydrothermal" solutions which have penetrated through the intergranular and have altered the plagioclases despite the surrounding cover of quartz (see also Chapter 16).

Often sericitisation may result in the extensive replacement of K-feldspars. Fig. 610 shows K-feldspar sericitised, the alteration has advanced along the crack and the intergranular of the feldspars. Quartz initially associated with feldspars is left as relics in the sericite. The disintegration of the feldspar has resulted in the complete alteration of the granitic rocks, since feldspars constitute the greatest part of the granitic rocks.

The alteration and sericitisation process is most selective, a typical case being the sericitisation of perthites in contradistinction to the non-altered K-feldspar host (Fig. 611).

The alteration of plagioclases may often show a preferential sericitisation of certain twin lamellae while other plagioclase lamellae show no alteration (Fig. 612). This may be due to greater penetrability along certain twin planes.

In addition to sericitisation, chloritisation may play an important role in the alteration of granitic rocks and components. Fig. 613 shows a chloritised mass with extensions of it penetrating in veinlet form through quartz and feldspars. An intersection of chloritic veinlets is also indicated. The penetration of quartz and feldspar by the chloritic veinlet occurs rather through intracrystalline metasomatic infiltration of the chloritic substances than due to interleptonic penetration, since the chloritic veinlet penetrates through a quartz and does not merely fill cracks in the quartz or intergranular cavities. Similarly, Fig. 614 shows chloritic veinlets bifurcating and re-uniting, crossing the boundary of K-feldspar and quartz. Metasomatic intracrystalline penetration as well as interleptonic penetration have played a role in the formation of this chloritic veinlet.

In contrast to the chloritic veinlets, intergranular cavities between idiomorphic and sub-idiomorphic quartz and feldspars may be filled with secondary chlorite (Fig. 615). In contradistinction to the fine grained chloritic mass filling the intergranular space, well-developed crystals of chlorite may be filling again intergranular cavities of quartz (Fig. 616).

Often kidney-shaped chloritic aggregates may be formed in K-feldspar representing a late-phase metasomatic replacement (Fig. 617). Chloritisation of biotite is a late-phase "hydration" alteration of micas and may take place along directions of cleavage of the mica (Fig. 618). Similarly, marginal chloritisation of the biotite takes place due to "hydration" reaction (Fig. 619).

The chloritisation of biotite may proceed along cracks and cleavages of the biotite resulting in a cell-like structure. This type of alteration is due to hydration which eventually results in the complete alteration of the biotite by secondary formed chlorite (Fig. 620). In contradistinction, chloritisation may take the form of "veinlets" in biotite (parallel to the mica's cleavage) with reaction margins between mica and the chloritic mass (Fig. 621).

Fig. 622 shows quartz with chlorite or chloritised bodies present in the marginal part of the quartz. Similarly, Fig. 623 shows three different quartz grains in contact sharing chloritic or chloritised inclusions in the margins of their contact. These textural patterns are dubious since they could be interpreted as either being due to infiltration of chloritic material marginal or as representing relics of a mafic mineral resorbed by quartz.

In addition to chlorite mobilisation, biotite may be mobilised and as a secondary mineral may "invade" feldspars or biotite-forming solutions, may "infiltrate" along cracks, cleavage planes or twin planes of plagioclases. Fig. 624 shows a twinned plagioclase with secondary fine laths of biotite formed by infiltration along cracks, having a tendency to follow the twinning and to be orientated perpendicular to the twin planes. In contrast, due to biotite mobilisation, corrosion of the feldspars by the biotite may take place with infiltrations of micaceous granules along the cleavage of the feldspars. Also micaceous mobilisations extend irregularly into the feldspar (Fig. 625).

Within the replacement and metasomatic substitution of secondary nature, i.e., deuteric processes not directly related to protogenic — granite forming — processes, are the replacement textures whereby secondary calcite replaces and substitutes quartz and feldspar within a granite. Fig. 626 shows microcline and quartz corroded and replaced by calcite. Similarly, Fig. 627 shows K-feldspar and plagioclase extensively corroded and replaced by calcite.

Such textural patterns undoubtedly represent corrosion and replacement, however, the question: "what happened to the feldspar and quartz substances that originally occupied the space now occupied by the calcite?", remains to be answered. The calcite cannot accommodate in its lattice — assimilate — the feldspar and quartz that originally occupied its space. One has to assume that a solution and transportation of these substances preceded the calcite formation. The solution and transportation processes preceded the replacement of quartz and feldspar by calcite.

Late-phase metasomatic crystallisations

In contrast to the plastically mobilised muscovite along the non-distortion planes of the strain ellipsoid (Fig. 569), a late-phase muscovite crystallisation is observed in intergranular space-cavities between quartz. Fig. 628 shows fan-shaped muscovite (the fan-texture is due to the radiating arrangement of muscovitic plates) occupying intergranular cavities between quartz. Similarly, Fig. 629 and 630 show textural patterns formed by the orientation and arrangement of a muscovitic "shell" in the intergranular cavity delimited by feldspar and quartz. In both cases, the muscovite is formed as a late phase in the granitic rock, i.e., after the crystallisation of quartz.

Of particular interest is the tourmaline in granitic rocks, which also is a late-phase crystallisation by metasomatic mobilisation. A series of photomicrographs shows the late-phase metasomatic formation of tourmaline in quartz veins and granitic rocks. Fig. 631 shows zoned quartz formed under free-space crystallisation (e.g., well-developed quartz crystals) with tourmaline infiltrations interzonally between the quartz. The infiltration nature of the interzonal tourmaline is also illustrated in Fig. 632, 633 and 634.

Fig. 632 shows a photomicrograph indicating quartz in the extinction position with interzonal tourmaline. The tourmaline-forming solutions have infiltrated along the interleptonic spaces provided by the interzonal spaces. The tourmaline infiltrations transverse the boundaries of quartz crystals. Fig. 633 shows, in detail, tourmaline crystals following directions of greater penetrability within the quartz host.

The later infiltration nature of the interzonal tourmaline is indicated in Fig. 634 which shows tourmaline infiltrations filling interzonal spaces of quartz and transversing quartz crystals differently orientated. It should, however, be emphasised that the tourmaline infiltrations also followed — in addition to the interzonal spaces — the boundaries between the differently orientated quartz, thus supporting an infiltration origin of the tourmaline.

In cases, the tourmaline infiltration has followed directions of greater penetrability which have been produced due to straining in the quartz (Fig. 635). The infiltration of tourmaline-forming solutions along directions of strain illustrates the post-quartz formation of the tourmaline.

In contradistinction to tourmaline infiltrations along interzonal spaces and penetrability direction due to strain, tourmaline may metasomatically infiltrate along cracks of quartz. Hydrothermal quartz shows cracks

(Fig. 636 and 637) occupied by metasomatically formed later tourmaline. Fig. 637 shows prismatic tourmaline crystals which have been formed by metasomatic replacement of the quartz along its cracks.

In addition to the infiltration textural pattern, metasomatic replacement of quartz by tourmaline is often observed. Fig. 638 shows tourmaline metasomatically corroding and replacing quartz. Tourmaline infiltrations follow the penetrability directions of the host quartz. Often the quartz is corroded and replaced by aggregates of tourmaline crystals; relics of quartz are left in the metasomatically formed tourmaline. On the basis of observations introduced, it can be seen that the tourmaline is formed after the quartz, either along penetrability directions provided by interzonal spaces or cracks, or by replacement, partial corrosion and assimilation of the latter (Fig. 639).

In contradistinction to the magmatic hypothesis which regards tourmaline as a typical mineral of the pneumatolytic phase, a metasomatic origin later than the hydrothermal quartz is indicated on the basis of the present observations. In accordance with the magmatic hypothesis, the pneumatolytic phase belongs to the following sequence of events: orthomagmatic crystallisation of granitic melt, pegmatitic-phase, pegmatitic-pneumatolytic and hydrothermal phase. As pointed out, the observations introduced in Fig. 631–639 showed a post-quartz (hydrothermal) metasomatic tourmaline formation.

A corollary to the post-quartz tourmalinisation is the blastogenic tourmaline transversing the boundary of ankerite–prochlorite in hydrothermal veins (Augustithis, 1967c) (Fig. 640).

In contrast to the post-hydrothermal quartz tourmalinisation, tourmaline is often a component of pegmatites and granites. Also in contrast to the magmatic interpretation whereby tourmaline is considered to belong to the pneumatolytic phase formed by pneumatolytic emanations of a consolidating granitic magma, Goldschmidt (1954) and Drescher-Kaden (in Goldschmidt, 1954) introduced the hypothesis of boron metasomatism from an initial sedimentary source. They showed that the boron in a granite of the Harzburg district was picked up from sediments. A comparable origin is proposed by Oftedahl (1964) for the formation of B-minerals in some Norwegian pegmatites.

Similarly, Drescher-Kaden (1969) describes a pegmatite from Piona, Lake Como, where the pegmatite transverses country rocks in which tourmaline gneiss is included. He suggests a mobilisation of the boron of the country rock metasediments as a source for the tourmaline formation in the pegmatite. The tourmaline in

the pegmatite often is perpendicular to the contact wall with the country rock. Fig. 641 shows tourmaline in the pegmatite perpendicular to the contact wall with the tourmaline-containing gneiss of the country rock.

An early crystallisation of tourmaline in a liquid pegmatitic intrusion would have, as a consequence, the sinking of the heavy tourmaline in the liquid magma of the yet not solidified pegmatitic intruding material. A gravitation differentiation would have been expected. However, the tourmaline is either perpendicular to the contact wall of the pegmatite or is in the pegmatite again perpendicular to its contact wall. Fig. 642 shows a handspecimen of tourmaline in the pegmatite, perpendicular to its contact with the tourmaline gneiss. Comparable structural patterns of tourmaline crystals, perpendicular to the contact walls yet extending in the pegmatite, have been observed in banded pegmatites–aplites from Cornwall.

Two alternative explanations are put forward to explain the non-gravitational sinking of the relatively heavy tourmaline in the pegmatite:

(a) The tourmaline was held in a "suspension" within a semi-liquid–semi-solid environment, i.e., the feldspar and quartz were in colloform phase while the tourmaline crystallised.

(b) The tourmaline has been formed in an already crystallised background of feldspar and quartz by crystalloblastic growth and due to its great corrosion and replacement capacity has attained large crystal forms due to its crystalloblastic force. As already shown, tourmaline needles metasomatically formed have a crystalloblastic force which makes the tourmaline to have a penetration capacity. A corollary to the great crystalloblastic force of tourmaline, are the radiating needles of tourmaline "Maltese cross-structures" and the elongated tourmaline autometasomatic growths in Luxillianites, whereby later metasomatic tourmaline has — by replacement and crystalloblastic force — penetrated through an already formed texture of feldspar and quartz of the granitic environment in which it was formed (Fig. 643 and 644). Similarly, observation of metasomatic crystalloblastic tourmaline penetrating through microfossils are known. In all these cases tourmaline is a late-phase crystalloblastesis.

Textural patterns of tourmaline

As already pointed out, graphic tourmaline may occur in symplectic intergrowth with K-feldspar (Fig. 322). Similarly, Fig. 645 shows tourmaline with extensions of it, intergranular between quartz and enclosing quartz. The tourmaline is a late blastogenic growth. The tourmaline often encloses accessory zircons (with radioactive halos produced) and corroded laths of biotite which are pre-blastic components enclosed by the late crystalloblastic tourmaline growth (Fig. 646 and 647). Whereas the zircon has maintained its idiomorphic shape (due to its great resistance), the enclosed biotite is corroded by the tourmaline.

In cases, the tourmaline crystalloblasts are infiltrated and corroded by a later-phase quartz. Fig. 648 shows tourmaline with a quartz worm-like body (myrmekite-like) invading a tourmaline. Similarly, late quartz has infiltrated and invaded a tourmaline along cracks and interleptonic spaces (Fig. 649). Also the tourmaline is corroded and replaced by the late-phase quartz.

Fig. 650 shows mobilised quartz following the contact tourmaline–quartz and extending into cracks of the tourmaline. The mobilised quartz is clearly a post-tourmaline formation.

In cases, tourmaline crystals may be enclosed in a blastic garnet. Fig. 651 shows tourmaline crystals both outside (in a background of quartz and feldspar) and included by the later garnet crystalloblast.

Chapter 21 | Radioactive minerals in granitic rocks

On the basis of X-ray fluorescence spectroanalysis of selected pegmatitic and hydrothermal uranium oxides, it has been determined that Th, Y and rare earths occur more abundantly in the uranium oxides of pegmatitic origin than in those of hydrothermal origin. These results are in accordance with previous determinations by other authors. However, studies by Augustithis (1964d) have shown that a number of exceptional cases exist, e.g., more particularly pegmatitic UO_2 occurrences, without noticeable Th or Y, have also been determined. Moreover, analyses have shown that Ti and Zr can occur in both pegmatitic uraninite and pitchblende.

TABLE I

CELL DIMENSIONS OF SYNTHETIC UO_2, PITCHBLENDE AND URANINITE (a_o IN Å)

Source, locality	Synthetic UO_2	Pitchblende (hydrothermal)	Uraninite (pegmatitic)
Albermann and Anderson, (1950) Pure UO_2	5.456		
Atomic Energy Commission U.S. General Statement	5.46	5.36 (minimum)	5.50
Berman, (1955) Widely different localities	5.4682	5.39–5.44	5.447–5.490
Gruner, (1951/52) Uraninite obtained at 50–215°C by the reduction of uranyl sulphate solution with H_2S, $FeSO_4$ or ether	5.39–5.40		
Ingerson, (1938) Haddam Neck, Connecticut Uraninite with columbite			5.454
Leutwein, (1957) Erzgebirge		5.40–5.43	
Robinson and Sabina, (1955) Grenville sub-province of the Canadian shield (a) 10% ThO_2 or less (b) 10%–18% ThO_2 (c) High thorian uraninites containing more than 20% ThO_2 and all thorianites			Less than 5.47 i.e., 5.449–5.470 5.47–5.50 5.51–5.65
Strunz, (1961) Hagendorf, Bavaria Uraninite with columbite Other occurrences Pure synthetic UO_2 Pitchblende (oxidised)	5.468	5.35	5.50 5.449–5.540
Wasserstein, (1954) Gordonia, South Africa Uraninite			5.444

TABLE II

CELL DIMENSIONS OF HYDROTHERMAL PITCHBLENDE AND PEGMATITIC URANINITE

a_0 in Å	Locality	Form and occurrence	Remarks
5.40	Schneeberg, Saxony	pitchblende (hydroth.)	spectrochemically, only traces of Th
5.430 ±0.001	Joachimsthal (Jáchimov, C.S.S.R.)	pitchblende gel → crystalline UO_2 (hydroth.)	X-ray fluorescence spectroanalysis, Th present
5.447 ±0.004	Ruggles mine, Center Grafton, New Hampshire	uraninite (pegmat.)	X-ray fluorescence spectroanalysis, Th in small quantities
5.48	Shinkolobwe, Katanga	relatively large crystals (hydroth.) ? recrystallised, originally gel-pitchblende	X-ray fluorescence spectroanalysis, traces of Th
5.490 ±0.001	Gordonia South Africa	uraninite (pegmat.)	X-ray fluorescence spectroanalysis, Th and Y both present
	Stackebo, Wästergötland, Sweden	uraninite (pegmat.)	X-ray fluorescence spectroanalysis
5.540	Faraday (Lockwood Farm), Canada	uraninite in lenses of rock made up of coarse-grained tremolite and white calcite containing rounded grains of diopside	U_3O_8 46% ThO_2 35% PbO 9%

Comparing the analytical results from colloform pitchblende (Fig. 652) with those from crystalline hydrothermal uraninite (Fig. 653), it can be seen that in both cases the elements forming the uranium oxides do not include Th, Y, and the rare earths as important constituents. In contrast to hydrothermal pitchblende, the pegmatitic uraninites are characterised by the presence of higher contents of Th, Y and the rare earths. Studies by X-ray fluorescence spectroanalysis of uraninite cubes (Fig. 654) of pegmatitic origin from Stackebo, Wästergötland, Sweden, show a relatively high content of Th, Y and rare earths in comparison with the analysed uraninite cubes of hydrothermal origin from Shinkolobwe, Katanga (Fig. 652).

On the basis of the studies by X-ray fluorescence spectroanalysis of fergusonite, malacon, naegite and of an unidentified mineral containing U, Nb and Y from Harrar, Ethiopia, it can be seen that elements similar to those in uraninites of pegmatitic origin are present, e.g., U, Th, Zr, (Hf), Ti, Ta, Nb and the rare earths. The quantities in which they occur can vary with their crystal structures. In the pegmatitic uraninites U is dominant, in fergusonite Nb and Y, and in malacon and naegite Zr.

The presence of U, Th, Y, Nb, Ta, Ti, Zr in pegmatitic uranium minerals is, as expected, in accordance with the presence of the same elements as mineral-building elements in the paragenesis of pegmatitic uranium minerals (Augustithis, 1964d, p. 53).

In addition to the difference in composition between hydrothermal (gel pitchblende) and pegmatitic uraninite there is also a difference in the dimension of the unit cell. Both the crystalline uraninite and the colloform (röntgenomorph) pitchblende crystallise in the cubic system and have a fluorite-type unit cell. Tables I and II show the variations in the cell of synthetic UO_2, hydrothermal pitchblende and pegmatitic uraninite.

It can be seen from Tables I and II that the pure synthetic UO_2 has a cell-unit dimension of $a_0 = 5.468$ Å, (although this value contrasts with that obtained for non-thorian pure pitchblende the unit cell of which is given as $a_0 = 5.40$ Å and (oxidised) pitchblende shows a value as low as 5.35 Å). Nevertheless the cell unit of the synthetic UO_2 obtained at $50-215°C$ by the reduction of uranyl sulphate solution with H_2S, $FeSO_4$ or ether is approximately that of pure natural pitchblende (a_o = 5.39–5.40 Å). Table II shows that the cell-unit values of hydrothermal and pegmatitic UO_2 converge between 5.447–5.48 Å.

Comparing the hydrothermal paragenesis consisting of groups[1] A: (U, (Th), Pb, Bi, As, Sb, (Se, Sn, Mo)) and B: (Fe, (Mn), Co, Ni, Ag, Zn, Cu, Au) with the pegmatitic uranium paragenesis which mainly consists of group C: (U, Th, Zr, Hf, Y, Nb, Ta, Ti and the "Rare earths"), certain geochemical tendencies become apparent.

Table III indicates the abundance of C-group elements in the earth's crust.

TABLE III

ABUNDANCE OF C-GROUP ELEMENTS IN THE EARTH'S CRUST (p.p.m.)

U	4
Th	11.5
Y	28.1
Zr	220
Hf	4.5
Nb	20
Ti	4,400
Ta	2.1
Ce	41.6

It is consequently more than coincidence that *the rare elements occur together in mineral paragenetic associations of world-wide distribution.*

Between these elements there appears to exist a chemical–geochemical affinity and some kind of interrelationship. These can be best understood by considering the periodic system and its empirical laws which determine the broad lines of the affinities of all elements.

The elements comprising group C show interrelationships. Th, Hf, Zr, Ti are homologous and belong to the subgroup of family IV. Y and Nb are interrelated to Zr as elements next to it in the periodic table, and also are related to Hf. Ti is related both to Nb (homologous) and to Hf as next to it. The rare earths are related to Hf as elements next to it. It can consequently be suggested that the elements which comprise group C and which are often the main mineral-building elements in pegmatitic uranium paragenesis are interrelated in accordance with the periodic system (see Chapter 25).

Present geochemical studies show that Th is the key element for the understanding of uranium paragenesis.

According to Dwight (1960), there is also a geochemical interrelationship between U and Th. Besides their interrelation in accordance with the periodic system, UO_2 and ThO_2 form an isomorphous series. Th is for group C: (Th, Zr, Hf, Ti, Y, Nb, Ta and the rare earths) the key element, and investigations have shown that, when in an uranium paragenesis, thorium is in excess, the other elements of the group are also present.

The textural patterns of the pegmatitic uraninite paragenesis

A series of photomicrographs illustrate some characteristic examples of textural patterns of pegmatitic uraninite and their intergrowth with other pegmatitic minerals. Fig. 320 shows graphic-like intergrowth of uraninite with microcline. These textural patterns are comparable to the graphic intergrowths of quartz and K-feldspar. Also Fig. 655 shows a skeleton crystal of uraninite again in intergrowth with microcline. If the uraninite develops, it will attain a eucrystalline form. Both the graphic and skeleton textures indicate that they are intermediate phases to idiomorphic uraninites in pegmatites.

In contrast, pegmatitic uraninite may be associated with zircon (malacon). Fig. 656 shows a zoned malacon which is "pushed into" or included by uraninite and magnetite. In contrast, uraninite is included as an intergrowth within malacon (Fig. 657).

Another characteristic textural pattern is shown in Fig. 658. Crystalline pegmatitic uraninite is transversed by cassiterite. A radioactive margin (due to the radioactive influence of the uraninite) is produced along the contact of uraninite and cassiterite.

Moreover pegmatitic uraninite may occur as an intergrowth in columbite. Fig. 659a shows ex-solution-like bodies of uraninite in columbite. In cases, the uraninite may attain idiomorphic form with the uraninite, as epitaxis of uraninite on columbite (Fig. 659b), (see Ramdohr, 1960 ; Strunz, 1961). The geochemistry and mineralogy of primary uranium-containing minerals is extensively discussed by Augustithis (1964d).

Radioactive halos in granitic rocks

The study of the accessory minerals has illustrated numerous cases of radioactive halos surrounding zircons (and apatites) enclosed in biotite. In general, the zircons contain radioactive elements, i.e., U or Th which are responsible for the emission of α rays. Fig. 660 shows a double radioactive halo surrounding zircon enclosed in biotite.

_____
[1] A and B groups: the mineral-building metallic elements of hydrothermal paragenesis, and Group C: the mineral-building elements of the pegmatitic uranium paragenesis.

About radioactive halos and the influence of radio-active minerals on the colour of their hosts Ramdohr and Strunz (1967) remark the following: "Das auffallendste Merkmal radioaktiver Einwirkung in Gesteinen sind die radioaktiven Höfe. Sie entstehen dort, wo kleine Mineralkörnchen, die Gehalte an U, Th oder auch Sm besitzen, in "verfärbbaren" Mineralien liegen und dort lange genug einwirken können. Radioaktiv verfärbbar sind besonders Biotit, Chlorit, Cordierit, Hornblende, Fluorit, Zinnstein, seltener Turmalin, Spinell, Korund, Triphylin, Triplit, Baryt, Siderit, Astrophyllit und Albit. Durch die einwirkende α-Strahlung wird das Gitter dieser Mineralien teilweise zerstört, die entionisierten Atome wirken wie eine kolloidale Färbung. Die Färbung reicht natürlich nur so weit, wie die energiereichsten α-Teilchen (die des RaC′ und ThC′) in dem betreffenden Material fliegen. Die Reichweite beträgt ungefähr 1/2000 der Reichweite in Luft."

A corollary to the radioactive behaviour of zircon is the X-ray fluorescence analysis of malacon from Hittero, Norway and Takayama Mino, Japan (Fig. 661 and 662). In both cases, besides Zr, also U, Th (in addition to Y and Hf) are constituents of the pegmatitic zircon (metamictic malacon). Furthermore, Zr, Hf, Y, Th, U are interrelated on the basis of empirical laws of the periodic system and their joint occurrence is to be expected. It is, therefore, not surprising to find radioactive halos surrounding zircon included in granitic biotites.

In addition to the radioactive halos of zircons in bio-tite, numerous other examples have been studied, i.e., pegmatitic uraninite in intergrowth with microcline showing radioactive halos surrounding the uraninite (Fig. 320); uraninite in epitactic intergrowth with columbite shows a radioactive margin along the contacts of uraninite with columbite Ramdohr (1960); uraninite in contact with cassiterite shows a radioactive margin bordering the uraninite along its contact with the cassiterite (Fig. 658). Also zircon in tourmaline indicates radioactive halos surrounding the accessory (Fig. 646). Indeed, these are only some well known cases of radioactive halos — the prerequisite conditions are a radioactive mineral (a mineral containing a radioactive element in sufficient amount that the emission of α rays can bring about alteration effects on the neighbouring mineral) and the susceptibility of the neighbouring minerals to the effect of the emitted α rays.

A relatively common radioactive mineral in granitic rocks is orthite (allanite),

$$Ca\,(Ce, Th)\,(Fe''', Mg, Fe'')\,Al_2\,[O/OH/SiO_4/Si_2\,O_7]$$

It is often associated with biotite causing a radioactive margin on the mica. Orthite is often converted into metamictic aggregates (radioactive isotropisation), (Fig. 663).

In contradistinction to the radioactive halos described, radioactive halos can be also produced due to mobilisation of U and Th oxides secondarily along cracks and fissures of biotite (Fig. 664A and 664B).

Chapter 22 | The intrusive character of granitic rocks

From the vast literature on granites, a selection of excerpts is quoted here to show the wide spectrum of theories introduced at different times by geologists and petrographers, each trying to formulate a hypothesis that would, according to him, explain at best his observations and experiences gained either in the field, in the laboratory or under close examination of specimen under the microscope.

Hutton (1795)

"Without seeing granite actually in a fluid state, we have every demonstration possible of this fact: that is to say, of granite having been forced to flow, in a state of fusion, among strata broken by a subterraneous force . . ." (1795, p. 52)

Lyell (1838, 1875)

In his early treatment of the metamorphic rocks, Lyell (1838) states: "The metamorphic theory does not require us to affirm that some contiguous mass of granite has been the altering power; but merely that an action, existing in the interior of the earth at an unknown depth . . . analogous to that exerted near intruding masses of granite, has, in the course of vast and indefinite periods, and when rising perhaps from a vast heated surface, reduced strata thousands of yards thick to a state of semifusion, so that on cooling they have become crystalline, like gneiss. Granite may have been another result of the same action in a higher state of intensity, by which a thorough fusion has been produced; and in this matter the passage from granite into gneiss may be explained." (1838, p. 251)

"The transmutation has been effected by the influence of subterranean heat acting under great pressure, and aided by thermal water or steam and other gases permeating the porous rocks, and giving rise to various chemical decompositions and new combinations, the whole of which action has been termed "plutonic", as expressing in one word all the modifying causes brought into play at great depths and under conditions never exemplified at the surface. To this plutonic action the fusion of granite itself in the bowels of the earth as well as the development of the metamorphic texture in sedimentary strata may be attributed." (1875, p. 164)

Sederholm (1967)

"I therefore do not expect that the opinions presented here will be generally accepted immediately, particularly by all those who have travelled in gneissic terrains without realising the enormous importance of granitic injection phenomena and their wide-spread occurrence. What I do hope for is that hereafter such travellers will not completely deny the existence of such phenomena, and that they will admit that I have arrived by inductive study, and not by trust in authority or by armchair geology, at an opinion about a rebirth or palingenesis of granitic magma.

I venture to suggest this new name *Palingenesis*[1]) in spite of the great number of terms already in existence in this field, because of my wish to stress strongly the philosophical (if I may be permitted to use the word) significance of the process, which is in a true sense regional, and can be regarded as of at least the same importance as metamorphism and other great geological processes. According to the point of view I have attempted to defend here, regional metamorphism is a weaker form of the kind of alterations which in greater depth give rise to palingenesis. We thus return to an idea which is essentially the same as the old doctrine of plutonic metamorphism." (1967, pp. 48—49)

Niggli (1924)

"In summary, we can well say that granite and granodiorite with the usual chemical, mineralogical, structural and textural characteristics have the typical characters of magmatic rocks and that their explanation as normal metamorphic rocks, for example as metasomatically altered sediments, appears impossible to all petrographers who have investigated a great deal of eruptives and metamorphic rocks in the field and in the laboratory. The new idea that granite is a metamorphic rock rests on no kind of fundamental investigation. True migmatites are marginal to granite as Sederholm, Gruben-

---

[1]) Palingenesis synonymous to anatexis

mann, Niggli, Holmquist, Barth, Scheumann readily agree. So-called 'granitised' metamorphic rocks must be separated from the granites and granodiorites." (Grubenmann and Niggli, 1924, pp. 39–40)

Harker (1932, 1950)

"The phenomena of thermal metamorphism are best studied in the rocks surrounding a large plutonic intrusion of a type not clearly connected with orogenic movements. Here the heat, which is the proximate cause of metamorphism, is of course drawn from the earth's internal store, but has been carried by an ascending molten magma. If, for a rough estimate, we suppose the temperature of intrusion to range from 1,000 to 600°C, according to the nature of the magma, and assume 0.3 as the mean specific heat of the solid igneous rock, we have from 300 to 180 calories as the measure of the heat given out in cooling; to which must be added about 100 calories for the latent heat of fusion. From a large body of plutonic rock, therefore, an enormous amount of heat will be set free, and the whole of this passes by conduction into and through the surrounding rocks, raising their temperature in its passage . . .

Inasmuch as the effects are due, not to contact, but to heat and high temperature, the term thermal metamorphism seems more appropriate. The belt of metamorphosed rocks surrounding a plutonic intrusion, conveniently styled a metamorphic aureole, has a width which depends upon more than one factor, but mainly upon the size of the intrusive mass." (1950, p. 21)

". . . In favourable circumstances it is then possible to divide the aureole into successive zones of metamorphism, possessing distinctive characters and representing successive grades of metamorphism. This was first attempted by Rosenbusch in the metamorphosed Palaeozoic slates known as the Steiger Schiefer round the granite mass of Barr-Andlau in the Vosges. He distinguished three zones:

(I) Knotenschiefer or spotted slates, (II) Knotenglimmerschiefer or spotted mica schists, and (III) Hornfels, rocks totally reconstructed." (1950, p. 24)

Green (1882)

"We have found that granite occurs under three forms. Under the first it still retains traces of bedding or is interstratified with undoubtedly bedded rocks; here there can be little doubt that it is an intensely metamorphosed rock. Under the second form granite occurs in amorphous masses, which melt away insensibly on all sides into unaltered strata, show no signs of having burst violently through the adjoining beds, but look as if they filled up spaces once occupied by rocks similar to those that surround them. Such appearances are best explained by supposing that portions of the rock-mass, in the heart of which these bosses occur have been altered into granite, the metamorphism having been more intense than that which produced the first form of the rock because the bedding is effaced, but yet not energetic enough to cause the granite to behave irruptively. Under the third form, granite gives proof of having been forcibly intruded into the rocks among which it occurs, and its irruptive behaviour may reasonably be attributed to an increased degree of energy in the metamorphic process which gives rise to it." (1882, p. 58)

Termier (1912)

"If a granite is surrounded by a narrow aureole, it is certain that the granite has not been made in situ – it has come from somewhere else, ready made. If, on the other hand, a granite is surrounded by a vast aureole of metamorphic rocks, it has certainly been formed in place, by complete fusion of a eutectic, whilst the neighbouring rocks were regionally metamorphosed." (1912, pp. 592–593).

Read (1957)

"Wegmann concludes (Wegmann, 1931, pp. 58–59) that the greater part of the Hangö Granite was not a molten silicate mass in the usual sense of the word, but a mass soaked with granitic solutions coming from below. Where this soaked mass moved and met with enough resistance at the walls it presents to us the characters of an intrusion; movement gives an intrusion, no movement gives an area of granitisation. The pegmatite dykes are the part of the granitising solutions which crystallises in joint and opened spaces arising in the permeated mass." (1957, p. 124)

"According to Backlund, granitisation in situ (i.e., granitisation in Read's sense) causes an increase in the amount of material in a given space; the result is that a mobilisation or rheomorphism of the granitisation products takes place. This mobilisation leads to flow movements, differential movements, flow folds, penetration and intrusion in the direction of least resistance (Backlund, 1938b). Granitisation is controlled by the capacity of the country-rocks to allow diffusion both as regards quality and quantity of material. Diffusion will increase with temperature and will depend also upon textures, such as schistosity and upon the make-up of the sediment. Granitisation thus may become the culmination of metasomatism and find its expression in rheomorphism leading to sharp contacts." (1957, p. 133)

"De Beaumont (De Beaumont, 1847) accepts Virlet's (Virlet, 1847) proposals that some granites are of metamorphic origin and discusses how such granites can yet display the characteristic minerals of the aura granitica." (1957, p. 97)

"Scheerer (Scheerer, 1847) has stated about the character of the plutonic matter at the time of its intrusion: 'All granites formed at one time a kind of watery paste 'une bouillie aqueuse' or moistered magma.'" (1957, p. 62)

"Similarly Scope accepts the physical state of the granitic intrusive material to be a type of broth, mesh, or 'Brei' which could theoretically arise in various ways. One kind would be a mesh consisting of 'magma' and of minerals already crystallised from this magma 'ein Brei, bestehend aus magma und aus diesen Magma bereits auskristallisierten Mineralien.' (P. Niggli, 1942, p. 41)." (1957, p. 63)

"The plutonic origin of granite has been thought to be shown by its contact phenomena and by the resemblance in its composition to that of some true volcanic rocks. In Scheerer's opinion, neither of these are serious proofs of an igneous origin of granite and the problem can only be solved by a study of the intimate structure (i.e., texture) of the rock itself." (1957, p. 96)

Drescher-Kaden (1948, 1969)

"Die grosse Ähnlichkeit, ja Übereinstimmung der Granitgefüge mit solchen der metamorphen Bildungen kann damit aus ihrer nur graduell verschiedenen, generell aber einheitlichen Genese erklärt werden." (1948, p. 249)

"Die mitgeteilten Beobachtungen haben genügend Beispiele für die hydatogene Entstehung der einzelnen Gefügeformen granitischer Gesteine erbracht. In Zukunft wird es notwendig sein, die beobachteten Merkmale besonders in solchen Granittypen aufzusuchen, aus deren Auftreten man bisher geglaubt hat, auf selbständige magmatische Schmelzen der Tiefe (woher?) schliessen zu können, bzw., zur Auffindung desjenigen Bildungsbereichs zu kommen, in dem die Umformung des Gefüges das ehemalige Strukturbild so weitgehend geändert hat, dass keine Merkmale des ursprünglichen früheren Zustandes mehr erhalten geblieben sind und nur noch abgeleitete Gefügeeigenschaften die durchlaufene Entwicklung andeuten." (1969, p. 564)

The granite problem

The above quotations show stages in the evolution of thoughts regarding the intrusive character and origin of granitic rocks, without though the evolution following a conformity of thoughts. The extreme theories, magmatic origin of granites and transformation in situ, are extrapolations of the problem. On the other hand, paligenesis—anatexis (palingenesis) of magma is a compromise.

The return to Lyell, namely that there is a plutonic class of rocks which comprises the granites and the metamorphics (Read, 1957), allows a great margin of magma-rebirth palingenesis (fusion of rocks).

In contradistinction, Wegmann (1931), Backlund (1935), De Beaumont (1847), Virlet (1847) and Scheeter (1847)—on the basis of the aforementioned quotations—tend to accept granitisation and a granitic intrusion without magmatic palingenesis.

Whereas there is a tendency to accept the transmutation of initial sediments or metasediments to granites, this is generally only acceptable for the non-intrusive "granitised" masses, i.e., there are granites and granites (Raguin, 1965; Read, 1957; Green, 1882; Termier, 1912).

In contrast, Drescher-Kaden (1948) concludes that there is a great similarity of textures of metamorphic rocks and granites and that they are both of the same (metamorphic—metasomatic) origin. Furthermore, Drescher-Kaden (1969) concludes: "Observations reveal the "hydrogenic" origin of certain textural forms in granitic rocks. It remains to find these (hydrogenic textural forms) also in granites which are considered previously to be magmatic and in which the transformation of the initial structure is so advanced that no vestiges are left and in these granites in particular the evolution of the textural changes must be traced." In addition to Drescher-Kaden (1969) also Michel-Levy (1874) and Scheerer (1847) believe that the ultimate solution of the granite problem depends on the study of the intimate structure (i.e., textures) of the granites themselves.

It has been the task of the present atlas to study the intimate structure of granites and granitic rocks and, on the basis of the comparative anatomy of the textures observed in more than five hundred different granitic massifs from a world-wide distribution, to study the evolution (changes which resulted) of the textural patterns observed in granitic rocks, whether they are granitised masses or intrusive granites. The hydrogenic textures observed in granitic rocks by Drescher-Kaden (1969) and in fact the hydrogenic textural patterns and their variations are found as the main textural patterns in all granites, whether they are granitised masses or intrusive with "aura granitica".

More work is needed for the understanding of the evolution of the textural patterns of granitic rocks. The

"Reaktionsgefüge" and *"Granitprobleme"* by Dre-scher-Kaden (1948, 1969) and the present atlas should be considered only a beginning, i.e., an introduction in this vast field of granitic textural patterns. Moreover, the intrusive character of granites and the aura granitica should be studied and explained on the basis of the gained experience of the "hydrogenic" evolution of the granitic intimate structures, i.e., in which state and at what stage of the granite's evolution an intrusion and aura granitica can be formed.

Chapter 23 | Contact metamorphism and metasomatism

Harker (1950, pp. 21—28) gives an account of "aureoles of thermal metamorphism". One gains the impression that a thermal effect is indisputable and chilled contacts characterise the intrusive granitic masses. Both Harker and Rosenbusch (1877) believe in pure thermal metamorphism due to granitic intrusive magma. However, Harker's metamorphism does not produce evidence of such thermal metamorphic aureoles, also the description of the different stages of thermal metamorphism by Rosenbusch, i.e., from without inward: [*(1)* "Knotenschiefer", spotted slates (spots are marked by aggregation of the disseminated carbonaceous matter — now reduced to graphite — and fine magnetite formation); *(2)* "Knotenglimmerschiefer" or spotted mica ,schists, (a more advanced stage, fine micaceous material and amorphous relics); *(3)* "Hornfels" andalusite— cordierite-hornfels] is difficult to accept as evidence of pure thermal metamorphism. Particularly the cordierite formation in the hornfels denotes some Mg-metasomatic influences. In general, solution phases could account for the metamorphic alteration considered as pure thermal by Rosenbusch.

Contact metamorphism has been extensively studied by both magmatists and transformists; the following are some publications concerning contact metamorphism-metasomatism: Lacroix (1898/99), Goldschmidt (1911), Eskola (1922a), Harvey (1931), Reynolds (1947a, b, c), Holmes and Reynolds (1947), Drescher-Kaden (1961d), Fonteilles (1962), Seim (1963), Beavis (1964), Weibel and Locher (1964), Tilton et al. (1964).

The celebrated alteration of limestone to marble as pure contact thermal metamorphism is contrary to experimental data. The limestone—marble transformation is either pre-intrusive or synchronous to the granite implacement in the sense of concurrent metamorphism with granite emplacement under conditions of "regional metamorphism".

In contrast to the pure thermal metamorphism, evidence is introduced whereby country rocks in contact with intrusive granites, as well as enclosed sedimentogenic "xenoliths" in granites, show no influence of reconstitution as would be expected by the enormous heat released by an intrusive batholith or large granitic mass as it is imagined by Harker, Rosenbusch and magmatists in general. In this connection, it should be recalled that phyllitic xenoliths occur in the tunnel of Mt. Blanc without evidence of thermal metamorphism. Fig. 665 shows a handspecimen of a phyllite xenolith with "double-inclusions" of K-feldspar. According to the magmatic hypothesis, a thermal metamorphism (transformation of phyllite to hornblende schist) should have taken place. Similarly, Fig. 32 shows a sandstone enclosed as a xenolithic relic in granite. Here again, no recrystallisation or melting of the enclosed sandstone nodule has taken place.

In contrast to the absence of pure thermal influences, often granitic contacts are characterised by metasomatic alterations.[1] Here again no rules and regulations can be made regarding the relation of the intrusive granitic body and the presence and extent of contact metasomatic effects. Granitic intrusions may or may not show extensive contact metasomatic influences on the country rocks in which they intrude. In cases, whereas the contact metasomatic effects may be absent at the contact with the country rock, nevertheless metasomatic effects may be formed at a distance from the contact boundary within the metamorphic—metasomatic aureole. Often granitic veins or granitic apophyses, meters apart, may or may not show contact metasomatic influences. Also cases are known where the same vein-granitic body may have a metasomatic contact only on one side of the vein intrusion. In cases, the granitic vein may show metasomatic alteration within the granitic mass, but not as contact in adjacent country rock. Fig. 666 shows a granitic intrusive vein in contact with marble. No contact metasomatic effects are visible in the marble, however, there is a metasomatic alteration. Epidote formation is noticeable within the granite, forming a margin in the granite itself as it is in contact with the marble.

In cases, granitic intrusions with very extensive contact metasomatic influences on the country rock may have apophyses devoid of metasomatic contacts. Fig. 40 shows a granitic apophysis (Seriphos Granite, Greece) without a metasomatic contact. Also a xenolith enclosed

---

[1] The metasomatic contacts are often more spectacular when the country rock consists of marble. Epidote-garnet and often epidote-garnet-skarns are formed.

in the granite shows no metasomatic contacts. In contra-distinction, a granitic apophysis of the same granite (Fig. 667) has folded the marbles into an arch and shows a metasomatic contact.

Contact metasomatism is complex and in general depends on the nature and composition of the country rock and the metasomatic substances either of the granite, or elsewhere mobilised, which react with the country rock. Contact metasomatism is a vast subject and an enormous amount of literature exists in this field. Only some cases are considered here illustrating the complexity of the subject and introducing some suggestions on the possible mechanism involved. Special cases of contact metasomatism are the skarn bodies formed as contact reactions of the intrusive granites with marbles. It should be noted that the limestone—marble transformation is either pre-granitic or synchronous to the intrusion under regional metamorphism and is an event of complex metamorphic—metasomatic processes.

Different hypotheses have been introduced in order to explain the skarn bodies and the contact metasomatic alterations in general. According to the early magmatic interpretation of Goldschmidt (1911), the Fe is of pneumatolytic derivation from the granitic intrusive magma. Goldschmidt (1911, p. 214) has suggested that the iron is introduced as a volatile chloride or fluoride, and that it has reacted with the calcite as follows:

$$Fe_2Cl_6 + 3CaCO_3 \rightarrow Fe_2O_3 + 3CaCl_2 + 3CO_2$$

The chloride or fluoride would then go to make scapolite or fluor minerals, which do occur but neither generally nor in abundance. As Harker (1950, p. 127) comments: "The ordinary pneumatolytic minerals are not usually a prominent feature of the iron skarns."

The skarn bodies are indeed complex and such a schematic interpretation does not provide a satisfactory interpretation. In addition to Fe, also Mg and Cu—Zn sulfides as well as traces of W, Mo, and Au, Ag, etc., have often been found. In this connection, it should be mentioned that in contact metasomatism, in addition to Fe, Mg introduction plays a predominant role. Often Mg metasomatism is predominant in contact metasomatism.

Modern magmatists, e.g., Oen (1968), reject the possibility that (Mg, Fe) is derived from the granite, mainly on the consideration that residual granitic fluids will normally be devoid of magnesia.

As a corollary to the non-granitic derivation of Mg and Fe, I would like to quote the summary of the work of Oen (1968) regarding the contact metamorphism of amphibolites near Farminhao, Portugal:

"Contact metamorphism of amphibolites near Farminhao has involved three phases:

(1) Early phase of moderately high t and lower pH_2O; a tremolitic hornblende rich in the cummingtonite molecule is formed together with spinel and forsterite in amphibolites which have been considerably enriched in Mg; in less magnesian rocks the hornblende is correspondingly less Mg-rich; plagioclase is stable instead of spinel and forsterite.

(2) Main phases of contact metamorphism under higher t and pH_2O; (hornblende—hornfels facies); tschermakitic hornblendes rich in the richterite molecule are formed in mineral assemblages as hornblende—spinel—orthopyroxene, and hornblende—plagioclase—gedrite (cummingtonite).

(3) Waning phase with relatively high t and low pH_2O involving the formation of pargasite-rich hornblendes.

Mg-metasomatism is related either to the early phase of contact metamorphism or to a preceding hydrothermal chloritisation; the Mg is derived from metamorphosed pelitic sediments surrounding the amphibolites. Na, Ca and Si are the chief elements removed on Mg-metasomatism; part of the Ca is involved in an internal Ca-metasomatism causing the local formation of vesuvianite-rich amphibolites."

In contrast to the magmatic interpretation of the basic metasomatic contact and skarn bodies, Sederholm (1926) noticed the disappearing of basic rocks included in granitised—migmatised regions and has thus prepared theoretically the way for the "Mg-front" hypothesis of Wegmann (1935b).

Reynolds (1947a) has summarised the evolutionary development of thoughts leading to the "basic front" hypothesis and she has discussed the geochemical involvement (migrations) associated with granitic intrusion and the development of basic metasomatic margins and skarns surrounding intrusive granites. The following are some quotations from Reynolds' (1947a) paper:

"The transformation of leptite into grey gneissic granite, and of the latter, together with its added swarm of basic dykes, into Hangö Granite was naturally not accomplished without chemical changes. In each instance the change included addition of alkali, and decrease of other constituents, and, since some of the rocks transformed to Hangö Granite were originally of andesitic and basaltic composition, the amount of material transferred must indeed have been large. Sederholm attributed these changes to the agency of granitic ichor, which he envisaged as a granitic juice 'showing gradations between an aqueous solution and a very diluted magma', or as 'magma containing much water in a gaseous state'. The astounding thing, however, is that each particular granite conforms to a recognisable chemical type, and maintains its composition even where large masses of basic rock have disappeared from within it. The amazing homogeneity of the Hangö Granite led Sederholm to deduce that in its formation 'assimilation' of a diversified assemblage of country rocks by ichor must have been followed by some form of differentiation. Although he left unsolved the problem as to the method whereby this differentiation, involving the displacement and removal of cafemic[1] materials, might have been achieved, he nevertheless threw out a significant suggestion as to where the solution might be sought when he wrote: 'The basic rocks dissolved in the granite seem to disappear as by magic, perhaps escaping together with the volatile or fluid constituents. Only in rare cases phenomena are observed that seem to give an indication of what has happened. So the "basic halos" around fragments in the Obnäss Granite tell of a diffusion extending to a certain limit.' "

"Both leptites and sedimentary rocks in the peripheral zones of migmatite regions were found to be enriched in mafic[2] minerals such as cordierite, garnet and biotite. Wegmann (1935b) correlated this Fe—Mg enrichment with the loss of Fe and Mg from the rocks overcome by migmatisation, and for this zone of enrichment in cafemic constituents he coined the term 'Mg-front'. Thus the view originated that the development and upward progress of migmatites in orogenic belts is accompanied by a frontal zone of Fe—Mg enrichment."

"In order to explain the aureole of Fe—Mg enrichment around granite stocks, it has to be assumed either (a) that considerable proportions of Fe and Mg remain in the residual solutions of granite magma, which is contrary to experimental evidence; or (b) that gaseous or volatile compounds of Fe and Mg are given off from granite magma, i.e., that the process is one of pneumatolysis; or (c) that the aureole of Fe and Mg enrichment is a basic front, to be explained by the fixation of material that migrated from a central locus, now occupied by granite, at the time the granite was emplaced."

In contrast to the magmatic interpretations of Goldschmidt and Oen, field studies and the granitisation origin of the intrusive granites in marbles (at Seriphos, Greece, Kimmeria — Xanthe, Greece and Frerone — Malga Basena, Italy) have led the author to scepticism regarding both the pneumatolytic interpretation and the non-granitic derivation of (Mg, Fe) at the contact metasomatic aureoles of his studied examples.

---

[1]) Cafemic: a term for an assemblage of Ca, Fe and Mg.
[2]) Mafic: a term applied to minerals rich in Mg and Fe.

The pneumatolytic interpretation is considered unsatisfactory mainly on the ground that intrusive granites are not magmatogenic but products of granitisation. Furthermore, close study of granitic apophyses in marbles have revealed contact metasomatism restricted to a narrow zone within the marbles at the contact with granitic apophyses. Due to the fact that garnet—epidote formation is restricted within the marble (can be a few centimetres in width) in the immediate vicinity of the contact with the granite, this suggests a genetic relation of these metasomatic contacts and its granite.

In its evolutionary history, a granite may have passed through phases that differ from its present form. As has been pointed out in the case of the Melca-Guba gneissgranite, a paragneissic pre-granitic phase has been granitised mainly by K-feldspar blastesis, relics of this pregranitic gneissic phase are the xenolithic relics and the pre-blastic components interspersed (palaeosoma) within the granitic feldspar. Similarly, a comparable pre-granitic phase consisting mainly of hornblende schist (has been granitised by feldspar blastesis) has existed as a pre-granitic phase in the case of the Seriphos, and Kimmeria granite abundant relics of this hornblende schist phase are the hornblende schist xenolithic relics. Granitisation of a hornblende-rich schist or paragneisses would result in the liberation of Fe and Mg which would move out of the granite, i.e., a basic front, and produce a Fe—Mg metasomatic contact.

Theoretically, the liberation of Fe and Mg under granitisation can be understood on the basis of K-feldspar and plagioclase blastesis, whereby the blastic feldspar encloses, replaces and assimilates mafic mineral components, e.g., biotite, hornblende and pyroxenes. On the basis of crystallochemical equilibrium of the petrogenetic process, biotite, hornblende, pyroxene — corroded and assimilated by feldspar blasts — should account for Mg and Fe liberation and the liberation of other cations of the mafic minerals that cannot be incorporated in the crystal lattice of the blastic feldspars. We have, therefore, a petrogenetic mechanism within granitisation which could liberate Mg and Fe, and give rise to Fe—Mg front solutions which will tend to move out of the granite. The nature of the metasomatic contacts will depend on the reactions that take place between the metasomatically introduced substances and the country rock which is the recipient of the introduced metasomatism.

Microscopic evidence supports the transformation of mafic minerals to feldspar. Augustithis (1959/60) has shown pyroxenes (augites) assimilated by later plagioclase formation (Fig. 1 and 2). Moreover, Pieruccini (1962) has introduced the hypothesis of gradoseparation whereby mafic minerals may be transformed to feldspars, i.e., a separation of Mg and Fe with reconstitution of the residual Al and Si components into silicates.

As a corollary to these interpretations, Drescher-Kaden (1969) describes textural patterns where hornblende is in the stage of assimilation by a blastic plagioclase in a xenolithic inclusion in tonalite:

"Anzahl und Menge der in den Plagioklasen vorhandenen Reste der älteren Kornarten ändern sich in weiten Grenzen: von fast relikt-freien Typen bis zu solchen, die mit eckig begrenzten Bruchstücken geradezu vollgestopft sind, gibt es alle Übergänge."

Photomicrographs (Fig. 61 and 67) show hornblende rests in all phases of transition from unaffected to small rests of assimilation in blastically formed plagioclase. The assimilations and "transmutation" of hornblende to colloform plagioclase are in accordance with the gradoseparation hypothesis whereby Fe and Mg would be free as a result of the assimilation of a mafic mineral by a colloform plagioclase crystalloblast (see Drescher-Kaden, 1969, Fig. 438).

Chapter 24 | The state of the granitic material at the time of intrusion

In contrast to the textural studies which can be understood on the basis of an inductive way of thinking, the state of the granitic material at the time of intrusion can only be a matter of deduction. Different explanations have been proposed regarding the emplacement of granites, e.g., Geijer (1916), Lewinson-Lessing (1933), Backlund (1936), Scholtz (1946), Noble (1952), Walton (1955), Butler et al. (1962), Marmo (1956, 1958, 1971).

Interconnected with this question is the formation period of a granite and, in particular, the time-span of the formation of its components, e.g., geochronological studies have determined a difference in the formation of zircons within the same granitic mass (see Chapter 18). Similarly, the study on the blastic sequence of granitic rocks has shown different periods of blastic growths. In addition, there can be a great time difference (in terms of millions of years) between the age of pre-blastic components (palaeosoma) and the later blastic growths which resulted in the granitisation of metasediments.

Textural studies have shown that different blastic phases characterise the "evolutionary" development of a granite. When a granite shows a certain geological age of intrusion (on a geological–structural basis), it does not necessarily imply that all its components have been crystallised at the time of its intrusion. On the basis of the textural patterns and their interpretation, we have seen that each granite has a distinct evolutionary history which primarily depends on its blastic sequence.

Termier (1912) has suggested that granites with a narrow metamorphic aureole have not been made in situ but come from elsewhere ready-made. The geochronological evidence of the variation in the age of the zircons and the concept of evolutionary changes – blastic sequence – supports a greater time-span for the formation of a granitic rock which is in contradistinction to the time required for the consolidation of the granitic magma. The question is: in which state a ready-made or partly made[1] granite would intrude?

A series of photographs illustrate the structural field behaviour of intrusive granitic bodies. Fig. 667 shows an intrusive "apophysis" of the Seriphos Granite (Greece)

with a narrow epidote–garnet skarn. Due to the intrusion of the granite, a folding – bending – of the intruded marbles has taken place. It should be pointed out that the structure as shown in Fig. 667 is of small dimensions and is not due to large scale intrusion effects. Considering the strength of the calcareous rocks, such a deformation suggests that the intrusive body must have been in a plastic form, i.e., had a certain degree of resistance. One is hardly to expect such a folding (bending of marble) by a liquid intrusion.

Furthermore, Fig. 668 shows a granitic "vein-like" body intrusive in marble and a basic xenolith is enclosed by the granitic vein. It should be pointed out that the xenolith is not an engulfed country rock from the immediate vicinity of the intrusion. The granitic vein has intruded into the marble "bearing" the basic xenolith. Moreover, the granitic vein intrusion must have been in a state, at the time of intrusion, that could hold in suspension a basic xenolithic body. It is most likely that the granitic vein is a "mobilised" apophysis of an already or partly made granite which has been forced in the marble.

Fig. 669 shows a polymictic mylonite from Masino Bangi Sondrio, with a gneissic–granite body forming a deformed "augen" or lense-shaped body, giving a "plastically deformed" appearance. The deformed-augen granitic body has been intruded into the banded "gneissic material" within the polymictic mylonitic zone under tectonic influence. The thinning out of the augen granitic body is in accordance with a plastic deformation (see Fig. 669, arrow a). Similarly, Fig. 670 shows a plastically deformed granitic–gneissic body in a slightly folded and mobilised gneissic background. In contrast, Fig. 671 shows an augen body of granitic rock in marble. The banding of the marble curves smoothly around the granitic "augen" body. The intrusion of the granitic body plastically and the folding of the marble must have taken place under tectonic deformation.

In the region of Kebra-Mangist (Adolla, S. Ethiopia), irregular and lense-shaped bodies of "pegmatoids" occur in gneissic schists. Microscopic observations (Fig. 672) reveal that they consist of rounded microcline–quartz with a later blastic quartz partly enclosing the rounded microcline and the rounded quartz. The textural pattern of the pegmatoid reveals a meta-sedimentogenic material

---

[1] In the sense that certain mineral components have been already formed.

mobilised and intrusive within the gneiss—schist. In this connection it should be pointed out that sediments, e.g., sandstones, may show an intrusive behaviour (Holmes, 1964). Also, tectonically mobilised, dyke-like in form and isolated bodies of cretaceous limestones may tectonically be pushed in diabase ophiolites (Fig. 673). Such tectonically mobilised intrusions are described by Augustithis (1967d). In contrast, often solution streams, either within the granite itself, or as granitising impregnations in metasediments, may exist giving an intrusive impression.

Graton (1940) has expressed the opinion that that which crystallises from the fluid is not longer be called an igneous rock and it may well be that the dominant cause of liquidity has changed from the effect of heat to the effect of solvent. Fig. 33 shows feldspar-forming solution having impregnated an amphibole gneiss and as a result of feldspar blastesis (hydrogenic formation) granitisation has taken place. In contrast, solution streams which lead to hydrogenic feldspar formation may be seen transversing the Adamello Granite (Fig. 674). Similarly, Fig. 675 shows a K-feldspar-rich vein transversive in character, extensions of which infiltrate into the granite giving rise to hydrogenic blastic K-feldspar formation.

In order to explain the intrusive behaviour of granites and in particular the intrusive phenomena illustrated in Fig. 667 and 668, some theoretical considerations are here introduced regarding crystal plasticity, rheidity, visco-elastic properties of inorganic polymers and colloform state.

(1) Considering the plastic properties of granitic mineral components (see Chapter 19), quartz under shearing force or under all-sided pressure may pass into a plastic phase more readily than feldspars would. In a granitic rock, a component of the abundance of quartz, if it attains a plastic phase, will render a plastic character to the entire rock which, by plastic flow, will attain an intrusive character.

(2) A corollary to the plastic study of granitic mineral components is the theory of rheidity, introduced by Carey (1962), which is briefly summarised by Holmes (1964, p. 206) as follows:

"The three familiar states of matter — solid, liquid and gaseous — are clearly defined by reference to the melting and boiling points of the particular substance concerned. A liquid is at a temperature above its melting point and flows in virtue of this fact. A solid is below its melting point, and yet it, too, is capable of flow given the proper conditions. This raises the difficult question of the nature of the conditions that determine whether a substance behaves as an elastic solid or a viscous solid, or in some intermediate way. A whole new border-line science, known as rheology, is now devoted to the investigation of these phenomena. Here it must suffice to say that the essential control depends on the relationship between two properties: viscosity = resistance to viscous flow, and rigidity = resistance to elastic deformation.

S. Warren Carey has proposed the term rheidity for this relationship, which turns out to be expressible in terms of time. For given conditions of temperature, confining pressure and deforming stress, rheidity is arbitrarily defined by Carey as the time required for deformation by viscous flow to become more than 1,000 times the elastic deformation."

(3) The plastic properties of crystalline quartz (which is due to visco-elastic behaviour) lead us to ponder about properties of polymeric materials.

(4) Furthermore, in contrast to the plastic and visco-plastic phases, microscopic observations have revealed colloform blastoids (see Chapter 12). On a textural basis, both quartz and plagioclases may show an indication or relics of an initial colloform phase. The physical properties of a "Brei" consisting of crystalline substances and colloids would give it a semi-solid character. Intrusion of such a "Brei" would be comparable to plastically mobilised diapirs.

_____

[1] In the sense that certain mineral components have been already formed.

Chapter 25 | The relation of hydrothermal metallogenesis and granitisation

In contrast to the magmatogenic theory, namely that the ore deposits represent a hydrothermal end-phase segregation of rare elements dispersed in the granitic magma and that they become "concentrated" after the orthomagmatic phase of crystallisation in the pegmatitic–pneumatolytic and finally in the hydrothermal phase, a hypothesis is here proposed based on the concept of granitisation.

On the evidence introduced by transformists, the granitic rocks are considered to be granitisation products of initial sedimentary or metasedimentary rocks. If, in principle, the granitisation hypothesis satisfactorily explains the origin of granitic rocks, it is within the processes of granitisation that a mechanism should be proposed attempting to explain the segregation of relatively rare elements in the form of ore deposits. Vast geological evidence exists in support of a relationship between granitic intrusion or granitic bodies and "hydrothermal" metallogenesis.

In the realm of metamorphism, and particularly under conditons where ultragranitisation takes place, i.e., plutonic–metamorphic conditions, sedimentogenic rocks are transformed into granites and intrusive granites. Concurrently with granitisation or as a concluding phase of it under "hydrogenetic conditions", element segregation processes occur which result in the concentration of relatively rare elements interspersed in the original sediments, ultimately resulting in the formation of vein ore deposits.

In an attempt to understand the "causes" of element segregation which result in mineral paragenesis, a brief consideration is here introduced of the empirical laws of the periodic system which seem to play a role in the joint segregation of relatively rare elements into paragenetic associations. It is also necessary to redefine (in a geochemical sense) the concept of paragenesis and to attempt to explain it in terms of element similarities and affinities as outlined in the empirical laws of the periodic system.

The concept of paragenesis

Broadly speaking, the term paragenesis is used to signify genetic associations of minerals. We should bear in mind, however, that a mineral association can be the result either of a single period of crystallisation or of more. Tishkin et al. (1958), in describing types of uranium paragenesis from the U.S.S.R., use the following terms:

(1) Period of mineralisation: a long period of time during which a complex of asynchronous hydrothermal formations connected with a definite tectonomagmatic cycle was produced.

(2) Stage of mineralisation: a space of time within the period of mineralisation during which hydrothermal formations were produced (veins, nests, zones of dissemination, metasomatic bodies, etc.). Hydrothermal formations formed during the same stage of mineralisation have more or less similar compositions and, chronologically, are separated from other stages by tectonic movements.

(3) Association: a group of minerals in the same place, irrespective of their genesis or age.

(4) Paragenetic association: a group of minerals as a rule formed together and at the same time, deposited from only one portion of a single solution.

(5) Generation: asynchronous separation of a single mineral deposited during the same stage of mineralisation.

In contradistinction to the above terms, however, other authors have introduced other terms describing the periodic formation of minerals in other uranium parageneses (Augustithis, 1964d, pp. 33–34). It should also be pointed out that the Russian term *stage of mineralisation* corresponds to the following terms used by their respective authors:

(a) Formation: term used by Leutwein (1957) in describing the mineralisation stage of the Erzgebirge uranium paragenetic associations.

(b) Type: term used by Kidd and Haycock (1935) in describing the mineralisation stages of the Great Bear Lake deposits. These authors have also introduced the term "stage" which corresponds rather to the Russian term "period of mineralisation".

(c) Phase: term used by Derriks and Oosterbosch (1958) to describe the mineralisation stages of the Shinkolobwe, Swambo and Kalongwe deposits.

TABLE IV

GROUPING OF THE ELEMENTS AROUND THE INERT GASES
(after Remy, 1956)

Main Groups of the Periodic System

	III	IV	V	VI	VII	VIII (O)	I	II
Principal valence states	+III	+IV / −IV	+V / −III	+VI / −II	+VII / −I	− / O	− / +I	− / +II
Simplest hydrides			Volatile			—	Solid, salt-like	
					[1H] / 2He	3Li / 4Be		
	5B	6C	7N	8O	9F	10Ne	11Na	12Mg
	13Al	14Si	15P	16S	17Cl	18A	19K	20Ca
	31Ga	32Ge	33As	34Se	35Br	36Kr	37Rb	38Sr
	49In	50Sn	51Sb	52Te	53I	54Xe	55Cs	56Ba
	81Tl	82Pb	83Bi	84Po	85At	86Rn	87Fr	88Ra
Magnetism			All elementary ions are diamagnetic					
Color			Form *colorless* elementary ions exclusively					

The properties of the last element of each series are related in each case to those of the first element in the next series. ᵇB forms volatile hydrides, like C.

Lanthanides
58Ce, 59Pr, 60Nd, 61Pm, 62Sm, 63Eu, 64Gd, 65Tb, 66Dy, 67Ho, 68Er, 69Tm, 70Yb, 71Lu

Sub-groups of the Periodic System

	III	IV	V	VI	VII	VIII			I	II
Principal valence states	+III	+IV	+V	+VI	+VII	+VIII Readily variable valence … …			(+I)	+II
Simplest hydrides			Hydrides quasi-metallic							
	21Sc	22Ti	23V	24Cr	25Mn	26Fe	27Co	28Ni	29Cu	30Zn
	39Y	40Zr	41Nb	42Mo	43Tc	44Ru	45Rh	46Pd	47Ag	48Cd
	57La	72Hf	73Ta	74W	75Re	76Os	77Ir	78Pt	79Au	80Hg
	89Ac	90Th	91Pa	92U	Transuranics 93Np 94Pu 95Am 96Cm 97Bk 98Cf 99E 100Fm 101Mv					
Magnetism			Some elementary ions paramagnetic							
Color			Form *colored* elementary ions in many cases							

The empirical laws of the periodic system: segregation of elements into parageneses

The following empirical laws and discussion of their causes are based on the work of Remy (1955):

(1) The similarity between the main and the subgroup elements of the same family increases strongly from families I–IV and decreases strongly from IV–VIII.

In trying to understand this empirical law, the very recognition of the main and subgroups depends on the conception of the ordinal number and on the rare gases (inert gases), the recognition of which depends in turn on their valency. Consequently, *valency* is the main factor on which this law depends.

The relation expressed in this law can be understood by considering Table IV, listing the elements on the basis of the inert gases. If families I–III are considered, the valency of the elements of the main and subgroups is positive and uniform within each separate family, even though in proceeding from family I to family III the value of the valency nevertheless increases. Consequently, the increase in similarity of the main and subgroup elements as one proceeds from family I to family III is in accordance with this increase in the valency.

Comparing the valencies of the main and subgroups of families IV–VII, however, it can be seen that whereas the valencies of the subgroups are positive and increasing, those of the main groups can be both positive and negative, with the positive increasing and the negative decreasing from family IV to family VII. Thus the main and subgroups can differ in their valency, and this explains the decrease in similarity of the main and subgroups from family IV to family VII. In general, it is from a consideration of the valency that an explanation should be sought for the increasing and decreasing similarity of the main and subgroups.

(2) Between the main and the subgroup belonging to the same family, there is a marked similarity between the second element of the main group and the first element of the subgroup. This law is subject to an increase from families I–IV and to a decrease from IV–VII (the interrelationship between the main and subgroup in family VIII being almost non-existent). This tendency should be viewed from the aspect of valency, since it depends on the relationship between the elements of the main and subgroups.

(3) The similarities and affinities between the elements are illustrated by two additional empirical laws, which also depend on the valency and the atomic structure of the elements:

(a) Among the elements belonging to the same subgroup there are always two that are particularly similar to each other, and for those subgroups which are made up of transitory elements, the following is applicable: of elements (within the same subgroup) listed vertically within the same column, the second element, reading downwards, shows a greater similarity with the third than with the first, and also a similarity greater than that which exists between the third element and the fourth.

(b) The similarity in behaviour of elements listed along the same horizontal row increases from subgroups III–VIII but decreases from subgroups I–III.

Augustithis (1964d) has used the term paragenesis, not to describe every type of mineral association in rocks, but only for the special case of metallic minerals in hydrothermal and pegmatitic uranium parageneses (e.g., two specific examples of hydrothermal and pegmatitic parageneses). Furthermore, he considered the paragenetic association of minerals (provided that the minerals are genetically interrelated) actually to represent a geochemical interrelationship between elements segregated at one or more stages of mineralisation. Irrespective of whether the minerals belong to one or more of these stages, two groups of elements forming the metallic minerals of hydrothermal pitchblende paragenesis have been recognised. The two groups of elements recognised (in the ideal case by considering the metallic elements present in a number of "pitchblende parageneses" of world-wide distribution) are: Group A = U, Th, Pb, Bi, Sb, Se, Mo, Sn and Group B = Fe, Co, Ni, Cu, Zn, Au, Ag.

In addition, he considered that the crystallisation of minerals in a paragenesis depends on the physico-chemical conditions, i.e., temperature, pressure, and crystallochemical factors (as most extensively shown in the work of Goldschmidt, 1954).

The relation between crystal structure and chemical composition can be summarised as depending on: *(1)* the relative proportions of the various kinds of atoms (or ions) in the chemical formula, and *(2)* the relative sizes of the various kinds of particles, i.e., atoms (or ions) in a crystal.

Regarding the interrelationship of elements in Group A and B in accordance with the empirical laws of the periodic system, the following conclusions are tentatively suggested:

(1) In Group A only the elements As, Bi and Sb are interrelated as homologues, so that the recognition and acceptance of this group as a whole is no more than tentative, i.e., no strict interrelationships in accordance with the periodic system exist.

(2) The elements of the B group show an interrelationship more in accordance with the periodic system.

Nevertheless, their affinities are not as great as is theoretically possible, since other elements not present in the group show stronger bonds of affinity with elements which are present in the group.

(a) More than one unit of element assemblage can occur in paragenesis, e.g., the A and B groups in the case of uranium hydrothermal paragenesis. In such cases, no affinity or interrelationship exists between the groups.

(b) The elements present in the above-mentioned groups (A, B, and the special group C) do not strictly follow the rule that elements with the strongest affinities and relationships are always paragenetically associated i.e., occur as mineral-building elements in the paragenesis. Elements with greater affinities (as stated by the empirical laws of the periodic system) than those of the elements included in a group may be absent.

(c) The empirical laws of element affinities and interrelationships should not be considered as rules governing the segregation of elements forming parageneses, but only as an explanation of relationships existing among the elements of the three groups recognised. Nevertheless, the fact that uranium parageneses of world-wide distribution show similarities in the elements comprising their metallic minerals can to some extent be understood in view of the chemical and geochemical affinities of these elements. Notwithstanding, a number of observed cases suggest that, in nature, elements strongly homologous or analogous tend to occur together. This tendency derives from similarities and analogies, and indeed the repetition of analogies in the atom structures. Consequently, for element segregation there is an internal cause, i.e., the segregation depends on the structure of the atoms themselves, which is a fundamentally important factor in understanding the joint segregation of the less abundant elements in the earth's crust (ions) in the chemical forms (of ions) in a crystal.

Regarding the interrelationship of elements in Group A and B in accordance with the empirical laws of the periodic system, the following conclusions are tentatively suggested:

(1) In Group A only the elements As, Bi and Sb are interrelated as homologues, so that the recognition and acceptance of this group as a whole is no more than tentative, i.e., no strict interrelationships in accordance with the periodic system exist.

(2) The elements of the B group show an interrelationship more in accordance with the periodic system.

genesis may serve only as a "model" in order to understand the "causes" of element segregation and mineral paragenesis formation. It should be, however, emphasised that each hydrothermal mineral paragenesis should be judged on its own merits and, despite the aforementioned causes of the joint segregation of relatively rare elements in paragenetic association, no theory is proposed to explain this rather complex problem. In addition to the "causes" of element segregation to build paragenetic associations, of fundamental importance is the presence of these elements and their distribution in the initial sedimentogenic or pre-granitic rocks that have been granitised. Consequently, valency is a factor on which this law depends.

The relation expressed in granite is shown by considering Table IV, listing the elements on the basis. In contrast to the element segregation and granitisation and the formation of vein deposits, the hydrothermal parageneses, studies of the trace element distribution in 'granitised' granites from Singhbhum, India, by Gunnar S. Roonwal (pers. communication), suggest that the atomic (or ionic) radii of the trace elements determine their presence in minerals of granitic rocks. Accordingly, the size of ionic radii plays a determinative factor which controls the presence and the possibility of incorporation of trace elements in the lattice patterns of granitic mineral components. The following relationships of trace elements and elements building up granitic minerals are recognised. Ti is present in magnetites and substitutes Fe^{3+}; Ga replaces Al^{3+}; V follows Ca^{2+} and is more concentrated in hornblendes. Co generally follows Mg^{2+}, more evenly distributed between Mg^{2+} and Fe^{3+}, diadochically replacing the latter; Cu is concentrated in hornblendes, and follows Fe^{3+}. Ba is captured in the plagioclase lattice, increasing the plagioclase lattice.

From the cited examples it can be seen that the distribution of trace elements and incorporation in the lattice depends primarily on the ionic radii and their capacity to replace mineral-building elements of granites.

(2) ... the second element of the subgroup. This law is subject to an increase from families I–IV and to a decrease from VI–VII (the interrelationship between the main and subgroup in family VIII being almost non-existent). This tendency should be viewed from the aspect of valency, since it depends on the relationship between the elements of the main and subgroups.

(3) The similarities and affinities between the elements are illustrated by two additional empirical laws, which also depend on the valency and the atomic structure of the elements:

(a) Among the elements belonging to the same subgroup there are always two that are particularly

Chapter 26 | On the petrogenetic and geochemical relationships of the Mo-Cu-W-Bi hydrothermal quartz veins and the Fe-Cu-W-Mo epidote-garnet skarn bodies (contact metasomatism) of the younger, intrusive granite of Kimmeria (Xanthe, Greece)

The present chapter discusses certain mineralogical and geochemical aspects of the hydrothermal Mo-Cu-W-Bi quartz veins in the Kimmeria Granite and similarly the Fe-Cu-W-Mo epidote-garnet skarns which are formed as a result of metasomatic influences of solutions of granitic derivation on the mainly calcareous rocks (marbles) into which the granitic body has "intruded".

Both the metasomatic contact aureole and the geological disposition of the granite indicate a granitic-boss character. However, despite its undoubtedly intrusive character, a granitisation origin is not precluded. The intrusive character of the granite indicates that the granitic material was, at the time of intrusion, in a state that could behave as an intrusive body.

In contrast to the orthodox petrogenetic views of a magmatic derivation of granitic rocks, the transformist school, on the basis of textural and geological evidence, regards granites as products of transformation of initial sedimentogenic material. The abundant xenolithic bodies, the sedimentogenic relics and furthermore the metasomatic textural patterns such as symantetic reactions (myrmekitisation) as well as the metasomatic and replacement structures such as graphic intergrowths, perthites, etc., are in accordance with transformists' evidence of granitisation. In addition, it should be mentioned that feldspar blastesis has played the most important role in the transformation of sedimentogenic initial material through granitisation into granites.

The intrusive character is not in contradiction with granitisation. Within the wide spectrum of granitisation possibilities, anatexis, i.e., palingenesis of melts, semisolid plastic flow of material, can take place through the granitisation of initial sedimentogenic material which, due to rheidity, under great pressure and relatively low temperatures, can be mobilised and intrude like a diapir under conditions of deep crust metamorphism into the country rocks.

It is with this petrogenetic background, namely a granitisation origin, that an attempt is made in the present chapter to interpret the origin of the Mo-Cu-W-Bi quartz hydrothermal veins and the Fe-Cu-W-Mo contact metasomatic skarn bodies. In addition to the discussion on the mineralogy and geochemistry of these types of mineralisation, an attempt is made to explain the petrogenetic relationship of the hydrothermal and skarn mineralisation on the basis of the 'granitisation' theory.

The Kimmeria Granite and the hydrothermal Mo-Cu-W-Bi quartz veins. The hydrothermal Mo-Cu-W-Bi quartz veins of the Kimmeria Granite (rich in hornblende, tonalite) follow a well-developed joint system in the granite. A petrographic description of the granite is given by Walenta and Pantzartzis (1969). On the basis of the ratio of plagioclases to orthoclase, which is 1:1, the granite is considered to be a calcalkaline type. In addition to feldspars, it contains biotite and hornblende. The plagioclases are zoned with the central parts exhibiting a composition of 50% An. In contradistinction, the external zones indicate an An content between 15-20%. Often the outer plagioclase zones show granophyric intergrowths. As accessories, zircon, sphene, tourmaline, zoisite and scheelite occur. Zeschke mentions also tungsite.

Within the Kimmeria Granite, impregnations (disseminations) of molybdenite and chalcopyrite occur which are independent of the vein mineralisation. Similarly scheelite occurs within the granite, again independent of the vein mineralisation.

There is a distinct relationship between the set of joints and the hydrothermal veins. The prevalent direction of the veins is 2-3°NW and the dips are between 60-70° in a westerly direction. The length of the main vein system is more than 400 m. However, additional Mo-Cu-W-Bi veins occur in the area, and on the whole they exceed a length of 800 m. Fig. 676 shows the constant direction of the veins which coincides with a prevalent direction of the joint-set system. The width of the veins is more or less constant; a width of about 1 m has been measured on the outcrop of the vein shown in Fig. 676. Occasionally, at the intersection point of two sets of joints (which are occupied by veins) the width may reach 2 m. The behaviour of mineralised veins in depths of about 100 m from the surface is similar, as measurements of exposed veins in underground galeries indicated. The greatest part of the main vein system remains uninterrupted and constant in its behaviour. However, small scale displacements of the vein outcrop are occasionally indicated and are due to small scale faulting (in the order of 2–3 m).

The mineralogical composition and textures of the Mo–Cu–W–Bi hydrothermal veins of Kimmeria, Xanthe

Ore-microscopic and thin-section studies reveal that the mineralisation mainly consists of molybdenite (MoS_2), chalcopyrite ($CuFeS_2$), pyrite (FeS_2), wolframite ($Fe,MnWO_4$), scheelite ($CaWO_4$), malachite ($CuCO_3$. $Cu(OH)_2$), and the main mass consists of quartz showing undulating extinction due to strain as a result of post-mineralisation tectonic influences. In addition to these minerals, Walenta and Pantzartzis (1969) have determined, on the basis of microscopic and X-ray investigations, the following primary minerals (however in small quantities) within the mineralised quartz veins: sphalerite, galena, tetrahedrite, aikinite, emplektite, wittichenite and luzonite.

In the primary veins, a number of secondary minerals have been determined by Walenta and Pantzartzis (1969) and by Zeschke (1961). The following secondary minerals are listed: covellite, digenite, cuprite, hydrotenorite, goethite, haematite, malachite, chalkanthite, brochantite, langite, devillin, jarosite, pisanite, sulphur and gypsum. Also, as alteration product of molybdenite and scheelite, powellite and cuprotungstite have been determined. Zeschke mentions also tungstite, hydrotungstite and ferritungstite.

In addition to the quartz, the mineralised veins contain calcite and siderite. The quartz shows undulating extinction and the molybdenite is bent and shows "deformation twinning" due to tectonic influences. Fig. 677 shows rich distributions of MoS_2 in quartz veins; the molybdenite is tectonically bent and shows twinning. Fig. 678 shows the association of molybdenite and chalcopyrite in the quartz vein. Often the molybdenite follows cracks in the quartz mass and binds cataclastic fragments of the chalcopyrite, as is indicated in Fig. 678. Also, small fragments of chalcopyrite are surrounded by molybdenite. In addition, Fig. 679 shows a fine band of

molybdenite following a strained zone in the quartz band and ending within the quartz mass.

Weathering of the MoS_2 and alteration by solutions have produced abundant molybdenum ochre. In addition, the alteration of chalcopyrite has resulted in secondary copper minerals such as malachite (which often gives a greenish colour to the veins). In addition to copper and molybdenum minerals, wolframite ($Fe,MnWO_4$) has been ore-microscopically determined. Abundant wolframite crystal grains have been determined in samples of the veins. Under oil immersion the following characteristics have been observed: weak reflection pleochroism, anisotropism, twinning and redbrown internal reflection. Fig. 680 shows paragenetic association of wolframite with (a twin lamella visible) molybdenite and chalcopyrite in quartz.

Examination of the Mo–Cu–W–Bi vein outcrops and of the exposures within the galleries under ultra-violet light (shortwave 2,537 Å) showed several fluorescent minerals. Samples of the bluish–whitish, creamish and yellowish fluorescent minerals have been separated and spectrographically analysed. Sig. 681f shows the spectrographic plate indicating the presence of W. Also, X-ray powder analyses have shown that the mineral is scheelite ($CaWO_4$). An average sample analysis of 10 kg Mo–Cu–W–Bi quartz veins has given: 0.07% W, 0.54% Mo and 0.53% Cu.

The skarn bodies

Several skarns and metasomatic reaction bodies occur at the intrusive contacts of the Kimmeria Granite with the surrounding country rocks.

The mineralogical composition of the skarn and contact metasomatic bodies is variable and depends on the composition of adjacent country rocks as well as on the nature of the metasomatic solutions which have reacted with it. In general, the contact metasomatic bodies vary from magnetite skarns to garnet–epidote-amphiboles (tremolite) wollastonite metasomatic bodies.

From the many skarn occurrences around the intrusive granite only two skarns, one representing a typical magnetite skarn and the other a garnet–epidote skarn, are here described.

The main magnetite skarn body is situated about 3 km N–NE of the Kimmeria village. Fig. 682 shows the outcrop of this skarn and its relation to the marble and granite. Ore-microscopic studies have shown that the prevalent ore mineral is magnetite (in cases, rhombododecahedra have been observed, which is typical of metasomatic magnetite). Ore-microscopically, the magnetite is free from ilmenite, ulvite and spinel exsolution, also no martitisation[1] is observed. In addition, ore-microscopically, a mineral — between chalcopyrite and pyrrhotite — has been observed, often in intergrowth with sphalerite. Fig. 684 shows the magnetite with copper mineral (the intermediate between chalcopyrite and pyrrhotite) which is partly surrounded by sphalerite which is including a fine intergrowth of it. Fig. 685 shows a spectrographic diagram of the separated and analysed intermediate mineral and is compared with a copper compound indicating intense copper lines in both. Furthermore, ore-microscopically, chalcopyrite is observed as an abundant ore mineral and often along its cracks and margins chalcocite is present (Fig. 686). Thin-section microscopy reveals the presence of typical skarn-minerals, e.g., garnets (andradite) and epidotes. In addition, examination of this skarn body under short-wave ultra-violet light, showed abundant bluish—whitish and yellowish fluorescent minerals (scheelite). Spectrographically examined samples of these showed the presence of tungsten (see Fig. 681 b and c).

As a "projection" along the contact of the granite with the country rock, another metasomatic contact body consisting of contact reaction minerals (mainly epidote and andradite) occurs. A general view of the outcrop is shown in Fig. 687. This body follows the contact zone of the granite and the adjacent marble and is excellently exposed forming prominent small hills on the surface, starting from an elevation of about 200 m and extending to an elevation of about 500 m. The length, with some very small interruptions on the surface, is over 700 m and the average width about 20 m. In view of its general geological disposition, it is most probable that this body continues to a considerable depth in the order of hundreds of meters along the contact of this gneissic granite with the marble.

Detailed examination of the entire body under ultra-violet light (short-wave 2,537 Å), showed abundant scheelite mineralisation (as individual crystals and fine-grained ore) throughout its entire length. However, in many parts there was an increase in abundance. Samples have been taken at different parts along the length of this body and, after crushing blue, yellow and cream coloured crystals have been separated under the binocular microscope with the aid of ultra-violet light, and subsequently spectrographical analyses have been carried out, the results of which are illustrated in Fig. 681d and e.

For comparison purposes, scheelite crystals from Sax-

ony, Germany, have been similarly spectrographically analysed and the plates are shown in Fig. 681a to enable the comparison of intensities.

Also, 10 kg of samples taken at random from different parts of this main contact metasomatic body and chemically analysed by J. and H. S. Pattinson, gave a result of 0.45% W.

Suggestions on the origin of skarn and contact metasomatic bodies of the Kimmeria Granite

Different hypotheses have been introduced in order to explain the skarn bodies and the contact metasomatic affects in general (see Chapter 23). In its evolutionary history, a granite may have passed through phases that differ from its present form. As has been pointed out (Augustithis, 1967a) in the case of the Melca-Guba gneiss-granite, a paragneissic pre-granitic phase has been granitised mainly by K-feldspar blastesis. Relics of this pre-granitic gneissic phase are the xenolithic relics and the pre-blastic components interspersed (palaeosoma) within the granitic feldspar. Similarly, a comparable pre-granitic phase consisting mainly of hornblende—biotite schist (which has been granitised by feldspar blastesis) has existed as a pre-granitic phase in the case of the Seriphos, Ondonock and Kimmeria granites. Abundant xenolithic relics of this hornblende-biotite-schist phase are present.

Granitisation of a hornblende-rich schist or paragneisses would result in the libaration of Fe and Mg which would move out of the granite, i.e., a basic front, and produce a metasomatic Fe and Mg metasomatic contact. Theoretically, the liberation of Fe and Mg under granitisation can be understood on the basis of K-feldspar and plagioclase blastesis, whereby the blastic feldspar encloses, replaces and assimilates mafic mineral components, e.g., biotite, hornblende and pyroxenes.

On the basis of the crystallochemical equilibrium of the petrogenetic process: biotite, hornblende and pyroxene, corroded and assimilated by feldspar blast, should account for Mg, Fe liberation and the liberation of other cations of the mafic minerals which can not be incorporated in the crystal lattice of the blastic feldspars. We have, therefore, a petrogenetic mechanism within granitisation that could liberate Mg and Fe and give rise to Fe, Mg fronts of solutions which would tend to move out of the granite.

The nature of the metasomatic contacts will depend on the reactions that take place between the metasomatically introduced substances and the country rock-recipient of the introduced metasomatism.

---

[1] From other magnetite ore bodies, skarns maghemite has been determined as an alteration of Fe_3O_4 (see Fig. 683).

The significance of geochemical anomalies related to the Kimmeria Granite (Fersman's secondary dispersion halo)

As a corollary to the vein and skarn mineralisations and to the molybdenite, scheelite, chalcopyrite impregnations, geochemical soil sampling by W. G. Müller and J. R. Hillebrand (unpublished) of the Kimmeria Granite extending over the areas of contacts and over the adjacent metamorphosed country rocks, have determined geochemical anomalies for the following elements: Cu, Mo, Zn, Pb.

Cu: The cut-off limit employed was 100 ppm. The highest values were over 500 ppm, with a few values of 1000-4000 ppm.

Mo: The cut-off limit was 5 ppm. The anomalies ranged between 7-30 ppm, with some values over 50 ppm.

Zn: The cut-off limit employed was 100 ppm. The highest values ranged from 500-1000 ppm.

Pb: The cut-off limit employed was 100 ppm. The highest values ranged between 300-500 ppm.

The Cu geochemical anomalies are associated with the Cu-Mo-W veins and with the skarn bodies (this is in accordance with the mineralogical composition of the veins and skarn bodies). Furthermore, the Cu anomalies extend from the skarn bodies well into the adjacent country rocks. This is in accordance with the extension of Cu-mineralisation beyond the limits of the granite into the surrounding country rocks.

The Mo geochemical anomalies, as expected, are restricted within the granite and are centred around the quartz Cu-Mo-W veins and molybdenite impregnations. No anomalies were indicated along the contacts or in the adjacent country rocks. In contradistinction, it should be mentioned that Mo traces were determined in association with the scheelite in the contact metasomatic skarns.

The Zn anomalies were mainly associated with the skarn and beyond the limits of the granite in the adjacent country rocks. No Zn anomalies were determined in association with the vein bodies. Indeed, the most pronounced anomalies were determined outside the granite's limits in the adjacent country rocks, indicating Zn metallogenesis. However, sphalerite has been determined in the Mo-Cu-W quartz veins.

The geochemical anomalies of Pb are associated with Cu-Mo-W veins and skarns of the granite, and also extend beyond the granite's limit into the adjacent country rock.

On the basis of geochemical anomalies, and petro-

graphical and mineralogical studies, it can be concluded that the Cu and Pb-Zn mineralisation had a greater diffusion (mobilisation) also outside the granite's limits. In contrast, the Mo was mainly within the granite's limits (veins and disseminations within the granite), and only Mo traces were determined in association with skarn-scheelite. In contradistinction, the W distribution was within the granite, i.e., in the granite as accessory scheelite and in the veins as well as in the peripheral parts of the granite in its skarns. The mobilisation of Mo and W, generally speaking, has coincided and this is in accordance with their strong relationship according to the empirical laws of the periodic system.

Mo traces were determined in association with skarn-scheelite. In contradistinction, the W distribution was within the granite, i.e., in the granite as accessory scheelite and in the veins as well as in the peripheral parts of the granite in its skarns. The mobilisation of Mo and W, generally speaking, has coincided and this is in accordance with their strong relationship according to the empirical laws of the periodic system.

Granitisation and metallogenesis

On the basis of the mineralogical and geochemical comparisons of the Cu-Mo-W quartz veins and of the skarn bodies, it can be seen that the main ore-mineral building elements, i.e., Fe, Cu, Mo, W, (Zn), are present in both cases. Similarly, the geochemical dispersion halos have shown the presence of Cu, Mo, W in the granite itself.

In contradistinction to the orthodox mineralisation hypothesis, namely, that the skarn and the vein bodies are products of different phases of the granitic magma consolidation, i.e., liquimagmatic-pneumatolytic the skarns and hydrothermal the veins in the granitisation hypothesis, the metallogenesis of the (ore minerals containing) Fe, Mo, W (Cu) of the skarn bodies is to be associated with the Mg-Fe solution fronts as already mentioned. The Cu-Mo-W quartz veins represent lateral segregations as a last hydrogenic phase of the granite's formation, since the veins follow well-defined sets of joints within the granite.

In contradistinction to the vein and skarn mineralisations, which are respectively due to lateral segregation and solution front mobilisation of initial 'elements' interspersed in the pre-granitised sediments, the impregnations of the Mo, Cu, W in the granite indicate a redistribution within the granite. The metallogenic elements, e.g., Cu, Mo, W, Zn, Pb, Ag were originally present in the initial pre-granitised sediments.

[1] From other magnetite ore bodies, skarn magnetite has been determined as an alteration of Fe_3O_4 (see Fig. 683).

of granitisation with the formation of vein and contact deposits and providing an alternative to the magmatic metallogenetic theories

finities of elements and on the mobilisation and common segregation of elements under granitisation processes are here suggested, thus interrelating the mechanism

Chapter 27 | Conclusions

Comparative textural patterns based on detailed microscopic observations, show — whether we deal with granitised sediments or with intrusive granitic bodies — that the formation of their components belongs to *(1)* a pre-blastic phase (i.e., sedimentogenic relic components which vary in size and distribution within a granite from xenoliths to interspersed mineral components) and *(2)* to new blastic growths which are mainly responsible for the transformation of the initial sediments into granites.

The fact that the granitic components show differences in time of formation (e.g., pre-blastic and blastic mineral phases; accessory zircons geochronologically of different age) shows that:

(a) The time-span of the formation of the granitic rocks is greater than it would be if it was the consolidation period of a magmatic intrusion.

(b) The difference, which in some cases is established, between the age of granitic components and the geological age of the granitic intrusion supports the view that the intrusive granitic material was already partly formed.

The endoblastic growths, blastesis in granites, are metamorphic—metasomatic traits and their sequence of formation determines the crystallisation history of the rock.

The crystalloblastic, metamorphic—metasomatic, replacement, infiltration and recrystallisation in general textures of granitic rocks, as a whole, are of primary petrogenetic importance (protogenic and not deuteric), the result of recrystallisation after magmatic consolidation. Furthermore, these textural patterns do not represent rare exceptions but are most common and of primary petrogenetic significance.

One of the aims of the present atlas is to show the wide spectrum of textural possibilities and the possible diverse origin of each textural pattern described.

From the great number of cases described an example is here quoted, namely that of the graphic and micrographic textures which are observed in rocks of diverse petrogenetic origin, e.g., in volcanics (rhyolites) in granitised quartzitic pebbles of a conglomerate, in pegmatoids, in granites, in granitic cavities and even in lunar samples (volcanics from the moon's Sea of Tranquillity). Also, graphic intergrowths of different mineral phases, e.g., quartz—K-feldspar, uraninite—K-feldspar, hornblende—K-feldspar, quartz—plagioclase are described in granitic rocks indicating again that a wide spectrum of intergrowth possibilities exists, far greater than would be acceptable on the basis of a granitic magma consolidation. An eutectic crystallisation of uraninite—K-feldspar, hornblende—K-feldspar and quartz—plagioclase would be incompatible with the physico—chemical conditions of consolidation of a granitic magma.

Detailed microscopic observations support the explanation that the most common textural patterns of granites are hydrogenetic in origin (i.e., products of crystallisation from hydrogenetic solutions). As such are recognised: the infiltration, replacement, synantetic and symplectic intergrowths which in reality represent a common variant of all granitic textures (i.e., they are not the exception but the rule).

The fact that identical metamorphic crystalloblastic textures have been found in paragneisses and in both granitised sediments and intrusive granites, indicates that the intrusive character of granites is not incompatible with a granitisation origin.

The intrusive character of granites is reviewed in the light of the plastic behaviour of its components, the visco-elastic properties of the solids and rheidity. Furthermore, colloform relic structures in granites support the hypothesis that the intrusive granitic material has passed, or partly passed through a phase of a "Brei" which would explain the intrusive behaviour of the granitic material.

As a consequence of the granitisation origin of granites, the granitic aureole is not considered to be a thermal metamorphic effect; but instead due to geochemical mobilisations and element migrations within the granitisation processes. The basic front formation, as a result of granitisation, provides an explanation of contact metasomatic areas and skarn bodies.

One of the most important implications of the granitisation hypothesis is that it necessitates a diverse metallogenetic explanation rather than the orthodox magmatic theory which regards hydrothermal and contact deposits as derivatives of and belonging to phases of the granitic magma consolidation.

Metallogenetic explanations based on the chemical affinities of elements and on the mobilisation and common segregation of elements under granitisation processes are here suggested, thus interrelating the mechanism of granitisation with the formation of vein and contact deposits and providing an alternative to the magmatic metallogenetic theories.

ILLUSTRATIONS

Fig. 3. Plagioclase tecoblast in contact with pyroxene phenocryst. Here the whole the entire feldspar has partly assimilated and partly digested the pyroxene, with parts enclosed in the feldspar. Khidane/Meheret, Entoto, Addis-Abeba, Ethiopia. With crossed nicols; enlargement 100 x.

Fig. 1 and 2. Pyroxene phenocryst digested and assimilated along a crack by later tecoblastic plagioclase. The following zones are recognisable in the plagioclase: Zone I : 38–39% An., II : 44% An., III : 31–32% An., IV : 34% An. Zone II is as wide as the pyroxene. It also contains relics of pyroxene not assimilated by the blastic feldspar. In addition, pigment rests are present, representing elements which could not be incorporated in the lattice of the plagioclase. Khidane/ Meheret, Entoto, Addis-Abeba, Ethiopia. With crossed nicols; enlargement 100 x.

Fig. 4. A frame of plagioclase tecoblast with inclusions of plagioclase and pyroxene belonging to the ground-mass. Khidane/Meheret, Entoto, Addis-Abeba, Ethiopia. Enlargement 100 x.

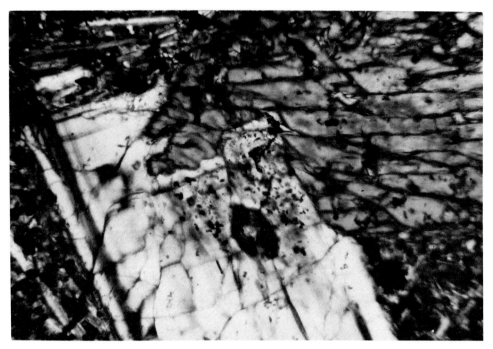

Fig. 3. Plagioclase tecoblast in contact with pyroxene phenocryst. Due to contact reaction, the later feldspar has partly assimilated and partly digested the pyroxene, with parts and relics enclosed in the feldspar. Khidane/Meheret, Entoto, Addis-Abeba, Ethiopia. With crossed nicols; enlargement 100 x.

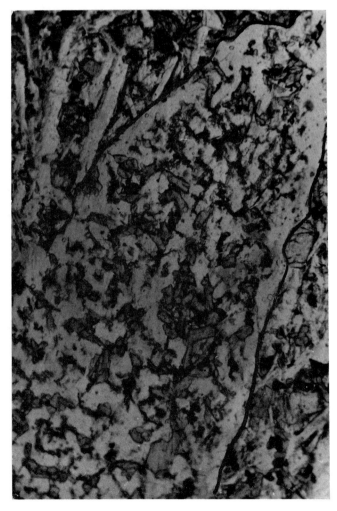

Fig. 4. A frame of plagioclase tecoblast with inclusions of plagioclase and pyroxene belonging to the ground-mass. Khidane/Meheret, Entoto, Addis-Abeba, Ethiopia. Enlargement 100 x.

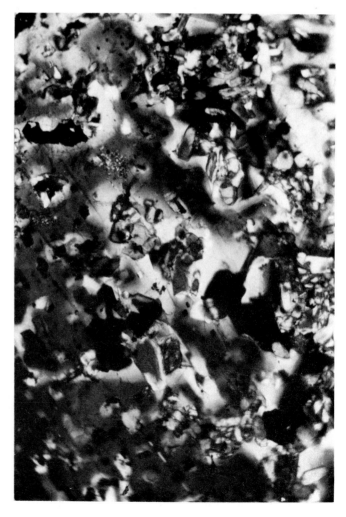

Fig. 5. A plagioclase tecoblast with inclusions of pyroxene and plagioclase components of the ground-mass. Khidane/Meheret, Entoto, Addis-Abeba, Ethiopia. With crossed nicols; enlargement 100 x.

Fig. 6. Ground-mass feldspars, pyroxenes and ore minerals enclosed in a tecoblastic feldspar. A strong reaction zone exists around the enclosed ground-mass components. Khidane/Meheret, Entoto, Addis-Abeba, Ethiopia. With crossed nicols; enlargement 100 x.

Fig. 7. Tecoblastic plagioclase with zoned structures due to variation in the composition. A great amount of ground-mass components (with various corrosion appearances) is enclosed in the tecoblast. Khidane/Meheret, Entoto, Addis-Abeba, Ethiopia. With crossed nicols; enlargement 100 x.

Fig. 8. Ground-mass components (unaffected) enclosed in the plagioclase: the rest pigments also enclosed represent relics of assimilated ground-mass. Khidane/Meheret, Entoto, Addis-Abeba, Ethiopia. With crossed nicols; enlargement 100 x.

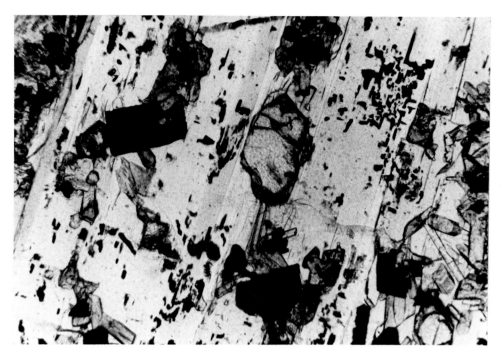

Fig. 9. Ground-mass components (also a large olivine) enclosed in a tecoblast plagioclase. Most of the ground-mass components are free from corrosion appearances. In contrast, rest pigments are shown clearly confined to, or at least partly following the cleavage of the feldspar. Khidane/Meheret, Entoto, Addis-Abeba, Ethiopia. Enlargement 100 x.

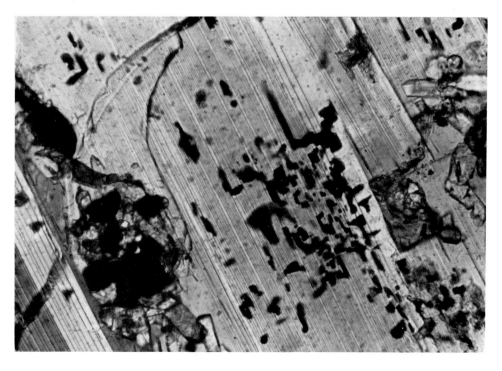

Fig. 10. Rest pigments partly following the tecoblast cleavage. Also shown are unaffected components of the ground-mass (see Fig. 9). Enlargement 200 x.

103

Fig. 11. A general view of a tecoblast plagioclase full of inclusions consisting of ground-mass material. Fig. 12–14 show the components of the ground-mass in greater detail. Khidane/Meheret, Entoto, Addis-Abeba, Ethiopia. Enlargement 20 x.

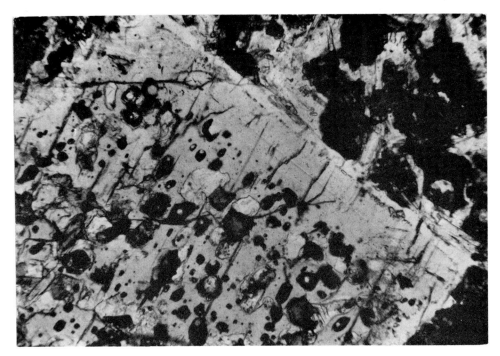

Fig. 12. Part of the tecoblast shown in Fig. 11. Corroded and assimilated ground-mass components in the tecoblast. In contrast, the ground-mass exterior to the tecoblast consists of large and non-corroded mineral components. Enlargement 100 x.

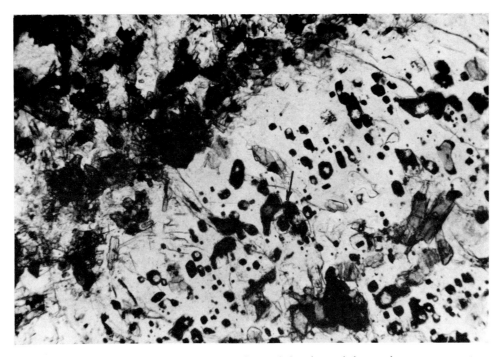

Fig. 13. A feldspar tecoblast with inclusions of corroded and rounded ground-mass components. (Arrow marks ground-mass components shown in greater detail in Fig. 14.) In comparison, the components of the ground-mass exterior to the tecoblast are larger and apparently free from corrosion. Khidane/Meheret, Entoto, Addis-Abeba, Ethiopia. Enlargement 100 x.

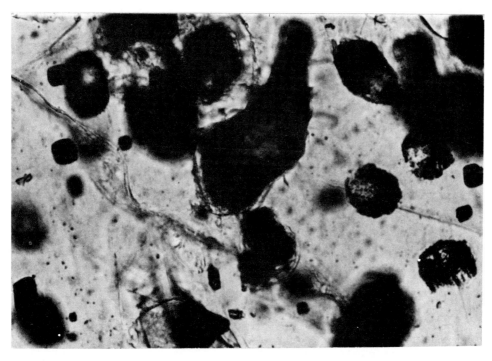

Fig. 14. Ground-mass components corroded and assimilated by the tecoblast (see also Fig. 8 and 9). Enlargement 400 x.

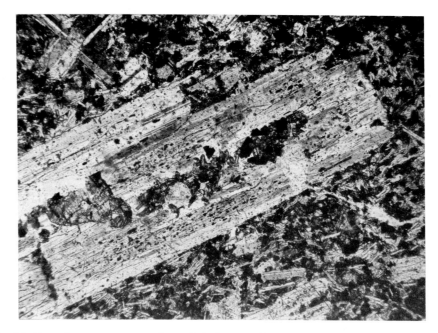

Fig. 15. Ground-mass components in a plagioclase tecoblast. Also, pigment rests are present as inclusions. A large corroded pyroxene of the ground-mass is also in the tecoblast. Khidane/Meheret, Entoto, Addis-Abeba, Ethiopia. Half-crossed nicols; enlargement 50 x.

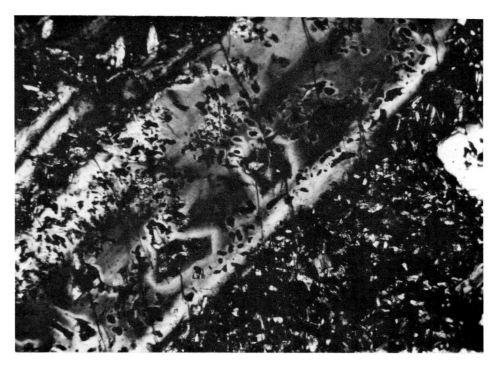

Fig. 16 and 17. Ground-mass components enclosed in tecoblast feldspar. Often the ground-mass is reduced to pigment forms. Surrounding the pigments and the ground-mass components there are marked reaction margins in the tecoblast. Fig. 17 shows in detail the ground-mass and pigments in the tecoblast. The arrow marks a reaction zone around an individual pigment. Khidane/Meheret, Entoto, Addis-Abeba, Ethiopia. With crossed nicols; enlargements 100 x, 200 x.

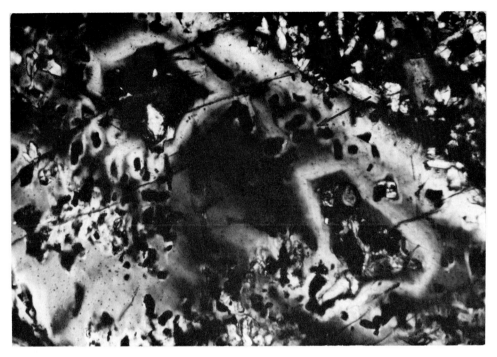

Fig. 17.

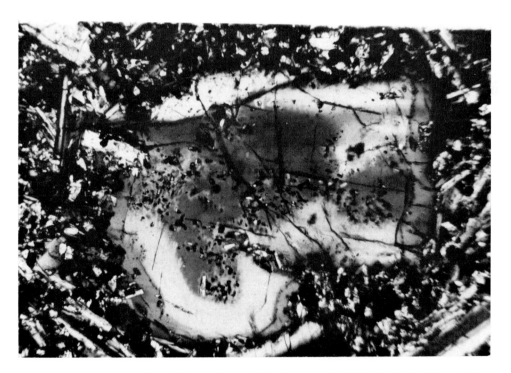

Fig. 18. A tecoblast plagioclase with rest pigments following a zonal distribution in the feldspar. It is interesting to note the coincidence of the feldspar "zone" with the pigment distribution. Khidane/Meheret, Entoto, Addis-Abeba, Ethiopia. With crossed nicols; enlargement 100 x.

Fig. 19. Ground-mass "extending" into a tecoblast (exceptional case). Also parts of the ground-mass are enclosed in the tecoblast. Khidane/Meheret, Entoto, Addis-Abeba, Ethiopia. With crossed nicols; enlargement 100 x.

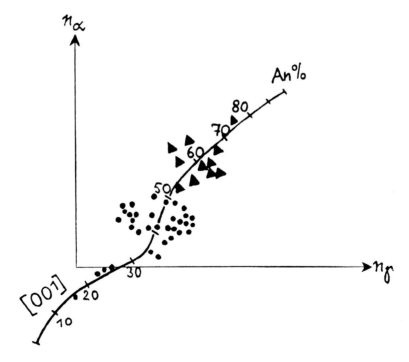

Fig. 20. The anorthite content of the ground-mass (small) plagioclase is shown by triangles. The composition of the large feldspar tecoblasts (phenocrysts) is indicated by dots.

Fig. 21 A and B. A tecoblast with an irregular type of zoning. The zones of the feldspar have the following An-content: Zone I : 25% An., Zone II : 15% An., Zone III : 24% An., Zone IV : 25—27% An. Zone I contains pigment rests. Also, parallel orientated cavities are present in the tecoblast. Khidane/Meheret, Entoto, Addis-Abeba, Ethiopia. With crossed nicols; enlargement 100 x.

Fig. 22. K-feldspar megablast due to crystalloblastic force transversing the foliation of a banded gneiss-granite. Arrows indicate directions of crystalloblastic growth of the K-feldspar megablast. Turbinasca, Val Bondasca, Alps.

Fig. 23. A gneiss-granite with an enclosed "xenolithic" relic of a gneiss (rich in mafic components). The foliation direction of the gneiss-granite corresponds to that of the xenolith. All transitions of the transformation of the xenolithic relic to the gneiss-granite are observed. Harrar, Ethiopia. Natural size approx. 1 m in length.

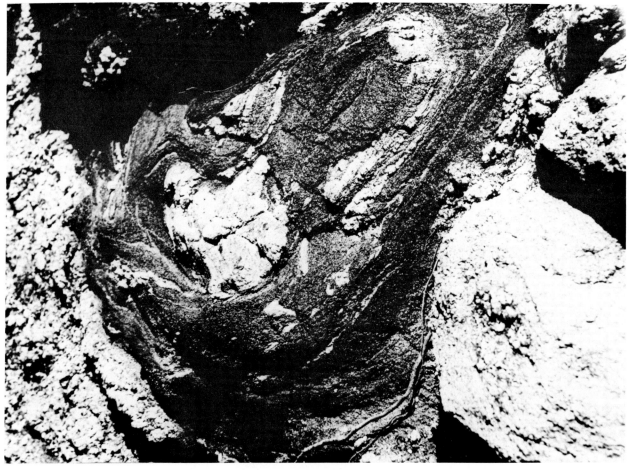

Fig. 24. A gneissic xenolith is enclosed in the granite. K-feldspar double inclusions are formed as patches in the gneissic xenolith following directions of greater penetrability, i.e., the schistosity–foliation directions. Harrar Granite, Ethiopia. Natural size approx. 1 m in length.

Fig. 25. Xenolithic relics enclosed in granite, indicating a different degree of preservation within the granitic mass. Some of the enclosed xenoliths are rounded, whereas others have been greatly influenced by feldspar forming solutions and show a high degree of assimilation (i.e., transformation to granite). Adamello Massif, Alps.

Fig. 26. Xenolithic relics representing a greater proportion than the enclosing granite. Bergeller Granite, Alps.

Fig. 27. Feldspar-forming solutions have penetrated the gneiss along its foliation direction. The gneissic relics (xenoliths) represent the pre-granitic phase which has been granitised by K-feldspar forming solutions. Piz Lagrev, Oberengadin, Alps.

Fig. 28. A granitic apophysis intruding in a vein-form into metamorphosed calcareous rocks. The granitic vein encloses gneissic xenoliths which were suspended in the granitic "Brei". The xenolithic bodies of the granitic veins have been "transported" along with the granitic vein intrusion. M=marble, G=granitic apophysis, X=gneissic xenoliths. Mt. Mattoni, Val Fredda, South Adamello, Italy.

113

Fig. 29. Portions of the granite rich in xenoliths in contact with xenolith-free granite. A sharp zig-zag margin (arrow "a") separates the relic rich with the relic-free portions of the granite. Arrow "b" shows random xenolithic relics within the relatively xenolith-free portions of the granite. Adamello Massif, Alps. Natural size approx. 2 m in length.

Fig. 30. Vein (gang) shaped hornblende-rich xenolithic body follows a tectonic fracture within the Seriphos Granite. Halara, Seriphos, Greece. Natural size approx. 10 m.

114

Fig. 31. Wedging-out of a hornblende xenolithic vein (gang) within the granite. Halara, Seriphos, Greece.

Fig. 32. "Sandstone nodule" between feldspar crystalloblast of the Mt. Blanc granitic body. q = quartz grains of the sandstone nodule, f = feldspar crystalloblasts. With crossed nicols; enlargement 50 x.

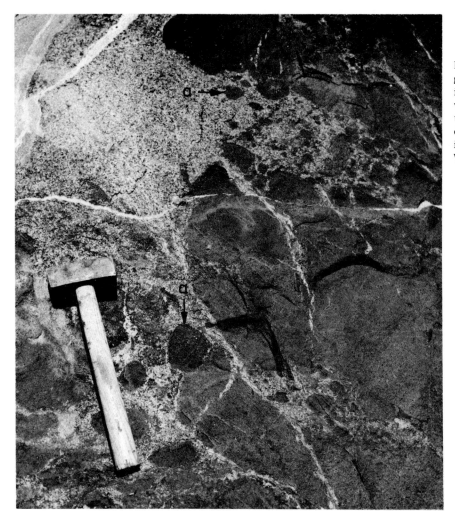

Fig. 33. Biotite–hornblende gneisses granitised by feldspar forming solutions impregnating into the gneiss, parts of which are left as xenolithic inclusions in the granitised portion. Arrow "a" indicates the gneissic parts left as xenoliths in the granitised portions. Ondonock, West Ethiopia.

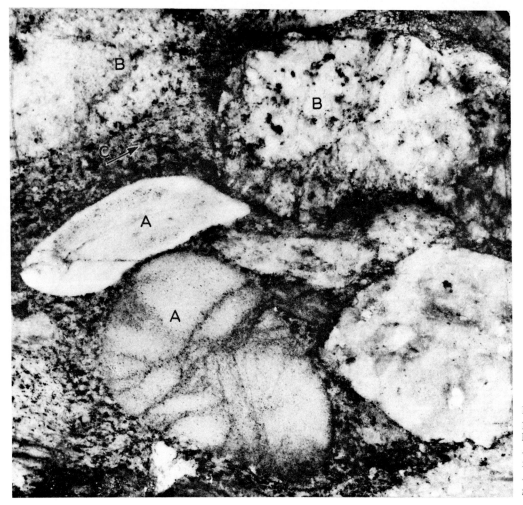

Fig. 34. Handspecimen of the metamorphosed (granitised) conglomerate of Buri-Rashitcha, Ula-Ulo, South Ethiopia. A = unaffected pebbles, B = pebbles resorbed and metasomatically affected. Arrow "C" shows the granitised (gneissic granitic) matrix. Enlargement about 2 x.

Fig. 35. General microscopic view of unaffected pebble of the granitised conglomerate of Buri-Rashitcha, Ula-Ulo, South Ehtiopia. With crossed nicols; enlargement 10 x.

Fig. 36. Fine grained quartzitic pebble consisting of interlocking fine quartz and containing micaceous laths. A coarse grained quartz veinlet is also shown. Buri-Rashitcha, Ula-Ulo, South Ethiopia. With crossed nicols; enlargement 100 x.

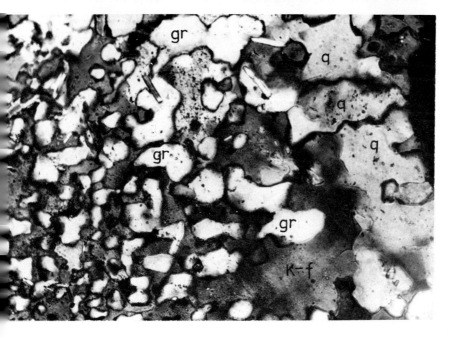

Fig. 37. A detailed view of a part of a pebble with recrystallised and mobilised quartz grains in a background-mass of a metasomatically formed K-feldspar. The texture of the quartz grains exhibited is a transition phase between the interlocking mosaic texture typical of the quartzites and the granophyric texture. gr = granophyric quartz, q = interlocking mosaic (quartzitic) texture, K-f = K-feldspar. Granitised conglomerate, Buri-Rashitcha, Adolla, Ethiopia. With crossed nicols; enlargement 250 x.

Fig. 38. Basic xenoliths in tonalite from Malga Macesso, Val di Selarno, Italy, representing an initial phase of conglomerate in the Werfener Formation. Due to resorption and incorporation of the conglomerate under granitisation basic xenoliths have been formed as relic structures in the tonalite.

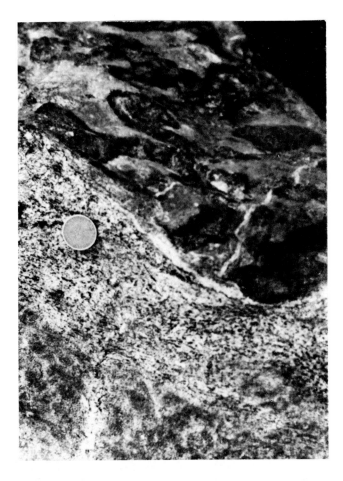

Fig. 39. Olivinefels xenoliths of an olivinefels mylonite in a fine-grained granite. Reaction (marginal formation of talk) and corrosion phenomena are noted on the xenolithic bodies as they are surrounded by the fine-grained granitic mass. Val Bondasca, Alps.

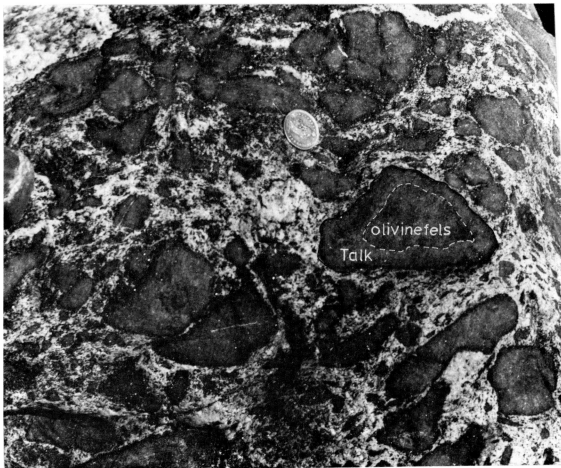

118

Fig. 40. An apophysis of the Seriphos Granite intruding in already metamorphosed calcareous rocks (marbles). No contact metamorphic and metasomatic phenomena are apparent. G = granite, C-X = calcareous xenolith, m = marble in contact with the granitic apophysis. Halara, Seriphos, Greece.

Fig. 41. "Augen structure" K-feldspar megablast in granite-gneiss. Melca-Guba, Borona, South Ethiopia ½X natural size

119

Fig. 42. K-feldspar "double inclusion" in a gneissic xenolith enclosed in the Naxos Granite, Greece. In the photograph only a part is shown indicating the contact of the xenolith with the granite and a K-feldspar double inclusion in the xenolith. Reference should be made to Fig. 144 and 145 which show components of the gneissic xenolith as inclusions in the K-feldspar double-inclusion. Enlargement 1½ x.

Fig. 43. K-feldspar megablasts following a penetrability direction within the Bergeller Granite, Alps.

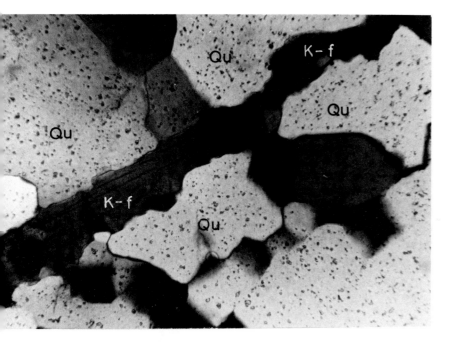

Fig. 44. A superindividual of K-feldspar as intergranular blastic growth between quartz grains. Qu = quartz, K-f = K-feldspar. Wänge Granite, Sweden. With crossed nicols; enlargement 100 x.

Fig. 45. K-feldspar megablast with a mylonitised ground-mass from Naxos Granite, Greece. Partly corroded pre-blastic plagioclases and biotites are following a zonal distribution in the later feldspar. In addition, other similar plagioclases and biotites are laying in random orientation in the K-feldspar megablast. The plagioclase and biotite inclusions are orientated. Bi = biotite, Pl = plagioclase, K-f = K-feldspar. With crossed nicols; enlargement 10 x.

121

Fig. 46 and 47. Blastic zoned K-feldspar with pre-blastic plagioclases and biotites (palaeosoma) following a strictly zonal distribution within the later formed K-feldspar host. K-f = K-feldspar, Bi = biotite, Pl = plagioclase. Hornblende syenite at Plauenscher Grund, Dresden, Saxony, Germany. With crossed nicols; enlargements 50 x, 100 x.

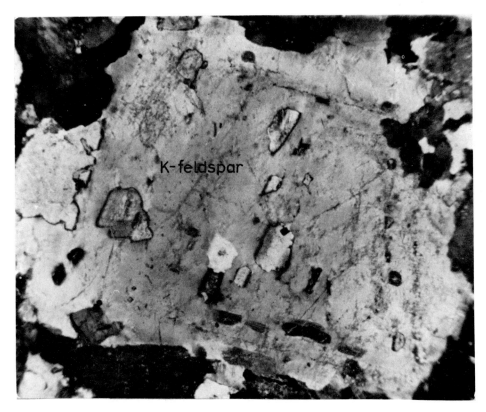

Fig. 48. Zoned K-feldspar megablast with plagioclase and biotite pre-blastic components, partly zonal, partly random in distribution within the later orthoclase. The pre-blastic components are corroded and assimilated by the later K-feldspar. Shap Granite. (rapakivi), Westmoreland, England. With crossed nicols; enlargement 50 x.

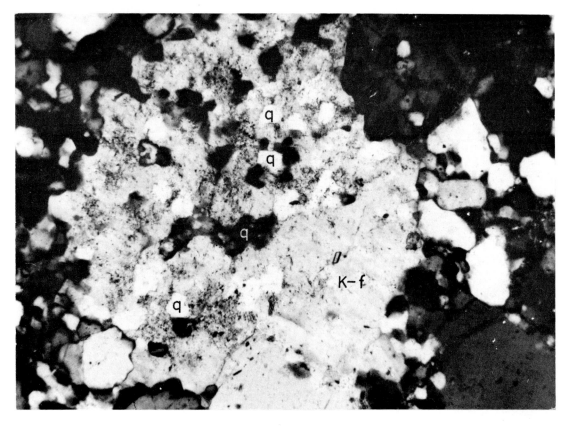

Fig. 49. Fine quartz grains differently orientated (some in the extinction position) surrounded, corroded and partly assimilated by a later K-feldspar blast. q = quartz, K-f = K-feldspar. Didessa Granite, Ethiopia. With crossed nicols, enlargement 100 x.

123

Fig. 50. Microcline blastesis in the ground-mass of a granitised conglomerate from Buri-Rashitcha, Adolla, West Ethiopia. Quartz and micas are partly assimilated, partly corroded by the microcline. With crossed nicols; enlargement 100 x.

Fig. 51. Corroded plagioclase with a reaction margin surrounded by later blastic perthitised K-feldspar. K-f = K-feldspar; Pl = plagioclase, r-m = reaction margin of plagioclase. Didessa Granite, Ethiopia. With crossed nicols; enlargement 100 x.

Fig. 52. Plagioclase in contact with later K-feldspar. Infiltration, corrosion and replacement of the plagioclase by the K-feldspar has taken place. Within the reaction margin of the plagioclase, protruding K-feldspar results in corrosion and replacements. Pl = plagioclase, K-f = K-feldspar, I-r = interzonal replacement of plagioclase by orthoclase. Granite at Cap Carbonara, Elba, Italy. With crossed nicols; enlargement 100 x.

Fig. 53. K-feldspar in contact with plagioclase. As a result of the synantetic reaction of these two feldspars, corrosion of the plagioclase and a reaction margin with reversing of the twin lamellae is indicated. Rapakivi, Finland. With crossed nicols; enlargement 100 x.

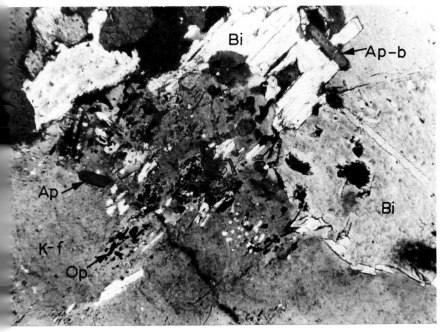

Fig. 54. Blastic K-feldspar in contact with biotites. Assimilation and replacement of the mica has taken place as a result of which apatites, opaque minerals and sillimanites originally associated with the mica are now liberated and lay in the K-feldsparblast (taken over by the K-feldspar due to the replacement of the mica). Also relic parts of the mica are present in the K-feldspar. Ap = apatite, K-f = K-feldspar, Bi = biotite, Op = opaque minerals. Ap-b = apatite associated with biotite. Granite at Proschwitz, Reichenberg, Bohemia. With crossed nicols; enlargement 100 x.

125

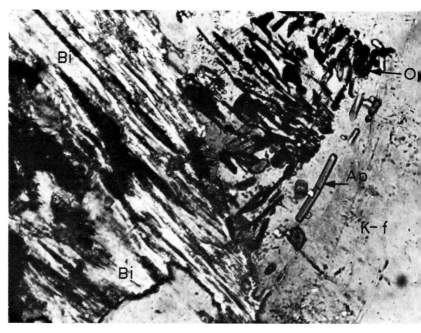

Fig. 55. Biotite with apatites, sillimanites and opaque minerals in contact with blastic K-feldspar. The orthoclase has assimilated and corroded the mica. As a result, opaque minerals, sillimanites and apatites, originally associated with the biotite, are now present in the K-feldspar. Bi = biotite. K-f = K-feldspar, Op = opaque minerals, Ap = apatite. Granite at Proschwitz, Reichenberg, Bohemia. Enlargement 200 x.

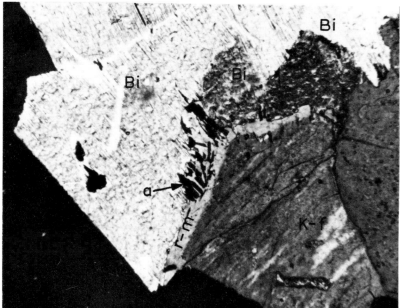

Fig. 56 and 57. Biotite in contact with K-feldspar. A synantetic reaction zone is produced in the K-feldspar. Opaque minerals originally in intergrowth with the biotite are now present in the K-feldspar reaction zone. In Fig. 57 arrow "a" shows an opaque intergrowth both present in the biotite and in the feldspar. Bi = biotite, K-f = K-feldspar, r-m = reaction margin in the K-feldspar. Ragunda Granite, Sweden. With crossed nicols; enlargements 100 x, 250 x.

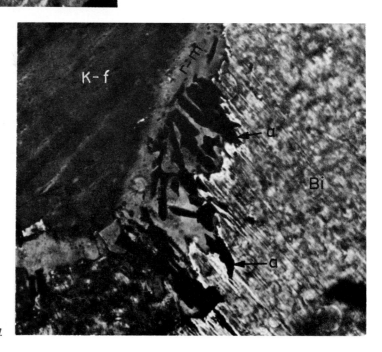

Fig. 57.

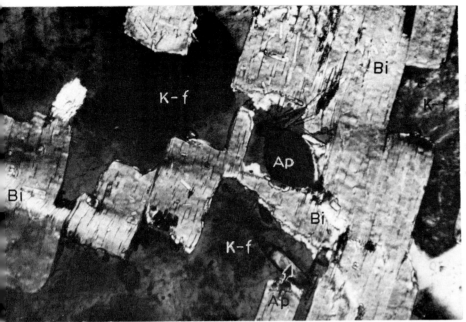

Fig. 58. Strained biotite (undulating extinction) corroded and replaced by blastic plagioclase. Also apatites, originally with the biotites, are partly freed and are now laying in the K-feldspar. Bi = biotite, K-f = K-feldspar, Ap = apatite. Hornblende granite at St. Diedler, Höhe, Vosges. With crossed nicols; enlargement 100 x.

Fig. 59. K-feldspar (in the extinction position) in contact with biotite which is corroded and is infiltrated by worm-like quartz myrmekitic bodies. B = biotite, r-m = reaction margin of the biotite, m-q = myrmekitic quartz. Two-mica granite at Altweier, Vosges. With crossed nicols; enlargement 100 x.

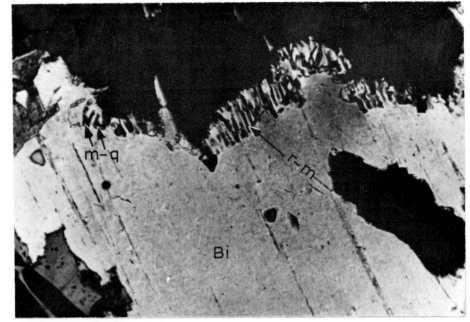

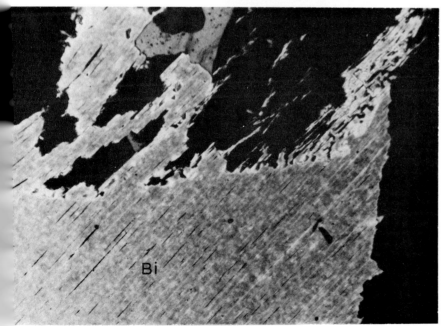

Fig. 60. K-feldspar in contact with biotite. The mica is corroded, replaced and indicates reaction effects as it comes in contact with the K-feldspar. The corrosion of the mica took place along the cleavage, with relics of it left in the feldspar. K-feldspar (in the extinction position), Bi = biotite. Two-mica granite at Altweier, Vosges. With crossed nicols; enlargement 100 x.

127

Fig. 61. The later K-feldspar has invaded and replaced the hornblende along its cleavage pattern. As a result, the outline of the hornblende is determined by its cleavage set, H = hornblende, K-f = K-feldspar (in the extinction position). Hornblende granite at Maryland, New South Wales, Australia. With crossed nicols; enlargement 100 x.

Fig. 62. Blastic plagioclase enclosing corroded biotite and quartz of the palaeosoma which are pushed at the periphery of the plagioclase due to autocatharsis (self-clearing processes). Bi = biotite, q = quartz, Pl = plagioclase. Granite at Trubinasca, Bergell Alps. With crossed nicols; enlargement 100 x.

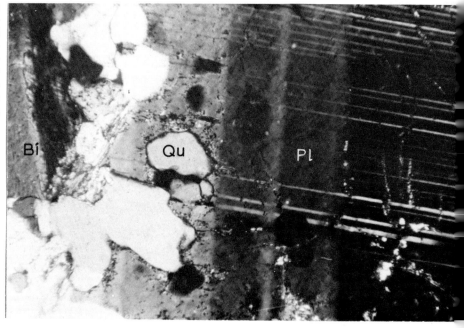

Fig. 63. Blastic plagioclase in contact with components of the ground-mass (palaeosoma). A reaction border with repeated zones indicating reversing of twinning is indicated. Within the reaction border are enclosed quartz grains corroded and partly assimilated. Qu = quartz, Bi = biotite, Pl = plagioclase. Granite at Krummhübel, Riesengebirge, Silesia, Germany. With crossed nicols; enlargement 100 x.

128

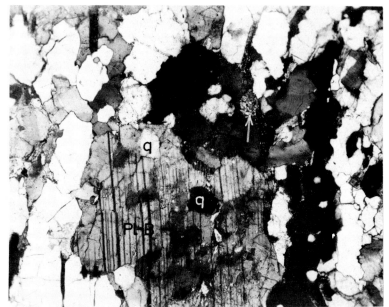

Fig. 64. Blastic plagioclase enclosing pre-blastic quartz. Antiperthitisation of the plagioclase has taken place. The blastic plagioclase is in contact with K-feldspar (in the extinction position) which encloses pre-blastic quartz and a myrmekitised plagioclase. The blastic plagioclase in contact with the K-feldspar is not myrmekitised. Pl-B = blastic plagioclase, q = pre-blastic quartz. Arrow shows myrmekitised plagioclase enclosed in the K-feldspar. Naxos Granite, Greece. With crossed nicols; enlargement 25 x.

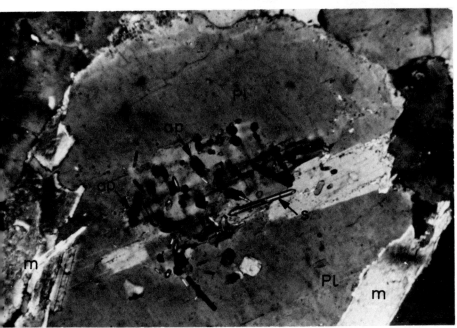

Fig. 65. Blastic plagioclase with accessory apatites, mica and sillimanite in the central part of the feldspar, simultaneously biotite is autocathartically pushed at the margins of the feldspar and shows corrosion effects. Pl = plagioclase, ap = apatite, m = mica, s = sillimanite. Fitchburg Granite, Mass., U.S.A. With crossed nicols; enlargement 100 x.

Fig. 66. Blastic plagioclase enclosing mafic mineral components which also build up a part of the ground-mass, outside the blastic growth. A reaction zone is indicated by the blastic plagioclase as it surrounds an amphibole grain. A = amphibole, Pl = plagioclase, Bi = biotite, r-z = reaction zone. Granite-gneiss at Museumberg, Bergen, Sweden. With crossed nicols; enlargement 100 x.

129

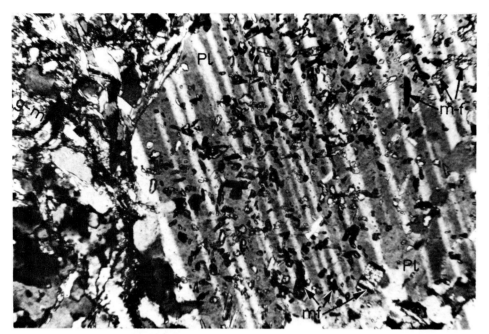

Fig. 67. Relics of mafic components interspersed within a later blastic plagioclase. Pl = plagioclase, m-f = mafic relics into the plagioclase, g-m = ground-mass outside the blastic feldspar. Granite-gneiss at Museumberg, Bergen, Sweden. With crossed nicols; enlargement 100 x.

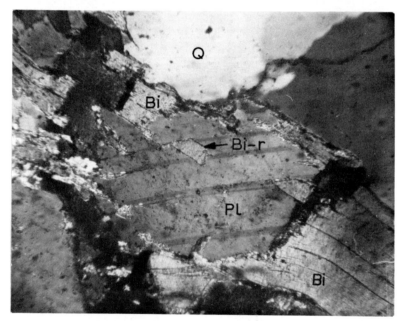

,Fig. 68. Blastic plagioclase enclosing biotite part and simultaneously pushing unassimilated parts of it (due to autocatharsis) towards its outer periphery. The biotite relic enclosed in the blastic plagioclase has the same orientation as the biotite outside the feldspar. Bi = biotite, Bi-r = biotite relic enclosed in blastic plagioclase, Pl = plagioclase (blastic), Q = quartz. Didessa Granite, West Ethiopia. With crossed nicols; enlargement 100 x.

Fig. 69. Blastic plagioclase in contact with biotite. Due to the blastic force of the feldspar strain-effects are produced on the mica indicated by undulating extinction. High relief mafic grains occur at the margin of the mica to the feldspar. Pl = plagioclase, Bi = biotite. Hornblende granite at Maryland, New South Wales, Australia. With crossed nicols; enlargement 100 x.

Fig. 70. Reaction contact of blastic plagioclase with biotite. A reaction margin is produced in the feldspar which is also protruding and replacing the mica along its cleavage. Bi = biotite, Pl = plagioclase, arrow indicates plagioclase protruding into the biotite. Hornblende Granite at Maryland, New South Wales, Australia. With crossed nicols; enlargement 100 x.

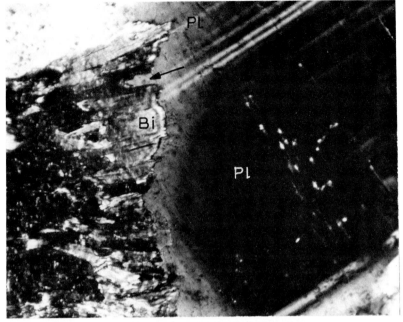

Fig. 71. Biotite in contact with later blastic plagioclase. Corroded outlines characterise the boundaries of these two mineral phases. Reaction margins are indicated in the plagioclase and a biotite part is partly engulfed by the feldspar. Bi = biotite, Pl = plagioclase, r-m = reaction margin of plagioclase; Bi-p = biotite part in plagioclase. Ballachulish Granite, Scotland. With crossed nicols; enlargement 100 x.

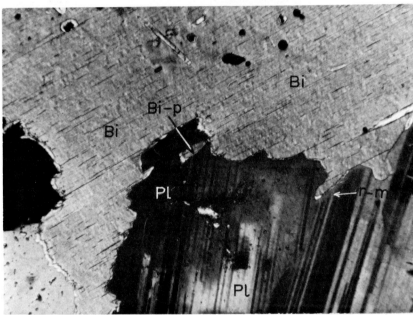

Fig. 72. Biotites corroded by blastic plagioclases. Most probably the two biotites were originally a continuous mineral grain which has been separated into two and is corroded by two independent plagioclase blastic growths. Bi(a) = biotite, Bi(b) = biotite; the two grains have the same orientation, Pl = plagioclase. Bergeller Granite, Albigna, Alps. With crossed nicols; enlargement 100 x.

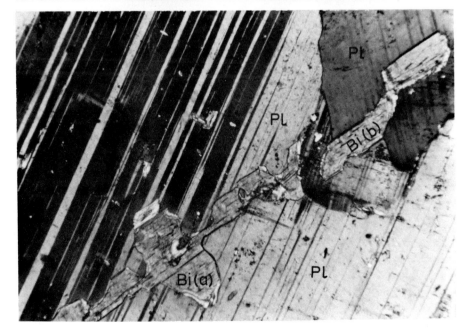

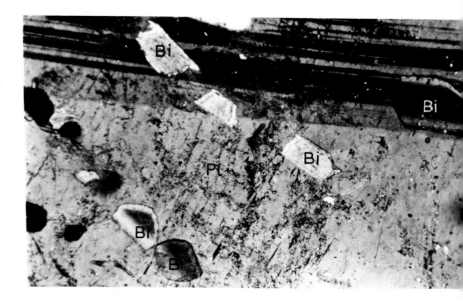

Fig. 73. Biotite grains following linear arrangement in plagioclase and indicating originally a single biotite which, due to corrosion and replacement by the blastic feldspar, has been "interrupted" in parts. In contrast to the linear arranged biotites (which cross the twinning) a biotite grain is present parallel to the plagioclase twinning. Pl = plagioclase, Bi = biotite. Bergeller Granite, Albigna, Alps. With crossed nicols: enlargement 100 x.

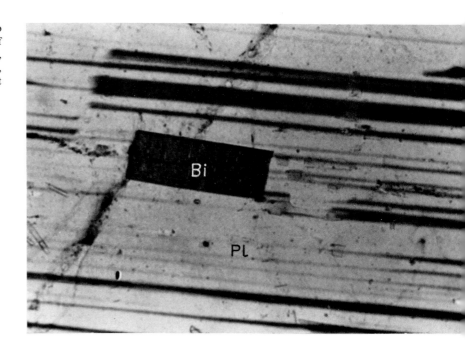

Fig. 74. Plagioclase with biotite parallel to the twinning of the feldspar; no corrosion of the biotite has taken place. Pl = plagioclase, Bi = biotite. Seussen Granite, Fichtelgebirge, Germany. With crossed nicols; enlargement 100 x.

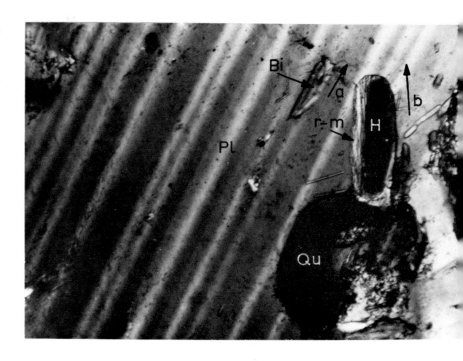

Fig. 75. Biotite and hornblende grains, both parallel to the feldspar twinning (arrow "a") and at an angle to it (arrow "b"). Pl = plagioclase, Bi = biotite, Qu = quartz, r-m = reaction margin of hornblende, H = hornblende. Bergeller Granite, Trubinasca, Alps. With crossed nicols; enlargement 100 x.

Fig. 76. Mica (biotite) infiltrated and replaced along directions of cleavage by plagioclase, later quartz infiltrates into the mica (also along the cleavage) and partly surrounds and replaces the feldspar as well. M = mica, Pl = plagioclase, Pl-i; Plagioclase infiltrating into the cleavage of the mica, q = quartz, q-i = quartz infiltrating along the cleavage of the mica, arrow indicates quartz surrounding the feldspar. Pegmatite near Piona, Lake Como district, Italy. With crossed nicols; enlargement 100 x.

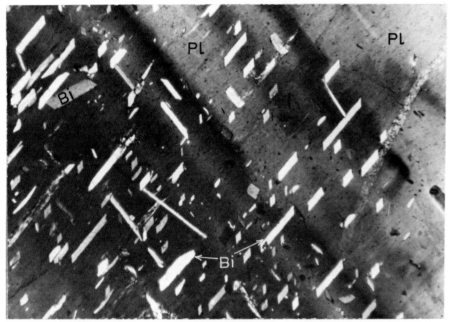

Fig. 77. Plagioclase with the orientated biotites, parallel and at an angle to the polysynthetic twinning of the feldspar. Pl = plagioclase, Bi = biotites. Seussen Granite, Fichtelgebirge, Germany. With crossed nicols; enlargement 100 x.

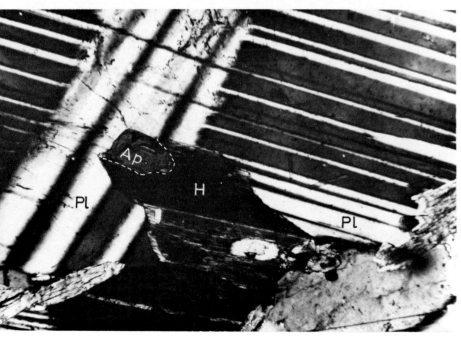

Fig. 78. Blastic plagioclase (two twinned individuals) with different orientations surrounding twinned hornblende and apatite (in the apatite a small zircon is included). Pl = plagioclase, H = hornblende, Ap = apatite (zircon in the apatite). Bergeller Granite, Trubinasca, Alps. With crossed nicols; enlargement 100 x.

Fig. 79. Plagioclase (generation I) surrounded by later blastic plagioclase which corrodes adjacent hornblende. Pl-I = plagioclase generation I, Pl-b = blastic plagioclase, H = hornblende. Bergeller Granite, Trubinasca, Alps. With crossed nicols; enlargement 100 x.

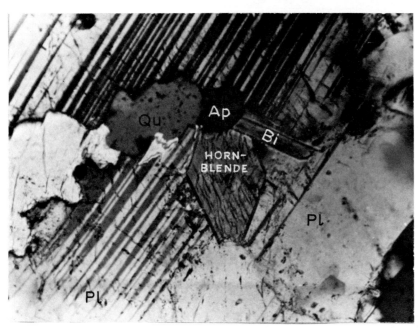

Fig. 80. Idiomorphic hornblende, apatite, quartz, biotite (all mineral components of the palaeosoma) surrounded and enclosed by a blastic later plagioclase. Pl = plagioclase, Qu = quartz, Ap = apatite, Bi = biotite. Bergeller Granite, Trubinasca, Alps. With crossed nicols, enlargement 100 x.

Fig. 81 and 82. K-feldspar (orthoclase) surrounded by blastic later plagioclase. No myrmekitisation is present in the plagioclase. K-f = K-feldspar, Pl = plagioclase. Two-mica granite at Kaibach, Schenkenzell, Schwarzwald (Black Forest), Germany. With crossed nicols; enlargements 50 x, 100 x.

Fig. 82.

Fig. 83. Plagioclase transversed by a band consisting of interlocking quartz grains and micaceous minerals. Pl = plagioclase, m = micaceous minerals, q = interlocking quartz. Phyllite "xenolith", Mt. Blanc. With crossed nicols; enlargement 100 x.

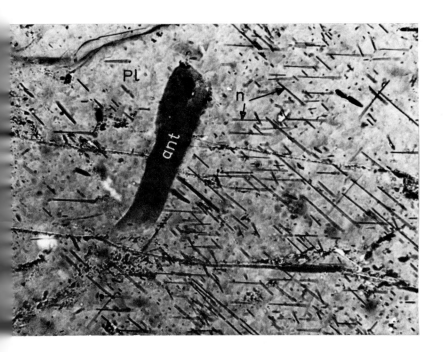

Fig. 84. Plagioclase with antiperthite and needles of an unidentified mineral (sillimanite?) following different orientations in the plagioclase. Pl = plagioclase, n = needles, ant = antiperthite.
Hornblende syenite at Ben Cruachen, Loch Awe, Scotland. With crossed nicols; enlargement 100 x.

135

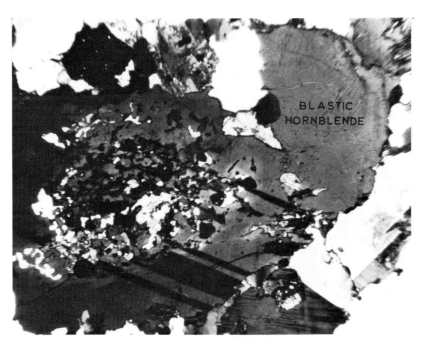

Fig. 85. Quartz, opaque minerals and feldspars as pre-blastic components (palaeosoma) enclosed by a twinned horn-blende megablast. Ondonock Granite, West Ethiopia. With crossed nicols; enlargement 25 x.

Fig. 86. (Detail of Fig. 85.) Blastic hornblende enclosing components of the pre-blastic phase (palaeosoma). Qu = quartz, opaque-minerals (black), Ap = apatite, mf = pre-blastic mafic components. With crossed nicols; enlargement 100 x.

136

Fig. 87. An idioblastic hornblende megablast with pre-blastic plagioclases (either as intact idiomorphic grains or as corroded components) interzonal in the amphibole megablast. H = hornblende, pl = plagioclase, K-f = K-feldspar (microcline). Hornblende granite at Rikitujn, Rikucho, Japan. With crossed nicols; enlargement 50 x.

Fig. 88. (Detail of Fig. 87.) Hornblende megablast with enclosed idiomorphic and corroded plagioclase. Pl = plagioclase, H = hornblende. With crossed nicols; enlargement 100 x.

137

Fig. 89. Feldspars and quartz of ground-mass included and partly corroded by blastic hornblende. Arrows show blastic protuberances of the hornblende into the intergranular spaces of the ground-mass. H = hornblende, q = quartz, f = feldspar. Malga, Bazena, Alps. With crossed nicols; enlargement 100 x.

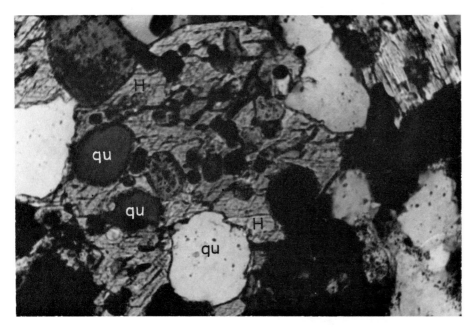

Fig. 90. Blastic hornblende enclosing different size of rounded and corroded quartz grains. H = hornblende, qu = quartz. Biegelsberg Granite, Eberstadt, Hessen, Germany. With crossed nicols; enlargement 100 x.

Fig. 91. Blastic hornblende megablast with enclosed corroded and assimilated relics of plagioclase. Also, plagioclases outside the hornblende blastic phase are present. H = hornblende, Pl = plagioclase, Pl-i = plagioclase inclusions in blastic hornblende. Granite at Malga Mecesso, Val di Selarno, Adamello, Italy. With crossed nicols; enlargement 100 x.

138

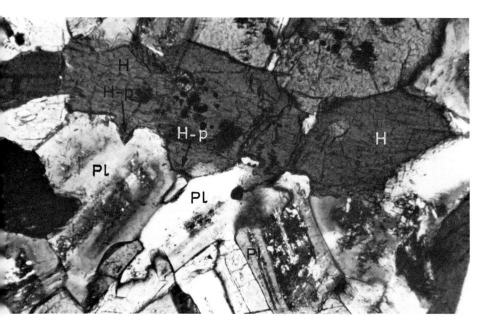

Fig. 92. Blastic hornblende partly surrounding plagioclases and sending intergranular protuberances. H = hornblende, Pl = plagioclase, H-p = intergranular protuberances of hornblende. Granite at Malga Macesso, Val di Selarno, Adamello, Italy. With crossed nicols; enlargement 100 x.

Fig. 93. Plagioclase corroded (rounded) by later blastic hornblende. Quartz replacement has taken place in the enclosed feldspar (probably pre-hornblende in sequence). H = hornblende, Pl = plagioclase, Qu = quartz. Granite at Malga Macesso, Val di Selarno, Adamello, Italy. With crossed nicols; enlargement 100 x.

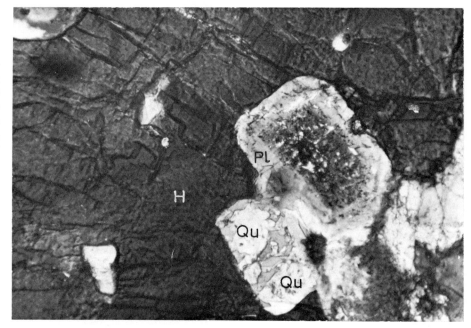

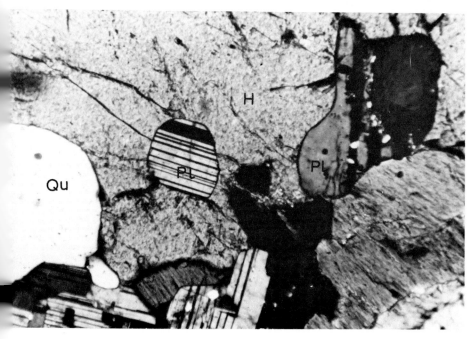

Fig. 94. Hornblende blastic growth enclosing rounded and corroded plagioclases and quartz. H = hornblende, Pl = plagioclase, Qu = quartz. Granite at Malga Macesso, Val di Selarno, Adamello, Italy. With crossed nicols; enlargement 100 x.

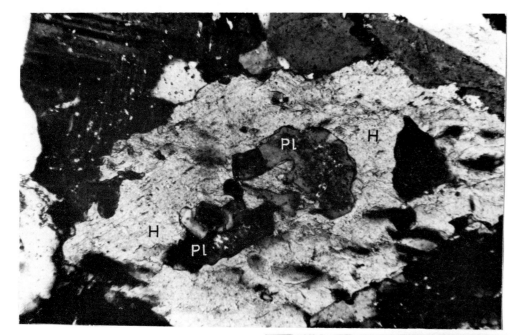

Fig. 95. Hornblende with enclosed and assimilated plagioclase relics. H = hornblende, Pl = plagioclase. Mte. Cadino, Malga Bazena, Alps. With crossed nicols; enlargement 100 x.

Fig. 96. Plagioclase partly surrounded by a later hornblende blastic growth. Pl = plagioclase, H = hornblende, Qu = quartz. Granite at Malga Macesso, Val di Selarno, Adamello, Italy. With crossed nicols; enlargement 100 x.

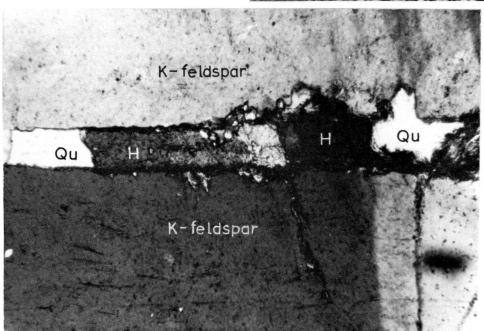

Fig. 97. Veinlet partly occupied by quartz, partly by amphiboles (hornblende) between K-feldspars. Qu = quartz, H = hornblende. Granodiorite at Ondonock, West Ethiopia. With crossed nicols; enlargement 100 x.

140

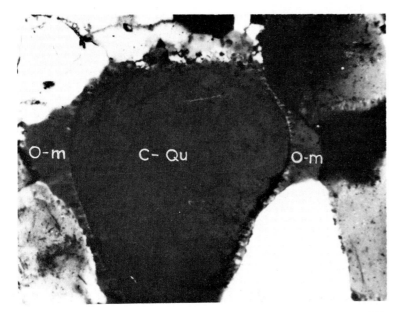

Fig. 98. A clastic quartz grain with a regrowth margin due to diagenetic processes. The clastic quartz and overgrowth margin are having the same optical orientation. C-Qu = clastic quartz, O-m = overgrowth margin. Sandstone, Guder, Blue Nile, Ethiopia. With crossed nicols; enlargement 100 x.

Fig. 99. A clastic quartz surrounded by an aggregate of fine granular quartz forming an overgrowth of the quartz. C-Qu = clastic quartz, O-A = overgrowth aggregate. Sandstone, Guder, Blue Nile, Ethiopia. With crossed nicols; enlargement 100 x.

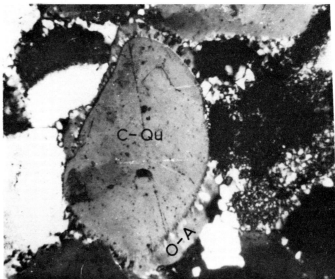

Fig. 100. Blastic quartz filling intergranular space and pushing the feldspars to its periphery due to autocatharsis. Qu = quartz, f = feldspars. Didessa Granite, Ethiopia. With crossed nicols; enlargement 100 x.

141

Fig. 101 and 102. Blastic quartz corroding and assimilating components of the palaeosoma, which are restricted in a zonal distribution within the blastic quartz, f = feldspar, m = mica, Qu = quartz. Königshain Granite, Silesia, Germany. With crossed nicols; enlargements 50 x, 100 x.

Fig. 102.

Fig. 103. Blastic quartz partly enclosing and corroding plagioclase and biotite of the palaeosoma, also the pre-blastic grains are pushed at the periphery of the blastic quartz due to autocatharsis. Qu = quartz. Bi = biotite, Pl = plagioclase. Melibokus Granite, Odenwald, Germany. With crossed nicols; enlargement 100 x.

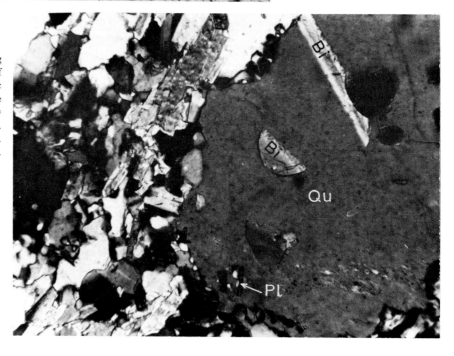

142

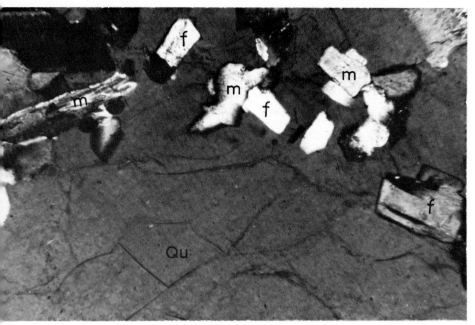

Fig. 104. Feldspars and micas of the palaeosoma (pre-blastic components) in zonal distribution within the quartz blastic growth. The zonal distribution of the palaeosoma components in the quartz is due to autocathartic processes. Qu = quartz, f = feldspars, m = mica. Granite at Gorxheimertal, Weinheim, Germany. With crossed nicols; enlargement 100 x.

Fig. 105. Biotite in contact with quartz (in the extinction position). A reaction margin with interleptonic penetration of quartz has taken place in the synantetic zone of the mica. Bi = biotite mica, Qu = quartz, r–m = reaction margin of biotite. Two-mica granite at Altweir, Vosges. With crossed nicols; enlargement 100 x.

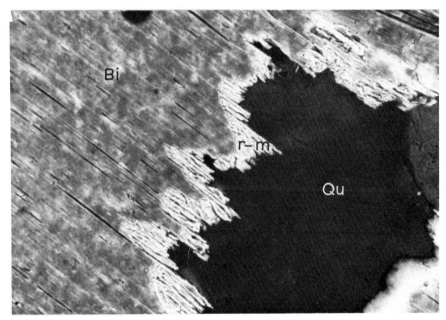

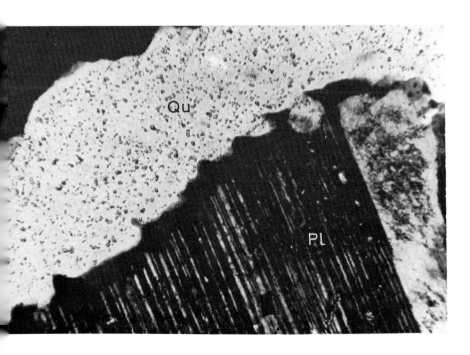

Fig. 106. Quartz in contact with corroded and affected plagioclase. In addition to a corrosion outline a reaction margin with reversing of the twinning is indicated by the feldspar. Pl = plagioclase, Qu = quartz. Granite, Wänge, Sweden. With crossed nicols; enlargement 100 x.

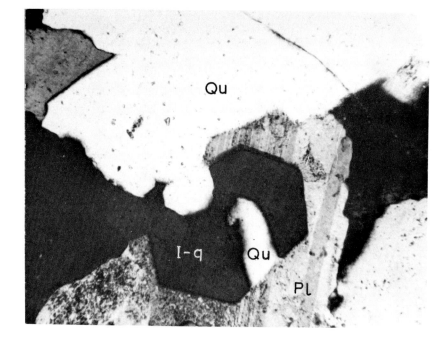

Fig. 107. Idiomorphic quartz in plagioclase. Later quartz corrodes both the feldspar and the idiomorphic quartz. Pl = plagioclase, Qu = quartz, I–q = idiomorphic quartz. Baveno Granite, Italy. With crossed nicols; enlargement 100 x.

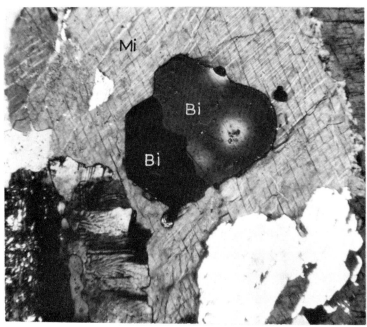

Fig. 108. "Twinned biotite" with accessory minerals showing a radioactive halo, in microline. Bi = biotite, Mi = microcline. Thalhorn Granite, St. Amarintal, Vosges. With crossed nicols; enlargement 100 x.

Fig. 109. Biotite enclosing apatites, some rounded and corroded by mica growth. Quartz and K-feldspar are in contact with the mica. Myrmekitic quartz is formed in the biotite in contact with the K-feldspar. Bi = biotite, Ap = apatite, Qu = quartz, m-q = myrmekitic quartz. Buchwald Granite, Silesia, Germany. With crossed nicols; enlargement 100 x.

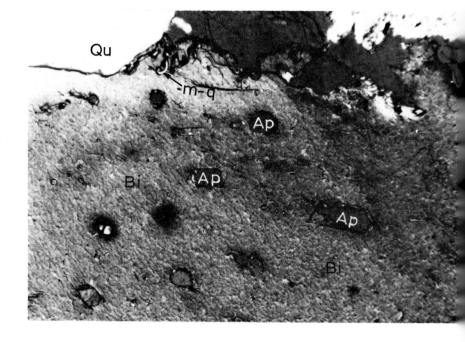

144

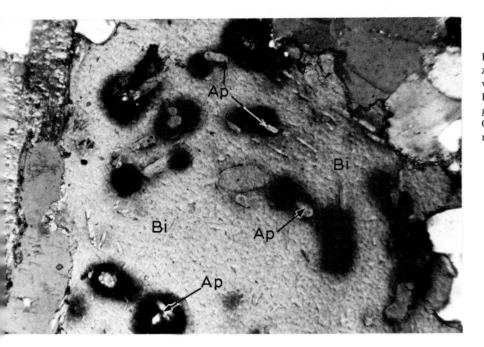

Fig. 110. Biotite blastic growth with zonal arranged accessories (apatites), which show a strong radioactive halo. Bi = biotite, Ap = apatite. Two-mica granite at Gleesberg, Schneeberg, Saxony, Germany. With crossed nicols; enlargement 100 x.

Fig. 111. Biotite with accessories (apatites) following a zonal or interzonal arrangement of the mica. Radioactive halos are present around the accessories. Bi = biotite, Ap = apatite. Granite at Bergen, Vogtland, Saxony, Germany. With crossed nicols; enlargement 100 x.

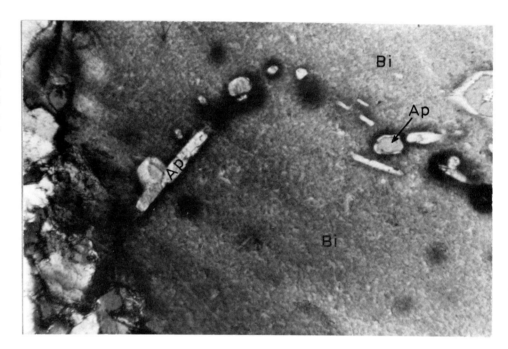

Fig. 112. Plagioclase enclosed in biotite crystalloblast. Pl = Plagioclase, Bi = biotite crystalloblast. Granite at Pitz Lagrev, Oberengadin, Switzerland. With crossed nicols; enlargement 100 x.

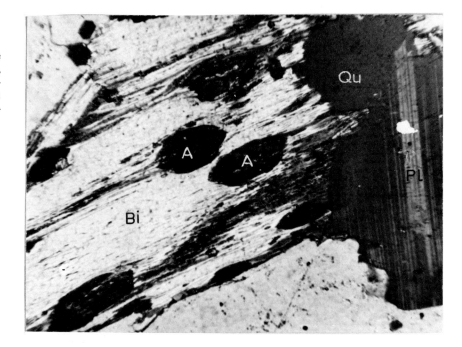

Fig. 113. Amphibole "augen" structure in biotite. A = amphibole, Bi = biotite, Pl = plagioclase, Qu = quartz. Hornblende syenite at Ben Cruachen, Loch Awe, Scotland. With crossed nicols; enlargement 100 x.

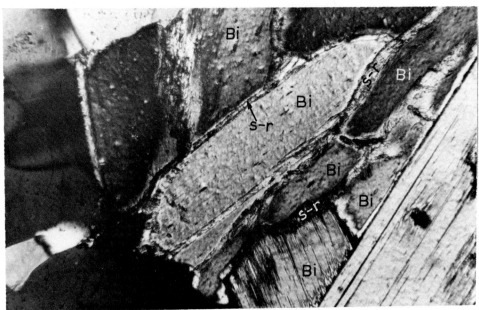

Fig. 114. Synantetic reaction margins of biotite as they come in contact with one another. Bi = biotite, s-r = synantetic reaction margin. Granite, southwest of Torn, Sweden. With crossed nicols; enlargement 100 x.

Fig. 115. Veinlet of chalcedony in birbirite, transgressing from the margins to the centre from a mass of chalcedony to fine grained quartz which maintains gel relic structures (see Fig. 116). Chalalaca/Chambe, Adolla, South Ethiopia. With crossed nicols; enlargement 100 x.

146

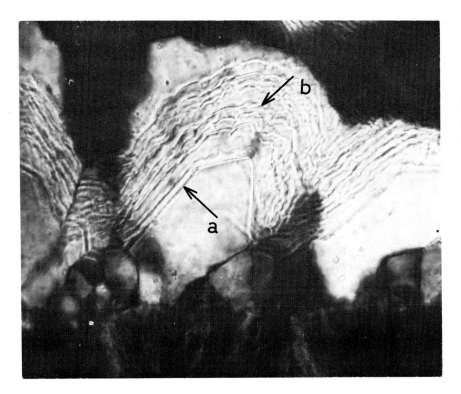

Fig. 116. (Detail of Fig. 115.) Gel and crystalline structures co-existing in the same individual. Arrow "a" shows a crystalline outline of the quartz nucleus; arrow "b" indicates relic gel-structure in the same quartz individual. With crossed nicols; enlargement 400 x.

Fig. 117. Relic gel-structure with "edged" outline resembling zonal growth structure. Chalalaca/Chambe, Adolla, South Ethiopia. With crossed nicols; enlargement 400 x.

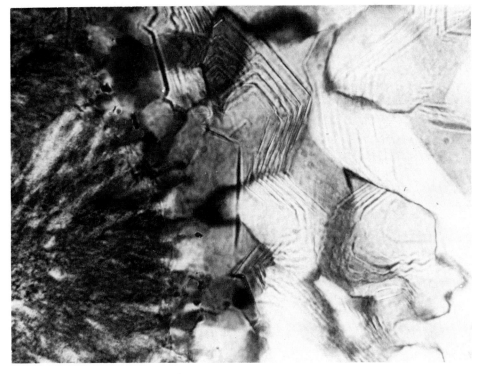

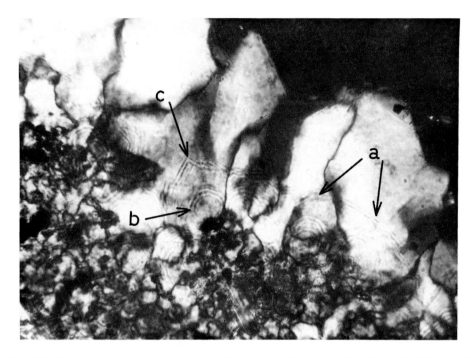

Fig. 118. Relic gel-structure in quartz aggregate of a veinlet in serpentine. Arrow "a" shows gel-structure traversing different quartz individuals; arrow "b" indicates a ring-like relic gel-structure in a quartz grain; arrow "c" indicates that the relic gel-structure simulates zonal growth. Dubitcha, Adolla, South Ethiopia. With crossed nicols; enlargement 400 x.

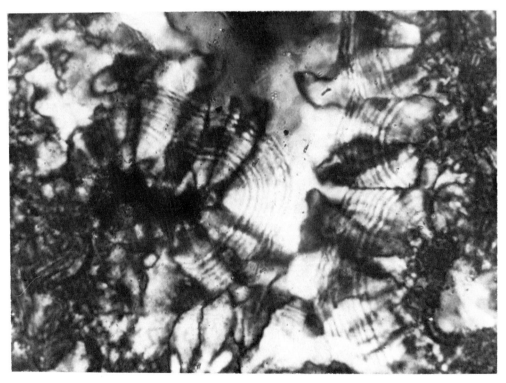

Fig. 119. Colloform relic structure preserved after the crystallisation of the original gel-structure into a quartz aggregate. Quartz veinlet in serpentine. Dubitcha, Adolla, South Ethiopia. With crossed nicols; enlargement 400 x.

148

Fig. 120. Pigment bands traversing quartz grains. The pigments consist of limonite granules originally interspersed in the silica-gel phase. With subsequent formation of quartz from the silica-gel, the original pattern of the pigment bands have been preserved. Birbirite from Daleti, Wollaga, West Ethiopia. With crossed nicols; enlargement 400 x.

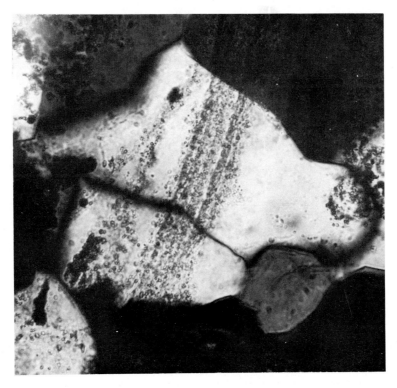

Fig. 121. Limonite granules (forming bands) relics of an initial gel-phase "traversing" quartz individuals. Birbirite from Daleti, Wollaga, West Ethiopia. With crossed nicols; enlargement 100 x.

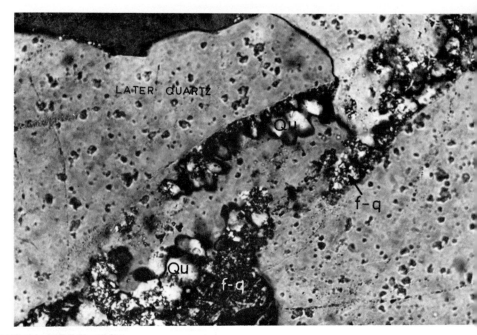

Fig. 122. Fine quartz indicating a gel-structure (partly resorbed, partly recrystallised) in a later quartz. f-q = fine quartz, a crystallisation product out of a gel. Qu = quartz, recrystallised. Two-mica granite at Kaibach, Schenkenzell, Schwarzwald (Black Forest), Germany. With crossed nicols; enlargement 100 x.

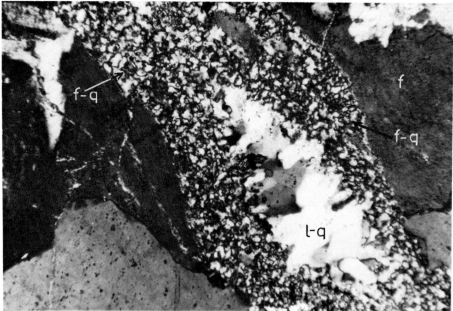

Fig. 123. A veinlet of fine quartz with larger quartz grains in the central part transversing feldspars. The fine and the larger quartz of the veinlet represent the latest phase in the transition from "gel", crypto-crystalline, fine crystalline, to well-crystalline forms in the transformation series from colloforms to well-crystalline forms. f = feldspars, f-q = fine quartz, l-q = larger quartz. Two-mica granite at Kaibach, Schenkenzell, Schwarzwald (Black Forest), Germany. With crossed nicols; enlargement 100 x.

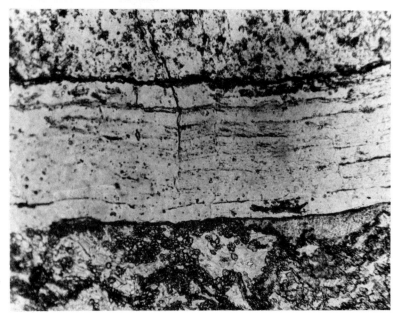

Fig. 124 and 125. A band consisting of larger quartz grains transverses a mass of fine quartz. Within the quartz band are lines of fine inclusions indicating an original colloform structure for the band. Granite in Bernina region, Alps. Without and with crossed nicols; enlargement 100 x.

150

Fig. 125.

Fig. 126. Linear distribution of fine pigments (representing an initial gel-structure) in crystallised quartz grains, indicating relics of the transformation from silica gels to crystalline quartz. It should be noted that the linear distribution of the relic pigments transverses the differently orientated quartz grains. For comparison see Fig. 124 and 125. Harrar Granite, Ethiopia. With crossed nicols; enlargement 100 x.

Fig. 127. Mega phenocryst of oscillatory zoned plagioclase in an olivine basaltic ground-mass. The plagioclase zoning simulates gel-like structure. Where the zonal structure is transversed by the twinning of the plagioclase a packet structure is formed (indicated by arrows). Olivine basalt at Debra-Sina, Ethiopia. With crossed nicols; enlargement 25 x.

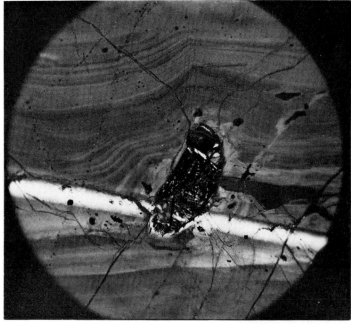

Fig. 128. Zoned plagioclase with the zoning surrounding a pocket of ground-mass. The zonal texture of this basaltic phenocryst simulates gel-structure. Olivine basalt at Debra-Sina, Ethiopia. With crossed nicols; enlargement 50 x.

Fig. 129. Plagioclase phenocryst in olivine basalt ground-mass. The feldspar shows a fine zoning "oscillatory in nature" simulating the appearance of gel-like structures. Polysynthetic twinning transverses the feldspar zoning. Olivine basalt at Debra-Sina, Ethiopia. With crossed nicols; enlargement 50 x.

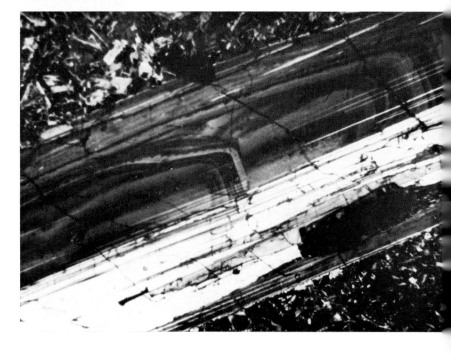

Fig. 130. Plagioclase twinning and fine feldspar zoning. The phenocryst zoning simulates gel-like structure. Olivine basalt at Debra-Sina, Ethiopia. With crossed nicols; enlargement 50 x.

Fig. 131. Zoned plagioclase megablast with the zoning attaining gel-like form. Granite at Passo di Val Fredda, Adamello, Italy. With crossed nicols; enlargement 25 x.

Fig. 132. Zoned plagioclase with corroded interzonal biotite. Also zoning simulating a colloform structure is between bands of fine zoning of the plagioclase; a biotite is also present. Seccheto Granite, Elba, Italy. With crossed nicols; enlargement 100 x.

153

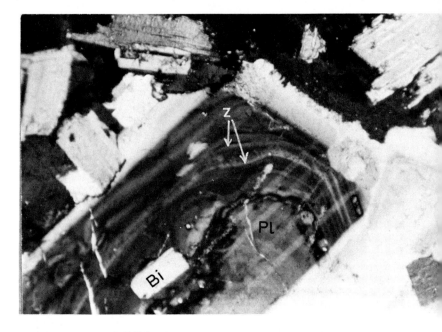

Fig. 133. Plagioclase megablast with fine zoning following defined crystalline faces (outlines). Biotites are orientated parallel to the fine zoning. Local disturbances in the development of the zoning produce gel-like structural patterns. Pl = plagioclase with fine zoning, G-z = gel-like zones, Bi = biotite. Seccheto Granite, Elba, Italy. With crossed nicols; enlargement 100 x.

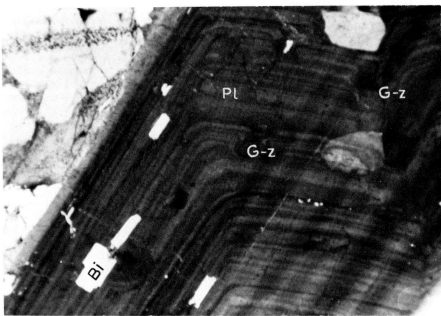

Fig. 134. Zoned plagioclase with the zoning attaining gel-like structure. Two zones running parallel diverge apart (see arrows). Pl = plagioclase, z = zones diverging apart, B = biotite. Granite at Passo di Val Fredda, Adamello, Italy. With crossed nicols; enlargement 25 x.

Fig. 135. Zoned and twinned plagioclase megablast enclosing biotite and quartz of the ground-mass. A reaction margin is formed as the plagioclase encloses biotite and comes in contact with part of the ground-mass (see arrow "a"); a corrosion outline (see arrow "b") is also indicated between a resorption and regrowth phase of the plagioclase. Bi = biotite, Qu = quartz, Pl = plagioclase, R-Pl = regrowth plagioclase. Granite at Passo di Val Fredda, Adamello, Italy. With crossed nicols; enlargement 100 x.

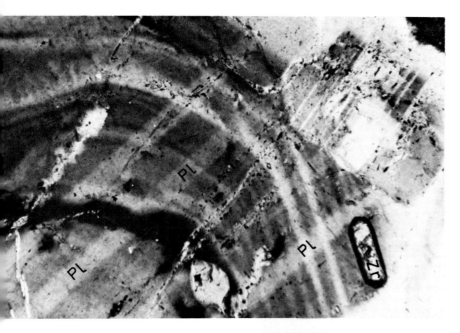

Fig. 136. Gel-like zonal structure of plagioclase crystalloblast with gel-structure and polysynthetic twinning transversing the zoning. A zircon parallel to the plagioclase zoning is also indicated. Pl = plagioclase, Zr = zircon. Seccheto Granite, Elba, Italy. With crossed nicols; enlargement 100 x.

Fig. 137. Zoned plagioclase megablast. The central part indicates a gel-simulating structure. A biotite flake is parallel to the plagioclase zoning. Pl = plagioclase, Bi = biotite. Elzach Granite, Schwarzwald (Black Forest), Germany. With crossed nicols; enlargement 100 x.

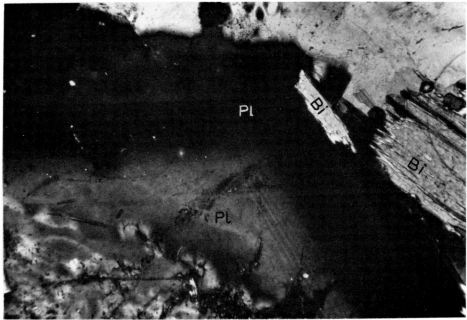

Fig. 138. Zonal development in plagioclase crystalloblast with resorption phases intervening between the zoning of the plagioclase. Zoned bands exist indicating gel-like structure. Arrow "a" indicates resorption phase, arrow "b" shows width of feldspar zone indicating gel-like structure. Seccheto Granite, Elba, Italy. With crossed nicols; enlargement 100 x.

155

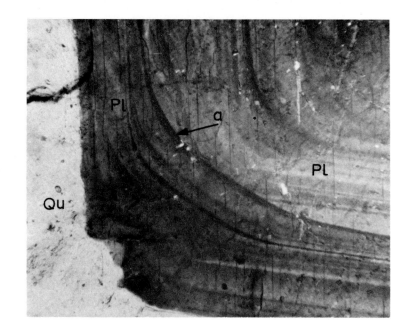

Fig. 139. Zoned plagioclase crystalloblast with an "unconformity" in the zoning (see arrow "a") indicating a resorption phase intervening between the zoning of the plagioclase. Pl = plagioclase, Qu = quartz. Seccheto Granite, Elba, Italy. With crossed nicols; enlargement 100 x.

Fig. 140. Zoned plagioclase with external fine zoning forming an "unconformity" with the central zoning. A smaller plagioclase (Pl-2) is interzonal to the external zoning. Interrupted line indicates "unconformity" in the plagioclase zoning. Elzach Granite, Schwarzwald (Black Forest), Germany. With crossed nicols; enlargement 100 x.

Fig. 141. Plagioclase megablast. Arrow "a" indicates zoning of central part of plagioclase, and arrow "b" indicates a border of fine zoning. Unconformity in the zoning is indicated between case "a" and case "b". Pl = plagioclase. Granite at Malga, Macesso, Val di Sondrio, Adamello, Italy. With crossed nicols; enlargement 100 x.

Fig. 142. Plagioclase megablast with broad zones corresponding to a geometrical crystalline outline. Complex and irregular zones ("a" and "b") developed between the well defined broader zones (interrupted lines). Seccheto Granite, Elba, Italy. With crossed nicols; enlargement 100 x.

Fig. 143. Fine plagioclase zones, due to disturbances in the development of the zoning, transgress into the "gel-like zonal patterns". Arrow shows a nucleus of disturbance feldspathic in composition which caused the development of gel-like structures. The polysynthetic twinning transgresses the feldspar zoning. Pl = plagioclase, T = polysynthetic twinning. Seccheto Granite, Elba, Italy. With crossed nicols; enlargement 100 x.

Fig. 144. Corroded and myrmekitised plagioclases included in later K-feldspar megablast (a double inclusion). The xenolithic ground-mass is partly included in the K-feldspar. Pl = plagioclase, K-f = K-feldspar. Naxos Granite, Greece. With crossed nicols; enlargement 25 x.

157

Fig. 145. Corroded and myrmekitised plagioclases in K-feldspar megablast (double inclusion). Pl = plagioclase, K-f = K-feldspar. Naxos Granite, Greece. With crossed nicols; enlargement 50 x.

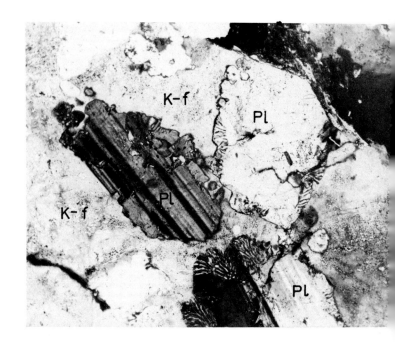

Fig. 146. K-feldspar megablast in contact with preblastic ground-mass (palaeosoma). Also recrystallised quartz in the preblastic phase. K-f = K-feldspar, Q-r = recrystallised quartz. Melca-Guba Granite, South Ethiopia. With crossed nicols; enlargement 20 x.

Fig. 147. (Detail of Fig. 146.) K-feldspar megablast in contact with corroded and myrmekitised plagioclase of the preblastic ground-mass (palaeosoma). Pl = Plagioclase, Qu.M = Myrmekitic quartz, K-f = K-feldspar. With crossed nicols; enlargement 100 x.

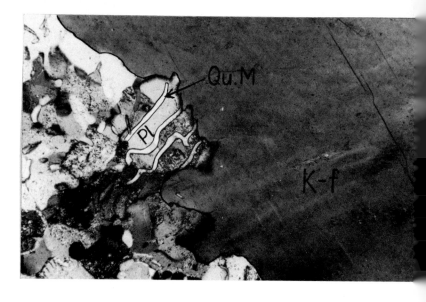

Fig. 148. K-feldspar megablast including and in contact with components of a xenolith. A plagioclase of the xenolith is partly corroded and myrmekitised by the younger K-feldspar of the granite. Naxos Granite, Greece. With crossed nicols; enlargement 50 x.

Fig. 149. Plagioclase included in K-feldspar and showing an outline due to corrosion. Myrmekitisation occurs only in a restricted part of the plagioclase margin. Arrow indicates an apophysis of the K-feldspar (most probably due to orientation of the section). K-f = K-feldspar, Pl = Plagioclase, myr = myrmekitisation. Didessa Granite, Ethiopia. With crossed nicols; enlargement 100 x.

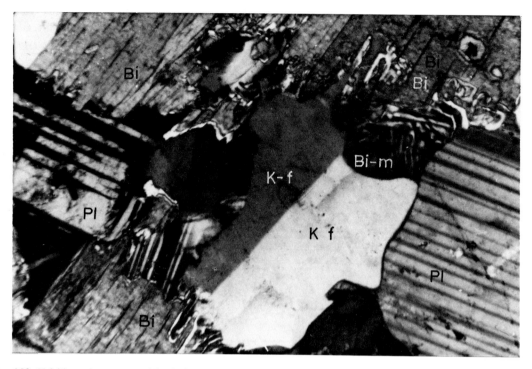

Fig. 150. K-feldspar in contact with plagioclase (corroded but not myrmekitised) and with biotite extensively myrmekitised. K-f = K-feldspar, Pl = plagioclase, Bi-m = myrmekitised biotite, Bi = biotite. Augite syenite at Groba, Saxony, Germany. With crossed nicols; enlargement 100 x.

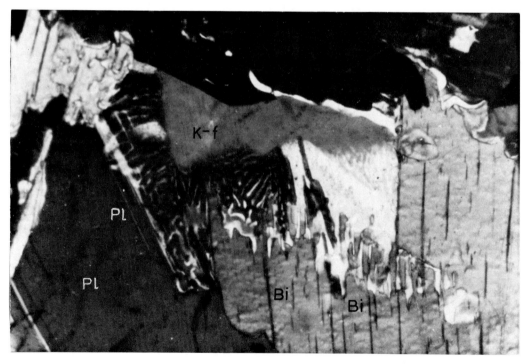

Fig. 151. K-feldspar in synantectic contact with both biotite and plagioclase. Both the plagioclase and the biotite in contact with the orthoclase are corroded and myrmekitised. K-f = K-feldspar, Pl = plagioclase, Bi = biotite. Augite syenite at Groba, Saxony, Germany. With crossed nicols; enlargement 100 x.

160

Fig. 152. U- and Y-shaped myrmekitic quartz in plagioclase surrounded (in contact) by a later K-feldspar (in the extinction position). K-f = K-feldspar, m-q = myrmekitic quartz. Norra Granite, Udde, Sweden. With crossed nicols; enlargement 100 x.

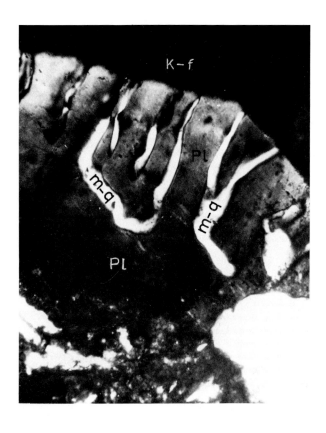

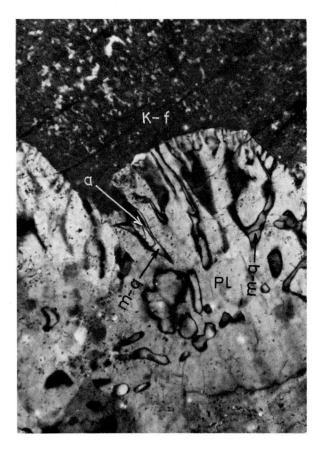

Fig. 153. Arrow "a" shows a transitional stage in the process of replacement of the plagioclase part between a V-shaped myrmekitic quartz body. An intermediate stage between the cases indicated in Fig. 152 and 154. Pl = plagioclase, K-f = K-feldspar, m-q = myrmekitic quartz. Port d'Oo Granite, Pyrenees, France. With crossed nicols; enlargement 100 x.

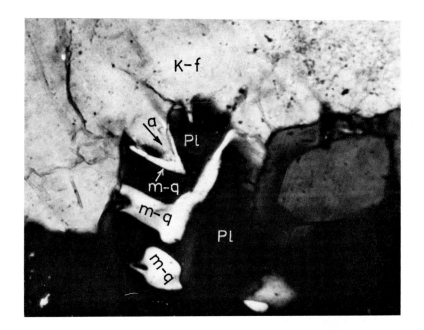

Fig. 154. Myrmekitised plagioclase surrounded and corroded by later K-feldspar. Arrow "a" indicates the part of the K-feldspar which corroded and replaced the plagioclase that was originally between the V-shaped myrmekitic quartz. K-f = K-feldspar, Pl = plagioclase in the extinction position, m-q = myrmekitic quartz. Fitchburg Granite, Mass., U.S.A. With crossed nicols; enlargement 100 x.

Fig. 155. Myrmekitised plagioclase partly surrounded and corroded by later K-feldspar. Arrow "a" indicates corrosion and replacement of plagioclase by K-feldspar as a result of which myrmekitic quartz is partly freed from the plagioclase. Pl = plagioclase, K-f = K-feldspar, m-q = myrmekitic quartz. Fitchburg Granite, Mass., U.S.A. With crossed nicols; enlargement 100 x.

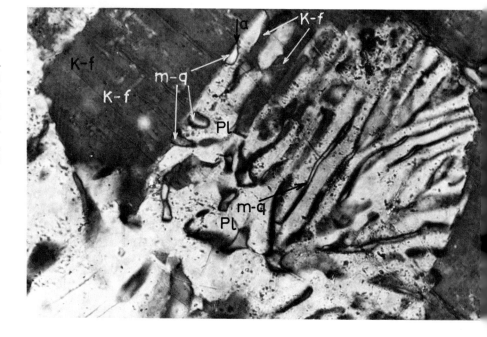

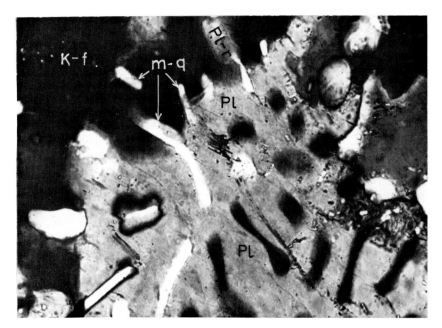

Fig. 156. Myrmekitised plagioclase partly surrounded and corroded by K-feldspar (in the extinction position). Due to the myrmekitised corrosion by a later K-feldspar relic, parts of the plagioclase and partly freed quartz myrmekitic bodies are laying in the K-feldspar. Pl = plagioclase, K–f = K-feldspar, Pl-r = plagioclase relic in K-feldspar, m-q = myrmekitic quartz bodies freed from myrmekite and laying in the K-feldspar. Val Rusein Granite, Switzerland. With crossed nicols; enlargement 250 x.

162

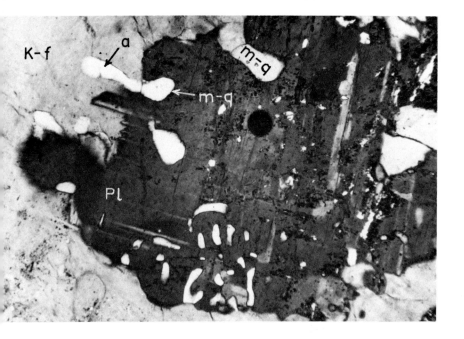

Fig. 157. Plagioclase myrmekitised and corroded by later K-feldspar. Due to the corrosion of the already myrmekitised plagioclase, quartz–myrmekitic bodies are partly freed and protrude into the K-feldspar (see arrow "a"). Pl = plagioclase, K-f = K-feldspar, m-q = myrmekitic quartz. Fitchburg Granite, Mass., U.S.A. With crossed nicols; enlargement 100 x.

Fig. 158. Plagioclase (in the extinction position) corroded and replaced by later K-feldspar. Myrmekitic quartz which was originally in intergrowth with the plagioclase is freed and now entirely surrounded by K-feldspar. K-f = K-feldspar, q = quartz, m-q = myrmekitic quartz. Didessa Granite, West Ethiopia. With crossed nicols, enlargement 100 x.

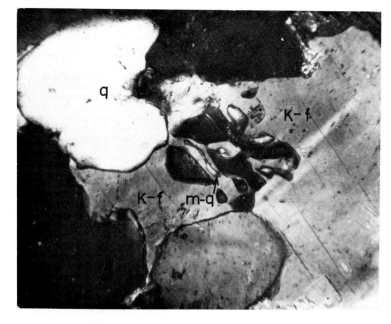

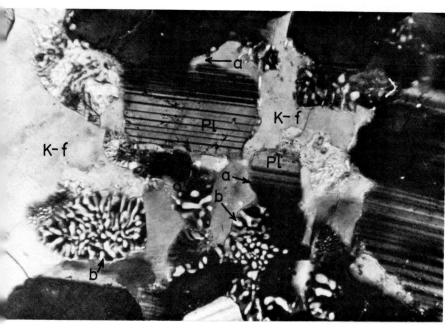

Fig. 159. Plagioclase corroded by later K-feldspar. The orthoclase partly encloses, partly infiltrates and replaces the plagioclase. The myrmekitisation of the plagioclase is related with the later K-feldspar infiltration and reaction effects. Arrow "a" shows corrosion outline of plagioclase; arrow "b" shows myrmekitised plagioclase contact, Pl = plagioclase, K-f = K-feldspar. Hornblende syenite at Berosowsks, Denejkin, Kamen, U.S.S.R. With crossed nicols; enlargement 100 x.

Fig. 160. Myrmekitised plagioclase partly surrounded and corroded by later K-feldspar. Arrow "a" shows K-feldspar extending into the plagioclase; arrow "b" shows K-feldspar in the plagioclase and in this case it is probably an extension of the K-feldspar in the plagioclase. Pl = plagioclase, K-f = K-feldspar, q = quartz. Hornblende syenite at Berosowsks, Denejkin, Kamen, Ural, U.S.S.R. With crossed nicols; enlargement 100 x.

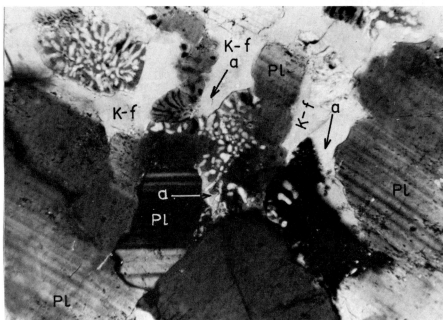

Fig. 161. Plagioclase crystal grains partly surrounded, infiltrated and corroded and myrmekitised by later K-feldspar. Arrow "a" shows K-feldspar extending intergranularly between crystal grains of plagioclase. Pl = plagioclase, K-f = K-feldspar. Hornblende syenite at Berosowsks, Denejkin, Kamen, Ural, U.S.S.R. With crossed nicols; enlargement 100 x.

Fig. 162. K-feldspar infiltrating intergranularly between plagioclase crystal grains partly replacing the plagioclase and freeing myrmekitic quartz grains. Pl = plagioclase, K-f = K-feldspar, m-q = myrmekitic quartz. Hornblende syenite at Berosowsks, Denejkin, Kamen, Ural, U.S.S.R. With crossed nicols; enlargement 250 x.

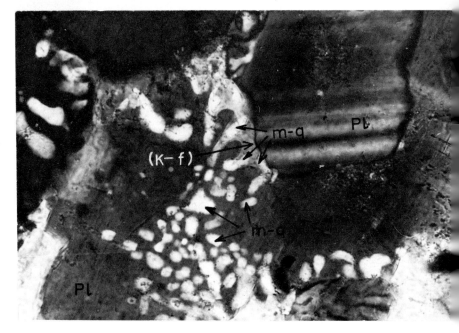

164

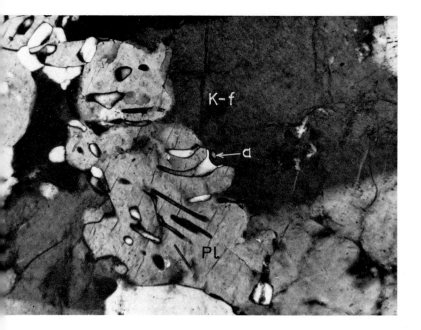

Fig. 163. Myrmekitised and corroded plagioclase in contact with K-feldspar. Due to the corrosion by the later K-feldspar of an already formed myrmekite (plagioclase with quartz worm-like bodies), parts of the quartz worm-like bodies are freed and are now present in the K-feldspar. Arrow "a" indicates quartz worm-like part in K-feldspar. Pl = plagioclase, K-f = K-feldspar. Fitchburg Granite, Mass., U.S.A. With crossed nicols; enlargement 100 x.

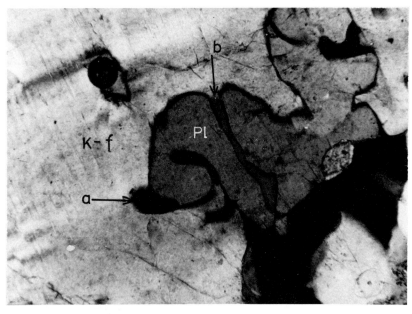

Fig. 164. Myrmekitised plagioclase corroded by the later K-feldspar. Myrmekitic quartz body acts as a delimiting margin to the corrosion of the myrmekite (see arrow "a"). Due to K-feldspar corrosion a worm-like quartz body is partly corroded (see arrow "b"). Pl = plagioclase, K-f = K-feldspar. Fitchburg Granite, Mass, U.S.A. With crossed nicols; enlargement 100 x.

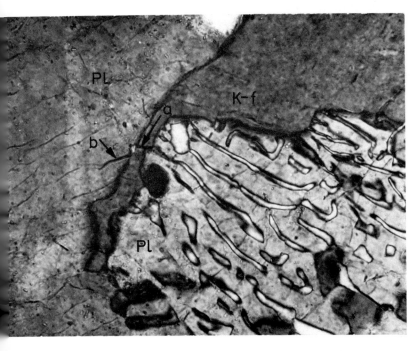

Fig. 165. Myrmekitised plagioclase with an apophysis of protruding K-feldspar replacing the plagioclase. However, a worm-like myrmekitic body is left in the K-feldspar (see arrow "a"). It can be seen that myrmekitic quartz is associated with a crack system in the plagioclase (also arrow "b"). K-f = K-feldspar, Pl = plagioclase. Port d'Oo, Granite, Pyrenees, France. With crossed nicols; enlargement 250 x.

165

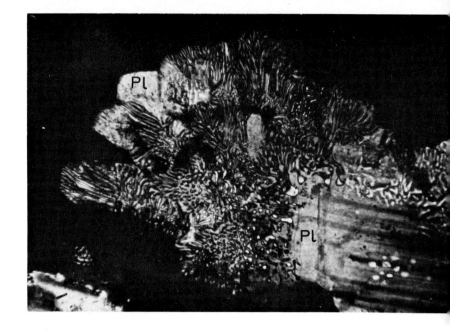

Fig. 166. Plagioclase surrounded by K-feld-spar (in the extinction position). Both extensively myrmekitised and quartz free parts of the plagioclase are shown. Pl = plagioclase. Hornblende syenite at Berosowsks, Denejkin, Kamen, Ural, U.S.S.R. With crossed nicols; enlargement 100 x.

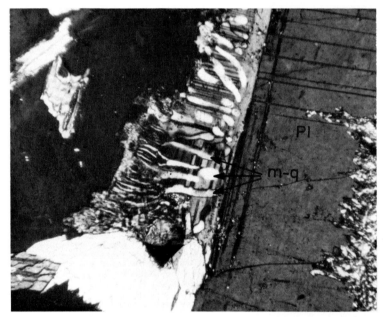

Fig. 167 and 168. Plagioclase in contact with K-feldspar (in the extinction position). Fine quartz canals unite forming wider canals and penetrating the plagioclase perpendicular to the direction of the twin lamellae. Arrow "a" indicates the influence exercised on the wall of the myrmekitic quartz canal by the pre-existing plagioclase twinning. Pl = plagioclase, m-q = myrmekitic quartz. Hornblende granite at Laudenbach, Vosges. With crossed nicols; enlargements 100 x, 250 x.

Fig. 168.

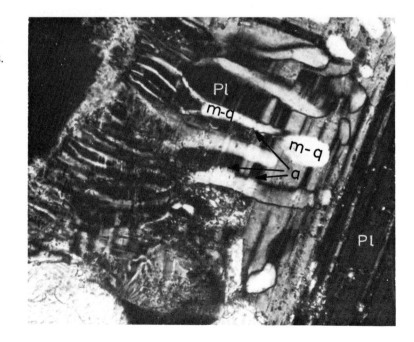

166

Fig.169 and 170. Twinned plagioclase myrmekitised. The shape of the myrmekitic quartz
body is influenced by the presence of a plagioclase
twin lamellae. Arrow indicates influence of twinning on the shape of the quartz myrmekite.
Ragunda Granite, Sweden. With crossed nicols; enlargements 100 x, 250 x.

Fig. 170.

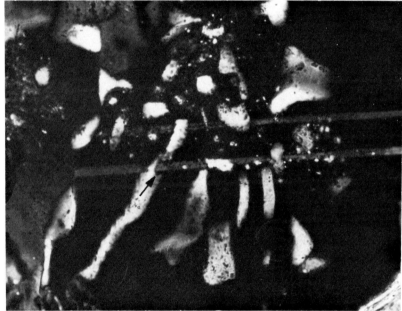

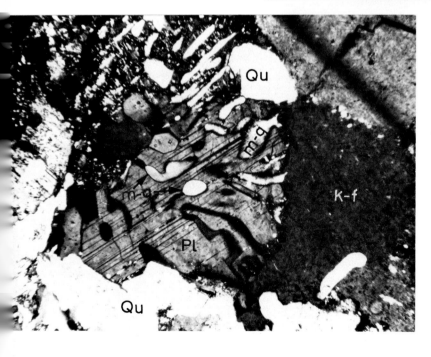

Fig. 171 and 172. Myrmekitised plagioclase in contact with K-feldspar and quartz. Myrmekitoid
quartz bodies (arrow "a") partly assimilating the
plagioclase (see Fig. 172). Pl = plagioclase, Qu =
quartz, K-f = K-feldspar, m-q = myrmekitoid
quartz. Wallbach Granite, Odenwald, Germany.
With crossed nicols; enlargements 100 x, 250 x.

Fig. 172.

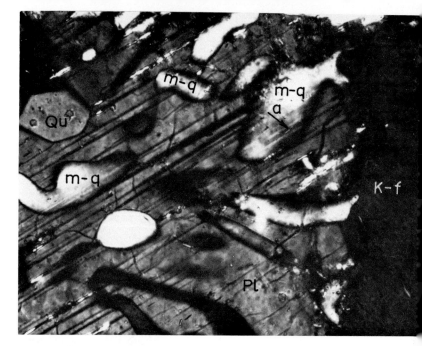

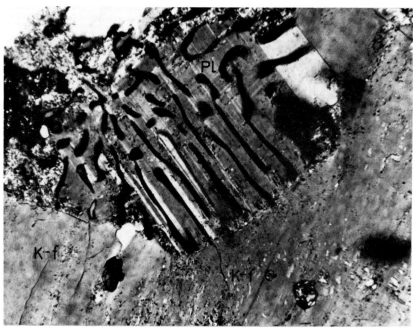

Fig. 173. Myrmekitised plagioclase partly surrounded by K-feldspar. The quartz myrmekitic bodies (in the extinction position) partly follow the plagioclase twinning and partly are orientated perpendicular to it, penetrating twin lamellae. Pl = plagioclase, K-f = K-feldspar. Wallbach Granite, Odenwald, Germany. With crossed nicols; enlargement 100 x.

Fig. 174. Myrmekitised plagioclase, with a fine reaction margin, is surrounded by K-feldspar (in the extinction position). Curved myrmekitic quartz bodies and rhabdites are indicated. Pl = plagioclase, r-m =reaction margin. Justila Granite, Saimakanal, Finland. With crossed nicols; enlargement 100 x.

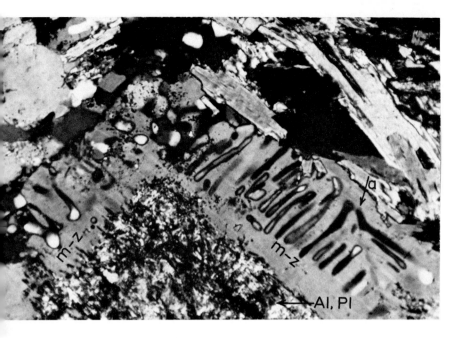

Fig. 175. Myrmekitised plagioclase with its central part greatly altered. Quartz rhabdites are arranged perpendicular to the margin of the plagioclase. Arrow "a" shows rhabdites forming a right angle. The myrmekitised outer zone of the plagioclase differs in composition from the altered central part. Al.Pl = altered plagioclase, m-z = myrmekitised outer plagioclase zone. Melibokus Granite, Odenwald, Germany. With crossed nicols; enlargement 100 x.

Fig. 176. Twinned plagioclase myrmekitised and surrounded by K-feldspar. Quartz rhabdites (myrmekitic quartz rods) and myrmekitised bodies are present in the plagioclase following different orientation. Hornblende granite at Laudenbach, Vosges. With crossed nicols; enlargement 100 x.

Fig. 177. Myrmekitised plagioclase in the extinction position surrounded by K-feldspar. Rhabdites (myrmekitic quartz rods) are also shown. K-F = K-feldspar. Fitchburg Granite, Mass., U.S.A With crossed nicols; enlargement 100 x.

169

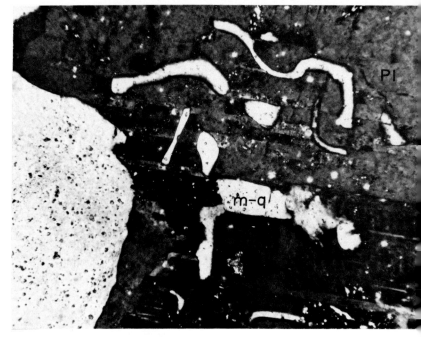

Fig. 178. Plagioclase twinned and myrmekitised. The relation of the myrmekitic quartz to the plagioclase twinning is most variable. The same myrmekitic quartz body can be seen partly following the twinning and partly extending perpendicular to it. Pl = plagioclase, m-q = myrmekitic quartz (parallel and transversing the plagioclase twinning). Hanga Granite, Finland. With crossed nicols; enlargement 100 x.

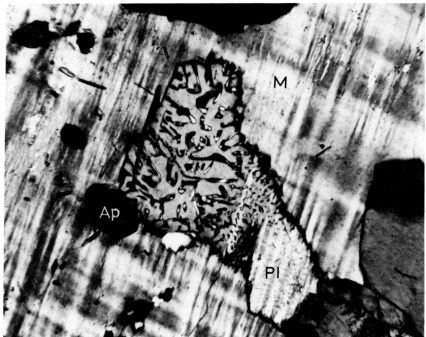

Fig. 179. Microcline surrounding myrmekitised plagioclase. The myrmekitic quartz tends to follow two main planes of orientation within the plagioclase. One parallel to the plane of the section, the other perpendicular (fine circles indicate cross-sections of myrmekitic quartz canals). Pl = plagioclase, M = microcline, Ap = apatite. Harrar Granite, Ethiopia. With crossed nicols; enlargement 100 x.

Fig. 180. Myrmekitised plagioclase with myrmekitic quartz in the extinction position including a myrmekitic quartz differently orientated (see arrow "a"). Pl = plagioclase, m-q = myrmekitic quartz. Fitchburg Granite, Mass., U.S.A. With crossed nicols; enlargement 100 x.

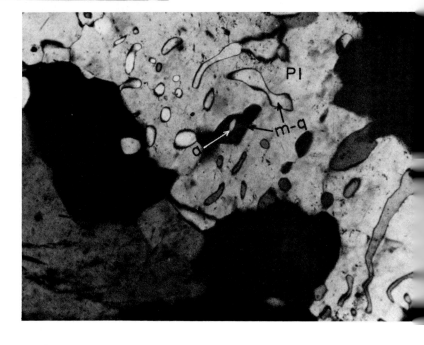

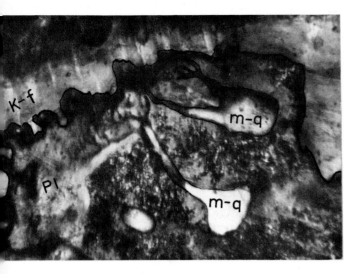

Fig. 181. Plagioclase corroded and partly surrounded by K-feldspar. Fine quartz canals unite and finally form a myrmekitoid quartz body. K-f = K-feldspar, Pl = plagioclase, m-q = myrmekitoid quartz body. Didessa Granite, West Ethiopia. With crossed nicols; enlargement 250 x.

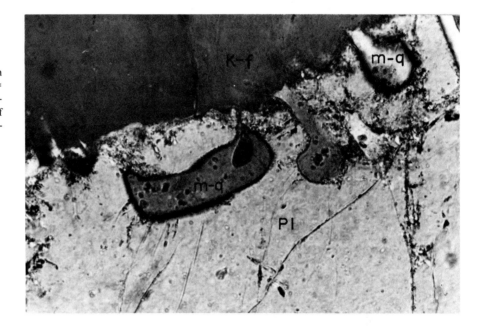

Fig. 182. Myrmekitoid quartz bodies in plagioclase in contact with K-feldspar. K-f = K-feldspar, Pl = plagioclase, m-q = myrmekitoid quartz. Granite southwest of Torn, Sweden. With crossed nicols; enlargement 250 x.

Fig. 183. K-feldspar in contact with myrmekitised plagioclase. Also quartz grain with an extension into plagioclase attaining a myrmekitoid form. K-f = K-feldspar, Pl = plagioclase, Qu = quartz. Granite at Aberdeen, Scotland. With crossed nicols; enlargement 100 x.

171

Fig. 184. Plagioclase myrmekitised and transversed by a quartz which extends in the plagioclase and attains a myrmekitic form. K-f = K-feldspar, Pl = plagioclase, Qu = quartz transversing the plagioclase and attaining myrmekitic form. Wallbach Granite, Odenwald, Germany. With crossed nicols; enlargement 100 x.

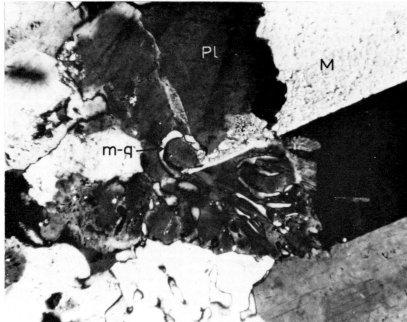

Fig. 185 and 186. Plagioclase texturally associated with mica (biotite) and having quartz myrmekitic bodies. Note a quartz myrmekite attaining a ring-like structure. Pl = plagioclase, m-q = myrmekitic quartz, M = mica. Gneis at Aar, Switzerland. With crossed nicols; enlargements 100 x, 200 x.

Fig. 186.

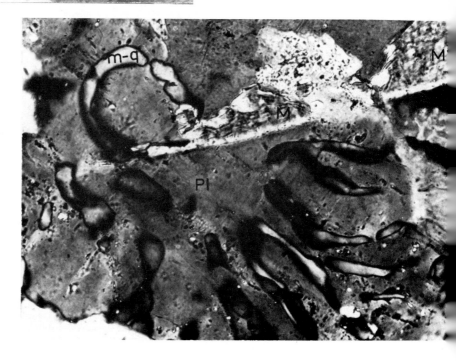

Fig. 187. Myrmekitised plagioclase; fine quartz canals uniting and forming myrmekitic quartz. Arrow "a" indicates an "egg-like" quartz body in association with myrmekite. Didessa Granite, Ethiopia. With crossed nicols; enlargement 100 x.

Fig. 188.

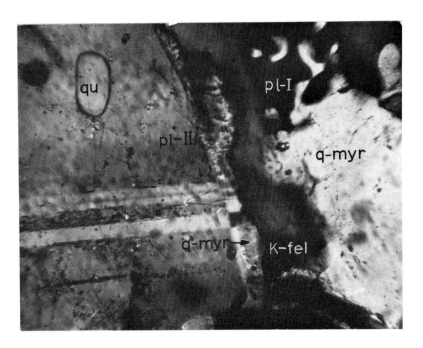

Fig. 188 and 189. Blastic plagioclase (generation II) including pre-blastic quartz (palaeosoma) is with a reaction margin (myrmekitised and showing reversing of twinning) in contact with K-feldspar. The K-feldspar in turn is in contact with a myrmekitised plagioclase (generation I) —(a pre-blastic component of the palaeosoma). pl-I = plagioclase (generation I), pl-II = plagioclase (generation II), q-myr = myrmekitic quartz, K-fel = K-feldspar. Didessa Granite, West Ethiopia. With crossed nicols; enlargement 100 x.

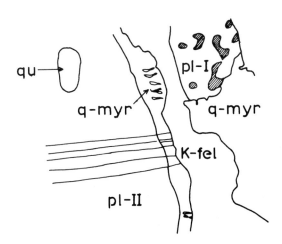

173

Fig. 190. Plagioclase with a myrmekitised marginal zone (no reversing of the plagioclase twinning in the reaction zone is indicated). Pl = plagioclase, M = microcline. Bautsen Granite, Saxony, Germany. With crossed nicols; enlargement 100 x.

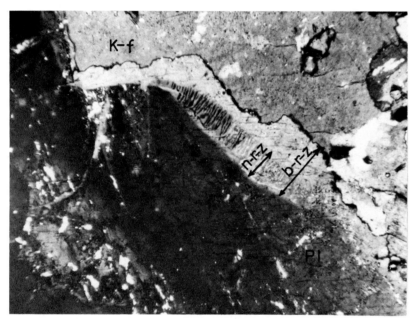

Fig. 191. Plagioclase in contact with K-feldspar. A broader reaction zone characterises the contact of the plagioclase with the K-feldspar. Within this reaction zone a narrower zone is distinguished which is myrmekitised. Pl = plagioclase, K-f = K-feldspar, b-r-z = broad reaction zone, n-r-z = narrow reaction zone with myrmekitic quartz. Baveno Granite, Italy. With crossed nicols; enlargement 100 x.

Fig. 192. Plagioclase in contact with K-feldspar. A reaction zone (dark margin of plagioclase, i.e., in the extinction position) is extending only half-way of the myrmekitisation border of the plagioclase. Pl = plagioclase, K-f = K-feldspar. Baveno Granite, Italy. With crossed nicols; enlargement 100 x.

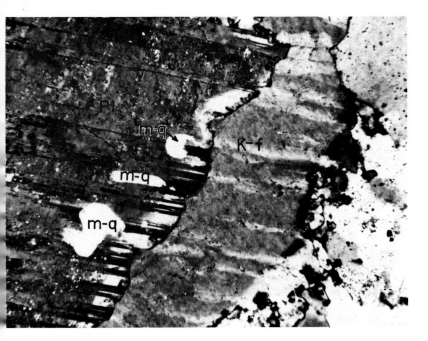

Fig. 193. Plagioclase with a reaction zone indicating reversing of twinning; myrmekitic quartz rhabdites and worm-like bodies are present in the plagioclase immediately after the reaction zone. Pl = plagioclase, K-f = K-feldspar, m-q = myrmekitic quartz. Hanga Granite, Finland. With crossed nicols; enlargement 100 x.

Fig. 194. Plagioclase with a reaction margin in contact with K-feldspar. Myrmekitic quartz is present in the inner margin of the reaction zone. Pl = plagioclase, K-f = K-feldspar, m-q = myrmekitic quartz. Granite at Mt. Mulatto, Tirol, Italy. With crossed nicols; enlargement 100 x.

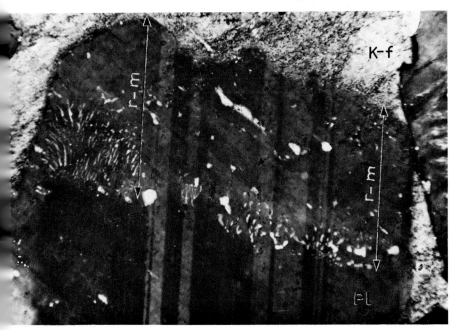

Fig. 195. Plagioclase with a broad reaction margin in contact with surrounding K-feldspar. Myrmekitic quartz is mainly present in the inner part of the reaction margin. Pl = plagioclase, r-m = reaction margin of plagioclase, K-f = K-feldspar. Buchwald Granite, Silesia, Germany.

175

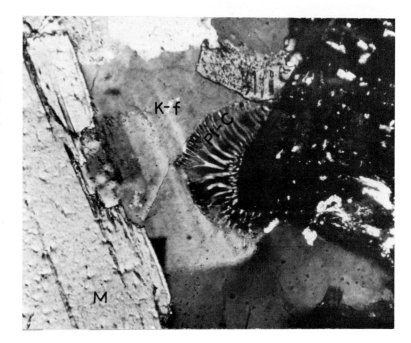

Fig. 196. K-feldspar in contact with plagioclase with a corona margin myrmekitised by fine quartz canals. K-f = K-feldspar, Pl-C = myrmekitised plagioclase corona, M = mica. Bautzen Granite, Saxony, Germany, With crossed nicols; enlargement 100 x.

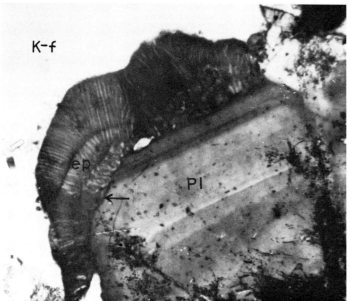

Fig. 197. Zoned plagioclase with an "epiphysis" extensively myrmekitised. Arrow shows the discordance between the zoned plagioclase and the epiphysis. Pl = plagioclase, K-f = K-feldspar, ep = epiphysis. Harrar Granite, Ethiopia. With crossed nicols; enlargement 100 x.

Fig. 198. Plagioclase myrmekitised and with a fine reaction margin surrounded by a later K-feldspar (in the extinction position). Pl = plagioclase, m-q = myrmekitised quartz, r-m = reaction margin of plagioclase. Harrar Granite, Ethiopia. With crossed nicols; enlargement 100 x.

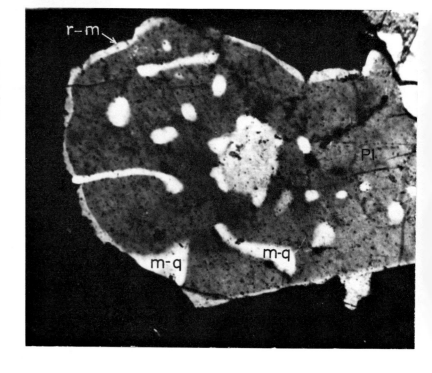

Fig. 199. Plagioclase with a margin of myrmekite. Pl = plagioclase, m-m = myrmekitised margin of plagioclase. Voigtsbach
Granite, Reichenbach, Bohemia. With
crossed nicols; enlargement 100 x.

Fig. 200. Plagioclase with a zonal structure. Myrmekitic quartz restricted in the outer plagioclase
zone and partly following the zonal margin. Pl =
plagioclase, K-f = K-feldspar. Harrar Granite,
Ethiopia. With crossed nicols; enlargement 100 x.

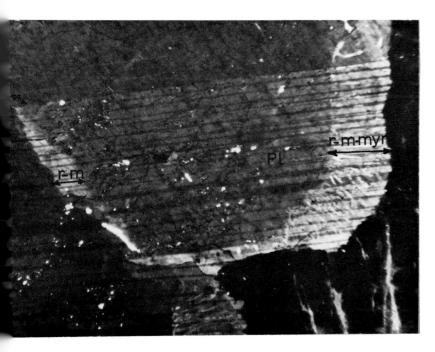

Fig. 201. Plagioclase in contact with K-feldspar indicates a reaction margin and is myrmekitised. The same plagioclase grain in
contact with another plagioclase is again
showing a reaction margin which is not myrmekitised. Pl = plagioclase, r-m = reaction
margin without myrmekite, r-m-myr = reaction margin myrmekitised. Buchwald
Granite, Silesia, Germany. With crossed
nicols; enlargement 100 x.

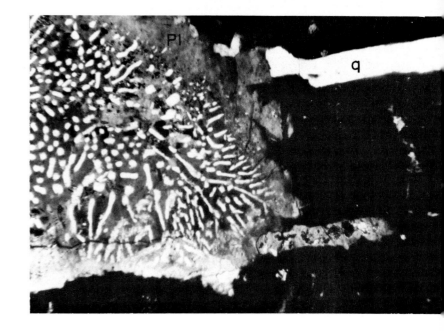

Fig. 202. Plagioclase with corroded margin included in K-feldspar. Myrmekitised quartz is present in the central part of the plagioclase, the marginal zone of which is mainly free of myrmekitic quartz. A quartz veinlet is present in the K-feldspar. Pl = plagioclase, q = quartz, K-feldspar in the extinction position. Wehmo Granite, Nystad, Helsingfors, Finland. With crossed nicols; enlargement 100 x.

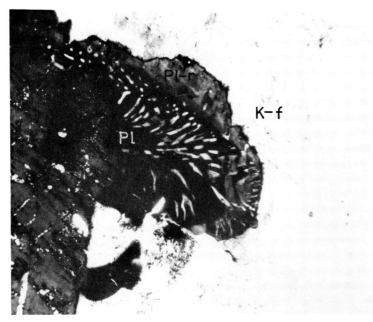

Fig. 203. Plagioclase with a reaction margin corroded and partly included by K-feldspar. Myrmekitic quartz is mainly present in the unaffected part of the plagioclase. Pl = plagioclase, Pl-r = plagioclase reaction margin, K-f = K-feldspar. Sornas Granite, Helsingfors, Finland. With crossed nicols; enlargement 100 x.

Fig. 204. Zoned plagioclase in contact with K-feldspars. Marginal myrmekitisation of the plagioclase has taken place with the worm-like quartz bodies extending from the outer margin inwards, and, when reaching a certain zonal "Wegsamkeit" penetrability, run parallel to the plagioclase zoning. K-f = K-feldspar, Pl = plagioclase, Qu = quartz. Didessa Granite, Ethiopia. With crossed nicols; enlargement 100 x.

178

Fig. 205. Microcline in contact with plagioclase showing a reaction margin with reversing of twinning and myrmekitisation. Bautzen Granite, Saxony, Germany. With crossed nicols; enlargement 100 x.

Fig. 206 and 207. Plagioclase with a reaction margin indicating reversing of twinning and myrmekitised. Pl = plagioclase, K-f = K-feldspar. Buchwald Granite, Silesia, Germany. With crossed nicols; enlargement 100 x.

Fig. 207.

179

Fig. 208. K-feldspar (microcline) in contact with plagioclase. The plagioclase shows a reaction margin with a small distortion and reversing of the twinning. In the plagioclase reaction margin fine myrmekitic quartz is present. K-f = K-feldspar, r-m = reaction margin, m = mica, Pl = plagioclase. Bautzen Granite, Saxony, Germany. With crossed nicols; enlargement 100 x.

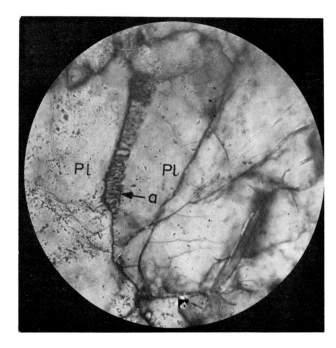

Fig. 209. Plagioclase with cracks. Fine myrmekitic worm-like bodies extend from a crack into the plagioclase. Pl = plagioclase, arrow "a" shows myrmekitic bodies. Naxos Granite, Greece. With crossed nicols; enlargement 100 x.

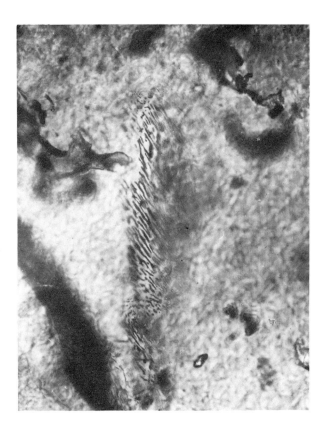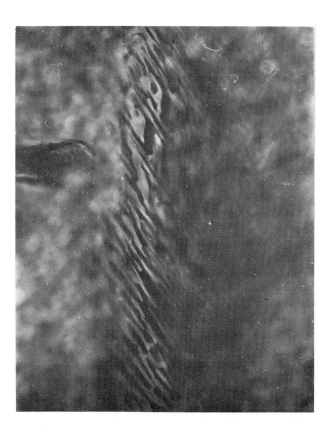

Fig. 210 and 211. Myrmekitic-like infiltration canals (of unknown composition) present in augite, in an olivine basalt from Batie/Dessie, Ethiopia. With crossed nicols; enlargements 600 x, 1200 x.

Fig. 212 and 213. Plagioclase with twinning and cleavage infilitrated by myrmekitoid quartz canals. The shape of the quartz body is restricted by cleavage margins (see arrow "a"). Pl = plagioclase, m-q = myrmekitoid quartz. Pegmatoid at Carrara, Giggiga, Ethiopia. With crossed nicols; enlargements 50 x, 100 x.

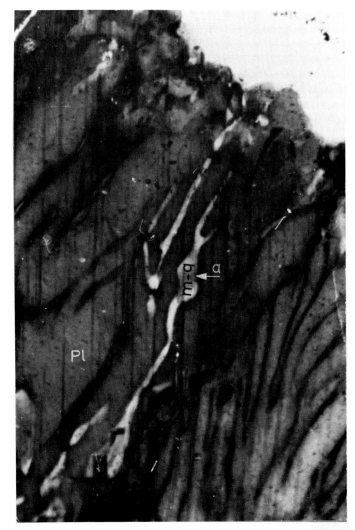

Fig. 213.

Fig. 214. Quartz associated with plagioclase sending protuberances into the feldspar attaining quartz myrmekitic character. Qu = Quartz, Pl = plagioclase, M = muscovite. Pegmatoid at Carrara, Giggiga, Ethiopia. With crossed nicols; enlargement 100 x.

Fig. 215. Plagioclase with muscovite. A muscovite lath is associated with the plagioclase. Quartz is associated with the muscovite and extends (as myrmekitoid infiltrations) in the muscovite lath included in the plagioclase. Pl = plagioclase, M = muscovite, Qu = quartz. Pegmatoid at Carrara, Giggiga, Ethiopia. With crossed nicols; enlargement 100 x.

Fig. 216. (Detail of Fig. 215.) Plagioclase with muscovite lath. Quartz has infiltrated into and partly replaced the mica and is extending between the cleavage of the plagioclase (see arrow). Pl = plagioclase, M = muscovite, Qu = quartz. With crossed nicols; enlargement 200 x.

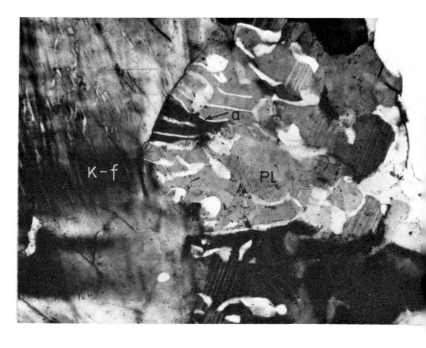

Fig. 217 and 218. Myrmekitised plagioclase in contact with K-feldspar. Arrow "a" indicates myrmekitic quartz following the junction of parts of the plagioclase differently orientated. Infiltration of myrmekitic quartz-forming solutions along the junction of plagioclase parts. Pl = plagioclase, K-f = K-feldspar, m-q = myrmekitic quartz. Fitchburg Granite, Mass., U.S.A. With crossed nicols; enlargements 100 x, 250 x.

Fig. 218.

184

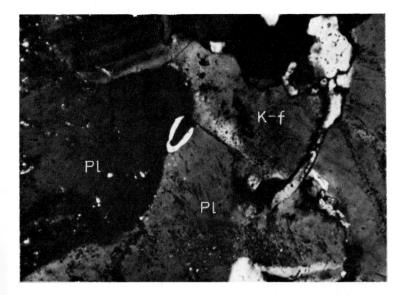

Fig. 219. Two plagioclase crystal grains with a U-shaped myrmekitic quartz. Whereas the one "leg" of the U-shaped myrmekitic quartz body is in the one plagioclase, the other follows the margin between the two plagioclases. Pl = plagioclase, K-f = K-feldspar. Bollstein Granite, Odenwald, Germany. With crossed nicols; enlargement 100 x.

Fig. 220. Myrmekitised plagioclase in contact with biotite. A quartz myrmekitic body extends in the plagioclase and when it comes in contact with the biotite it extends parallel to the contact of the two minerals. Pl = plagioclase, m-q = myrmekitic quartz, Bi = biotite. Wallbach Granite, Odenwald, Germany. With crossed nicols; enlargement 100 x.

Fig. 221. Special myrmekitic intergrowths of worm-like quartz bodies in biotite. There is a tendency of the myrmekitic quartz to follow the mica's cleavage. This myrmekitic quartz/biotite intergrowth is not a synantetic reaction, but rather due to the infiltration of quartz-forming solutions into the biotite. Augite syenite at Groba, Saxony, Germany. With crossed nicols; enlargement 100 x.

Fig. 222. Quartz myrmekite in biotite along its contact with K-feldspar. Bi = biotite, Zr = zircon, K-f = K-feldspar. Stoa Granite, Norway. With crossed nicols; enlargement 100 x.

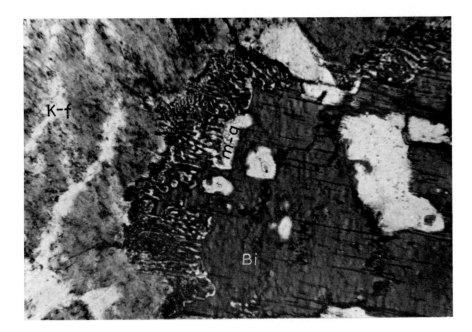

Fig. 223. K-feldspar in contact with myrmekitised biotite. K-f = K-feldspar, Bi = biotite, m-q = myrmekitic quartz. Stoa Granite, Norway. With crossed nicols; enlargement 100 x.

Fig. 224. Plagioclase and biotite both myrmekitised. Bi = biotite, Pl = plagioclase, m-q = myrmekitic quartz, K-f = K-feldspar. Tromm Granite, Furth, Odenwald, Germany. With crossed nicols; enlargement 100 x.

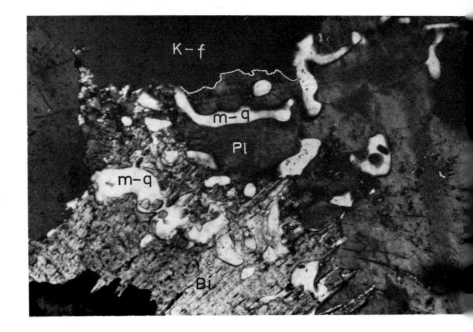

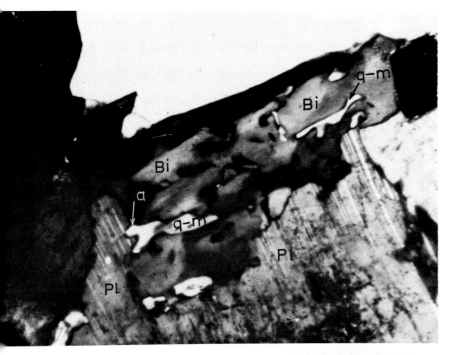

Fig. 225. Plagioclase in junction with biotite. Myrmekitoid quartz bodies are present in the biotite and one is intergrown with biotite and plagioclase. Bi = biotite, Pl = plagioclase, q-m = quartz myrmekitoid. Arrow "a" indicates myrmekitoid quartz transversing the boundary plagioclase/biotite. Kaptensgrube Granite, Gellivara, Sweden. With crossed nicols; enlargement 100 x.

Fig. 226. Myrmekitised biotite in contact with microcline. Bi = biotite, Mi = microcline. Granite at Aberdeen, Scotland. With crossed nicols; enlargement 100 x.

Fig. 227. Quartz marginal to biotite extends into the mica attaining myrmekitic forms. Qu = quartz, Bi = biotite. Tromm Granite, Furth, Odenwald, Germany. With crossed nicols; enlargement 100 x.

Fig. 228. Biotite surrounded by sericitised K-feldspar. Marginal quartz extends in the mica attaining myrmekitic intergrowth form. K-f = K-feldspar, Bi = biotite, Qu = quartz. Stoa Granite, Norway. With crossed nicols; enlargement 100 x.

Fig. 229. Biotite in contact with quartz. Quartz myrmekitic bodies are present in the mica at the contact with the quartz grain. Qu = quartz, Bi = biotite, m-q = myrmekitic quartz. Rapakivi Granite, Nystad, Finland. With crossed nicols; enlargement 100 x.

Fig. 230. Myrmekitised plagioclase entirely surrounded by later quartz. Pl = myrmekitised plagioclase, Qu = quartz. Granite at Ober-Krummhubel, Riessengebirge, Silesia, Germany. With crossed nicols; enlargement 100 x.

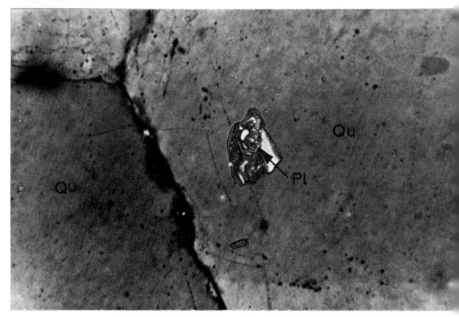

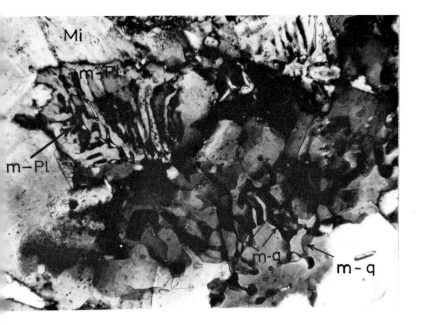

Fig. 231. K-feldspar (microcline) in contact with muscovite myrmekitised and with the quartz extending in the muscovite attaining a myrmekitoid form. Mi = microcline, m-Pl = myrmekitised plagioclase, m-q = myrmekitoid quartz in muscovite. Granite at Aberdeen, Scotland.

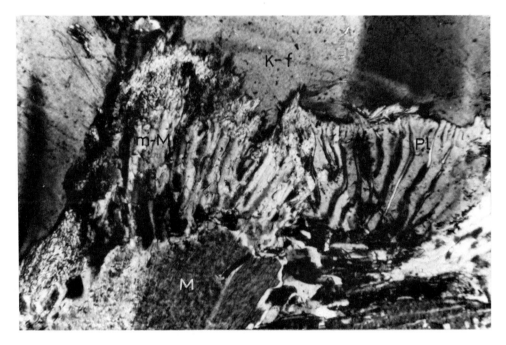

Fig. 232 and 233. K-feldspar in contact with myrmekitised plagioclase and muscovite. The muscovite shows a broad margin of reaction in which fine myrmekitic quartz bodies are present. K-f = K-feldspar, Pl = myrmekitised plagioclase, M = muscovite, m-M = myrmekitised reaction margin of muscovite. Granite at Aberdeen, Scotland. With crossed nicols; enlargement 100 x.

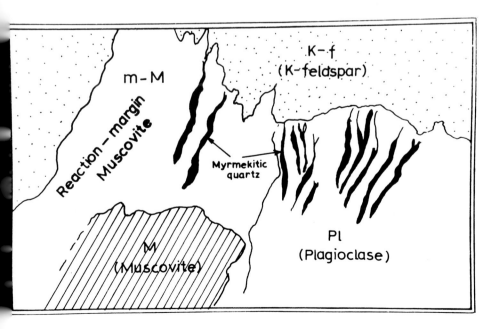

Fig. 233.

189

Fig. 234. Muscovite with marginal quartz myrmekitisation. M = muscovite, m-q = myrmekitic quartz. Bucksburn Granite, Aberdeen, Scotland. With crossed nicols; enlargement 100 x.

Fig. 235. A "sieve" -like structure of quartz with extensions into plagioclase attaining myrmekitic quartz character. Pegmatoid at Carrara, Giggiga, Ethiopia. With crossed nicols; enlargement 100 x.

Fig. 236 and 237. Part of the quartz "sieve" in contact with plagioclase. Quartz canals attaining myrmekitic character, extend from the quartz-sieve mass into the plagioclase. (No K-feldspar is present.) Pl = plagioclase, q-s = quartz sieve, q-c = quartz canal. With crossed nicols; enlargements 200 x, 400 x.

190

Fig. 237.

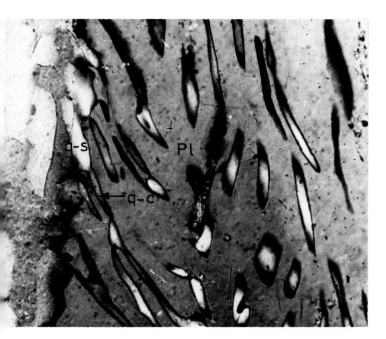

Fig. 238. Muscovite in contact with plagioclase with a myrmekitic reaction margin. Pl = plagioclase, M = muscovite. Harrar Granite, Ethiopia. With crossed nicols; enlargement 100 x.

Fig. 239. Myrmekitised epidote in contact with K-feldspar. E = epidote, K-f = K-feldspar, q = quartz. Didessa Granite, West Ethiopia. With crossed nicols; enlargement 200 x.

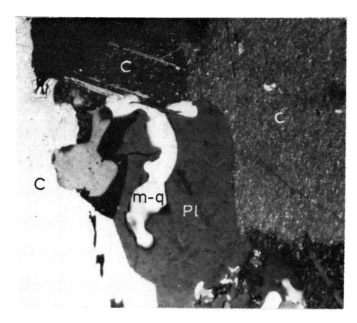

Fig. 240. Clastic plagioclase grain as a component of the coarse grained banded marble from Rukeli, Harrar, Ethiopia. The plagioclase is surrounded by calcite and a quartz myrmekitoid body extends in the feldspar partly protruding as well into the calcite (thus indicating a post-clastic-metasomatic origin of the myrmekitic quartz). C = calcite, Pl =plagioclase, m-q = myrmekitic quartz. With crossed nicols; enlargement 100 x.

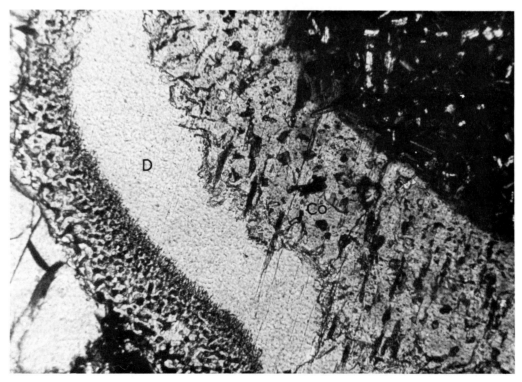

Fig. 241. Basaltic ground-mass infiltrating into a bronzite and forming a reaction corona intergrowth which simulates myrmekitic intergrowth. D = bronzite, Co = corona reaction margin. Olivine-pyroxene nodules in basalt at Nekempti, West Ethiopia. With crossed nicols; enlargement 100 x.

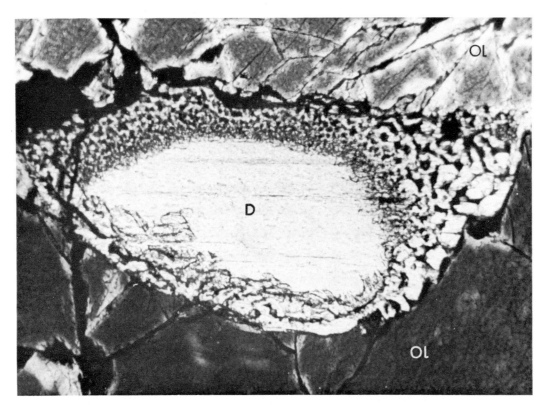

Fig. 242. Olivine infiltrated by basaltic liquid. The reaction corona structure simulates myrmekitic intergrowth. Ol = olivine, D = bronzite. Olivine-pyroxene nodules in basalt at Nekempti, West Ethiopia. With crossed nicols; enlargement 100 x.

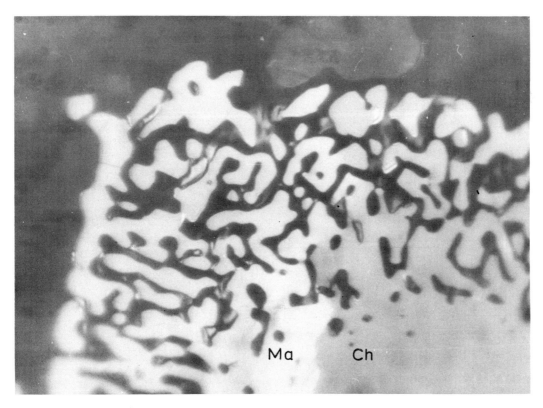

Fig. 243. Chromspinel and magnetite grain infiltrated and replaced by basaltic liquid; myrmekite-like intergrowths are thus formed. Ch = Chromspinel, Ma = magnetite. Olivine-pyroxene nodules in basalt at Nekempti, West Ethiopia, Polished section with one nicol, oil-immersion; enlargement 200 x.

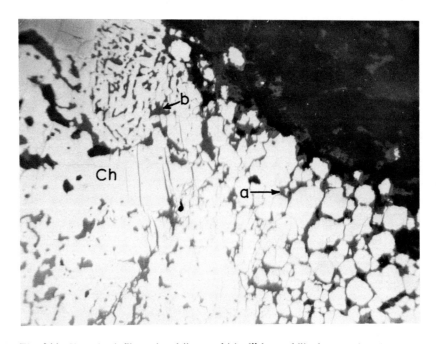

Fig. 244. Chromite infiltrated and "myrmekitised" by mobilised serpentine. Arrow "a" shows serpentine transitional from intergranular attaining myrmekitic-like inter-growth. Ch = chromite. Rodiani, Greece. Polished section; enlargement 200 x.

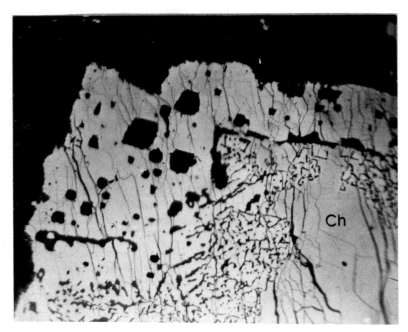

Fig. 245. Chromite with decoloration margin infiltrated and "myrmekitised" by mobilised serpentine. Ch = chromite. Rodiani, Greece. Polished section; enlargement 200 x.

Fig. 246. Quartz infiltrating into K-feldspar and attaining graphic appearance. Relics of feldspar are left in the metasomatically infiltrated quartz. Replacement process and greater penetrability of the quartz-forming solutions along certain directions of the feldspar resulted in graphic quartz intergrowths. F = feldspar, Qu = quartz, R-F = relics of feldspar in metasomatic quartz. Carrara, Giggiga, Harrar, Ethiopia. Enlargement 1½ x.

Fig. 247. Quartz vein (B) in contact with K-feldspar of a pegmatoid. In the quartz vein relics of K-feldspar (A) are present. The quartz vein extends as graphic quartz into the K-feldspars of the pegmatoid (C). Carrara, Giggiga, Harrar, Ethiopia.

Fig. 248 and 249. Quartz vein in contact with microcline of a pegmatoid. The quartz vein extends into the feldspar and eventually attains graphic quartz form and character. Qu.V = quartz vein, Qu.G = graphic quartz. Carrara, Giggiga, Harrar, Ethiopia. With crossed nicols; enlargement 4 x.

Fig. 249.

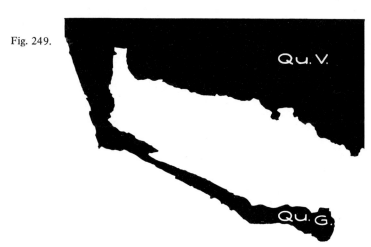

Fig. 250. Quartz vein in contact with microcline of pegmatoid. The quartz vein sends a protuberance (showing undulating extinction) in the feldspar. Perthitic veins are present in the microcline. Qu-v = quartz vein, U-Qu = Undulating quartz protuberance. Carrara, Giggiga, Harrar, Ethiopia. With crossed nicols; enlargement 10 x.

197

Fig. 251. Graphic quartz in intergrowth with K-feldspar. Extensions of the graphic quartz follow interleptonic spaces provided by the cleavage of the host K-feldspar. Qu = graphic quartz, arrow "q" graphic quartz following the interleptonic spaces of the K-feldspars cleavage, K-f = K-feldspar. Rapakivi granite, Finland. With crossed nicols; enlargement 50 x.

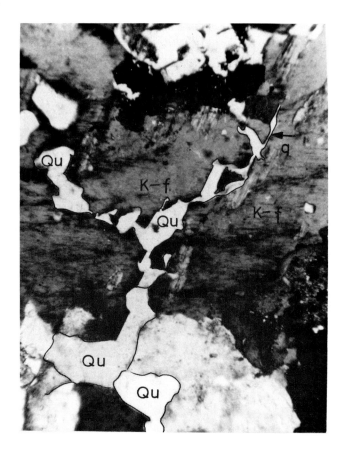

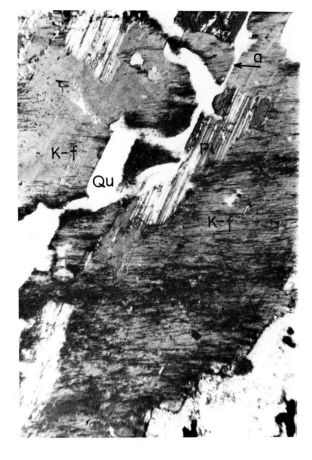

Fig. 252. (Detail of Fig. 251.) Granophyric quartz in K-feldspar. The shape of the graphic quartz is deliniated by the cleavage of the orthoclase. Also the quartz has interleptonically infiltrated into the cleavage openings (see arrow "a"). An extension of the granophyric quartz protrudes in plagioclase included in the K-feldspar. K-f = K-feldspar, Qu = granophyric quartz, Pl = plagioclase. Rapakivi granite, Wiborg, Finland. With crossed nicols; enlargement 100 x.

Fig. 253. Granophyric quartz, intergranular between K-feldspar crystal grains. $K\text{-}f_1$, $K\text{-}f_2$, $K\text{-}f_3$, $K\text{-}f_4$, $K\text{-}f_5$ = different K-feldspar crystal grains, Qu = quartz. Strathory, Ross-shire, Scotland. With crossed nicols; enlargement 100 x.

Fig. 254. Granophyric quartz, intergranular between differently orientated K-feldspar crystals. Qu = quartz, K-f = K-feldspar. Rapakivi granite, Wiborg, Finland. With crossed nicols; enlargement 100 x.

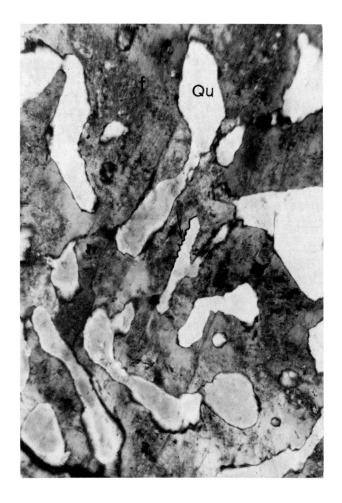

Fig. 255. Graphic quartz in K-feldspar. The quartz protrudes in the orthoclase by forming identations. Qu = quartz, f = feldspar. Strathory, Ross-shire, Scotland. With crossed nicols; enlargement 100 x.

Fig. 256. Graphic quartz with extensions (resembling indentations) into the K-feldspar. Qu = quartz, f = feldspar. Strathory, Ross-shire, Scotland. With crossed nicols; enlargement 100 x.

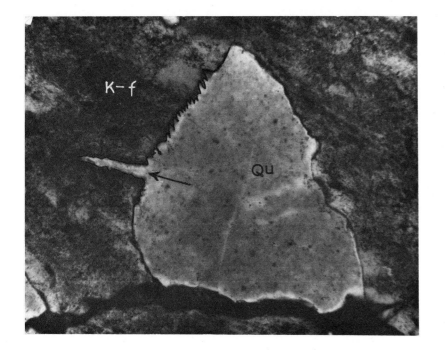

Fig. 257. Graphic quartz grain (typical in shape) with small identations following the K-feldspar cleavage. Also a quartz protuberance can be seen (marked by arrow). Qu = quartz, K-f = K-feldspar. Strathory, Ross-shire, Scotland. With crossed nicols; enlargement 100 x.

Fig. 258. Granophyric quartz in K-feldspar (in the extinction position). Quartz protuberances extending in the K-feldspar. Rapakivi granite, Finland. With crossed nicols; enlargement 100 x.

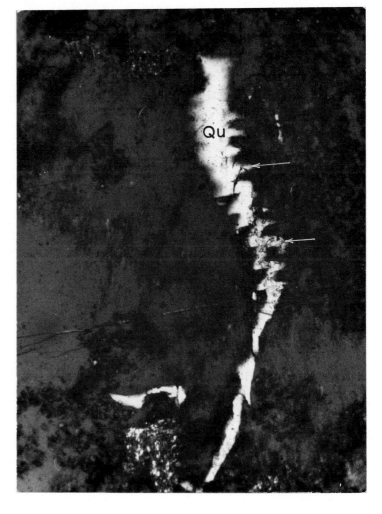

Fig. 259. Graphic quartz extending into and occupying cracks of the microcline (arrow marks graphic quartz part extending into the microcline crack). A quartz veinlet is also shown. Didessa Granite, Wollaga, West Ethiopia. Qu = quartz, M = microcline, Qu-v = quartz veinlet. With crossed nicols; enlargement 50 x.

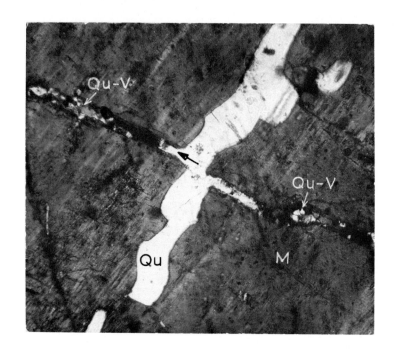

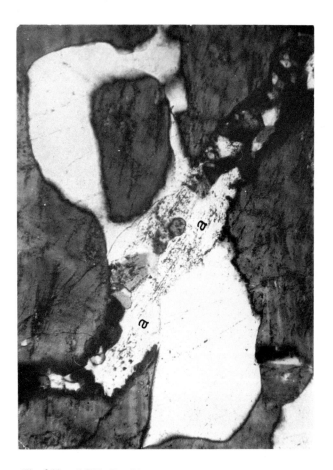

Fig. 260 and 261. Graphic quartz including and incorporating (by partial assimilation) a quartz veinlet. The parts of the graphic quartz extending into the veinlet are marked "a". The same graphic quartz in extinction position. The parts of the graphic quartz (extension in the veinlet) marked "a" in Fig. 260 as well as the main graphic quartz show the same orientation. The fine quartz grains of the veinlet are partly assimilated by the later graphic quartz and show a different orientation. Didessa Granite, Wollaga, West Ethiopia. With crossed nicols; enlargement 100 x.

202

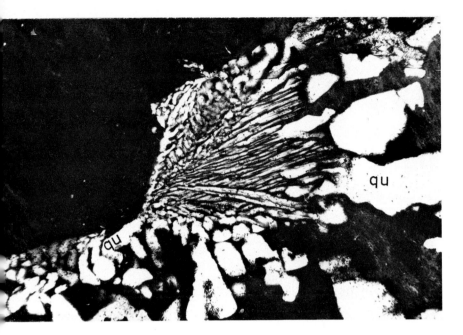

Fig. 262. K-feldspar, free of granophyric intergrowths and showing an eucrystalline outline, is surrounded by a K-feldspar zone in which granophyric quartz is intensely formed. K-feldspar (black) in the extinction position, qu = quartz. Rapakivi granite, Finland. With crossed nicols; enlargement 100 x.

Fig. 263. K-feldspar, free of graphic quartz, surrounded by a K-feldspar with graphic quartz intergrowths. A reaction margin is shown between the quartz-free K-feldspar and the outer zone with the graphic intergrowth. K-f = K-feldspar, r-z = K-feldspar reaction zone, q = graphic quartz. Bressoir Granite, Vosges. With crossed nicols; enlargement 100 x.

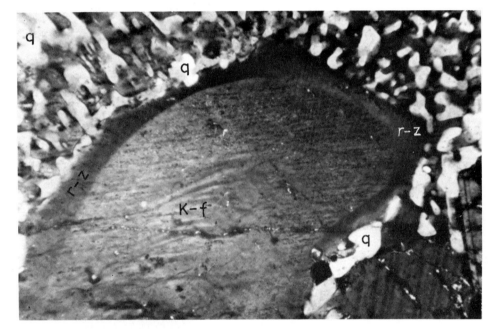

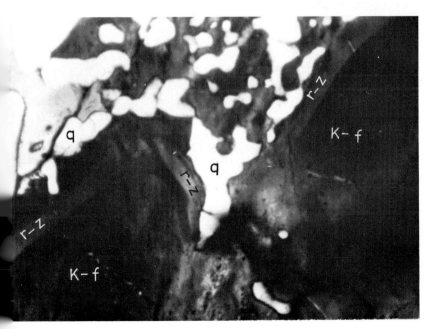

Fig. 264. (Detail of Fig. 263.) Quartz-free K-feldspar surrounded by an outer zone of K-feldspar with graphic quartz intergrowths. The reaction zone between the quartz-free K-feldspar part and outer zone (with graphic quartz) is greatly influenced by the shape of the graphic quartz. K-f = K-feldspar free of graphic quartz, r-z = reaction zone of K-feldspar, q = graphic quartz. With crossed nicols; enlargement 200 x.

203

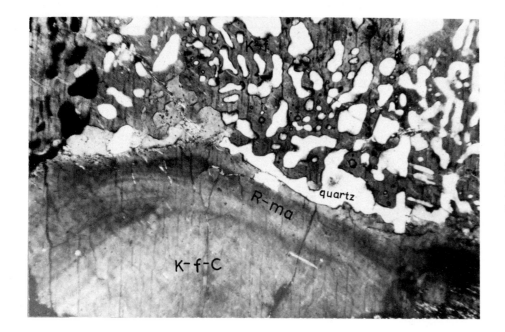

Fig. 265. An outer K-feldspar zone with graphic quartz intergrowths is surrounding a K-feldspar central part which is free of quartz. A reaction margin is noticeable in the central K-feldspar. Graphic quartz individuals follow the margins of the two K-feldspars. K-f-C = central K-feldspar free of quartz, K-f = K-feldspar with graphic quartz intergrowths, R-ma = reaction margin of the central K-feldspar. Kunnersdorf Granite, Hirschberg, Silesia, Germany. With crossed nicols; enlargement 100 x.

Fig. 266. Micrographic quartz in K-feldspar with parts extending into a plagioclase and sending a small protuberance following the twinning of the plagioclase (see arrow "a"). Qu = quartz, K-f = K-feldspar, plagioclase with polysynthetic twinning. Rapakivi granite, Finland. With crossed nicols; enlargement 100 x.

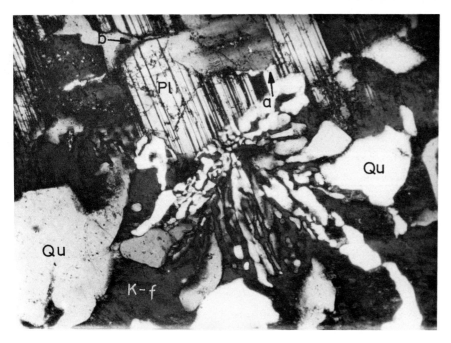

Fig. 267. K-feldspar surrounding a plagioclase. Granophyric (micrographic) quartz in the K-feldspar extends into the plagioclase, following its twinning (see arrow "a"). Another granophyric quartz (see arrow "b") extends from the K-feldspar and penetrates into the plagioclase perpendicular to its twinning. Qu = granophyric quartz, Pl = plagioclase, K-f = K-feldspar. Rapakivi granite, Finland. With crossed nicols; enlargement 100 x.

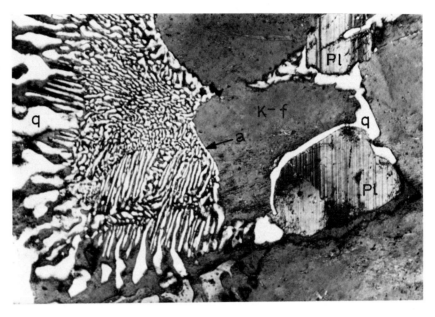

Fig. 268. K-feldspar including two plagioclase crystal grains. An outer zone of the K-feldspar is intensely intergrown with granophyric quartz. The demarcation of quartz forms a ring-like structure around the plagioclase. Pl = plagioclase, K-f = K-feldspar, q = granophyric quartz. Rapakivi granite, Finland. With crossed nicols; enlargement 100 x.

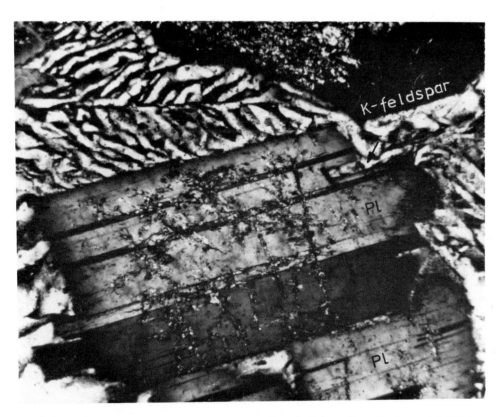

Fig. 269. K-feldspar with granophyric quartz surrounding plagioclase. Granophyric quartz infiltrates parallel to the plagioclase twinning (see arrow). Pl = plagioclase, quartz (white). Rapakivi granite, Finland. With crossed nicols; enlargement 100 x.

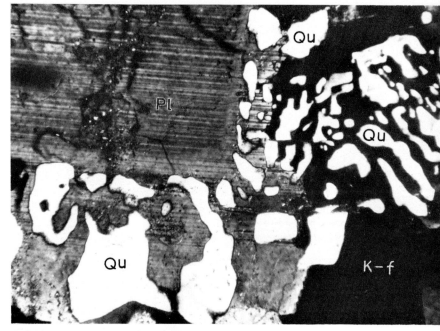

Fig. 270. K-feldspar in the extinction position with graphic quartz being in contact with fine-twinned plagioclase. Graphic quartz with the same orientation is present both in the K-feldspar and in the outer zone of the plagioclase. The presence of the graphic quartz in both feldspars and the fact that graphic quartz is in intergrowth with plagioclase, points out that the graphic intergrowths are not eutectics of K-feldspar/quartz. Qu = graphic quartz, Pl = plagioclase, K-f = Kfeldspar in the extinction position. Kunnersdorf Granite, Hirschberg, Silesia, Germany. With crossed nicols; enlargement 100 x.

Fig. 271. K-feldspar with graphic quartz in contact with plagioclase. A more or less idiomorphic plagioclase outline is maintained. However, when graphic quartz follows the margin K-feldspar/plagioclase, a reaction margin is noticeable in the plagioclase (see arrow "a"). Pl = plagioclase, Qu = graphic quartz, K-feldspar in the extinction position, Q-ma = graphic quartz following the margin and associated with the K-feldspar/plagioclase. Kunnersdorf Granite, Hirschberg, Silesia, Germany. With crossed nicols; enlargement 100 x.

Fig. 272. Plagioclase with graphic quartz perpendicular to the plagioclase twinning. K-f = K-feldspar, Pl = plagioclase, Qu = graphic quartz. Kunnersdorf Granite, Hirschberg, Silesia, Germany. With crossed nicols; enlargement 100 x.

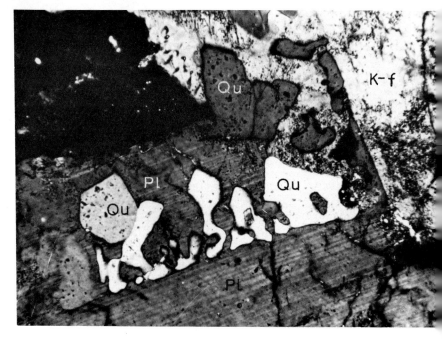

Fig. 273. Plagioclase free of graphic quartz surrounded by a plagioclase zone with graphic quartz. Reversing of twinning and a broad reaction zone is noticeable in the central plagioclase (quartz-free). The graphic quartz partly follows the reaction margin (see arrow "a"), partly stops at it as it extends from the outer plagioclase to the central. Pl-c = central plagioclase, quartz-free, O-Pl = outer plagioclase with graphic quartz, Qu = graphic quartz. Kunnersdorf Granite, Hirschberg, Silesia, Germany. With crossed nicols; enlargement 100 x.

Fig. 274. Perthitised K-feldspar with graphic quartz; a marked field is noticeable in which the graphic quartz is in a contrasted orientation. Qu = graphic quartz (graphic quartz with contrasted orientation in the extinction position), Se = sericitised K-feldspar, K-f-p = perthitised K-feldspar. Rapakivi granite, Finland. With crossed nicols; enlargement 100 x.

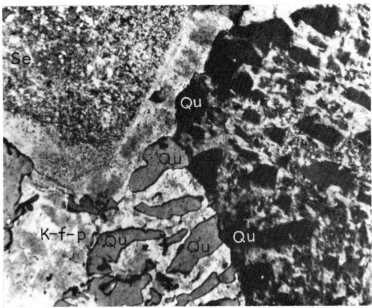

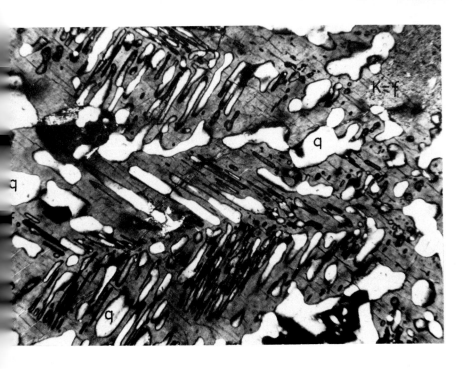

Fig. 275. In a single K-feldspar (uniform optical behaviour) individually orientated graphic quartz intergrowths follow a "fish bone" arrangement. The graphic quartz orientation pattern follows crystal penetrability directions (arrow indicates a feldspar cleavage direction which corresponds to a prevalent direction followed by a graphic quartz set). K-f = K-feldspar, q = graphic quartz. Kunnersdorf Granite, Hirschberg, Silesia, Germany. With crossed nicols; enlargement 100 x.

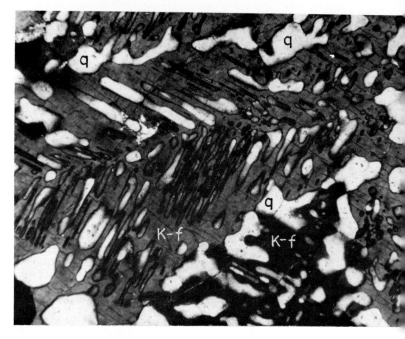

Fig. 276. The same graphic quartz textural pattern as shown in Fig. 275. However, in addition, a twin-wedge, in the extinction position, is also shown. Graphic quartz grains follow the contact of twinning and extend into the K-feldspar individual which is in the extinction position. With crossed nicols; enlargement 100 x.

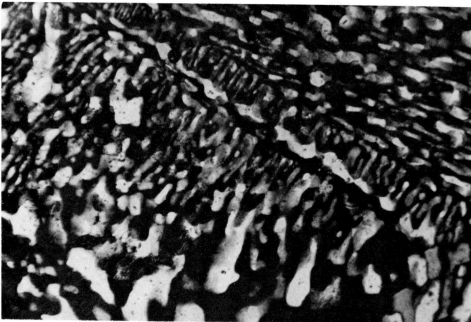

Fig. 277. K-feldspar in the extinction position, in intergrowth with graphic quartz which follows three different prevailing orientations. The K-feldspar is uniformly orientated. Hausmannsklippen Granite, Brocken area, Harz, Germany. With crossed nicols; enlargement 100 x.

Fig. 278. Orientated graphic quartz intergrowths in twinned K-feldspars. The graphic quartz follows two main orientations, q = graphic quartz, K-f = feldspar. Hausmannsklippen Granite, Brocken area, Harz, Germany. With crossed nicols; enlargement 100 x.

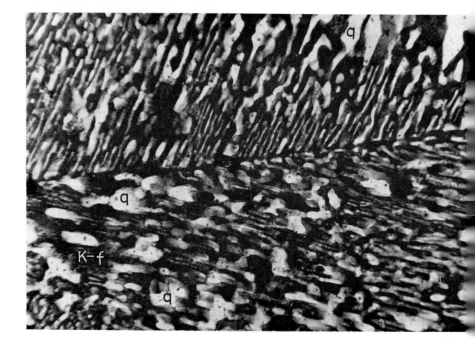

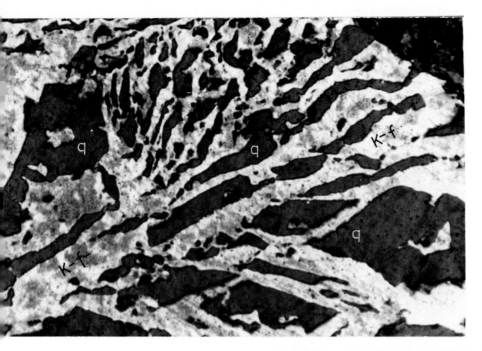

Fig. 279. Infiltration of quartz-forming solutions which resulted in equally orientated quartz, in intergrowth with perthitised K-feldspar. Q = quartz, K-f = K-feldspar. Rapakivi granite, Finland. With crossed nicols; enlargement 100 x.

Fig. 280. Graphic quartz attaining fully developed "idiomorphic" forms in K-feldspar, i.e., a phase of hieroglyphic skeleton-quartz to eucrystalline forms. K-f = K-feldspar, q = quartz. Rapakivi granite, Finland. With crossed nicols; enlargement 100 x.

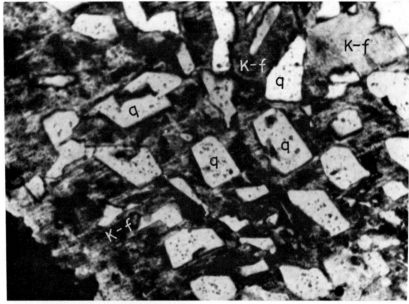

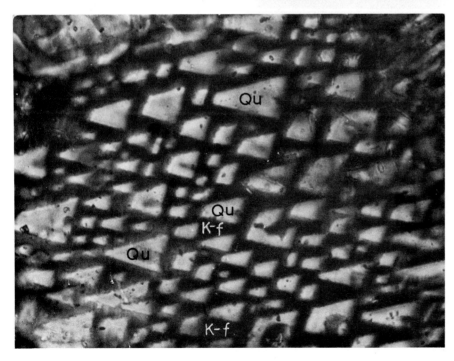

Fig. 281. Eucrystalline micrographic quartz grains are developed in K-feldspar. Skeleton and eucrystalline quartz grains are formed (a typical granophyric "hieroglyphic texture"). Qu = quartz, K-f = K-feldspar in the extinction position. Harrar Granite, Ethiopia. With crossed nicols; enlargement 250 x.

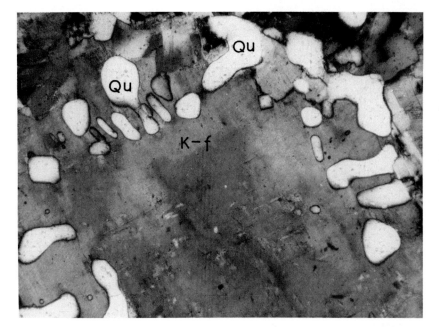

Fig. 282. In contrast to the eucrystalline micrographic quartz illustrated in Fig. 281, here granophyric quartz is orientated at the periphery of the K-feldspar. The micrographic quartz grains are rounded; their common orientation indicates late infiltration. This rounded granophyric quartz should not be confused with pre-blastic rounded quartz of the palaeosoma. K-f = K-feldspar, Qu = micrographic quartz. Rapakivi granite, Finland. With crossed nicols; enlargement 100 x.

Fig. 283 and 284. Orientated granophyric quartz in K-feldspar (in the extinction position). A biotite lath acts as a delimiting barrier in the development of a granophyric quartz grain. Q = granophyric quartz, Bi = biotite, K-f = K-feldspar. Kunnersdorf Granite, Hirschberg, Silesia, Germany. With crossed nicols; enlargements 100 x, 200 x.

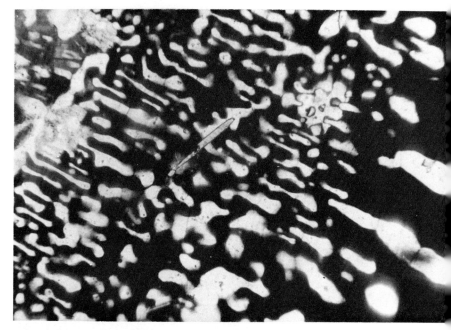

Fig. 284.

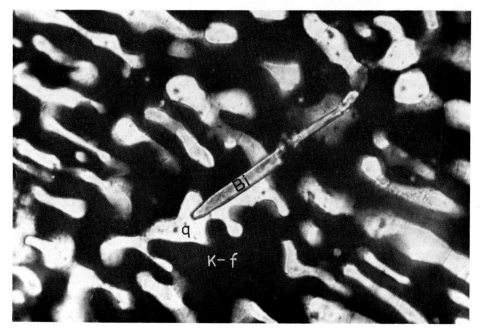

Fig. 285. Graphic quartz in microcline. Carrara, Giggiga, Harrar, Ethiopia. With crossed nicols; enlargement 10 x.

Fig. 286. (Detail of Fig. 285.) The graphic quartz consists of three differently orientated quartz individuals, a, b, and c. The quartz individual "a" indicates undulating extinctions and gives the impression that it is built up of "plates" of subindividuals. Mi = microcline. With crossed nicols; enlargement 50 x.

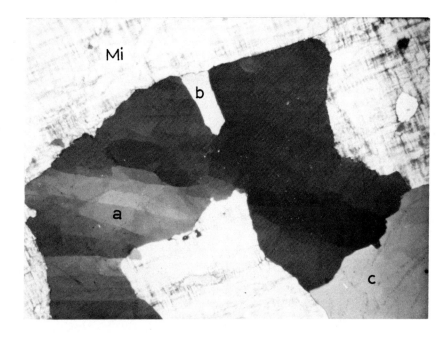

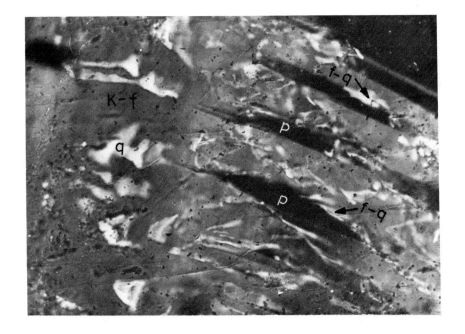

Fig. 287. K-feldspar with perthite (extinction position) and fine worm-like quartz canals, partly following the margin K-feldspar/perthite. In contrast to the myrmekitic quartz (which is associated with plagioclase) these quartz worm-like bodies are also present in K-feldspar. K-f = K-feldspar, f-q = fine quartz canals, p = perthite. Wehmo Granite, Nystad, Helsingfors, Finland. With crossed nicols; enlargement 250 x.

211

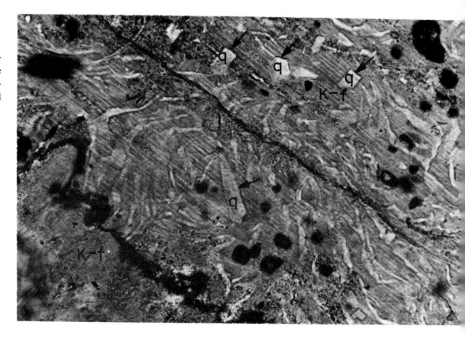

Fig. 288. K-feldspar with fine quartz worm-like bodies and fine idiomorphic quartz (see arrows). K-f = K-feldspar, q = quartz. Monzonite at Munzoni, Tirol, Italy. With crossed nicols; enlargement 100 x.

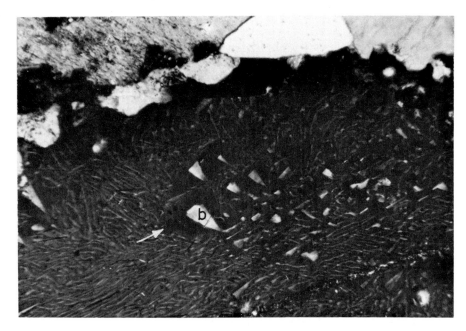

Fig. 289. Fine worm-like bodies, graphic in nature, often attaining eucrystalline form. A halo, free of worm-like bodies, surrounds the eucrystalline quartz grains (see arrow). K-feldspar in the extinction position, q = quartz. Monzonite at Munzoni, Tirol, Italy. With crossed nicols; enlargement 100 x.

Fig. 290. K-feldspar surrounding corroded and myrmekitised plagioclase. In the K-feldspar fine worm-like quartz bodies are present, often attaining idiomorphic forms. Pl = plagioclase, K-f = K-feldspar, q = quartz. Monzonite at Munzoni, Tirol, Italy. With crossed nicols; enlargement 100 x.

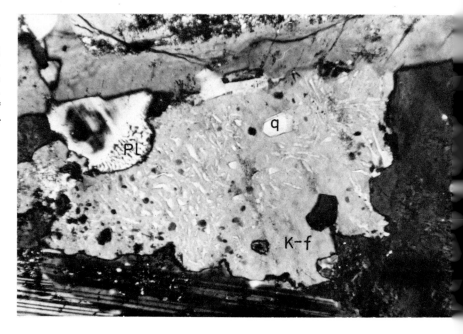

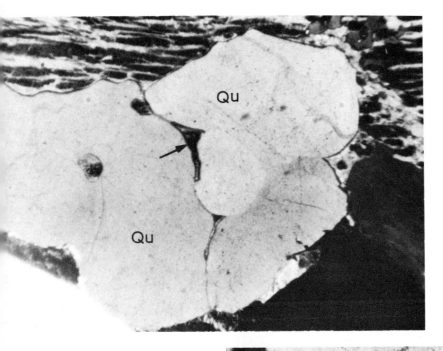

Fig. 291. Graphic quartz simulation globular-aggregate texture. Between the globules perthitised microcline forms isolated relics. Qu = graphic quartz "globules", arrow indicates interglobular perthitised K-feldspar. Ragunda Granite, Sweden. With crossed nicols; enlargement 100 x.

Fig. 292. (Detail of Fig. 291). Globular aggregate of graphic quartz with interglobular perthite K-feldspar. Arrow "a" indicates perthite running parallel to quartz margin. With crossed nicols; enlargement 250 x.

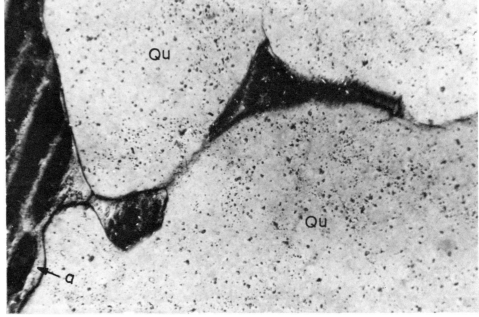

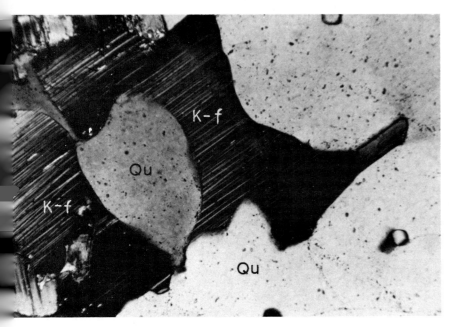

Fig. 293. Graphic quartz in intergrowth with K-feldspar (microcline). Curved contacts characterise these intergrowths. K-f = K-feldspar, Qu = quartz. Sornas Granite, Helsingfors, Finland. With crossed nicols; enlargement 100 x.

213

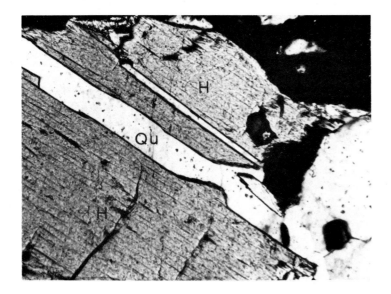

Fig. 294. Quartz infiltrating along the cleavage of hornblende. Qu = quartz, H = hornblende. Masino Granite, Bagni, Sondrio, Italy. With crossed nicols; enlargement 100 x.

Fig. 295. Hornblende with graphic intergrowth of quartz marginal to quartz with the same optical orientation as the graphic quartz. Plagioclase is adjacent to this intergrowth with granophyric-like quartz present. Qu = quartz surrounded by graphic quartz/hornblende intergrowth, Pl = plagioclase, gr-q = granophyric quartz in plagioclase, H = hornblende. Rapakivi granite, Wiborg, Finland. With crossed nicols; enlargement 100 x.

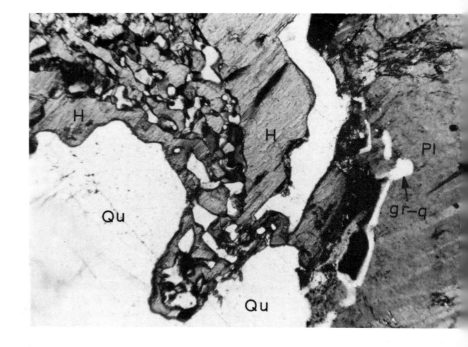

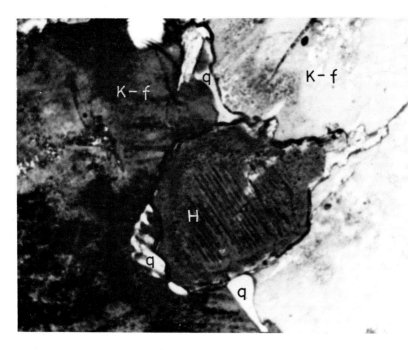

Fig. 296. Hornblende with schiller structures in K-feldspar. Graphic-like quartz follows the contact of two K-feldspars and partly that with the hornblende. Another graphic quartz marginal to the hornblende is partly intergrown with the amphibole. K-f = K-feldspar, H = hornblende, q = graphic quartz. Augite syenite at Kuhlerloch, Radantal, Harz, Germany. With crossed nicols; enlargement 100 x.

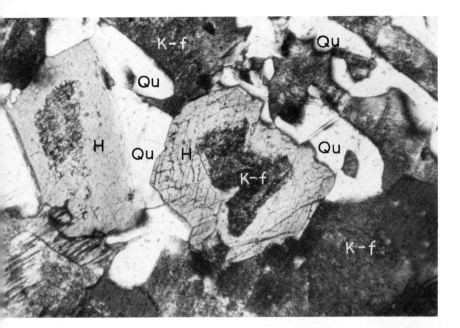

Fig. 297. Hornblende crystal grains in K-feldspar. Graphic quartz in intergrowth with the K-feldspar partly surrounding the amphibole. K-f = K-feldspar, H = hornblende, Qu = quartz. Monzonite at Atviken, Sweden. With crossed nicols; enlargement 100 x.

Fig. 298. Hornblende in K-feldspar. Graphic quartz in intergrowth with the K-feldspar extends also in the hornblende. H = hornblende, q = quartz (graphic), K-f = K-feldspar. Monzonite at Atviken, Sweden. With crossed nicols; enlargement 100 x.

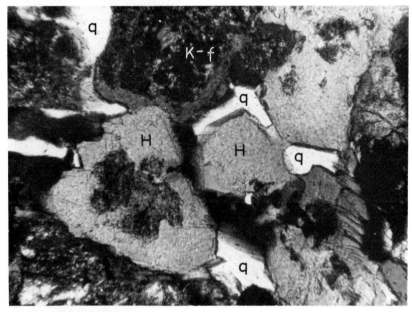

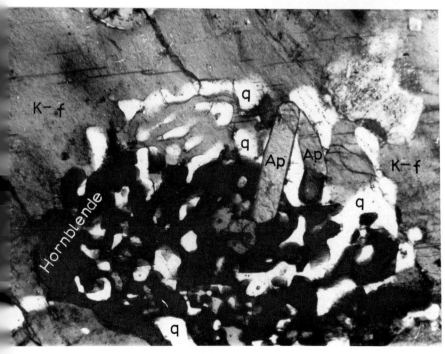

Fig. 299. K-feldspar surrounding hornblende (in the extinction position). Granophyric (micrographic) quartz is in intergrowth with both the K-feldspar and the hornblende. Apatites are also present. K-f = K-feldspar, hornblende (in the extinction position), q = micrographic quartz, Ap = apatite. Rapakivi granite, Wiborg, Finland. With crossed nicols; enlargement 100 x.

215

Fig. 300. Myrmekitised plagioclase surrounded by K-feldspar. Graphic quartz is in intergrowth with both the orthoclase and the myrmekitised plagioclase. The graphic quartz cuts the myrmekitised plagioclase, K-f = K-feldspar, Q = graphic quartz, m-pl = myrmekitised plagioclase. Bergeller Granite, Alps. With crossed nicols; enlargement 60 x. (Photomicrograph by courtesy of F. K. Drescher-Kaden.)

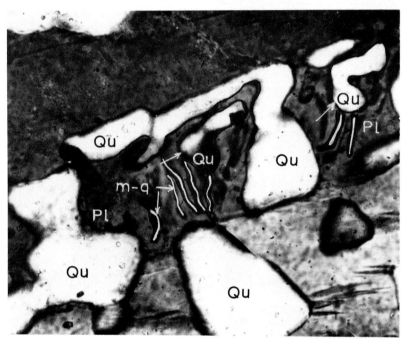

Fig. 301. Graphic quartz in intergrowth with K-feldspar. Graphic quartz grains also intersect myrmekitised plagioclase which is surrounded by K-feldspar. Arrow indicates graphic quartz intersecting myrmekitised plagioclase and cutting myrmekitic quartz bodies. Pl = plagioclase, Qu = graphic quartz, m-q = myrmekitic quartz. Kunnersdorf Granite, Hirschberg, Silesia, Germany. With crossed nicols; enlargement 200 x.

Fig. 302. K-feldspar with perthitic lines following the cleavage, partly in contact with myrmekitised plagioclase. Also another K-feldspar grain is shown. Graphic quartz is present in the K-feldspar and certain graphic quartz grains intersect both K-feldspar and myrmekitised plagioclase. K-f = K-feldspar, Qu = graphic quartz, Pl = plagioclase (myrmekitised), arrows show quartz intersecting the boundary K-feldspar/myrmekitised plagioclase. Kunnersdorf Granite, Hirschberg, Silesia, Germany. With crossed nicols; enlargement 100 x.

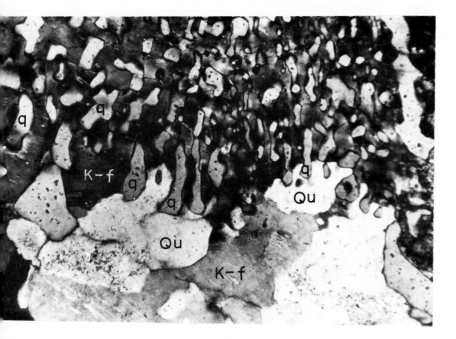

Fig. 303. Granophyric quartz grains (with common orientation) in K-feldspar. The granophyric quartz is also in intergrowth with non-graphic quartz. q = granophyric quartz, Qu = non-graphic quartz, K-f = K-feldspar. Kunnersdorf Granite, Hirschberg, Silesia, Germany. With crossed nicols; enlargement 100 x.

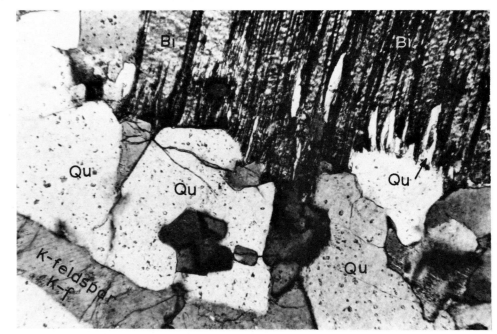

Fig. 304. Graphic quartz associated with K-feldspar. Graphic quartz sends apophyses (see arrow) into adjacent biotite. Also quartz infiltrations into the biotite are indicated. K-f = K-feldspar, Qu = quartz (graphic), Bi = biotite. Kunnersdorf Granite, Hirschberg, Silesia, Germany. With crossed nicols; enlargement 100 x.

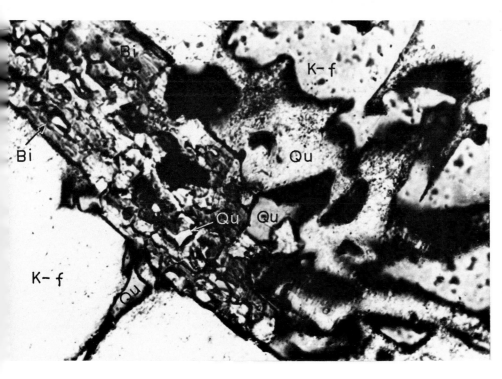

Fig. 305. K-feldspar with granophyric (micrographic) quartz including a biotite. The micrographic quartz-forming solutions have also "infiltrated" into the mica, and as a result granophyric quartz is intergrown also with the biotite. K-f = K-feldspar, Bi = biotite, Qu = granophyric quartz. Rapakivi granite, Finland. With crossed nicols; enlargement 100 x.

217

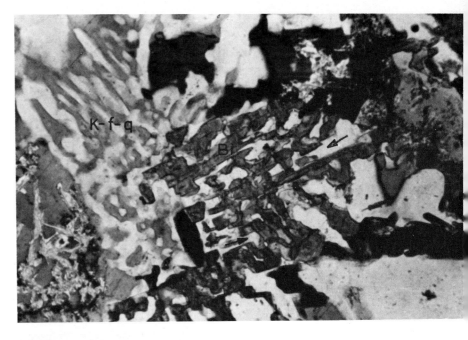

Fig. 306. Graphic quartz with K-feldspar. The quartz infiltrates into the biotite and replaces the mica along its cleavage. Also plagioclase is replaced by graphic quartz. K-f-q = K-feldspar/graphic quartz intergrowth, Bi = biotite. Arrows indicate graphic quartz replacing biotite. Bressoir Granite, Vosges. With crossed nicols; enlargement 100 x.

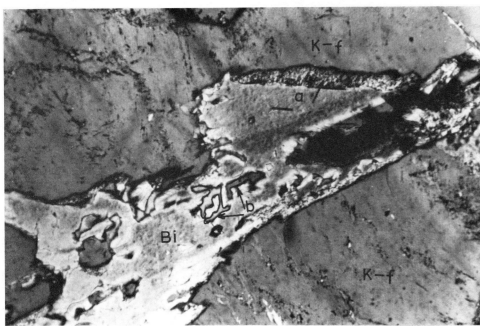

Fig. 307. Biotite surrounded by K-feldspar. Arrow "a" shows a fine myrmekitised biotite reaction margin. Also graphic-like quartz is present in the biotite (see arrow "b"). Bi = biotite, K-f = K-feldspar. Granite at Aberdeen, Scotland. With crossed nicols; enlargement 100 x.

Fig. 308. Muscovite in microcline of a pegmatoid. Graphic quartz in intergrowth with the muscovite and partly with the feldspar. M = muscovite, Qu = graphic quartz, Mi = microcline with cross-twinning. Carrara, Giggiga, Harrar, Ethiopia. With crossed nicols; enlargement 25 x.

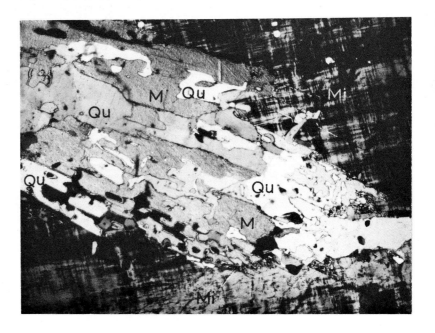

218

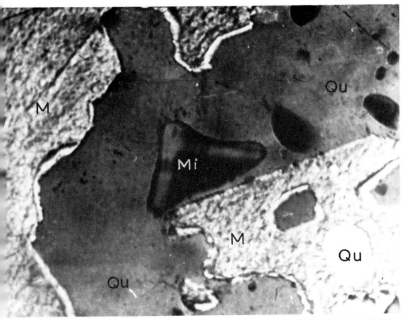

Fig. 309. Graphic quartz infiltrating and replacing muscovite which was originally associated with microcline. A microcline relic (with a corroded outline) is included in the later quartz. M = muscovite, Qu = quartz, Mi = microcline. Carrara, Giggiga, Harrar, Ethiopia. With crossed nicols; enlargement 100 x.

Fig. 310. (Detail of Fig. 308.) Graphic quartz in intergrowth with both the muscovite and microcline (in the extinction position). Corroded microcline relic is now present in the later graphic quartz from the original microcline/muscovite intergrowth. Qu = quartz, Mi = microcline (also in the extinction position), M = muscovite. With crossed. nicols; enlargement 100 x.

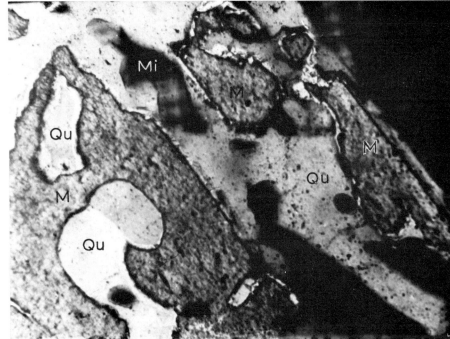

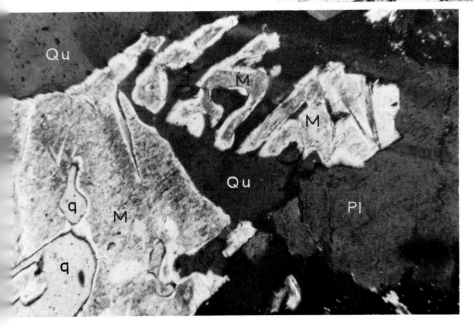

Fig. 311. Graphic-like muscovite textures associated with quartz and feldspar. In the adjacent muscovite graphic quartz is present. The graphic muscovite most probably represents corrosion relics. Qu = quartz, M = muscovite, q = graphic quartz in muscovite, Pl = plagioclase. Pegmatite at Piona, Lake Como district, Italy. With crossed nicols; enlargement 100 x.

219

Fig. 312. Muscovite infiltrated and replaced by quartz (simulating granophyric form) in plagioclase. A free quartz grain is also present. M = muscovite, q = granophyric-like quartz, Qu = quartz grain, Pl = plagioclase. Pegmatite at Piona, Lake Como district, Italy. With crossed nicols; enlargement 100 x.

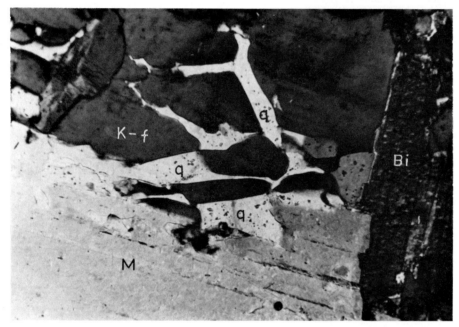

Fig. 313. Graphic-like quartz infiltrates K-feldspar and partly extends into the muscovite. K-f = K-feldspar, q = graphic-like quartz, M = muscovite, Bi = biotite. Hauzenberg Granite, Bavaria, Germany. With crossed nicols; enlargement 100 x.

Fig. 314. Hornblende and biotite associated with K-feldspar (in the extinction position). Later quartz infiltration into the biotite partly takes advantage of the mica's cleavage. H = hornblende, Bi = biotite, q = quartz. Hornblende syenite at Meissen, Saxony, Germany.

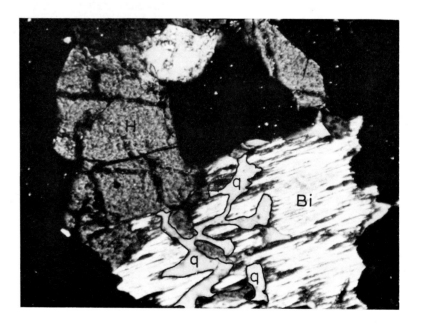

220

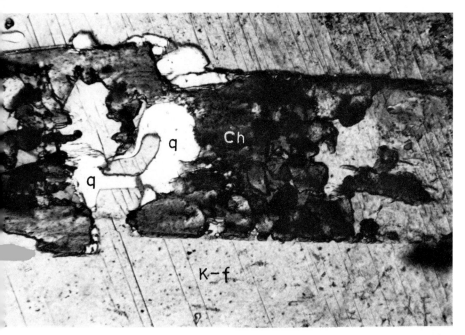

Fig. 315. Graphic quartz infiltrates into a K-feldspar which is chloritised. The quartz extends into the feldspar as well as into the chlorite. q = graphic quartz, K-f = K-feldspar, Ch = chlorite. Didessa, Ethiopia. With crossed nicols; enlargement 100 x.

Fig. 316. Two different minerals, quartz and hornblende, in graphic forms present in K-feldspar. Arrow "a" shows graphic quartz partly surrounding graphic hornblende. K-f = K-feldspar, Qu = graphic quartz, H = graphic hornblende. Monzonite at Atviken, Sweden. With crossed nicols; enlargement 100 x.

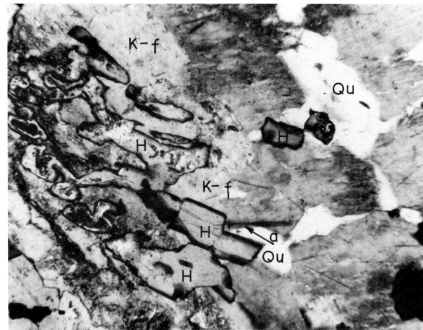

Fig. 317. A net-like texture of hornblende in intergrowth with K-feldspar adjacent to plagioclase. K-f = K-feldspar, Pl = plagioclase, H = hornblende. Bucksburn Granite, Aberdeen, Scotland. With crossed nicols; enlargement 100 x.

Fig. 318. Amphibole in intergrowth with K-feldspar. A = amphibole, K-f = K-feldspar. Masino Granite, Bagni, Sondrio, Italy. With crossed nicols; enlargement 100 x.

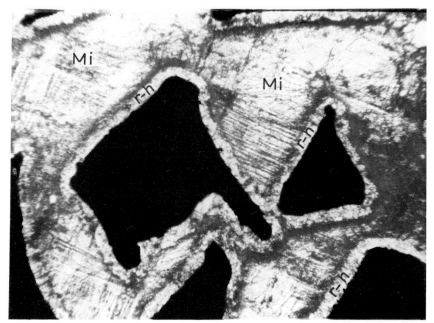

Fig. 319. Uraninite (black) with radioactive halo in pegmatitic microcline. Mi = microcline, r-h = radioactive halo. Ruggles mine, New Hampshire, U.S.A. With crossed nicols; enlargement 100 x.

Fig. 320. Graphic uraninite (with a radioactive halo) in pegmatitic microcline. Mi = microcline, U = uraninite, r-h = radioactive halo. Ruggles mine, New Hampshire, U.S.A. Polished section; oil-immersion with one nicol, enlargement 200 x.

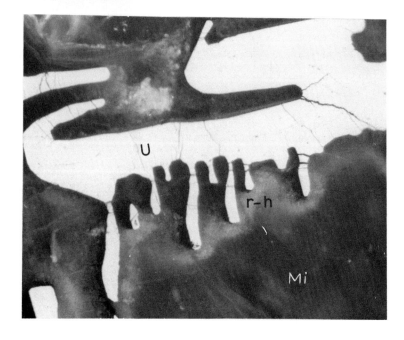

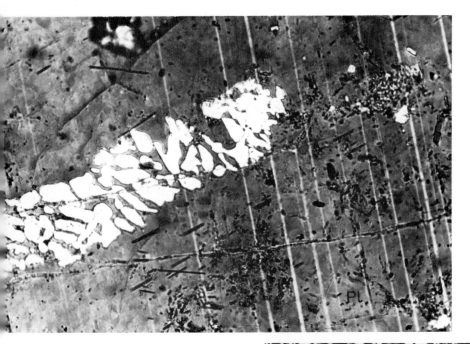

Fig. 321. Plagioclase in intergrowth with an unidentified mineral. A micrographic pattern is produced. Pl = plagioclase. Hornblende syenite at Ben Cruachen, Loch Awe, Scotland. With crossed nicols; enlargement 100 x.

Fig. 322. Graphic-like tourmaline in perthitised K-feldspar. T = tourmaline, pe = perthite in K-feldspar (in the extinction position). Ragunda Granite, Sweden. With crossed nicols; enlargement 100 x.

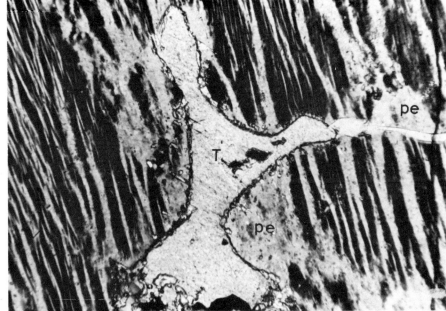

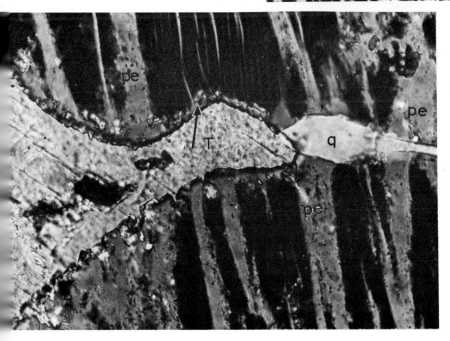

Fig. 323. (Detail of Fig. 322.) Tourmaline in perthitised K-feldspar. The perthite partly follows the tourmaline margin (see arrow). A graphic quartz is also present. T = tourmaline, pe = perthite following the tourmaline margin, q = graphic quartz. With crossed nicols; enlargement 200 x.

223

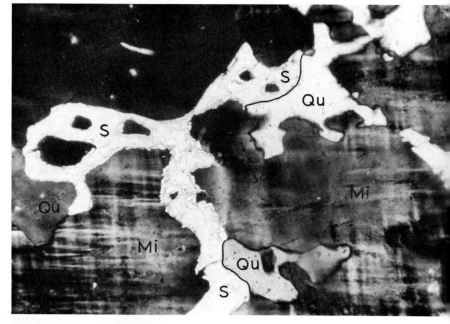

Fig. 324. Graphic-like sericite and quartz in intergrowth with microcline. S = sericite, Qu = quartz, Mi = microcline. Didessa Granite, Ethiopia. With crossed nicols; enlargement 100 x.

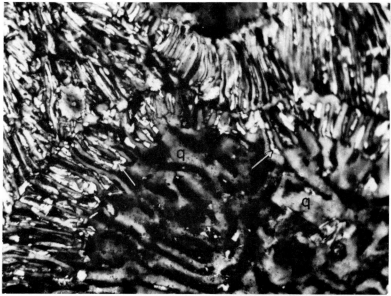

Fig. 325. Worm-like muscovite bodies (relics of mica due to replacement by quartz) in quartz. Arrows indicate individual muscovite worm-like bodies present in quartz. The textures thus produced simulate granophyric intergrowths. q = quartz. Didessa Granite, Ethiopia. With crossed nicols; enlargement 100 x.

Fig. 326. Muscovite infiltrated and replaced by quartz. Worm-like mica relics are in association with the infiltrated quartz; these intergrowths simulate granophyric textures. Didessa Granite, Ethiopia. With crossed nicols; enlargement 100 x.

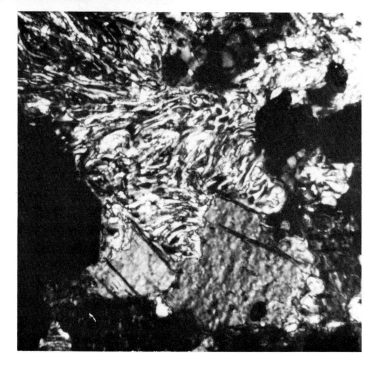

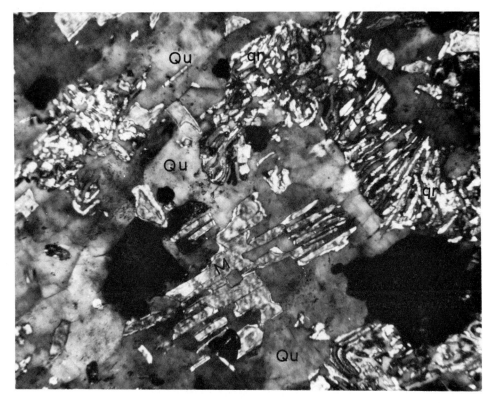

Fig. 327. Quartz replacing and infiltrating muscovite. The replacement often makes use of the muscovite cleavage. M = muscovite, Qu = quartz, qr = granophyric-like intergrowths of these two minerals phases which may be due to replacement. Didessa Granite, Ethiopia. With crossed nicols; enlargement 100 x.

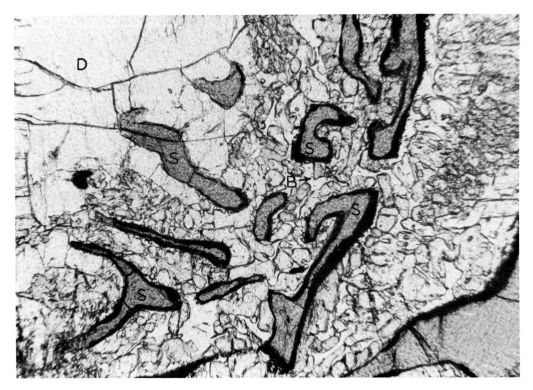

Fig. 328 and 329. Graphic spinel in intergrowth with forsterite and bronzite, in olivine pyroxene nodules of the olivine basalts of Nekempti, West Ethiopia. S = spinel, D = bronzite, B = basaltic ground-mass infiltrating in the pyroxene.

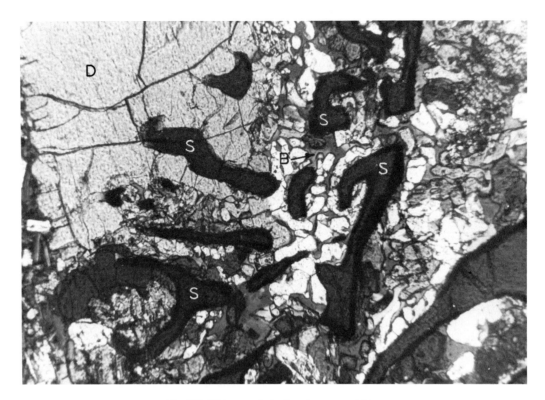

Fig. 329. With crossed nicols; enlargement 100 x.

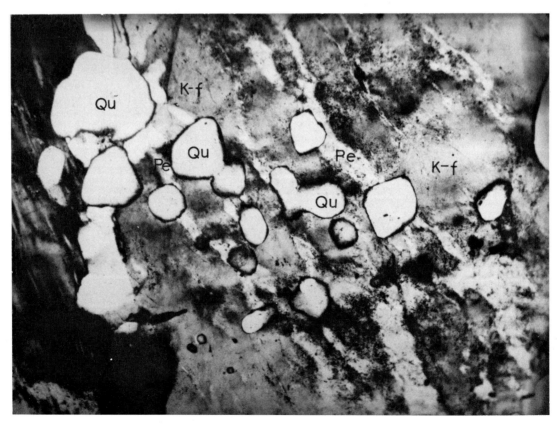

Fig. 330. Perthitic bands transversed by later graphic quartz (rounded quartz grains with common orientation). K-f = K-feldspar, Pe = perthite, Qu = graphic quartz. Rapakivi granite, Finland. With crossed nicols; enlargement 100 x.

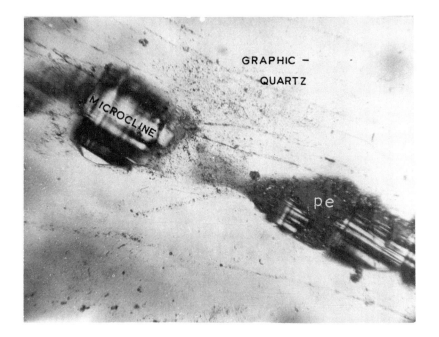

Fig. 331. Graphic quartz enclosing microcline with perthite (Pe). Both the microcline and the perthite are corroded and partly assimilated by the later graphic quartz. Pegmatoid at Carrara, Giggiga, Harrar, Ethiopia. With crossed nicols; enlargement 100 x.

Fig. 332. Microcline with graphic quartz. The graphic quartz in parts "surrounded" by perthite (black), shows extensions protruding into the plagioclase (perthite). Didessa Granite, Ethiopia. With crossed nicols; enlargement 100 x.

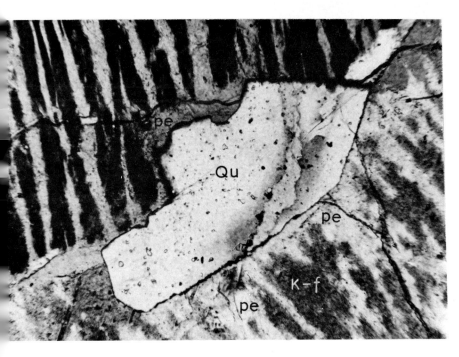

Fig. 333. Graphic quartz in perthitised K-feldspar. The perhite-forming solutions partly followed the contact graphic quartz/K-feldspar. Qu = graphic quartz, Pe = perthite following the quartz outline, K-f = K-feldspar (also in the extinction position). Ragunda Granite, Sweden. With crossed nicols; enlargement 100 x.

227

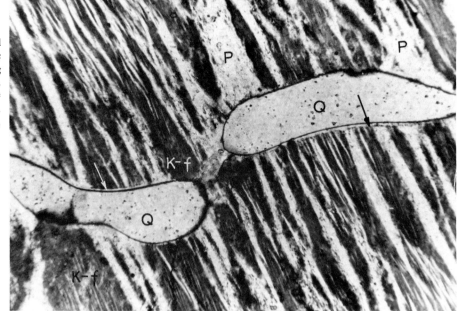

Fig. 334. Graphic quartz in perthitised
K-feldspar. Arrows show fine perthitic
infiltrations interleptonically following
the contact of graphic quartz/K-feldspar.
Q = graphic quartz, P = perthite, K-f =
K-feldspar. Ragunda Granite, Sweden.
With crossed nicols; enlargement 100 x.

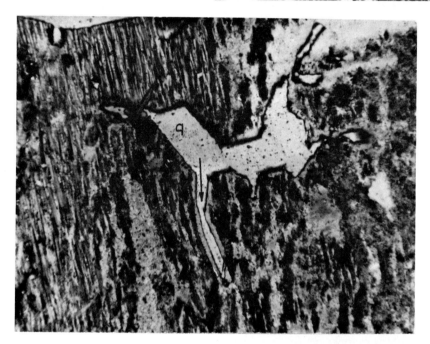

Fig. 335. Graphic quartz with protruding
apophyses in the K-feldspar. Perthitisation of K-feldspar coats a quartz protuberance indicating that perthitisation
took an advantage of the interleptonic
spaces between the quartz and K-feldspar.
q = graphic quartz (arrow indicates quartz
protuberance). Granite at "Jacobs Deal",
Turcoaja, Dobragea, Rumania. With
crossed nicols; enlargement 100 x.

Fig. 336. Graphic quartz in perthitised
K-feldspar. The perthite partly follows
the quartz outline (see arrow). Also perthitic bands cross the twinning plane of
K-feldspar. Qu = graphic quartz. Obertal
Granite, Harz, Germany. With crossed
nicols; enlargement 100 x.

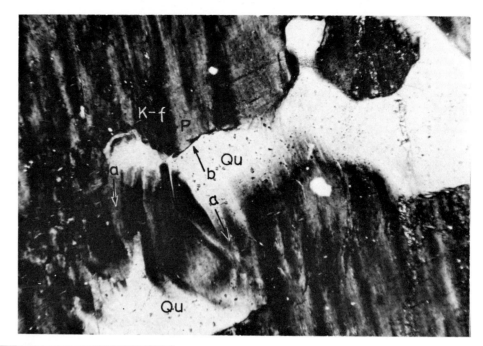

Fig. 337. Graphic quartz in intergrowth with perthitised K-feldspar. Arrow "a" shows extensions of graphic quartz attaining flame-like shape which eventually changes into flame perthite. In contradistinction arrow "b" indicates well-defined outlines of the graphic quartz. Qu = graphic quartz, P = perthites in K-feldspar (in the extinction position). Ragunda Granite, Sweden. With crossed nicols; enlargement 100 x.

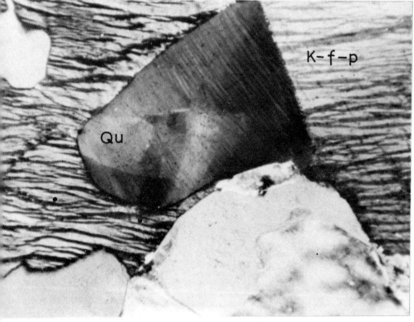

Fig. 338. Graphic quartz grains in perthitised K-feldspar. The graphic quartz grain shows undulating extinction and simultaneously "shadow" flame textures (probably perthitic patterns — relics of the initial phase of the graphic quartz formation by the replacement of an already perthitised K-feldspar). However, it should be pointed out that the flame-shadows in the graphic quartz follow a different orientation than that of the perthites in the K-feldspars, K-f-p = perthitised K-feldspar, Qu = graphic quartz with shadow patterns. Ragunda Granite, Sweden. With crossed nicols; enlargement 50 x.

Fig. 339. Graphic quartz with flame-shadow pattern in perthitised K-feldspar. The flame-shadow patterns in the quartz are differently orientated from those of the perthites in the K-feldspar. K-f-p = perhitised K-feldspar, Qu-s = graphic quartz with shadow patterns. Ragunda Granite, Sweden. With crossed nicols; enlargement 100 x.

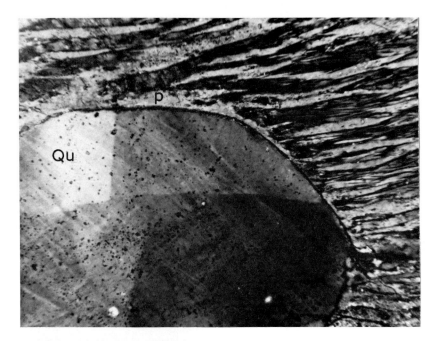

Fig. 340. Graphic quartz with undulating extinction (probably due to strain) with flame shadow patterns, partly surrounded by perthitised K-feldspar. K-feldspar perthite following the margins of graphic quartz thus giving the impression of a post-graphic quartz infiltration. p = perthite following the graphic quartz margin, Qu = graphic quartz with undulating extinction and flame-shadow patterns. Ragunda Granite, Sweden. With crossed nicols; enlargement 100 x.

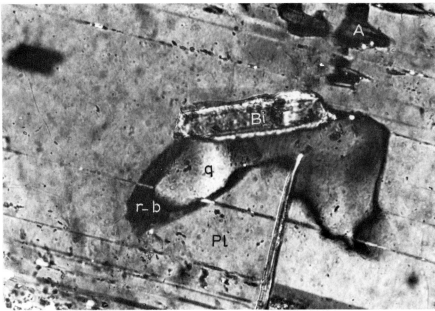

Fig. 341. A granophyric quartz in plagioclase. A reaction border with reversing of the plagioclase twinning is produced between the granophyric quartz and the plagioclase. Pl = plagioclase, q = quartz (granophyric), r-b = reaction border with reversing of plagioclase twinning, Bi = biotite, A = antiperthite. Gneiss-granite at Aar, Switzerland. With crossed nicols; enlargement 100 x.

Fig. 342. Graphic quartz with forms attained dependent on penetrability (mainly cleavage) of the K-feldspar. Quartz penetration has also affected plagioclase and a crystal grain of it is surrounded by quartz. K-f = K-feldspar (in the extinction position), Pl = plagioclase, Qu = graphic quartz. Hellewald Granite, Sewen, Vosges, Germany. With crossed nicols; enlargement 100x.

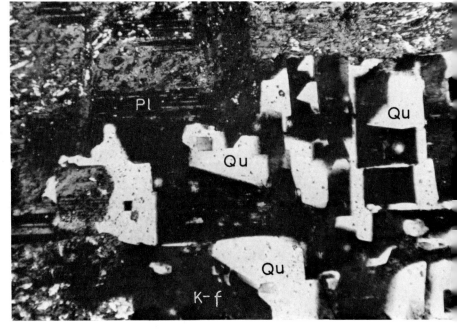

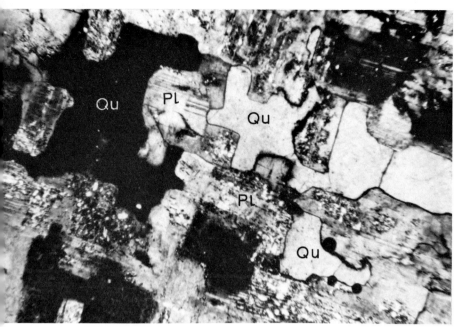

Fig. 343. Graphic quartz pattern comparable to that in Fig. 342. In this case, however, the graphic quartz is mainly associated with plagioclase and the pattern of the graphic intergrowth depends on the penetrability and control exercised by the host plagioclase on the later quartz-forming solutions. Pl = plagioclase, Qu = graphic quartz (black grain graphic quartz in extinction position). Ober Krummhubel Granite, Riesengebirge, Silesia, Germany. With crossed nicols; enlargement 100 x.

Fig. 344. Graphic quartz in intergrowth with twinned plagioclase. The shape of the graphic quartz is influenced by the twinning of the plagioclase. A reaction margin is produced in the plagioclase as it comes in contact with the graphic quartz. q = graphic quartz, r-m = reaction margin of plagioclase in contact with graphic quartz. Baveno Granite, Italy. With crossed nicols, enlargement 100 x.

Fig. 345 and 346. Graphic quartz in K-feldspar. A biotite lath is thinned off as it lays in between two graphic quartzes. Small-scale assimilation of the biotite has probably occurred. Qu = graphic quartz, Bi = biotite, K-f = K-feldspar. Kunnersdorf Granite, Hirschberg, Silesia, Germany. With crossed nicols; enlargements 100 x, 200 x.

231

Fig. 346.

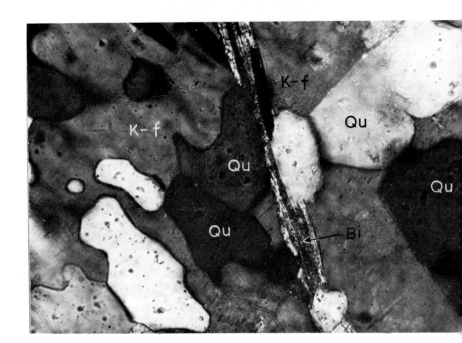

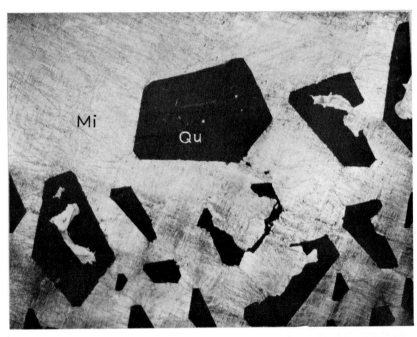

Fig. 347. Graphic pegmatoid. Graphic quartz in microcline cut perpendicular to the c-axis. All transitions from "hieroglyphic to six-sided crystal forms (cross sections) are illustrated, indicating that the graphic forms are skeleton structures., i.e., an incomplete development of the quartz crystal form. Mi = microcline, Qu = quartz (black). Pegmatite at Carrara, Giggiga, Harrar, Ethiopia. With crossed nicols; enlargement 5 x. (Details showing various transitions from "hieroglyphic" to six-sided crystal quartz cross-sections are shown in Fig. 348, 349 and 350.)

Fig. 348. A six-sided quartz in microcline, including microcline relics and perthite as relics of the metasomatic replacement process which resulted in the quartz formation. It should be noted that the sides of the six-sided quartz outline are unequal, resulting in a distorted six-sided form. Pe = perthite. Pegmatite at Carrara, Giggiga, Harrar, Ethiopia. With crossed nicols; enlargement 10 x.

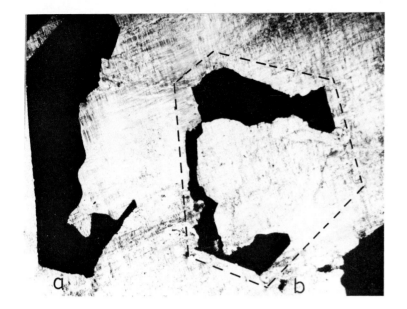

Fig. 349. Graphic quartz (cut perpendicular to the c-axis) shows well developed crystal faces (geometric outline) and irregular intergrowth with the microcline, resulting in a "hieroglyphic-form" at "a". At "b" the development of a six-sided quartz interfered with the microcline. The six-sided figure shows the form which the quartz would have attained if fully developed. Pegmatite at Carrara, Giggiga, Harrar, Ethiopia. With crossed nicols; enlargement 10 x.

Fig. 350. A six-sided quartz grain cut perpendicular to the c-axis in microcline. This can be regarded as a fully developed crystal in the transition from "hieroglyphic" (skeleton) to developed quartz forms. Pegmatite at Carrara, Giggiga, Harrar, Ethiopia. With crossed nicols; enlargement 10 x.

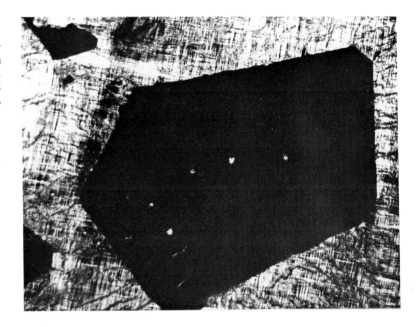

Fig. 351. Granitised quartzitic conglomerate. Quartz grains of a quartzitic pebble infiltrated by a K-feldspar blastesis. Small laths of mica are also present. The quartz grains are in the process of recrystallisation and re-orientation from random to granophyric. K-f = K-feldspar, Qu = quartz, m-l = mica laths. Buri-Rashitcha, Adolla, South Ethiopia. With crossed nicols; enlargement 250 x.

233

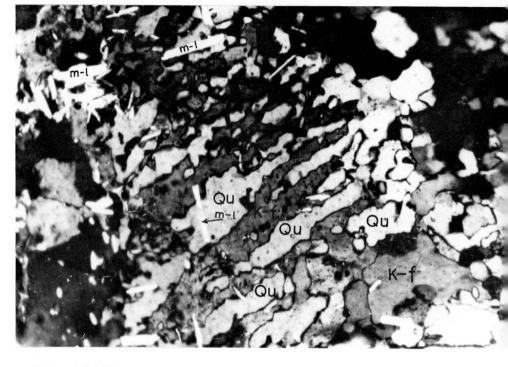

Fig. 352. Granitised quartzitic conglomerate. Quartz grains of a quartzitic pebble "infiltrated" by a K-feldspar crystalloblast. The quartz grains are recrystallised and re-orientated from random (quartzitic) to granophyric. Mica laths are present. K-f = K-feldspar, Qu = quartz, m-l = mica laths. Buri-Rashitcha, Adolla, South Ethiopia. With crossed nicols; enlargement 250 x.

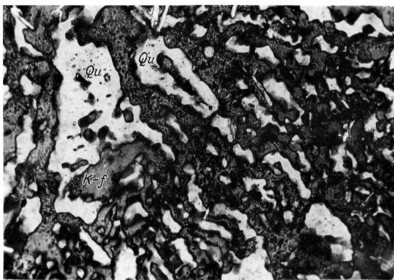

Fig. 353. Granitised quartzitic conglomerate. Quartz grains of quartzitic pebble "infiltrated' by a K-feldspar crystalloblast. The quartz grains are recrystallised and re-oriented from quartzitic mosaic to granophyric (micrographic). Qu = quartz, K-f = K-feldspar. Buri-Rashitcha, Adolla, South Ethiopia. With crossed nicols; enlargement 250 x.

Fig. 354 and 355. Granitised quartzitic conglomerate. Due to recrystallisation and K-feldspar blastesis the mosaic quartz has been transformed into a micrographic pattern. Qu = quartz, K-f = K-feldspar in the extinction position. With crossed nicols; enlargement 100 x, 250 x.

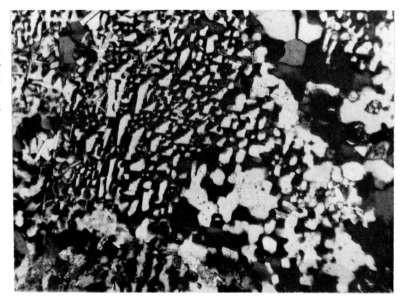

Fig. 355.

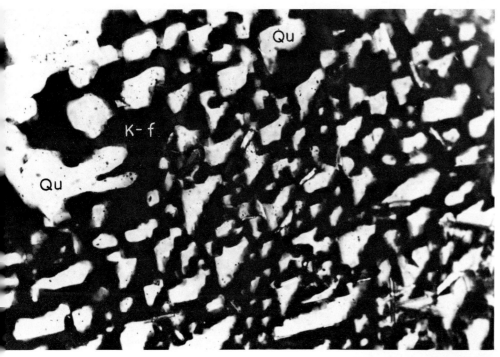

Fig. 356. Granitised quartzitic conglomerate. The extreme case of the transformation of the quartzitic texture due to recrystallisation of the quartz and K-feldspar topometasomatism, results in the intergrowth shown in this figure. Qu = micrographic quartz, K-f = K-feldspar crystalloblast. Buri-Rashitcha, Adolla, South Ethiopia. With crossed nicols; enlargement 250 x.

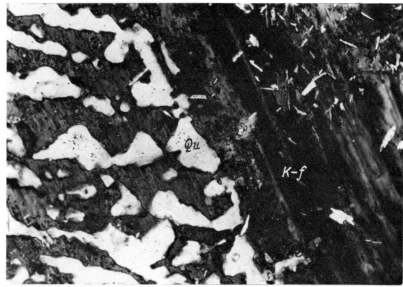

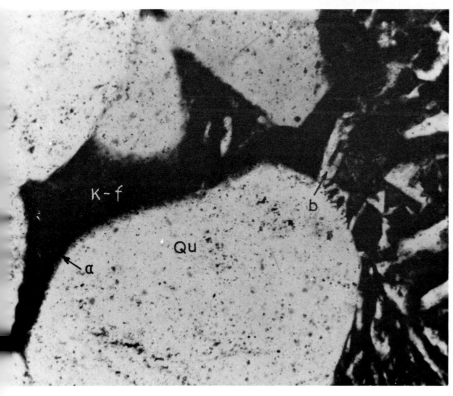

Fig. 357. Quartz with corroded outline infiltrated and replaced by K-feldspar. However, protruding parts of the quartz attain graphic form. Qu = quartz, K-f = K-feldspar in the extinction position, arrow "a" indicates corroded quartz outline, arrow "b" indicates protruding quartz attaining graphic form. Marblehead Granite, Massachusetts, U.S.A. With crossed nicols; enlargement 100 x.

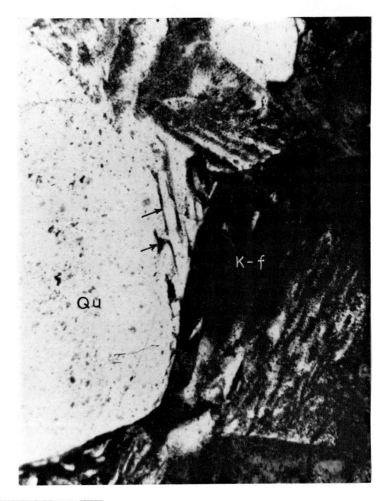

Fig. 358. Quartz infiltrated by K-feldspar, graphic-like intergrowths are produced. Qu = quartz, K-f = K-feldspar in the extinction position. Arrows mark infiltrations into quartz which result in or simulate graphic-like intergrowths. Marblehead Granite, Massachusetts, U.S.A. With crossed nicols; enlargement 100 x.

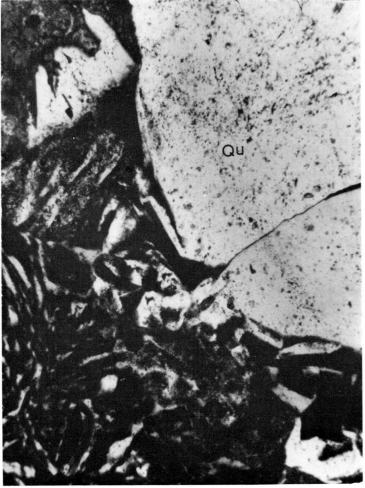

Fig. 359. Quartz infiltrated by K-feldspar (in the extinction position) gives rise to textures simulating graphic intergrowths. Qu = quartz. Marblehead Granite, Massachusetts, U.S.A. With crossed nicols; enlargement 100 x.

236

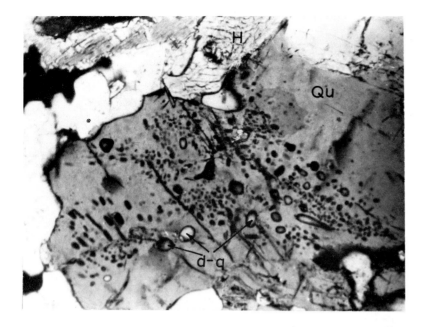

Fig. 360. A quartz with droplet-shaped fine quartzes. The quartz droplets most probably follow penetrability trends within the host quartz. H = hornblende, Qu = host quartz, d-q = quartz droplets. Bergeller Granite, Trubinasca, Alps. With crossed nicols; enlargement 100 x.

Fig. 361. Plagioclase with fine droplets of quartz. Pl = plagioclase, d-q = quartz droplets. Bergeller Granite, Trubinasca, Alps. With crossed nicols; enlargement 100 x.

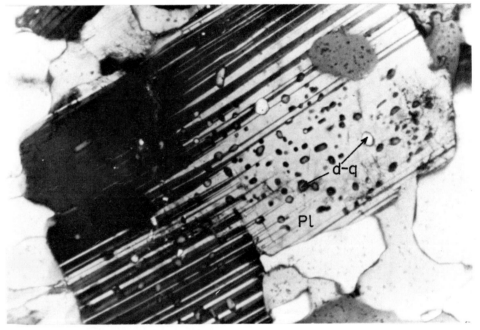

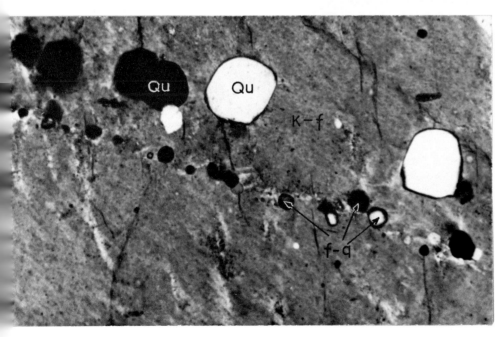

Fig. 362. K-feldspar with two types of quartz. The fine quartzes follow a linear arrangement in the K-feldspar which indicates a direction of greater penetrability of the host crystal. K-f = K-feldspar, Qu = quartz (larger), f-q = fine quartz. Fitchburg Granite, Massachusetts, U.S.A. With crossed nicols; enlargement 100 x.

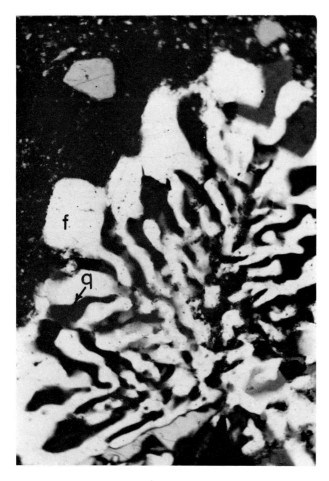

Fig. 363. Granophyric intergrowth of quartz–feldspar in a fine volcanic ground-mass, q = quartz, f = feldspar. Kuni, Asba-Tafari, Chercher, Ethiopia. With crossed nicols; enlargement 100 x.

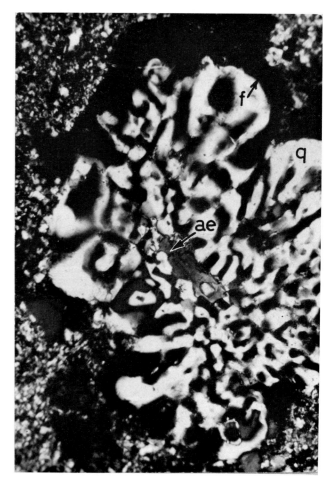

Fig. 364. Granophyric intergrowth of quartz–feldspar with an aegirine enclosed in the intergrowth. q = quartz, f = feldspar (orthoclase), ae = aegirine. Kuni, Asba-Tafari, Chercher, Ethiopia. With crossed nicols; enlargement 100 x.

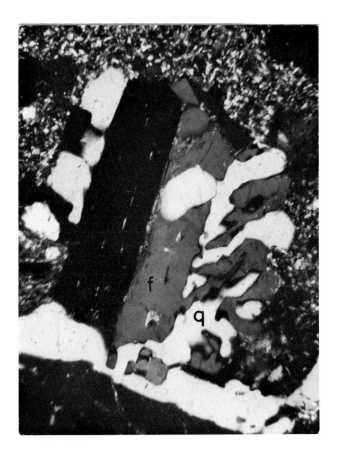

Fig. 365. Orthoclase (carlsbad twinning) in intergrowth with quartz. The granophyric texture is in a volcanic ground-mass, q = quartz, f = feldspar. Kuni, Asba-Tafari, Chercher, Ethiopia. With crossed nicols; enlargement 100 x.

Fig. 366. Feldspar with quartz in granophyric intergrowth. The granophyric intergrowth is restricted to an outer feldspar zone, almost geometrically delimited. f = feldspar (quartz-free), gr = granophyric intergrowth. Sea of Tranquillity, Moon. Photomicrograph; enlargement about 100 x. (Compare with Fig. 262.)

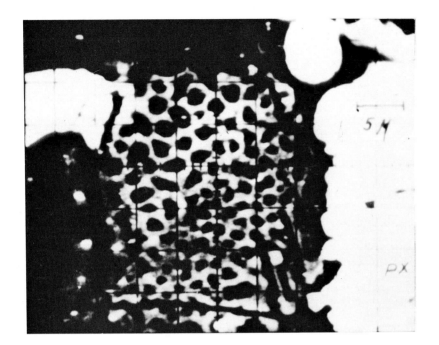

Fig. 367. An electron scanning microprobe picture indicating the graphic quartz—feldspar intergrowths picture of the granophyric texture shown in Fig. 366.

Fig. 368. A quartz—feldspar—muscovite tectonite in a pegmatoid. Symplectic textures (intergrowths of quartz—muscovite—feldspar); "sieve"-textures of quartz, recrystallisation and replacement, and corrosion textures are integral parts of this complex tectonite. A bending of the tectonite is shown in the photomicrograph. Details are shown in Fig. 369, 370 and 371. Pegmatoid at Carrara, Giggiga, Harrar, Ethiopia. With crossed nicols; enlargement 25 x.

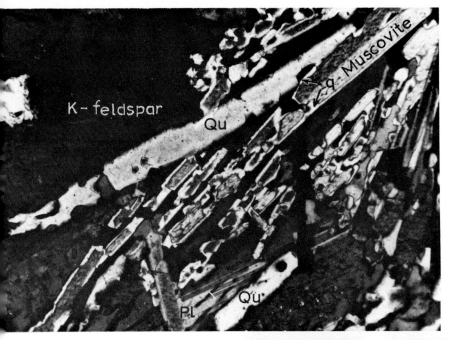

Fig. 369. Muscovite in K-feldspar (almost in extinction position) with metasomatic quartz partly as independent grains, partly intergranular between the mica. Often extensions of quartz grains corrode the muscovite and form a fine margin surrounding the mica. Qu = quartz, q = quartz margins surrounding corroded muscovite, K-feldspar in the extinction position, Pl = plagioclase. With crossed nicols; enlargement 25 x.

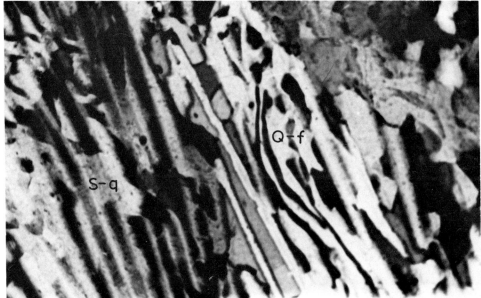

Fig. 370. Sieve intergrowth of recrystallised quartz texturally associated with quartz–feldspar symplectic intergrowth. S-q = sieve quartz, Q-f = symplectic quartz feldspar intergrowth. With crossed nicols; enlargement 100 x.

Fig. 371. Quartz–feldspar symplectic intergrowths with the crystalline components attaining idiomorphic shapes. Qu = quartz, f = feldspar. With crossed nicols; enlargement 100 x.

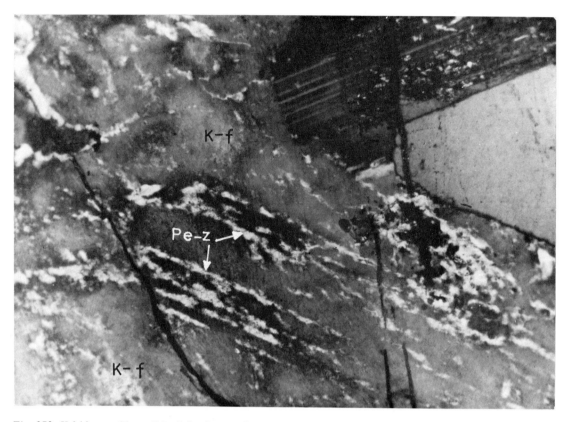

Fig. 372. K-feldspar with perthite following zonal arrangement in the host K-feldspar. K-f = K-feldspar, Pe-z = zonal perthite. Hornblende granite at Balma, Biella, Diemont, Italy. With crossed nicols; enlargement 100 x.

Fig. 373. Zoned K-feldspar with fine perthitic lines confined to a K-feldspar zone. K-f = K-feldspar, K-f-z = K-feldspar zone with fine perthitic bodies. Sandtal Granite, Werningerode, Harz, Germany. With crossed nicols; enlargement 100 x.

Fig. 374. Zoned K-feldspar with flame perthites transversing the orthoclase zoning. Markersdorf Granite, Saxony, Germany. With crossed nicols; enlargement 100 x.

Fig. 375. Zoned K-feldspar with perthite-free and perthite-containing zones. The intrazonal perthitisation consists of fine parallel arranged perthitic bodies. Also diffused perthitic masses transversing the K-feldspar are present. K-f = K-feldspar, d-p = diffused perthites transversing the K-feldspar zones. Hornblende granite at Balma, Biella, Piemont, Italy. With crossed nicols; enlargement 100 x.

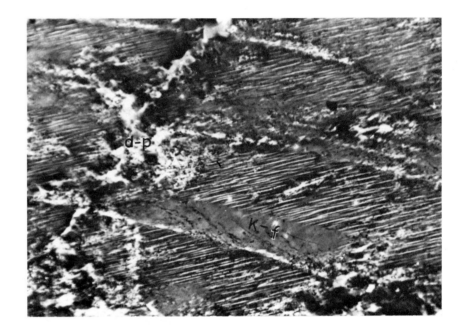

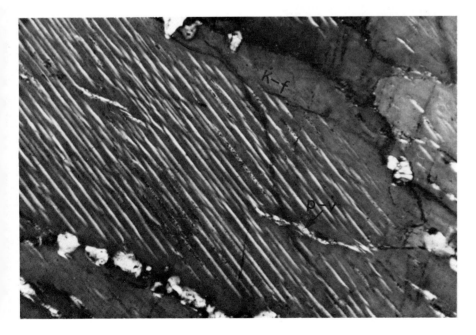

Fig. 376. K-feldspar with a perthite-free outer zone. In the central part of the K-feldspar perthitic lines are present. Where perthitic veinlets transverse the direction of the perthitic lines, perthite-free halos are shown. K-f = K-feldspar free of perthite, p-v = perthitic veinlet with a free-of-perthite halo. Schreirsgrun Granite, Vogtland, Saxony, Germany. With crossed nicols; enlargement 100 x.

243

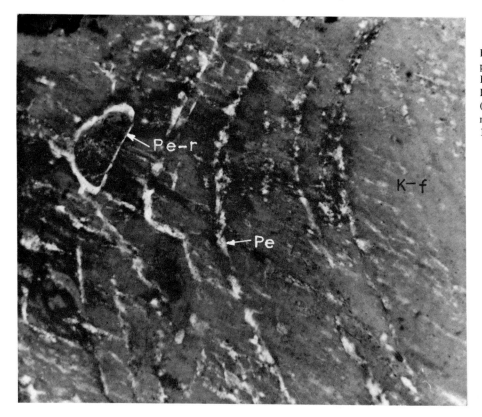

Fig. 377. Curved zonal perthite and a perthite ring structure in K-feldspar. K-f = K-feldspar, Pe = perthite curved zones, Pe–r = perthite ring structure. Hellewald (augite) Granite, Sewen, Vosges, Germany. With crossed nicols; enlargement 100 x.

Fig. 378. Diffused perthite masses zonal in arrangement in K-feldspar. K-f = K-feldspar, Pe = perthite. Hellewald, (augite) Granite, Sewen, Vosges, Germany. With crossed nicols; enlargement 100 x.

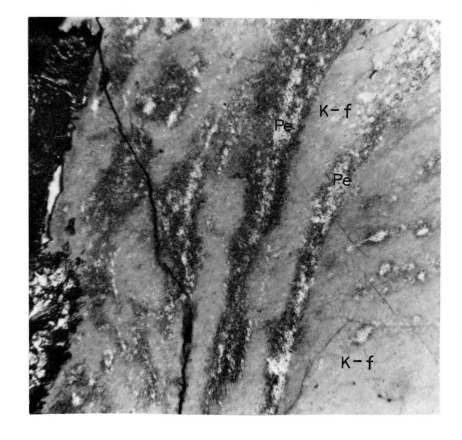

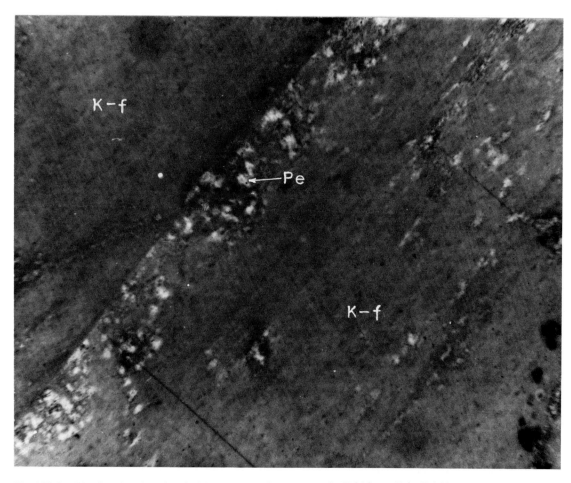

Fig. 379. Perthite dots forming a band which corresponds to a zone of a K-feldspar, K-f = K-feldspar, Pe = perthitic dots forming a band. Hornblende Granite at Rocheson, Vosges, Germany. With crossed nicols; enlargement 100 x.

Fig. 380. Perthitic veinlets terminating in perthitic cleavage-extensions following the K-feldspar. cleavage. Grubensgrund Granite, Schenkenzell, Black Forest, Germany. With crossed nicols; enlargement 100 x.

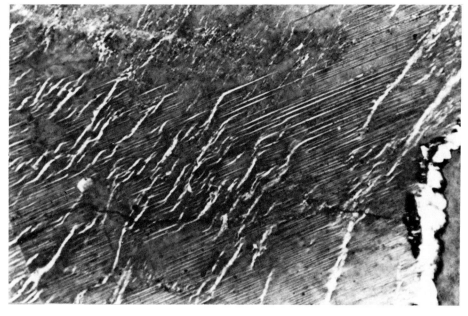

Fig. 381. Perthitic veinlets crossing the twinning plane of K-feldspar and with fine linear perthitic extensions. Grubensgrund Granite, Schenkenzell, Black Forest, Germany. With crossed nicols; enlargement 100 x.

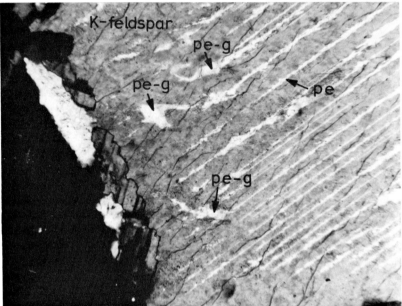

Fig. 382. K-feldspar with orientated perthitic lines. Small ganglia-like perthitic bodies are also present, pe = perthitic lines, pe-g = perthitic ganglia. Buchwald Granite, Silesia, Germany. With crossed nicols; enlargement 100 x.

Fig. 383. K-feldspar with perthite following its cleavage. Whereas the perthite formation in certain portions is restricted to the cleavage plane, in others it diffuses out of it. K-f = K-feldspar, Pe = perthite. Buchwald Granite, Silesia, Germany. With crossed nicols; enlargement 100 x.

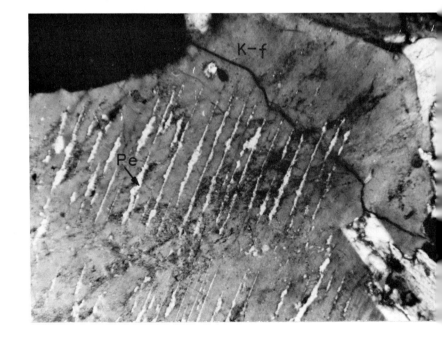

246

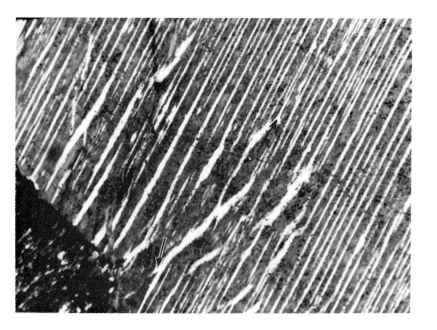

Fig. 384. K-feldspar with orientated perthitic lines. Arrows show that the perthitic lines are extensions of vein-shaped perthitic bodies. Buchwald Granite, Silesia, Germany. With crossed nicols; enlargement 100 x.

Fig. 385. Strained K-feldspar with perthitic veinlets parallel orientated (following the cleavage of the host). Arrow shows flame perthites associated with cracks of the K-feldspar. Norra Granite, Udde, Sweden. With crossed nicols; enlargement 100 x.

247

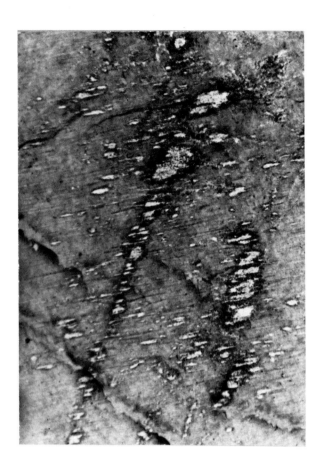

Fig. 386. K-feldspar with cleavage and with fine perthitic flakes situated along cleavage planes. Some kind of alteration is associated with the perthites. Hellewald Granite, Sewen, Vosges, Germany. With crossed nicols; enlargement 100 x.

Fig. 387. K-feldspar with metasomatic perthitic flakes. Also perthitic branches extend from the flakes. Arrow "a" shows a K-feldspar part deliniated by two cleavage cracks replaced by perthite. The flake and vein perthites shown most probably represent metasomatic replacements. K-f = K-feldspar, Pe = perthite. Yavello Granite, Borona, Ethiopia. With crossed nicols; enlargement 100 x.

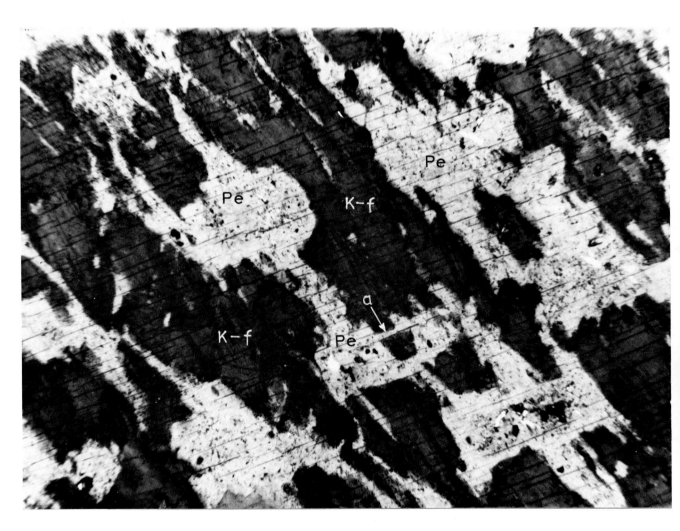

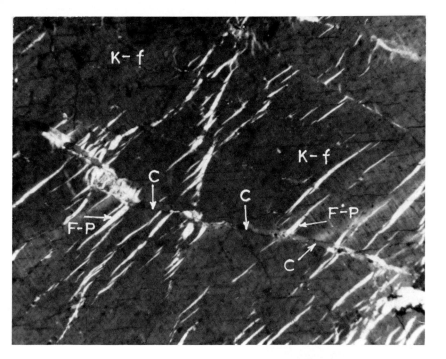

Fig. 388. K-feldspar with cracks out of which flame perthites extend. K-f = K-feldspar, F-P = flame perthites, C = cracks. Lavia Granite, Finland. With crossed nicols; enlargement 100 x.

Fig. 389 and 390. K-feldspar with a system of cracks following a pattern infiltrated by perthite-forming solutions. K-f = K-feldspar, Pe = perthite. Val Rusein Granite, Switzerland. With crossed nicols; enlargements 100 x, 200 x.

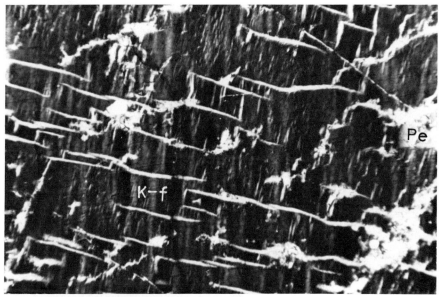

Fig. 390.

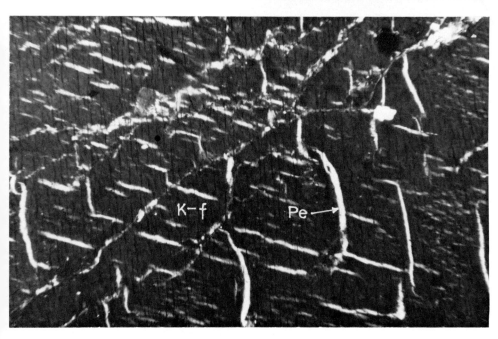

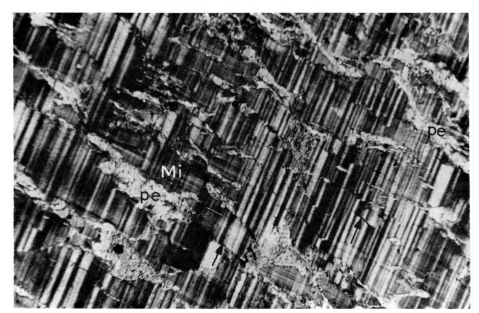

Fig. 391.

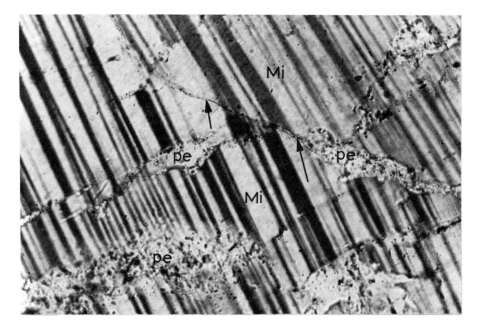

Fig. 391 and 392. Microcline affected by a system of cracks (resulting in microcline blocks) infiltrated by perthite-forming solutions. The perthites are selectively sericitised in comparison to the microcline. Arrows indicate cracks, pe = perthite, Mi = microcline. Cap Carbonara Granite, Elba, Italy. With crossed nicols; enlargements 100 x, 200 x.

Fig. 393. K-feldspar with strained plains occupied by perthite. K-f = K-feldspar, pe = perthite, qu = quartz. Didessa Granite, Ethiopia. With crossed nicols; enlargement 100 x.

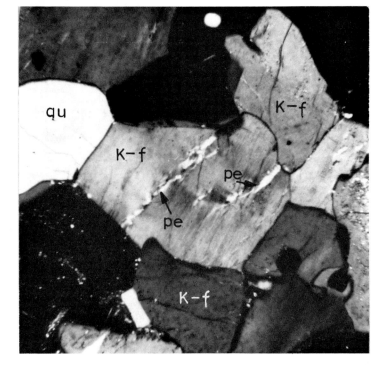

Fig. 394. K-feldspar with a restricted zone of intense perthitisation which seems to extend from a zone of weakness (greater penetrability) of the K-feldspar. The perthite is in the extinction position. K-f = K-feldspar. Didessa Granite, Ethiopia. With crossed nicols; enlargement 100 x.

Fig. 395 and 396. Perthitised microcline with perthite bodies sending extensions occupying partly a veinlet in which quartz is also present. Pegmatite at Strathory, Ross-shire, Scotland. With crossed nicols; enlargement 100 x.

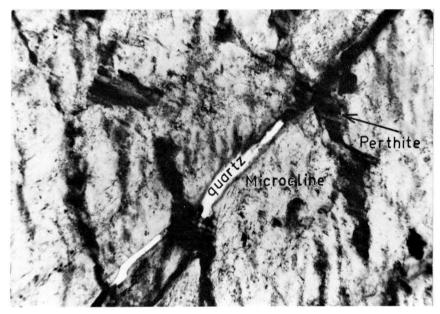

Fig. 396.

251

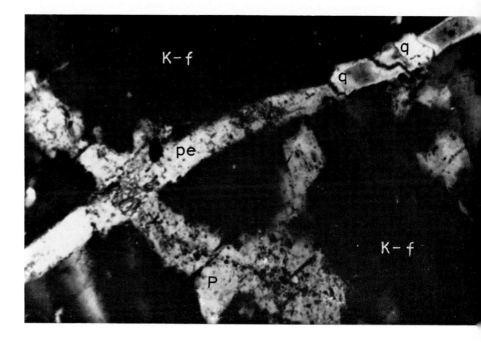

Fig. 397. K-feldspar in the extinction position in which perthitoid bodies are present. An extension of the perthite attains vein-like form; along this veinlet quartz is also present. K-f = K-feldspar (extinction position), P = perthitoid body, pe = perthite veinlet, q = fine quartz also present in the veinlet. Didessa Granite, Ethiopia. With crossed nicols; enlargement 100 x.

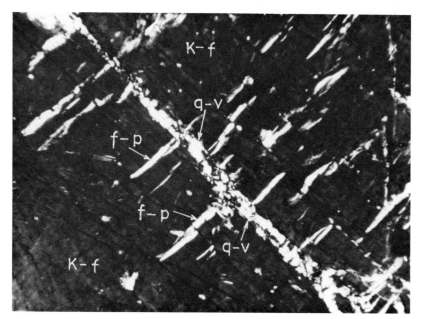

Fig. 398. K-feldspar with a veinlet of quartz. The quartz-veinlet is the starting point out of which fine flame perthites extend into the K-feldspar perpendicular to the quartz veinlet. K-f = K-feldspar (in the extinction position), q-v = quartz veinlet, f-p = flame perthites. Ondonock Granodiorite, West Ethiopia. With crossed nicols; enlargement 100 x.

Fig. 399. K-feldspar with two quartz veinlets out of which extend flame perthites perpendicular to the quartz veinlets. K-f = K-feldspar, f-p = flame perthite, q-v = quartz veinlet. Ondonock Granodiorite, West Ethiopia. With crossed nicols; enlargement 100 x.

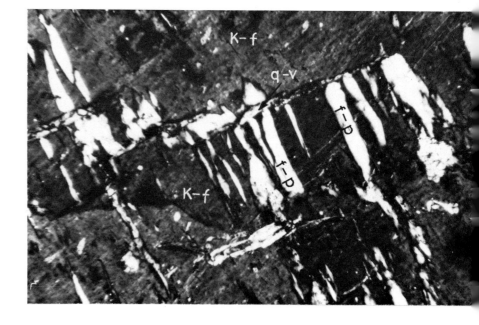

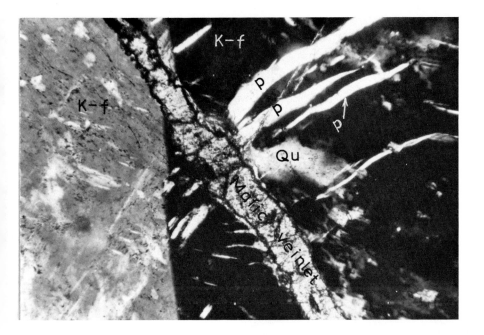

Fig. 400. K-feldspar with a veinlet of mafic minerals with perthite partly marginal and partly flame-like bodies extending perpendicular from the mafic veinlet into the K-feldspar. K-f = K-feldspar (also in extinction position), Qu = quartz, p = perthite. Ondonock Granodiorite, West Ethiopia. With crossed nicols; enlargement 100 x.

Fig. 401. K-feldspar with vein perthites, portions of which, due to tectonic influences, have changed into augen-shaped perthitic lenses. K-f = K-feldspar, Pe = perthite, p-l = lens augen-shaped perthitic body due to tectonic deformation. Chambe, Adolla, South Ethiopia. With crossed nicols; enlargement 100 x.

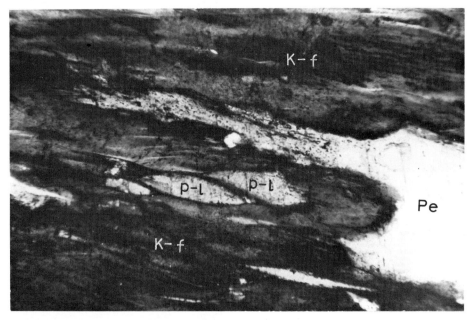

Fig. 402. Perthites in K-feldspar. In general the outline of the perthite is dependent on the influence exercised by the pre-existing K-feldspar. Due to tectonic deformation the perthites show an undulating deformation. K-f = K-feldspar, Pe = perthites, M = muscovite. Chambe, Adolla, South Ethiopia. With crossed nicols; enlargement 100 x.

253

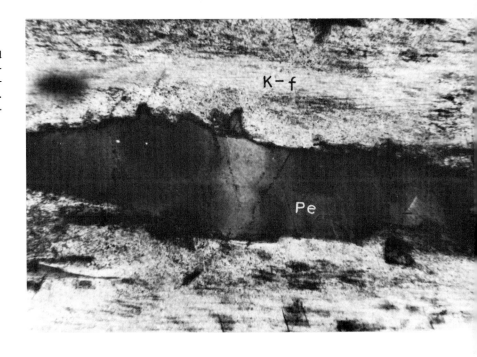

Fig. 403. K-feldspar with a perthite band (vein). Due to tectonic influences the perthitite shows strain effects, undulating extinction. K-f = K-feldspar, Pe = perthite. Pegmatite: Chambe, Adolla, S. Ethiopia. crossed nicols; enlargement 100 x.

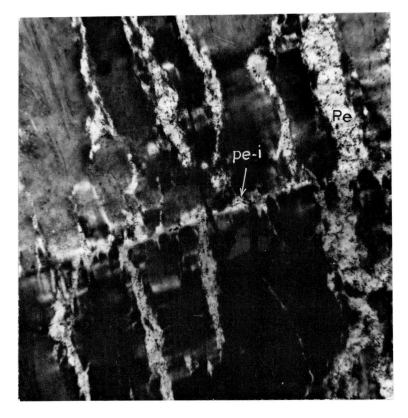

Fig. 404. Twinned K-feldspar with perthites crossing the twin-plane and with other perthite individuals partly following the twin plane. Pe = perthite crossing twin plane, pe-i = perthite following interspace of twinning. Granite: Wehmo, Nystad, Helsingfors, Finland. With crossed nicols; enlargement 100 x.

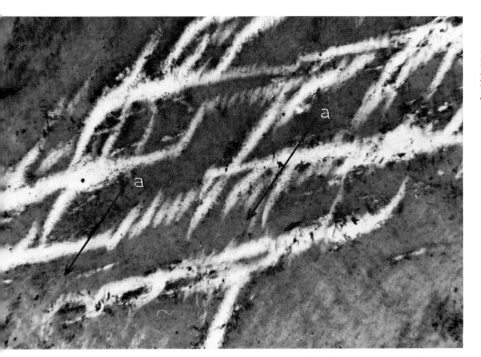

Fig. 405. Branching vein-perthites with flame perthitic branches which follow a parallel orientation as indicated by arrow "a". Yavello, Borona, South Ethiopia. With crossed nicols; enlargement 100 x.

Fig. 406. Different orientation from Fig. 405. Shows that the flame perthite extensions follow one of the cross-twinning directions of the microcline host. Yavello, Borona, South Ethiopia. With crossed nicols; enlargement 100 x.

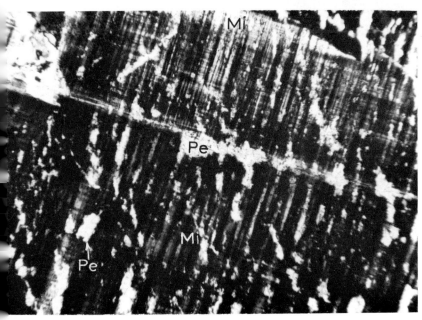

Fig. 407. Cross-twinned microcline metasomatically infiltrated by perthite. Pe = perthite, Mi = microcline. Wange Granite, Central Sweden. With crossed nicols; enlargement 100 x.

255

Fig. 408. Lamellar K-feldspar with replacement-perthitisation following and diffusing out of K-feldspar lamellae. Baveno Granite, Italy. With crossed nicols; enlargement 100 x.

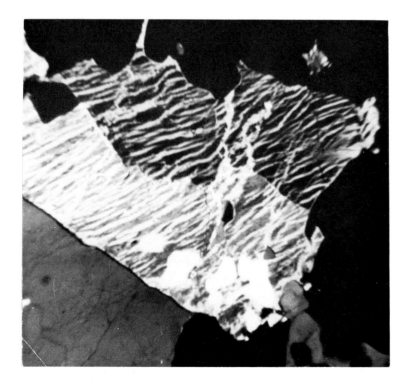

Fig. 409 and 410. Two differently orientated K-feldspars with perthitic veinlets trasnversing their common boundary; also fine perthite partly follows the boundary line. It should be pointed out that the proportion of perthite to the host K-feldspar is greater than what should be expected if it was an ex-solution phase. Pe = perthite transversing the boundary between the two K-feldspars, arrow indicates perthite situated between the two K-feldspars. Ragunda Granite, Sweden. With crossed nicols; enlargements 50 x, 100 x.

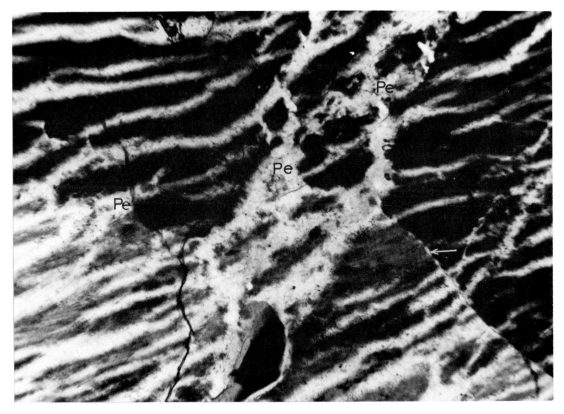

Fig. 410.

Fig. 411. Twinned K-feldspar with metasomatic plagioclase replacement affecting the K-feldspars from the margins and extending often across the twinning. K-f = K-feldspar, m-pl = metasomatic plagioclase, Qu = quartz. Quincy Granite, Massachusetts, U.S.A. With crossed nicols; enlargement 100 x.

Fig. 412. Intergranular plagioclase (A) with extensions (B) penetrating into the adjacent K-feldspar. Arrow "C" shows older plagioclase enclosed in the microcline. Pegmatoid at Yavello, Borona, South Ethiopia. With crossed nicols; enlargement 20 x.

Fig. 413. Intracrystalline extensions of plagioclase (see also Fig. 412) show continuations attaining flame perthitic form (see arrow "a"). With crossed nicols; enlargement 100 x.

Fig. 414. K-feldspar with flame perthitic bodies. These are marginal and outside the K-feldspar host. K-f = K-feldspar, f-p = flame perthite. Didessa Granite, Ethiopia. With crossed nicols; enlargement 100 x.

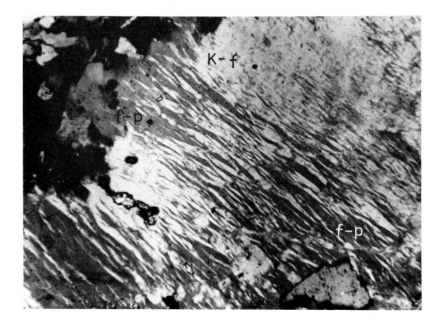

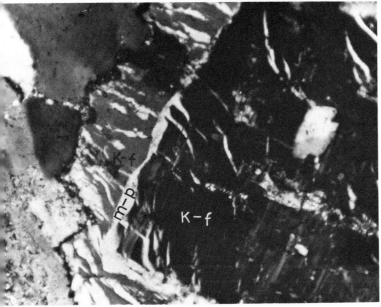

Fig. 415. K-feldspar in the extinction position in contact with another K-feldspar (K-f) which is perthitised. Marginal perthite (m-p) following the contact between the two K-feldspars sends flame-like extensions into the K-feldspar which is in the extinction position. Hornblende syenite at Tronitz, Saxony, Germany. With crossed nicols; enlargement 100 x.

Fig. 416. K-feldspar in the extinction position with marginal plagioclase infiltrating and replacing the orthoclase. The plagioclase infiltrations attain a perthitoid form. However, a metasomatic replacement appearance is characteristic for the plagioclase. Quincy Granite, Massachusetts, U.S.A. With crossed nicols; enlargement 100 x.

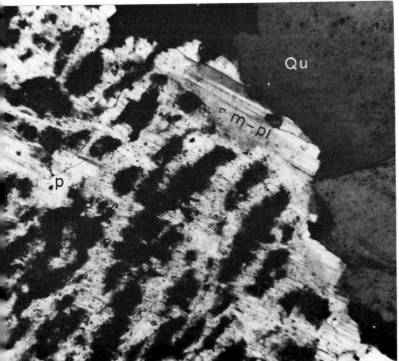

Fig. 417. K-feldspar in the extinction position with marginal plagioclase extending into the orthoclase and attaining a perthitic form and character. m-pl ; marginal plagioclase, p = perthite, Qu = quartz. Ragunda Granite, Sweden. With crossed nicols; enlargement 100 x.

259

Fig. 418. Two K-feldspars differently orientated with differently orientated perthitic bodies also. Nevertheless, the perthitisation of one of the K-feldspars partly follows the boundary of the two K-feldspars, K-f = K-feldspars, Pe = perthites. Didessa Granite, Ethiopia. With crossed nicols; enlargement 100 x.

Fig. 419. K-feldspar forming a broad margin around the quartz and extending into microcline, in irregular vein shapes. Often small parts of quartz (see arrow) are enclosed by the perthitic vein-like system. Qu = quartz, Mi = microcline, p = perthites. Granite near Red Sea, Egypt. With crossed nicols; enlargement 100 x.

260

Fig. 420. Intergranular plagioclase between older quartz and microcline grains has extensions continuing into the K-feldspar (almost extinction position) and attaining perthitic form and character. Pegmatoid at Yavello, Borona, South Ethiopia. With crossed nicols; enlargement 25 x.

Fig. 421. Quartz in contact with K-feldspar. A perthitic ganglion partly extends into the quartz (see arrow "a") and partly sends extensions attaining perthitic form. Qu = quartz, pe = perthite, p-g = perthitic ganglion. Mt. Mulatto Granite, Predazzo, Tirol, Italy. With crossed nicols; enlargement 100 x.

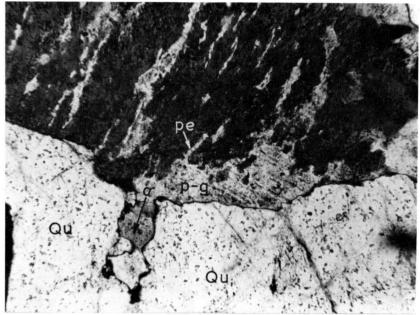

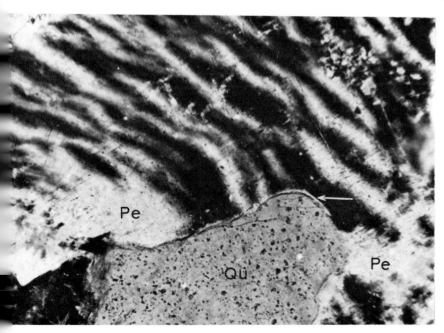

Fig. 422. Perthitised K-feldspar in contact with quartz. Arrow shows a fine perthitic margin bordering the quartz (representing infiltration of perthite interleptonically between the K-feldspar and the quartz). Qu = quartz, Pe = perthite, K-feldspar in the extinction position. Ragunda Granite, Sweden. With crossed nicols; enlargement 100 x.

261

Fig. 423. A system of anastomosing perthitic veins with parts following the intergranular of K-feldspar and quartz, Pe = perthite, Qu = quartz, K-f = K-feldspar. Ragunda Granite, Sweden. With crossed nicols; enlargement 100 x.

Fig. 424. Microcline with a border of plagioclase extending into the K-feldspar and attaining a perthitoid form. The plagioclase border and the perthite formation can be considered as metasomatic replacement processes. B-Pl = plagioclase border, pe = perthitic-metasomatic infiltrations. Didessa Granite, Ethiopia. With crossed nicols; enlargement 100 x.

Fig. 425. K-feldspar in contact with plagioclase which sends perthitic bodies in the orthoclase. The perthitic plagioclase extensions and the "independent" perthitic bodies follow curved lines of the K-feldspar. K-f = K-feldspar, pe = perthite, Pl = plagioclase. Wehmo Granite, Nystad, Helsingfors, Finland. With crossed nicols; enlargement 100 x.

Fig. 426. K-feldspar with a perthitic ganglion which sends off perthitic veinlets, one of which has infiltrated into a plagioclase along its twinning. Pe = perthitic ganglion, Pl = plagioclase. Didessa Granite, Ethiopia. With crossed nicols; enlargement 100 x.

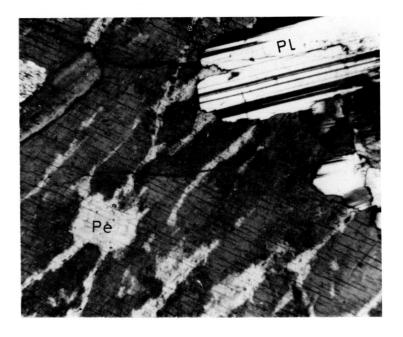

Fig. 427. Plagioclase partly surrounded, partly infiltrated by flame perthitic bodies, in a K-feldspar (extinction position). Uthammar Granite, Sweden. With crossed nicols; enlargement 100 x.

Fig. 428 and 429 (different orientations). Plagioclases enclosed in K-feldspar. A plagioclase grain is penetrated through by a branching and anastomosing perthitic veinlet. K-feldspar (almost in extinction position), Pl = plagioclase, v-p = perthitic veinlet. Granite at Linz-Margarethen, Austria. With crossed nicols; enlargement 100 x.

Fig. 429.

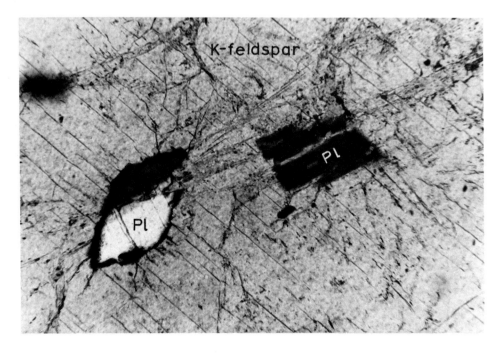

Fig. 430. Corroded plagioclase in contact with K-feldspar. Perthites from the adjacent K-feldspar extend along the corrosion "canals" into the plagioclase. Corroded plagioclase free of perthite infiltration. Pl = plagioclase, p = perthite, K-f = K-feldspar. Bergen Granite. Vogtland, Saxony, Germany. With crossed nicols; enlargement 100 x.

Fig. 431. Microcline in the extinction position with metasomatic veins of perthite which enclose or partly surround an independent plagioclase phase. Pe = perthite, Pl = plagioclase. Granite near Red Sea, Egypt. With crossed nicols; enlargement 100 x.

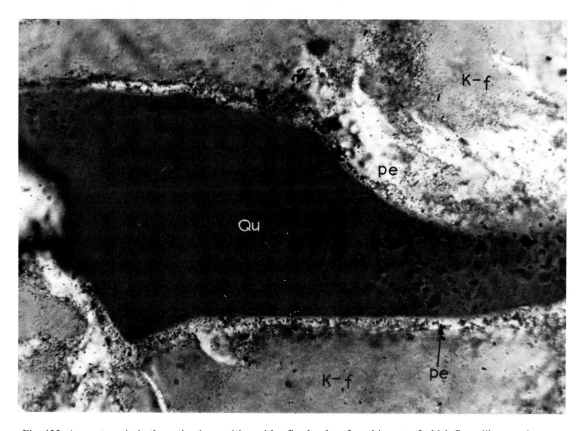

Fig. 432. A quartz grain in the extinction position with a fine border of perthite out of which flame-like protuberances extend into the K-feldspar. Qu = quartz (in extinction position), K-f = K-feldspar, pe = perthite. Ramsta Granite, Nordingra district, Sweden. With crossed nicols; enlargement 200 x.

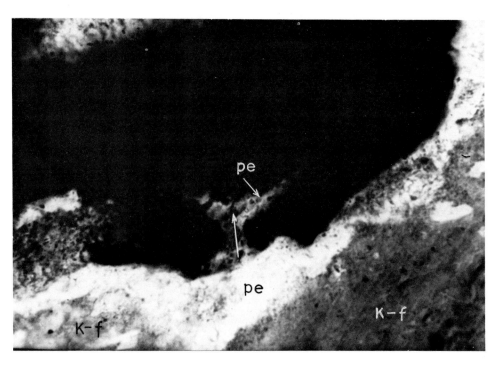

Fig. 433. Quartz (in extinction position) partly bordered by perthite, extensions of which infiltrate and extend into the quartz. K-f = K-feldspar, pe = perthite, arrows indicate perthitic extension in the quartz. Ramsta Granite, Nordingra district, Sweden. With crossed nicols; enlargement 200 x.

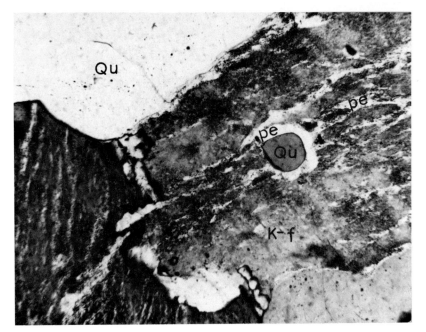

Fig. 434. Perthitised K-feldspar with a ring perthite surrounding a quartz grain. Anastomosing perthitic extensions extend from the ring perthite into the K-feldspar. Qu = quartz, K-f = K-feldspar, pe = perthite. Ragunda Granite, Sweden. With crossed nicols; enlargement 100 x.

Fig. 435. Perthitised K-feldspar, with a perthite individual extending into a biotite and following its cleavage. K-f = perthitised K-feldspar, Bi = biotite, Pe = perthite extending into the biotite's cleavage. Ragunda Granite, Sweden. With crossed nicols; enlargement 100 x.

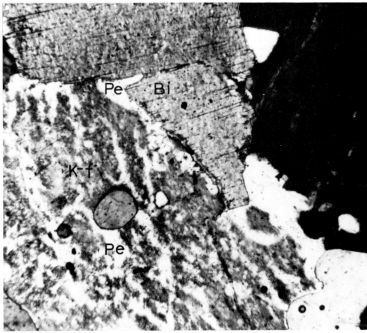

Fig. 436. K-feldspar with sphene. Fine perthites interleptonically occupy the margin sphene/K-feldspar. K-f = K-feldspar, S = sphene, Pe = perthite. Val Rusein Granite, Switzerland. With crossed nicols; enlargement 100 x.

267

Fig. 437. Perthitised K-feldspar intersected by an idioblastic sphene, which has cut across the perthitic veinlets in the K-feldspar. K-f = K-feldspar, S = sphene, pe = perthite. Val Rusein Granite, Switzerland. With crossed nicols; enlargement 100 x.

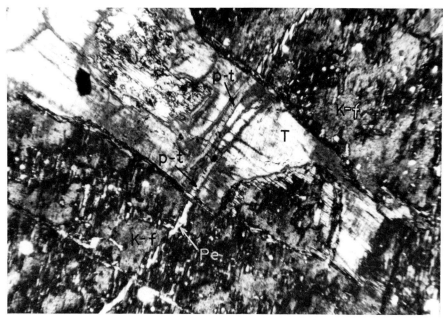

Fig. 438. Tourmaline in perthitised K-feldspar. Perthitic veinlets of the K-feldspar extend into the tourmaline. However, a reaction between the perthite-forming solutions and the tourmaline has taken place. T = tourmaline, Pe = perthites in K-feldspar, p-t = perthites in the tourmaline. Ragunda Granite, Sweden. With crossed nicols; enlargement 100 x.

Fig. 439. Two perthitised K-feldspars differently orientated. The perthites of the one form a marginal border between the two K-feldspars. Perthite extends into the border perthite of the other K-feldspar individual. K-f = K-feldspar, Pe = perthite. Ragunda Granite, Sweden. With crossed nicols; enlargement 200 x.

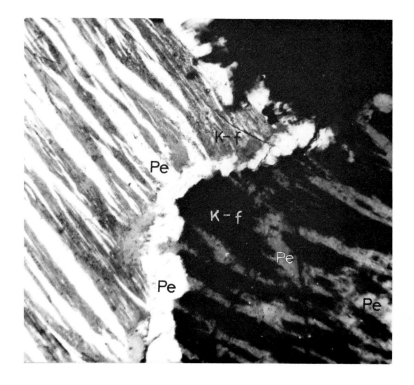

268

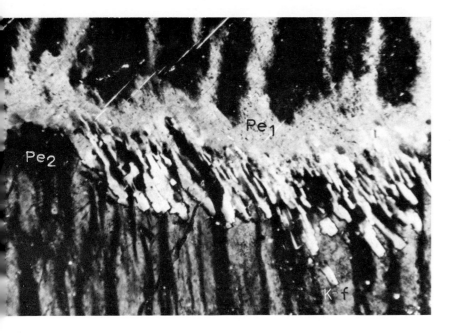

Fig. 440. A contact of two perthitised K-feldspars (differently orientated). The upper K-feldspar grain in the photomicrograph is in the extinction position with perthites marginally assuming a perthitic boundary which in turn is in intergrowth with the K-feldspar and perthites of the lower K-feldspar grain. Pe_1 = perthite of the upper K-feldspar, Pe_2 = perthite of the lower K-feldspar, K-f = lower K-feldspar. Ragunda Granite, Sweden. With crossed nicols; enlargement 100 x.

Fig. 441. K-feldspar with marginal phase of plagioclase. Perthite bodies extend and infiltrate along cracks of the marginal plagioclase (often resulting in characteristic infiltration and replacement phenomena). K-feldspar in extinction position, Pl = marginal plagioclase, pe = perthitic infiltration extending as well into the marginal plagioclase. Ragunda Granite, Sweden. With crossed nicols; enlargement 100 x.

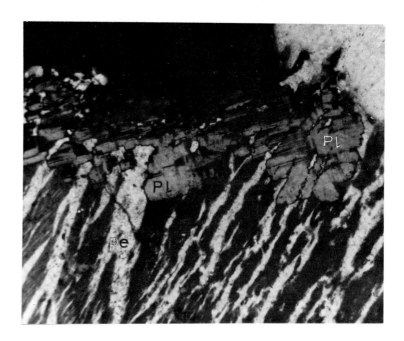

Fig. 442. K-feldspar in the extinction position with plagioclase and quartz grains included. Flake perthites with margins of vein perthites partly surround quartz and partly extend in the intergranular between the quartz grains. F-K = K-feldspar (also in extinction position), f-p = flake perthite, v-p = marginal vein perthite, Qu = quartz. Val Rusein Granite, Switzerland. With crossed nicols; enlargement 100 x.

269

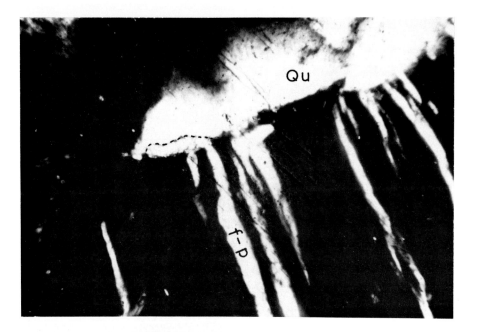

Fig. 443. K-feldspar (in extinction position) with quartz marginal to it. Perthitic bodies partly follow the margin quartz/K-feldspar and partly extend into the K-feldspar. Qu = quartz, f-p = flame perthites. Ondonock Granodiorite, West Ethiopia. With crossed nicols; enlargement 100 x.

Fig. 444. Microcline with quartz and mica from the contacts of which flame perthitic bodies extend outwards. Mi = microcline, Qu = quartz, f-p = flame perthite, m = mica. Hanga Granite, Finland. With crossed nicols; enlargement 100 x.

Fig. 445. Flame perthite partly surrounding the quartz and eventually attaining a perthitic lamellar shape. Qu = quartz, f = flame perthite, arrow indicates flame perthite attaining lamellar perthitic form. Obertal Granite, Harz, Germany. With crossed nicols; enlargement 100 x.

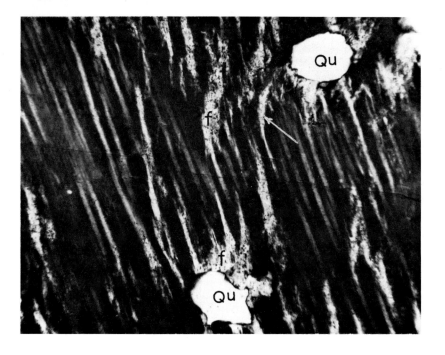

270

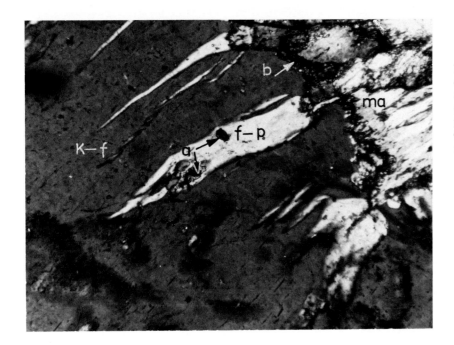

Fig. 446. K-feldspar with flame perthite enclosing mafic grain-components (arrow "a") and being in contact with other mafic grains (arrow "b"). K-f = K-feldspar, f-p = flame perthite, ma = mafic components. Ondonock Granodiorite, West Ethiopia. With crossed nicols; enlargement 100 x.

Fig. 447. Flake perthites with extensions attaining flame-like forms. f = flake perthites, fl = flame-like perthitic extensions. Damsgaard Granite, Kristiania area, Norway. With crossed nicols; enlargement 100 x.

Fig. 448. Metasomatic lens-like perthite due to infiltration and replacement of K-feldspar. These perthitoid bodies unite and form a ganglion-like body in the K-feldspar. Pe-g = perthitoid ganglion, K-f = K-feldspar. Hornblende syenite at Tronitz, Saxony, Germany.

271

Fig. 449. K-feldspar with a wave-like undulating extinction infiltrated along planes of penetrability by perthite-forming solutions, often forming ganglia-like bodies. There is a tendency for the perthitic veinlets to follow the undulating forms of the K-feldspar. Didessa Granite, Ethiopia. With crossed nicols; enlargement 100 x.

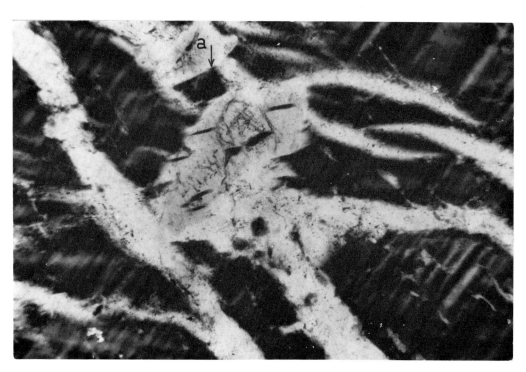

Fig. 450. Perthitic ganglion with flame-like extensions and vein perthitic branches. The branches of the "ganglion" often anastomose. Parts of microcline are enclosed in the perthite (arrow "a"). Yavello, Borona, South Ethiopia. With crossed nicols; enlargement 200 x.

272

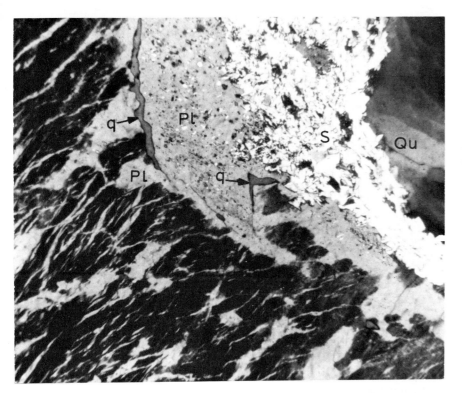

Fig. 451. K-feldspar in the extinction position in contact with a sericitised plagioclase which sends out many flame perthitic extensions. The transition from the plagioclase to the flame perthites suggests an infiltration origin of the latter. Qu = quartz with undulating extinction, q = quartz veinlet, Pl = plagioclase, S = sericitised plagioclase. Harrar Granite, Ethiopia. With crossed nicols; enlargement 100 x.

Fig. 452. Myrmekitised plagioclase corroded and partly surrounded by K-feldspar. Flame perthite of the K-feldspar follows the contact corroded-plagioclase/K-feldspar. K-f = K-feldspar, Pe = perthite following corroded plagioclase outline. Fitchburg Granite, Massachusetts, U.S.A. With crossed nicols; enlargement 100 x.

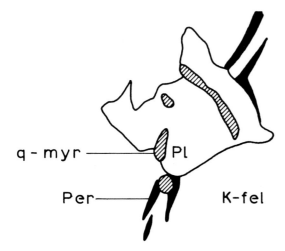

Fig. 453. Flame perthites enclosing myrmekitic quartz which has been freed from its initial symplectic association with the plagioclase due to the corrosion of the myrmekite by the later K-feldspar. The flame perthite is formed after the corrosion of the plagioclase by the K-feldspar. K-fel = K-feldspar, q-myr = myrmekitic quartz, Pl = plagioclase, Per = perthite. Didessa Granite, West Ethiopia.; enlargement 100 x.

273

Fig. 454. K-feldspar in contact with corroded plagioclase. Flame perthitic bodies extend into the corroded outline of the plagioclase. The perthitisation is later than the plagioclase corrosion. K-f = K-feldspar, Pl = plagioclase, f-p = flame perthite. Didessa Granite, Ethiopia. With crossed nicols; enlargement 100 x.

Fig. 455. K-feldspar with perthite. Both the high proportion of perthite to K-feldspar and the irregular perthitic shapes rather suggest a metasomatic origin for the plagioclase. K-feldspar in the extinction position. Peterhead Granite, Scotland. With crossed nicols; enlargement 100 x.

Fig. 456. Ganglia-like perthitic bodies with fine anastomosing perthitic veinlets extending in the K-feldspar. The orientation of the polysynthetic twinning planes in the different ganglia coincide. Pe-g = perthitic ganglia, K-f = K-feldspar. Stoa Granite, Kristiania area, Norway. With crossed nicols; enlargement 100 x.

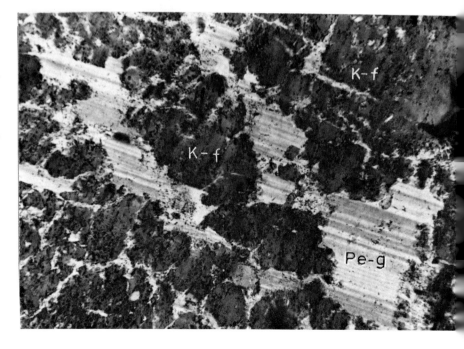

274

Fig. 457. Perthite band in K-feldspar in contact with biotite. Fine myrmekitic quartz intergrowths are produced as a reaction of biotite and the metasomatically formed plagioclase (perthite). Bi = biotite, Pe = perthite, K-f = K-feldspar, m-b = myrmekitised biotite. Stoa Granite, Kristiania area, Norway. With crossed nicols; enlargement 100 x.

Fig. 458. Perthitic bodies with branching apophyses in twinned K-feldspar. Perthitic branches and bodies transverse the boundary of the twinning. Pe = perthites, K-f = K-feldspar (also in the extinction position). Stoa Granite, Kristiania area, Norway. With crossed nicols; enlargement 100 x.

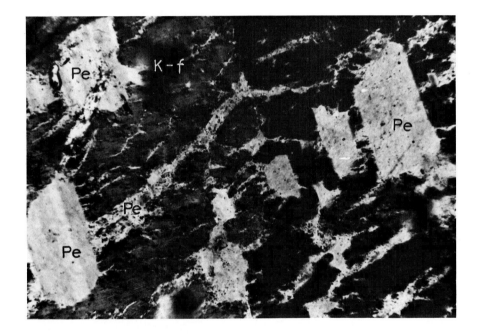

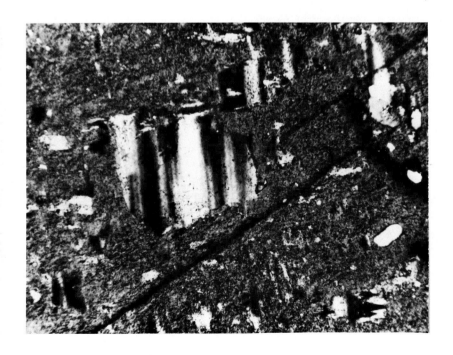

Fig. 459. Flake perthite with small apophyses in K-feldspar. Peterhead Granite, Scotland. With crossed nicols; enlargement 100 x.

275

Fig. 460. K-feldspar with perthitic veinlets associated with quartz veinlets and mobilised vein-like textures of muscovite. K-f = K-feldspar, Pe = perthite, M = muscovite, q = quartz, bi = biotite. Wehmo Granite, Nystad, Helsingfors, Finland. With crossed nicols; enlargement 100 x.

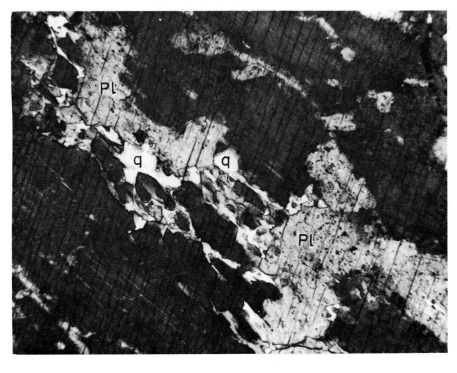

Fig. 461. Metasomatic perthitic replacements associated with fine quartz veinlets. A partial intergrowth of these two replacement phases has taken place. Pl = plagioclase (perthitic replacements); q = quartz. Harrar Granite, Ethiopia. With crossed nicols; enlargement 100 x.

Fig. 462. Plagioclase "ganglion-like" with branching extensions attaining vein perthitic form and character. A later quartz is formed in the perthitic ganglion with extensions of it infiltrating into the perthite and attaining myrmekitoid appearance and character. Also extension of quartz, worm-like in form, is present in the perthite. Yavello, Borona, South Ethiopia. With crossed nicols; enlargement 25 x.

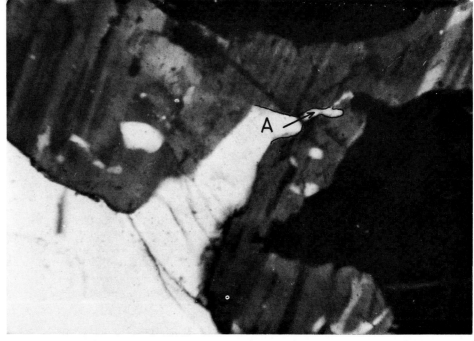

Fig. 463. (Detail of Fig. 462.) Quartz extends into the perthitic "ganglion" attaining myrmekitic quartz form (see arrow "A"). With crossed nicols; enlargement 100 x.

Fig. 464. Corroded plagioclase with relic attaining branch-like form. K-f = K-feldspar, Pl = plagioclase. Mt. Mulatto Granite, Predazzo, Tirol, Italy. With crossed nicols; enlargement 100 x.

Fig. 465. A well-developed crystalline form of a perthitic "ganglion" with vein extensions in K-feldspar (in extinction position). Melca-Guba Gneiss-granite, Borona, South Ethiopia. With crossed nicols; enlargement 100 x.

Fig. 466. A plagioclase body "ganglion" in K-feldspar; extensions of the plagioclase attain perthitic form and character. Also present are perthitoid bodies "disconnected" from the ganglion plagioclase. Yavello, Borona, Ethiopia. With crossed nicols; enlargement 100 x.

Fig. 467. A perthite in microcline. The perthite exhibits a noticeable reaction margin. Yavello, Borona, South Ethiopia. With crossed nicols; enlargement 100 x.

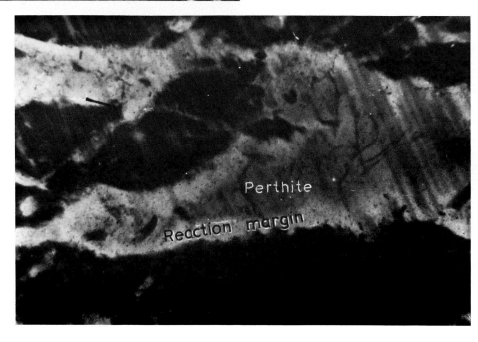

Fig. 468. Plagioclase enclosing portions of perthitised K-feldspar and simultaneously showing extensions of perthitised K-feldspar into the plagioclase (arrow "a"). Also perthite penetrating into the same plagioclase (arrow "b"). Pl = plagioclase almost in extinction position, K-f-p = perthitised K-feldspar, Pe = perthite penetrating into the plagioclase. Harrar Granite, Ethiopia. With crossed nicols; enlargement 100 x.

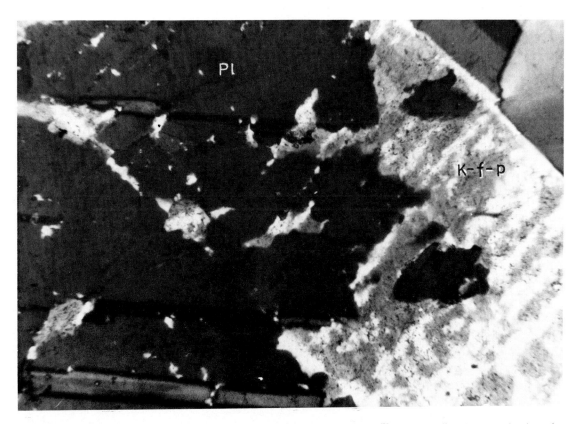

Fig. 469. Plagioclase (almost in extinction position) with perthitised K-feldspar "enclosed" and penetrating into the plagioclase. The portions of the perthitised K-feldspar enclosed in the plagioclase may represent actual penetration textures. Harrar Granite, Ethiopia. With crossed nicols; enlargement 100 x.

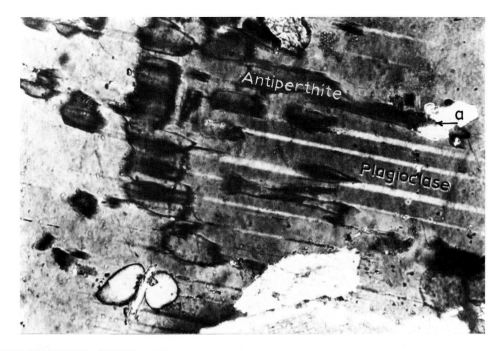

Fig. 470. Plagioclase with antiperthite infiltrations along the twin planes of the plagioclase. Also graphic-like quartz structure is present in the plagioclase, with a reaction margin between the quartz and the feldspar (see also Fig. 341). Arrow "a" shows antiperthite extending into mica enclosed in the plagioclase. Aar Gneiss-granite, Switzerland. With crossed nicols; enlargement 200 x.

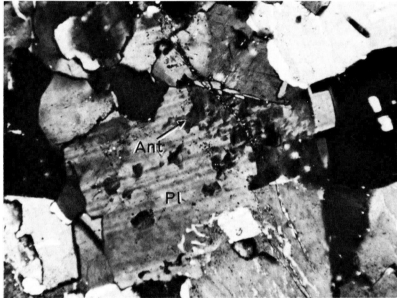

Fig. 471. Plagioclase with metasomatic antiperthite starting from the margin and extending into the plagioclase. Arrow shows protruding antiperthite in the plagioclase. Pl = plagioclase, Ant = antiperthite. Quartz—hornblende syenite at Beverly, Massachusetts, U.S.A. With crossed nicols; enlargement 100 x.

Fig. 472. Twinned plagioclase transversed by an anastomosing and branching K-feldspar "vein" system, comparable to vein-type perthitisation. Bergen Granite, Vogtland, Saxony, Germany. With crossed nicols; enlargement 100 x.

Fig. 473. Twinned plagioclase (Pl) with an outer zone (o-Pl) in which a veinlet-like anastomosing antiperthite system is present. The antiperthitic veinlets often follow directions of greater penetrability in the plagioclase. Ant = antiperthitic veinlets, H = hornblende grain outside feldspar. Malga Macesso Granite, Val di Selarno, Adamello, Italy. With crossed nicols; enlargement 100 x.

Fig. 474. Antiperthitic flakes in plagioclase. Ant = antiperthite, K-f = K-feldspar. Quartz–hornblende syenite at Beverly, Massachusetts, USA. With crossed nicols; enlargement 100 x.

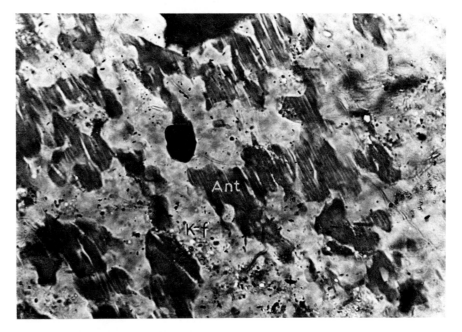

Fig. 475. Complex polysynthetic twinning of plagioclase with antiperthitic flakes. Pl = plagioclase, Ant = antiperthite. Granite, southwest of Torn, Sweden. With crossed nicols; enlargement 100 x.

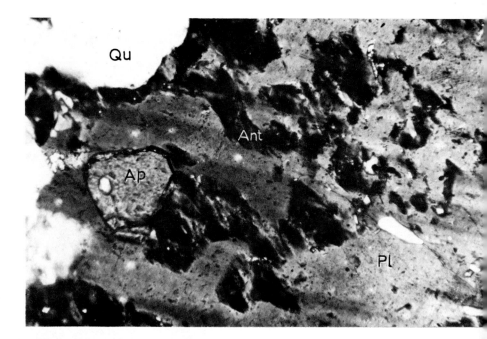

Fig. 476. PLagioclase enclosing apatite which is in contact with antiperthite. Pl = plagioclase, Ap = apatite, Ant = antiperthite, Qu = quartz. Hornblende syenite at Malmberget, Gellivara, Sweden. With crossed nicols; enlargement 100 x.

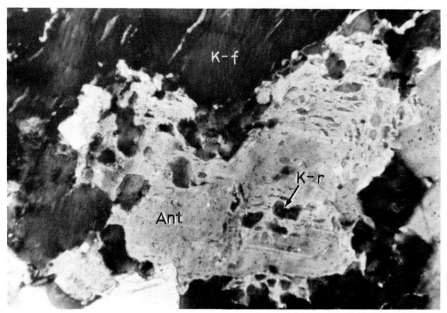

Fig. 477. K-feldspar with antiperthite. Zones of K-feldspar relics exist in the antiperthite which also sends protuberances attaining flame-like forms. K-f = K-feldspar, Ant = antiperthite, K-r = K-feldspar relics in zonal distribution in plagioclase (antiperthite). Voigtsbach Granite, Reichenbach, Bohemia. With crossed nicols; enlargement 100 x.

Fig. 478. Cross-twinned microcline antiperthites in plagioclase. As a synantetic reaction product of pre-existing plagioclase and later antiperthitic flakes, myrmekitic quartz is formed, mainly extending from the antiperthitic margin inwards to the plagioclase or into enclosed plagioclase within the K-feldspar flake. Ant = antiperthite (microcline flakes in plagioclase). Pl = plagioclase, q = myrmekitic quartz in plagioclase. Hornblende syenite at Malmberget, Gellivara, Sweden. With crossed nicols; enlargement 100 x.

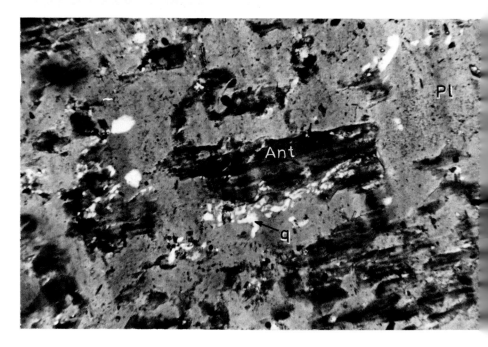

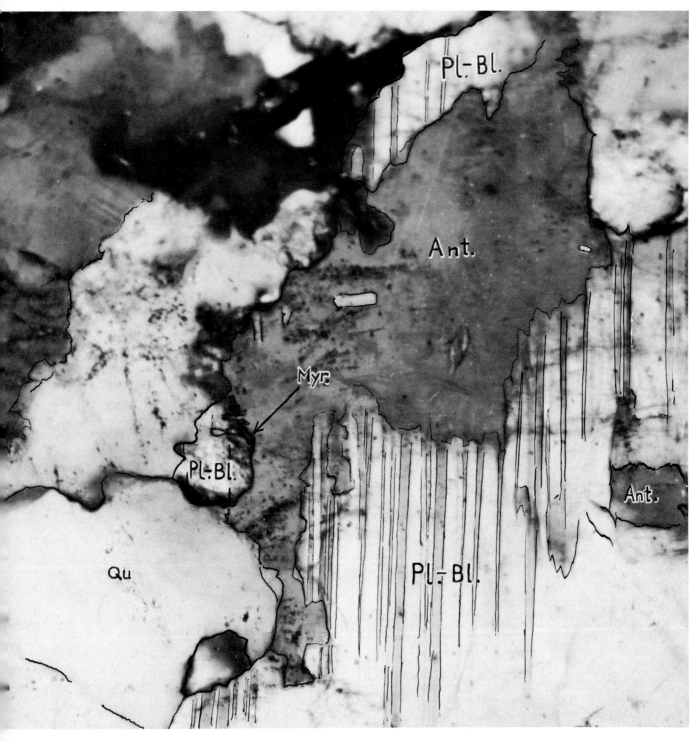

Fig. 479. Plagioclase with a large antiperthitic flake which, when in contact with a plagioclase, results into its myrmekitisation. Pl-Bl = blastic plagioclase, Ant = antiperthite, Qu = quartz, Myr = myrmekitic quartz. Naxos Granite, Greece. With crossed nicols; enlargement 100 x.

Fig. 480 and 481. Plagioclase transversed by a system of plagioclase veinlets often branching and anastomosing (see arrow). Reversing of the twinning of the plagioclase veinlet can be seen in comparison to the main plagioclase mass. Mt. Mattoni Granite, Val Fredda, South Adamello, Italy. With crossed nicols; enlargements 100 x, 200 x.

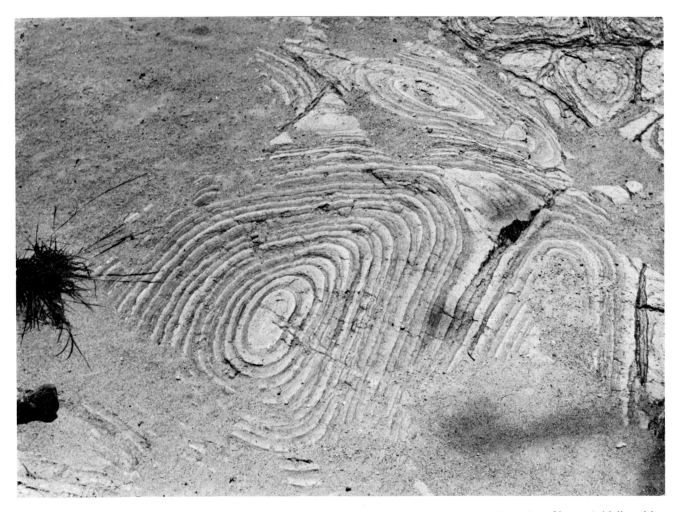

Fig. 482 Rhythmical spheroidal rings due to weathering of the Dangago (micro) Granite. There is an alternation of brown (with limonitic iron precipitation zones) and whitish bleached (depleated of iron). Dangago, Dire-Dawa, Ethiopia, Rhythmical spheroidal structure 1 m in diameter.

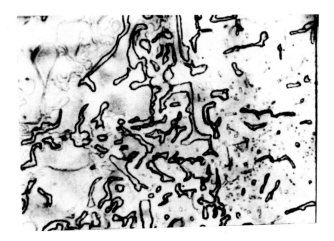

Fig. 483. Inclusions of xylol in natural salt crystal. The xylol inclusions are artificially produced. Enlargement about 100 x. (From Gerlach and Heller, 1966.)

Fig. 484. Intracrystalline penetration of solutions (a solution path) assuming myrmekitic-like appearance in the pyroxene. Arrows mark the direction of intracrystalline penetration of melts. Olivine and pyroxene nodules in basalts at Yubdo, West Ethiopia. Without crossed nicols; enlargement 100 x.

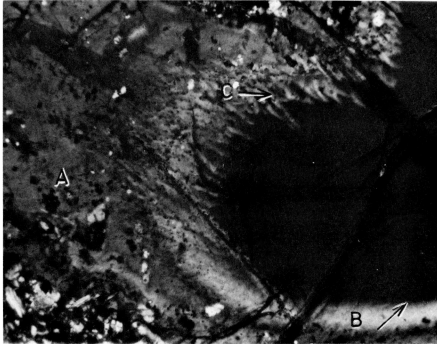

Fig. 485. Corrosion and alteration of pyroxene by basaltic ground-mass. A = altered pyroxene (these altered pyroxene margins are anisotropic), B = unaltered diopside (pyroxene), C = fine canals representing the alteration from advancing into the unaltered pyroxene. Olivine and pyroxene nodules in basalt at Yubdo, West Ethiopia. With crossed nicols; enlargement 100 x.

Fig. 486. A zircon composed of material of different generations. Perhaps the zonal structure exhibited could be interpreted: zircon (generation I) subjected to the geological cycle, zircon (generation II) overgrowth of material in a phase of granitisation in which case generation I represents the palaeosoma. A quartz grain is interzonal in the zircon. Zr-I = zircon (generation I), Zr-II = zircon (generation II), q = interzonal quartz, Qu = quartz, Bi = biotite. Seussen Granite, Fichtel mountains, Germany. With crossed nicols; enlargement 100 x.

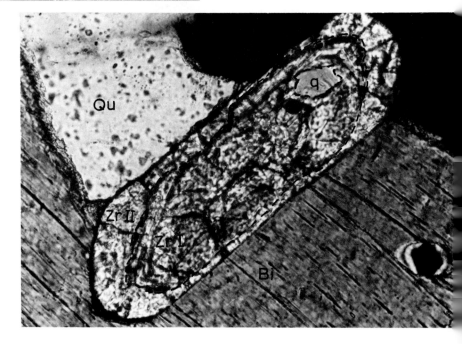

286

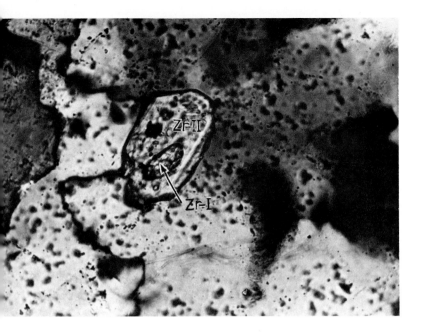

Fig. 487. Small zircon, rounded and surrounded by a zircon (generation II). Zr-I = zircon (generation I), Zr-II = zircon (generation II). St. Genes Granite, Pyrenees, France. With crossed nicols; enlargement 100 x.

Fig. 488. Zircon with an overgrowth attaining idiomorphic form. Zr = zircon, Zr-O = zircon overgrowth, Qu = quartz, Bi = biotite. Wehmo Granite, Nystad, Helsingfors, Finland. With crossed nicols; enlargement 100 x.

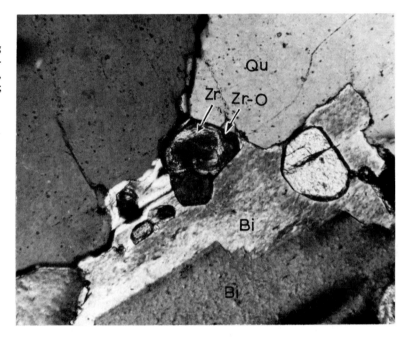

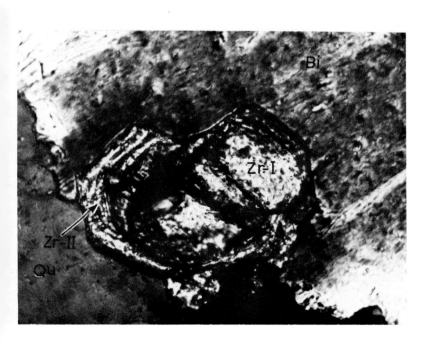

Fig. 489. Zircon (generation I) in biotite with an overgrowth of zircon (generation II) surrounding the first. The zircon overgrowth is only partially developed. Zr-I = zircon (generation I), Zr-II = zircon (generation II), Bi = biotite, Qu = quartz. Grubensgrund Granite, Schenkenzell, Black Forest, Germany. With crossed nicols; enlargement 200 x.

287

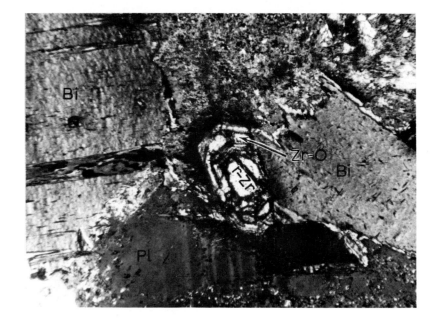

Fig. 490. Zircon with biotite and plagioclase. A rounded zircon is surrounded by a zoned overgrowth. Bi = biotite, Pl = plagioclase, r-Zr = rounded zircon, Zr-O = zircon overgrowth. Meissen Granite, Saxony, Germany. With crossed nicols; enlargement 100 x.

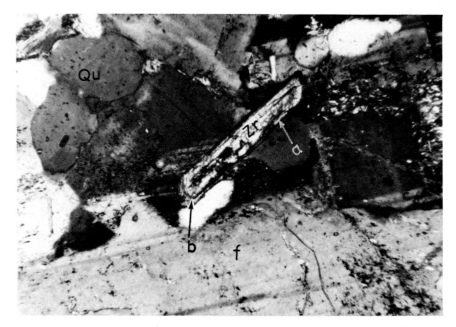

Fig. 491. Zircon showing simultaneously in different part of the crystal corrosion effects and overgrowth. Zr = zircon, arrow "a" indicates corrosion, arrow "b" indicates overgrowth, Qu = quartz, f = feldspar. Gleesberg (two-mica) Granite, Schneeberg, Saxony, Germany. With crossed nicols; enlargement 100 x.

Fig. 492. Zoned zircon associated with opaque mineral and plagioclase. A part, continuation of the zircon, is enclosed in the metallic opaque mineral. Ragunda Granite, Sweden. With crossed nicols; enlargement 100 x.

Fig. 493. Small apatite partly replaced and enclosed by zircon. Ap = apatite, Zr = zircon. Melca-Guba Gneiss-granite, Borona, South Ethiopia. With crossed nicols; enlargement 100 x.

Fig. 494. Apatite in the extinction position partly surrounded by zircon in biotite. Ap = apatite, Zr = zircon, Bi =biotite. Grubens-grund Granite, Schenkenzell, Black Forest, Germany. With crossed nicols; enlargement 100 x.

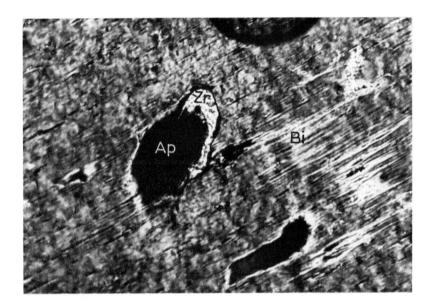

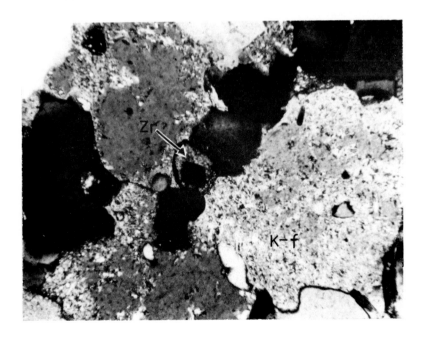

Fig. 495. Opaque grain mineral enclosed in zircon. Zr = zircon, K-f = K-feldspar. Melca-Guba Gneiss-granite, Borona, South Ethiopia. With crossed nicols; enlargement 100 x.

289

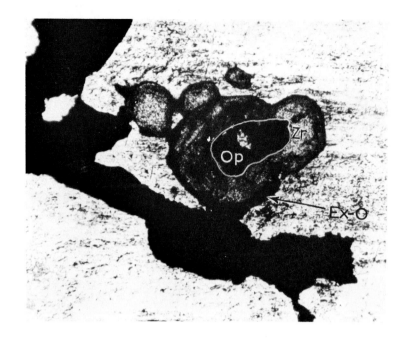

Fig. 496. Opaque mineral enclosed in zircon and also an opaque mineral forming an external margin of the same zircon grain. Op = opaque grain enclosed by zircon, Zr = zircon, Ex-O = external opaque mineral forming margin surrounding zircon. Melca-Guba Gneiss-granite, South Ethiopia. With crossed nicols; enlargement 100 x.

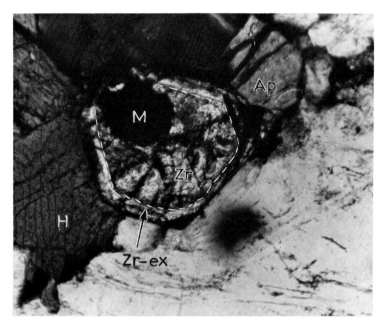

Fig. 497. Zircon enclosing magnetite (opaque) and with an external zone attaining idiomorphism. M = magnetite, Zr = zircon, Zr-ex = external zircon zone, Ap = apatite, H = hornblende. Hornblende syenite at Sachsdorf, Wilsdruff, Saxony, Germany. With crossed nicols; enlargement 100 x.

Fig. 498. Zircon built up of fine zones and partly showing idiomorphism. Hornblende granite at Belchen, Germany. With crossed nicols; enlargement 100 x.

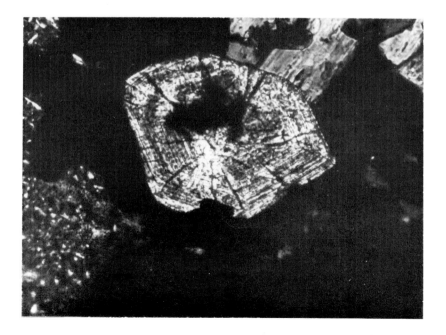

Fig. 499. Blastically grown accessory zircon, crossing the biotite cleavage and enclosing part of the mica. Also a radioactive halo surrounds the zircon. Bi = biotite, Zr = zircon, r-h = radioactive halo. Rapakivi granite at Nystad, Finland. Enlargement 100 x.

Fig. 500. (Detail of Fig. 499.) Blastic zircon, with radioactive halo, crossing the biotite cleavage and including part of the mica. The direction of the cleavage of the biotite part enclosed in the zircon is the same as the direction of the cleavage of the biotite outside the zircon. The zircon blastesis did not distort, or result in the disorientation of, the enclosed biotite. Bi = biotite, b = biotite enclosed in zircon, Zr = zircon, r-h = radioactive halo. Rapakivi granite at Nystad, Finland. Enlargement 100 x.

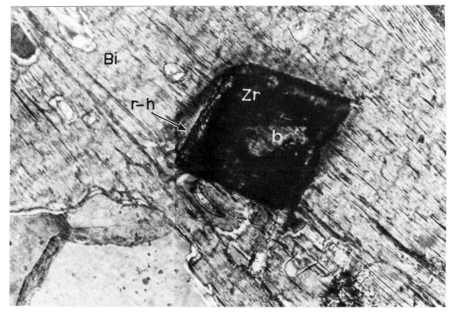

Fig. 501. Zircons in biotite with radioactive halos. Protruding extensions of a zircon grain partly engulf biotite part. Bi = biotite, Zr = zircon, arrows indicate zircon protruding parts, e-b = engulfed biotite part, r-h = radioactive halo. Wehmo Granite, Helsingfors, Finland. With crossed nicols; enlargement 100 x.

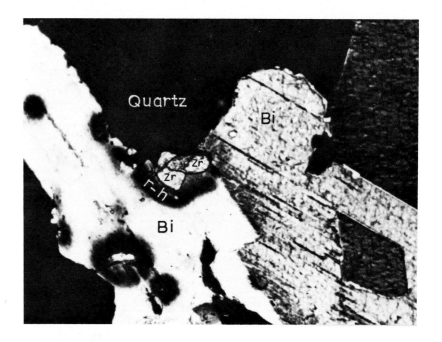

Fig. 502. Two intergrown zircons partly in biotite, partly in quartz. A radioactive halo is indicated in contact with the mica. Bi = biotite, Zr = zircon, r-h = radioactive halo. Wilschhaus Granite, Saxony, Germany. With crossed nicols; enlargement 100 x.

Fig. 503. Apatite (generation I), enclosed in apatite (generation II) in biotite. Ap-I = apatite (generation I), Ap-II = apatite (generation II), Bi = biotite. Monzonite at Munzoni, Tirol, Italy. With crossed nicols; enlargement 100 x.

Fig. 504. Hornblende with apatite included; as the amphibole is surrounded and corroded by later K-feldspar, apatites originally included in amphibole are now partly enclosed by the later K-feldspar. H = hornblende, K-f = K-feldspar, Ap = apatite. Hornblende granite at Maryland, New South Wales, Australia. With crossed nicols; enlargement 100 x.

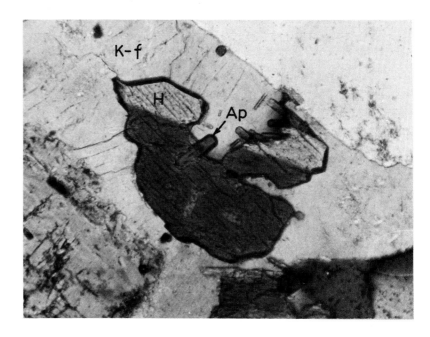

292

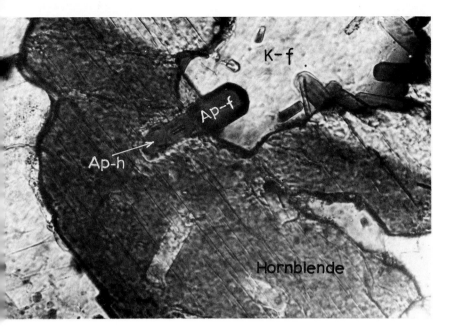

Fig. 505. (Detail of Fig. 504.) Hornblende with included apatite; also apatites which are laying partly in the amphibole and are partly enclosed by blastic feldspar as the latter corroded the hornblende. An apatite grain (enclosing a minute apatite) is partly freed and is now enclosed by the blastic K-feldspar. An overgrowth margin of apatite is formed and restricted to the apatite part which is surrounded by the K-feldspar. Ap-h = apatite in hornblende, and enclosing minute apatite, Ap-f = apatite in K-feldspar with an overgrowth zone, K-f = K-feldspar. With crossed nicols; enlargement 200 x.

Fig. 506. Zircon enclosed and corroded by later apatite in feldspar. Zr =zircon, Ap = apatite, f = feldspar. Bergeller Granite, Trubinasca, Alps. With crossed nicols; enlargement 100 x.

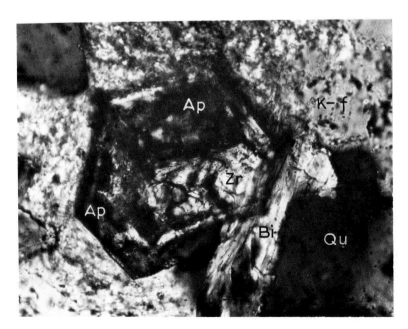

Fig. 507. Zircon surrounded by zoned apatite, hexagonal in outline. Zr = zircon, Ap = apatite, K-f = K-feldspar, Qu = quartz, Bi = biotite. Mt. Mattoni Granite, Val Fredda, South Adamello, Italy. With crossed nicols; enlargement 200 x.

293

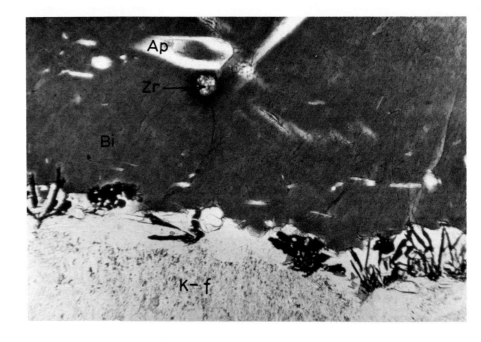

Fig. 508. Biotite in contact with feldspar and marginal transluscent metallic minerals. Zircons and apatites are present in the biotite. An apatite grain encloses a part of the biotite. K-f = K-feldspar, Bi = biotite, Ap = apatite, black = metallic minerals, Zr = zircon. Buchwald Granite, Silesia, Germany. With crossed nicols; enlargement 100 x.

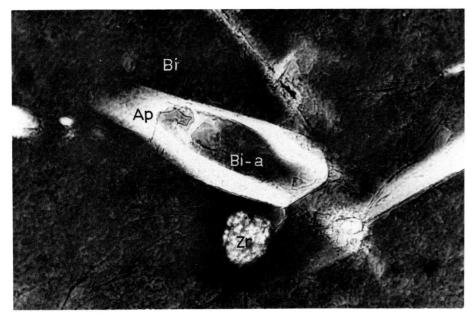

Fig. 509. (Detail of Fig. 508.) Apatite blastically grown enclosing parts of the biotite, indicating different degrees of assimilation by the blastic apatite. Bi = biotite, Ap = apatite, Zr = zircon, Bi-a = biotite parts in the apatite. With crossed nicols; enlargement 250 x.

Fig. 510. Myrmekitised plagioclase in contact with microcline. An apatite (mainly enclosed in the plagioclase) is indicating corrosion appearances (outline and a reaction margin). Pl = plagioclase, q = myrmekitised quartz, M = microcline, Ap = apatite, r-ap = reaction margin of apatite. Korenew Granite, Kiev, Russia. With crossed nicols; enlargement 100 x.

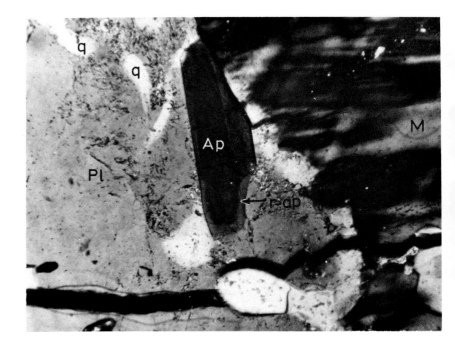

294

Fig. 511. Zoned apatite corroded and infiltrated by later crystallised quartz which partly surrounds the apatite and also extends into it. Ap = apatite (zoned), q = quartz. Korenew Granite, Kiev, Russia. With crossed nicols; enlargement 100 x.

Fig. 512. Apatite in plagioclase and biotite. Quartz partly infiltrating and replacing the plagioclase. Ap = apatite, Pl = plagioclase, Bi = biotite, q = quartz between plagioclase and biotite, Q = quartz. Meissen Granite, Saxony, Germany. With crossed nicols; enlargement 100 x.

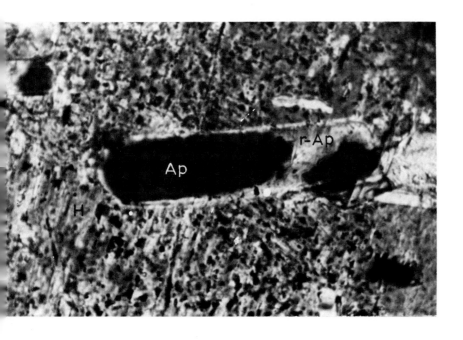

Fig. 513. Apatite in the extinction position partly corroded and replaced by blastic hornblende. Ap = apatite, H = hornblende, r-Ap = replaced apatite. Granodiorite, Ondonock, West Ethiopia. With crossed nicols; enlargement 100 x.

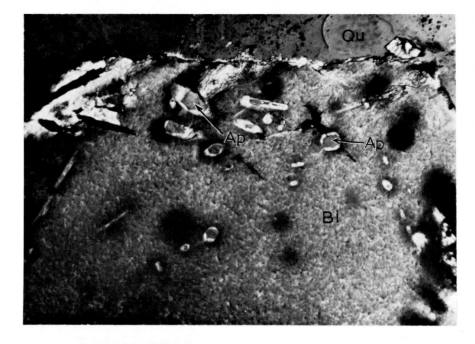

Fig. 514. Biotite with an outer zone relatively rich in accessory apatite; some opaque minerals are also present. The apatites are orientated parallel to the margin of the mica. The apatites are often indicating corrosion by the mica. Radioactive halos surround the accessories. Bi = biotite, Ap = apatite, Qu = quartz. Gleesberg (two-mica) Granite, Schneeberg, Saxony, Germany. With crossed nicols; enlargement 100 x.

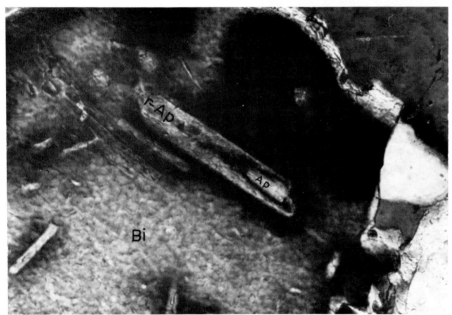

Fig. 515. Apatite in biotite. Partial replacement of the apatite by the biotite has taken place. Ap = apatite, Bi = biotite, r-Ap = replaced apatite by the mica. Ruthenbach (two-mica) Granite, Vogtland, Germany. With crossed nicols; enlargement 200 x.

Fig. 516. Apatite partly enclosed in biotite and partly in K-feldspar. The part of the apatite in the mica shows a corroded outline. In contrast the part of the apatite in the K-feldspar shows an overgrowth zone. A radioactive halo is present around the apatite in the mica. Ap = apatite, Bi = biotite, K-f = K-feldspar. Waldheim Granite, Saxony, Germany. With crossed nicols; enlargement 100 x.

296

Fig. 517. Apatite with corroded outline associated with biotite enclosed in K-feldspar. Ap = apatite, Bi = biotite, K-f = K-feldspar. Grubensgrund Granite, Schenkenzell, Black Forest, Germany. With crossed nicols; enlargement 100 x.

Fig. 518. Apatites between biotites and quartz. A corroded outline of the apatite and a radioactive halo-margin is shown as the mica comes in contact with the apatite. Ap = apatite, Bi = biotite, Qu = quartz, r-h = radioactive halo-margin as biotite is in contact with accessory. Wehmo Granite, Nystad, Helsingfors, Finland. With crossed nicols; enlargement 100 x.

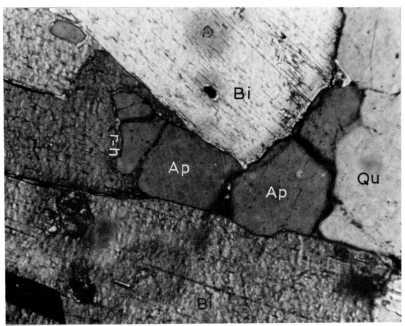

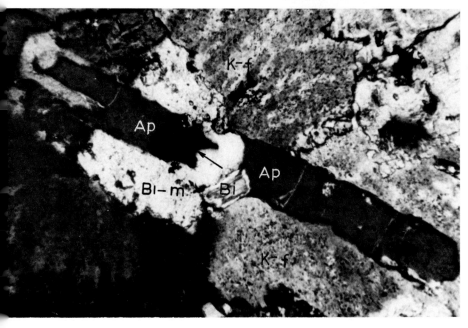

Fig. 519. Elongated large apatite corroded by K-feldspar (perthitised) and biotitic mica. The part of the apatite that is surrounded by the mica shows the more pronounced effects of corrosion and replacement. K-f = K-feldspar perthitised, Bi = biotite, Bi-m = biotitic mass. Arrow indicates corrosion outlines of the apatite. Hellewald Granite, Sewen, Vosges, Germany. With crossed nicols; enlargement 100 x.

297

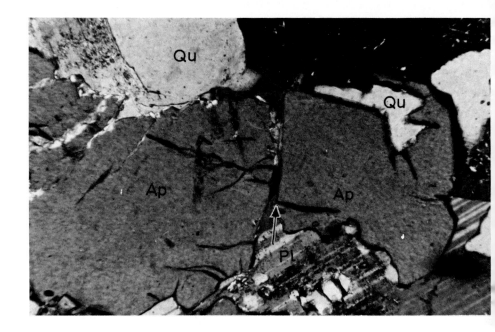

Fig. 520. Gigantic apatite partly enclosing quartz and in turn invaded and corroded by later blastic plagioclase. The plagioclase also partly surrounds and corrodes the quartz. Ap = apatite, Qu = quartz, Pl = plagioclase, arrow indicates plagioclase corroding both apatite and quartz. Wehmo Granite, Nystad, Helsingfors, Finland. With crossed nicols; enlargement 100 x.

Fig. 521. Zircon included in sphene. Zr = zircon, S = sphene, K-f = K-feldspar. Tromm Granite, Furth, Odenwald, Germany. With crossed nicols; enlargement 100 x.

Fig. 522. Twinned hornblende, with apatites, partly enclosed by later blastic sphene. Quartz is also enclosed by the blastic sphene growth. H = hornblende, q = quartz, S = sphene, Ap = apatite. Olsbach Granite, Gengenbach, Black Forest, Germany. With crossed nicols; enlargement 75 x.

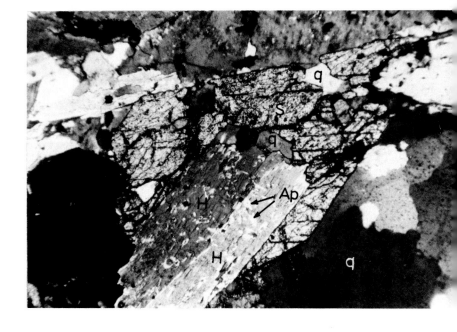

Fig. 523 (Detail of Fig. 522.) Twinned hornblende with apatite partly enclosed by later blastic sphene. Quartz is also present. H = hornblende, S = sphene, Qu = quartz. With crossed nicols; enlargement 200 x.

Fig. 524. Blastic sphene surrounded by later blastic hornblende. S = sphene, H = hornblende. Hornblende granite at Maryland, New South Wales, Australia. With crossed nicols; enlargement 100 x.

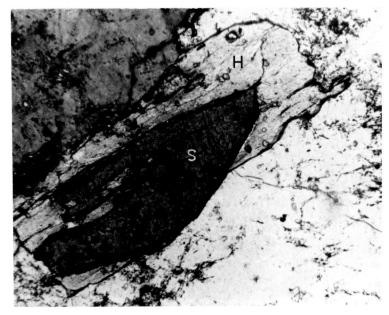

Fig. 525. Biotite enclosing quartz which in turn encloses an opaque mineral. Bi = biotite, Qu = quartz, arrow "a" indicates metallic substances following the cleavage of the biotite. Gleesberg (two-mica) Granite, Schneeberg, Saxony, Germany. With crossed nicols; enlargement 100 x.

299

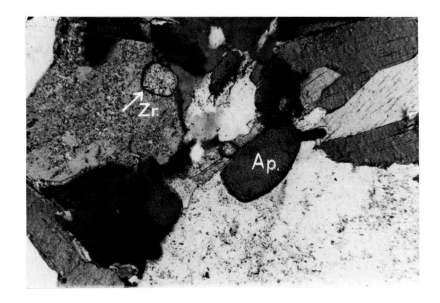

Fig. 526 and 527. Idiomorphic to sub-
idiomorphic zircons (Zr) and apatites (Ap)
associated with quartz, feldspars and biotites
of the paragneissic xenoliths. Melca-Guba
Granite, Borona, Ethiopia. With crossed
nicols; enlargement 100 x.

Fig. 527.

Fig. 528. Apatite (Ap), zircon (Zr), sphene
(Sph) and ore minerals (black) as components
of the paragneissic xenoliths. Melca-Guba
Granite, Borona, Ethiopia. Enlargement
100 x.

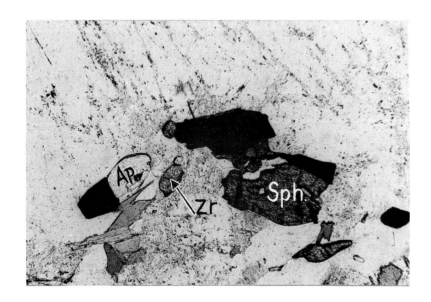

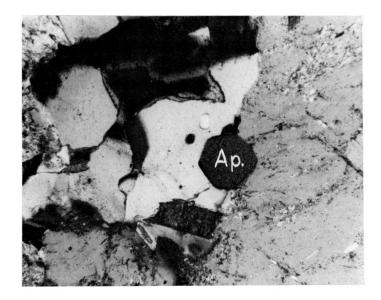

Fig. 529. Idiomorphic apatite (Ap) together with quartz, feldspars and biotite, as components of the paragneissic xenoliths. Melca-Guba Granite, Borona, Ethiopia. With crossed nicols; enlargement 100 x.

Fig. 530. Apatite (Ap) enclosed by biotite (Bi) of the xenoliths; biotite laths, feldspars and quartz are also shown. Melca-Guba Granite, Borona, Ethiopia. With crossed nicols; enlargement 100 x.

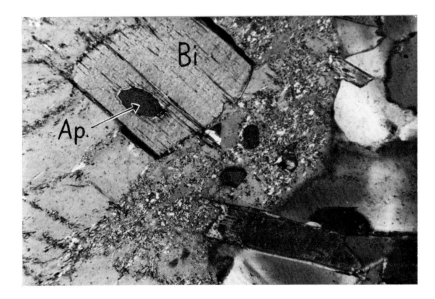

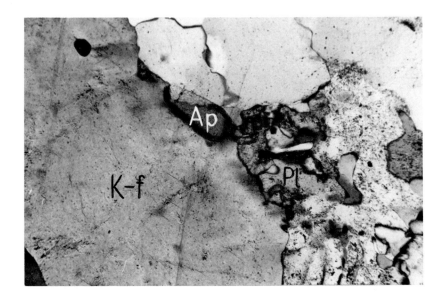

Fig. 531. Plagioclase (Pl) of the xenolith corroded and myrmekitised by a K-feldspar (K-f) crystalloblast of the granite. An apatite (Ap) component of the xenolith is partly engulfed by the blastic orthoclase. Melca-Guba Granite, Borona, Ethiopia. With crossed nicols; enlargement 100 x.

301

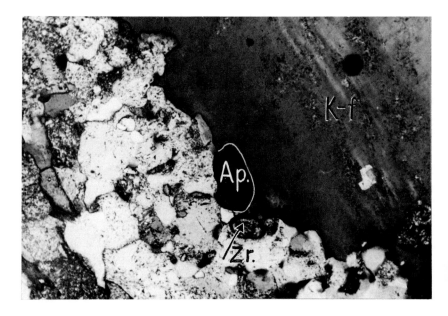

Fig. 532. Components of the xenoliths in contact with a K-feldspar crystalloblast of the granite. Apatite (Ap) and zircon (Zr) of the paragneissic xenolith are partly engulfed and taken over by the blastic K-feldspar (K-f). Melca-Guba Granite, Borona, Ethiopia. With crossed nicols; enlargement 100 x.

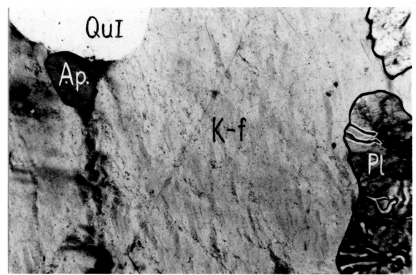

Fig. 533. K-feldspar crystalloblast (K-f) of the granite in contact with corroded and myrmekitised plagioclase (Pl) of the xenolith. Quartz (generation I) (Qu I) and apatite (Ap), components of the xenolith, lie entirely within the K-feldspar crystalloblast as non-assimilated relics. Melca-Guba Granite, Borona, Ethiopia. With crossed nicols; enlargement 100 x.

Fig. 534. A nodule consisting of fine grains of plagioclase, orthoclase, microcline quartz, biotite and accessory minerals, between K-feldspar crystalloblasts of the granite. Melca-Guba Granite, Borona, Ethiopia. With crossed nicols; enlargement 10 x.

Fig. 535. Zircon (Zr), apatite (Ap) and biotite (Bi) enclosed by neocrystallised quartz (generation II) (QuI) of the granite. Melca-Guba granite, Borona, Ethiopia. With crossed nicols; enlargement 100 x.

Fig. 536. Quartz (generation I) (Qu I) and apatite (Ap) engulfed and partly corroded by the later neocrystallised quartz (generation II) (Qu II) of the granite. The quartz (generation I) is more corroded than the apatite. Melca-Guba Granite, Borona, Ethiopia. With crossed nicols; enlargement 100 x.

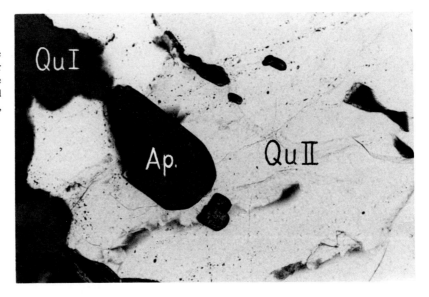

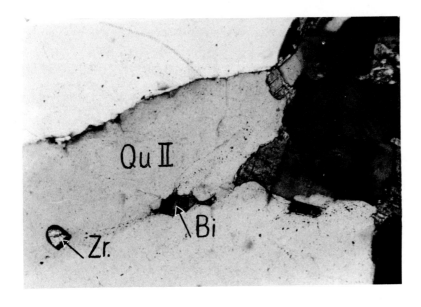

Fig. 537. Zircon (Zr), biotite (Bi) and other components of a nodule (corresponding to components of the paragneissic xenoliths) are corroded and enclosed by neocrystallised quartz (generation II) (Qu II) of the granite. In addition, it can be seen that the enclosed zircon and the corroded biotite belong to the components external to the quartz (Qu II). Melca-Guba Granite, Borona, Ethiopia. With crossed nicols; enlargement 100 x.

303

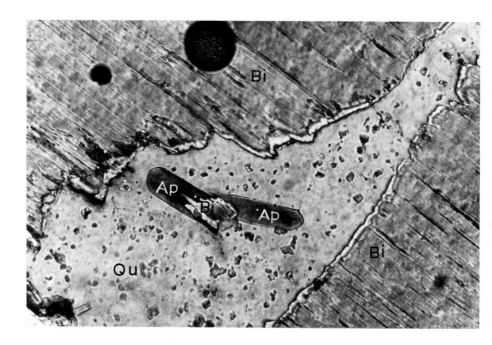

Fig. 538. Apatites with a part of a biotite enclosed in later grown quartz which has replaced biotite. The biotite part associated with the apatites is a relic of the biotite that has been replaced by the quartz. Bi = biotite, Qu = quartz, Ap = apatite. Ballachulish Granite, Scotland. With crossed nicols; enlargement 100 x.

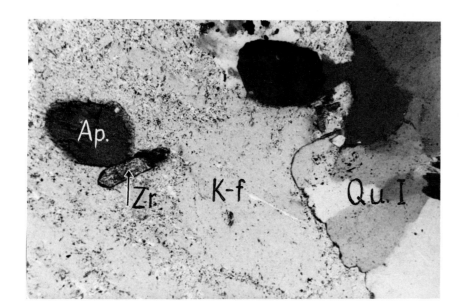

Fig. 539. A blastic K-feldspar (K-f), enclosing idiomorphic to subidiomorphic apatite (Ap) and zircon (Zr), is in contact with quartz (generation I) (Qu I). Melca-Guba Granite, Borona, Ethiopia. With crossed nicols; enlargement 100 x.

Fig. 540. A blastic plagioclase (Pl) of the Melca-Guba Granite enclosing apatite (Ap) which has a fine margin of quartz (generation I) (Qu I). The quartz margin represents a relic of quartz (generation I) associated with the apatite. Whereas most of the quartz (Qu I) has been corroded by the plagioclase crystalloblast, the apatite remained as unaffected relic. Other pre-blastic components are also shown in the photomicrograph. With crossed nicols; enlargement 100 x.

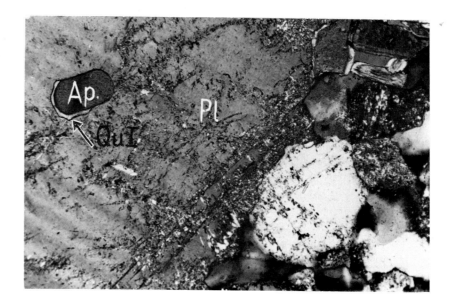

304

Fig. 541. Quartz veins with strain effects simulating a pattern produced by the non-distortion planes of the theoretical strain ellipsoid (Fig. 568). Ondonock Granodiorite, West Ethiopia. With crossed nicols; enlargement 100 x.

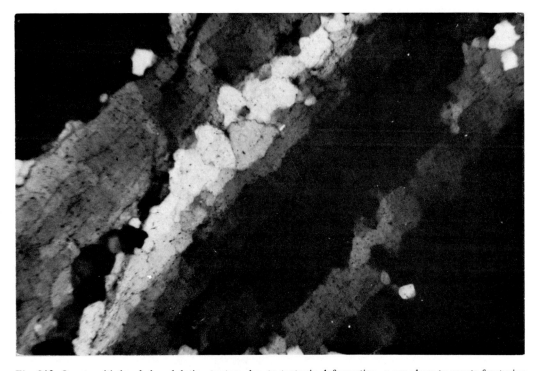

Fig. 542. Quartz with banded undulating texture due to tectonic deformation, a pre-phase to quartz fracturing (mylonitisation). Ondonock Granodiorite, West Ethiopia. With crossed nicols; enlargement 100 x.

Fig. 543. Quartz with strain effects simulating a pattern produced by the non-distortion planes of the theoretical strain ellipsoid. Among one of these planes, fracturing of the quartz has taken place. Ondonock Granodiorite, West Ethiopia. With crossed nicols; enlargement 25 x.

Fig. 544 (Detail of Fig. 543.) Initial mylonitisation phase; quartz fracturing along certain planes. The undulating extinction of the quartz indicates the beginning of grain separation due to mylonitisation. Ondonock Granodiorite, West Ethiopia. With crossed nicols; enlargement 100 x.

Fig. 545. Transition of tectonically affected quartz (undulating extinction) to a micro-mylonite with a pseudo-mosaic grain intergrowth texture. Ondonock Granodiorite, West Ethiopia. With crossed nicols; enlargement 50 x.

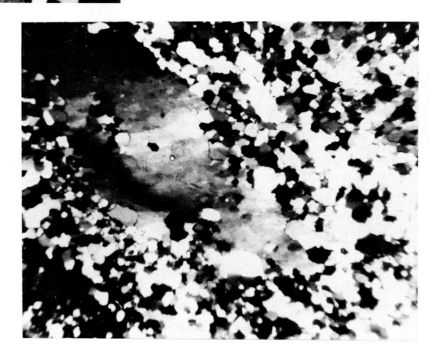

Fig. 546. Mosaic intergrowth texture of quartz due to tectonic deformation. A shearing plane marks differently orientated micro-mylonitised tectonites (tectonic units). Ondonock Granodiorite, West Ethiopia. With crossed nicols; enlargement 100 x.

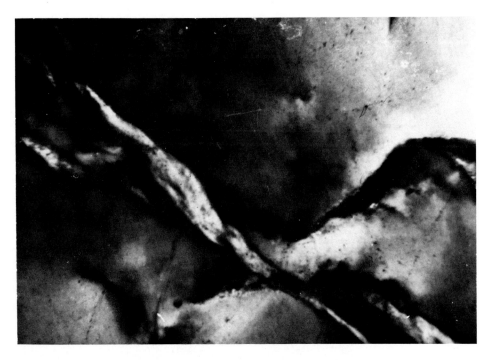

Fig. 547. An X-shaped undulation figure in deformed quartz due to tectonic influence. Orbicular granite at Tafi Viego, 60 km west of Treuman, Argentina. With crossed nicols; enlargement 100 x.

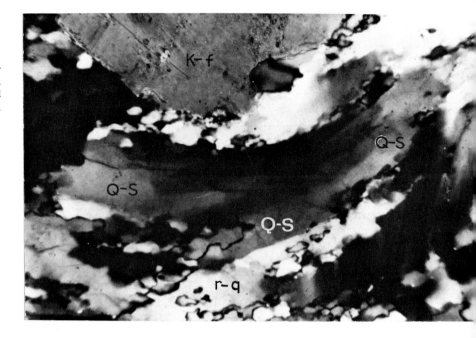

Fig. 548. A quartz "super-individual" with smaller quartz grains and K-feldspar. Q-S = "quartz super-individual", K-f = K-feldspar, r-q = recrystallised quartz. Naxos Granite, Greece. With crossed nicols; enlargement 100 x.

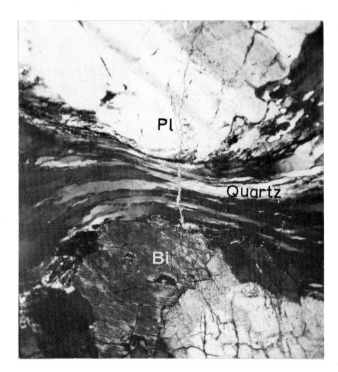

Fig. 549. Tectonically squeezed and plastically deformed (by plastic flow) quartz grains between plagioclase and biotite. Bi = biotite, Pl = plagioclase. Naxos Granite, Greece. With crossed nicols; enlargement 60 x.

Fig. 550. Quartz grains plastically deformed between plagioclase and microcline. Recrystallised quartz grains, due to plastic mobilisation and recrystallisation occupy cracks in the microcline (assuming vein-like form). Pl = plagioclase, q = quartz, Mi = microcline, r-q = recrystallised quartz extending as vein in the microcline. Naxos Granite, Greece. With crossed nicols; enlargement 100 x.

308

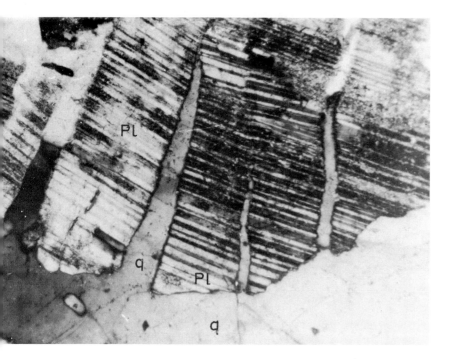

Fig. 551. Plagioclase with tectonic cracks into which plastic quartz is wedged. The strained quartz shows anomalous extinction. Pl = plagioclase, q = quartz. Ross Mull (biotite) Granite, Scotland. With crossed nicols; enlargement 100 x.

Fig. 552. Plastically mobilised and recrystallised quartz extending into fractures of a tectonically affected plagioclase. In addition a corrosion of the feldspar has taken place. Pl = plagioclase, Qu = quartz. Didessa Granite, Ethiopia. With crossed nicols; enlargement 100 x.

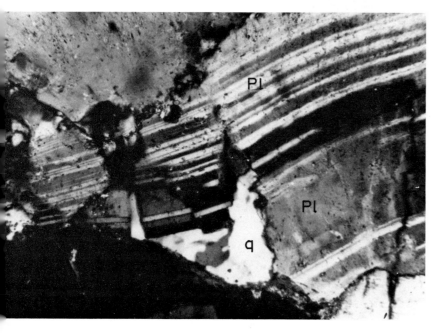

Fig. 553. Bending and fracturing of plagioclase twinning. Recrystallised quartz due to plastic deformation is wedged into plagioclase fractures. Pl = plagioclase, q = quartz. Naxos Granite, Greece. With crossed nicols; enlargement 100 x.

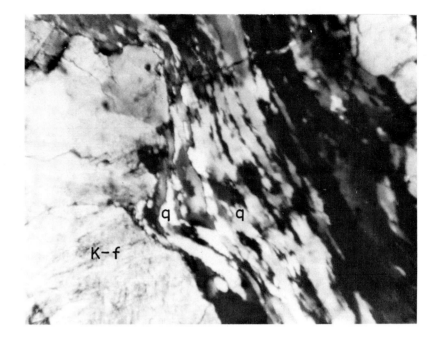

Fig. 554. Plastically deformed and recrystallised quartz of the ground-mass bulges into weak parts of an adjacent K-feldspar. K-f = K-feldspar, q = quartz. Naxos Granite, Greece. With crossed nicols; enlargement 100 x.

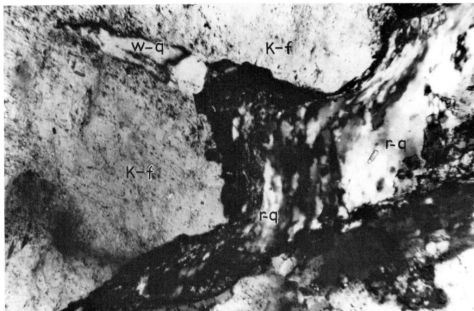

Fig. 555. Plastically deformed and recrystallised quartz of the ground-mass bulges into weak parts of an adjacent K-feldspar. Due to plastic deformation and recrystallisation, a wedge-shaped quartz body protrudes into the K-feldspar. K-f = K-feldspar, r-q = recrystallised and deformed quartz of ground-mass, w-q = quartz wedge protruding into K-feldspar. Naxos Granite, Greece. With crossed nicols; enlargement 100 x.

Fig. 556. Zoned plagioclase with mobilised plastic quartz penetrating along a reaction canal of the plagioclase. Pl = plagioclase, q = mobilised quartz (plastically), r-c = reaction canal in the plagioclase. Naxos Granite, Greece. With crossed nicols; enlargement 100 x.

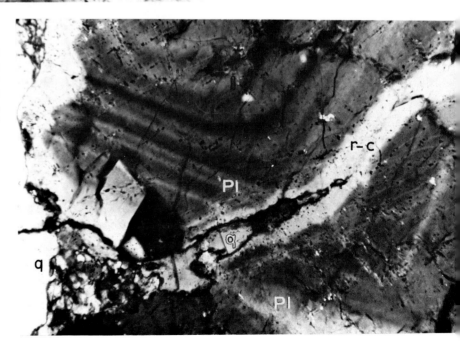

Fig. 557. Bending of biotite. Olsbach Granite, Gengenbach, Black Forest, Germany. With crossed nicols; enlargement 50 x.

Fig. 558. Bending of biotite. The accessories of the biotite (pre-deformation) have been displaced with the mica deformation. Bi = biotite, Ap = apatite. Olsbach Granite, Gengenbach, Black Forest, Germany. With crossed nicols; enlargement 100 x.

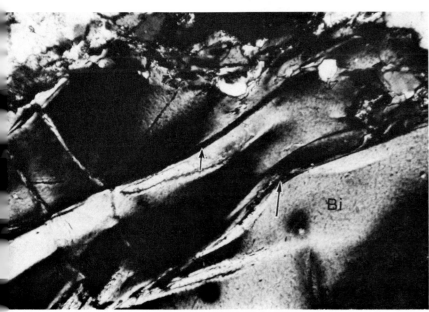

Fig. 559 and 560. (Different orientations.) Biotite with undulating extinction and curved micro-displacement planes. Bi = biotite, arrows indicate curved micro-displacements of the biotite itself. Hattula Granite, Finland. With crossed nicols; enlargement 100 x.

311

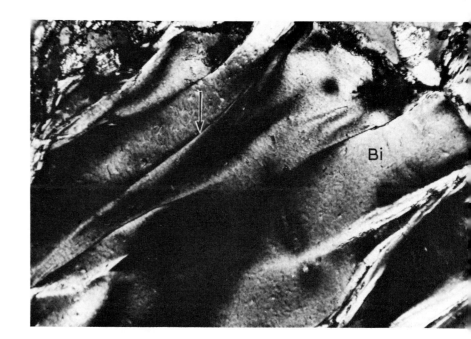

Fig. 560.

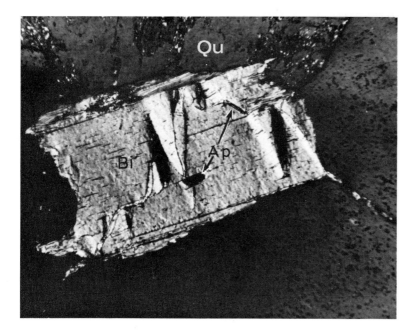

Fig. 561 and 562. (Two different optical orientations of the same grain.) Deformation wedges in biotite, due to tectonic influences. Whereas the biotite has been deformed, the apatites in the mica are not bent or influenced by the tectonic effects. Bi = biotite, Qu = quartz, Ap = apatites. Meissen Granite, Saxony, Germany. With crossed nicols; enlargement 100 x.

Fig. 562.

312

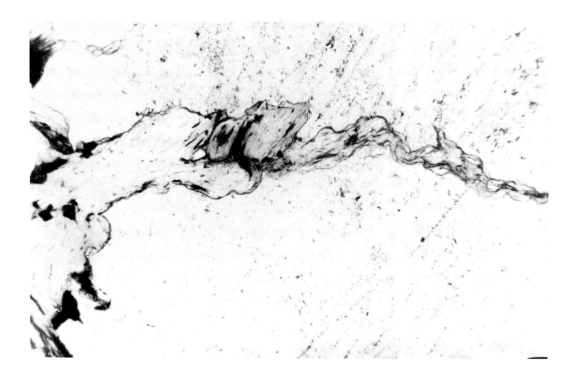

Fig. 563 and 564. Micaceous band in tectonically affected and recrystallised quartz. The micaceous band is also plastically deformed and eventually thins out. Didessa Granite, Ethiopia. Fig. 564 with crossed nicols; enlargement 100 x.

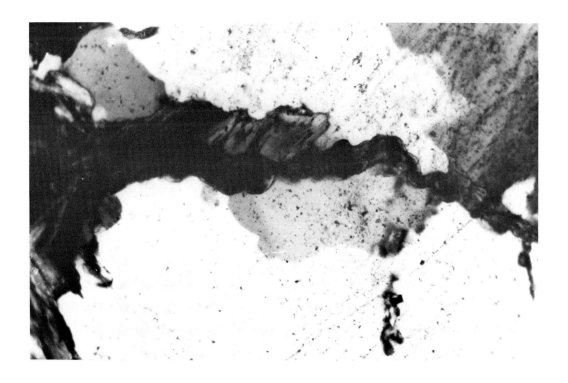

Fig. 565. String-like body of biotite resolving itself into minute granules in quartz grains with different orientations. Lörpys Kurn Granite, Tammersfors, Finland. With crossed nicols; enlargement 100 x.

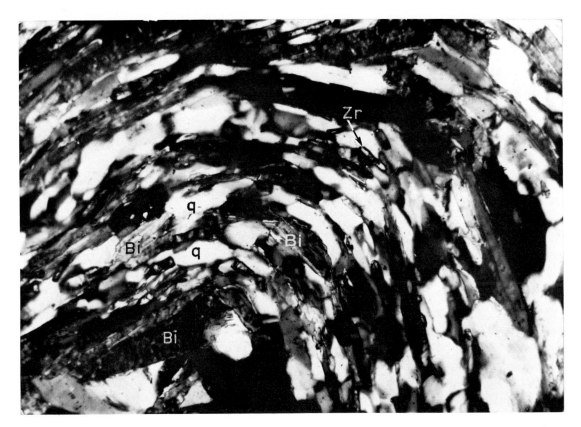

Fig. 566. Micro-fold a quartz-biotite gneiss. Small zircons are also present. The biotite flakes rearranged to conform to the micro-fold. No bending of the biotite flakes is observed. Plastic deformation and recrystallisation of the quartz grains is indicated. Bi = biotite, q = quartz showing bending due to plastic deformation, Zr = zircon. Mica gneiss at Didessa, Ethiopia. With crossed nicols; enlargement 100 x.

Fig. 567. Zigzag arrangement of biotite flakes due to folding. Recrystallisation of the quartz in the crests of the micro-folds is observed. Bi = biotite, qu = quartz (recrystallised). Mica gneiss at Didessa, Ethiopia. With crossed nicols; enlargement 100 x.

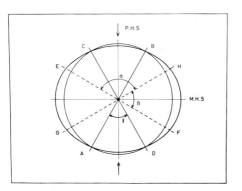

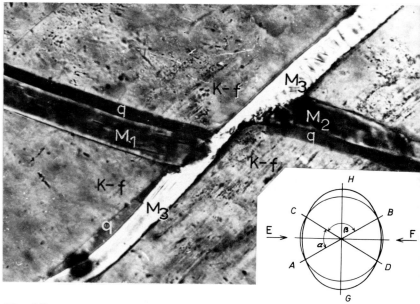

Fig. 568. Diagram from Means (1963) showing P.H.S. (principal horizontal stress) i.e., direction of maximum stress and M.H.S. (minimum horizontal stress) which correspond to the direction of maximum strain. AB, CD = non-distortion planes of the strain ellipsoid; EF, GH are perpendicular to the circular sections AB and CD respectively. The P.H.S. is the bisector of α and M.H.S, the bisector of β.α and β are formed by the intersections of the normals (EF and GH) to the circular sections (AB and CD) γ = the angle formed by the intersection of the non-distortion planes (γ = 60°).

Fig. 569. Muscovite following micro-fissures in K-feldspar (see Fig. 560). Displacement of the M_1, M_2 lamellae must have taken place, along the plane occupied by muscovite M_3. A fine border of mobilised quartz follows interleptonic spaces between k-feldspar and muscovite. K-f = K-feldspar, M = muscovite, q = quartz. Orbicular granite at Tafi Viego, 60 km west of Treuman, Argentina. With crossed nicols; enlargement 100 x.

Fig. 570. (General view of Fig. 569.) Muscovite (white lines) plastically mobilised and occupying micro-fissures in tectonically affected feldspar. The arrangement of the micro-fissures corresponds to the non-distortion planes of the theoretical ellipsoid. K-f = K-feldspar (extinction position), white lines = muscovite, Qu = quartz. Orbicular granite at Tafi Viego, 60 km west of Treuman, Argentina. With crossed nicols; enlargement 25 x.

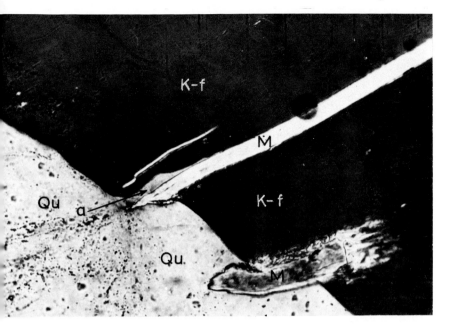

Fig. 571. Muscovite following micro-fissures of a K-feldspar host (extinction position). As the muscovite lamellae transverse the boundary feldspar/quartz, the latter is partly mobilised and sends an extension (see arrow "a") partly following the boundary feldspar/mica. K-f = K feldspar (extinction position), M = muscovite, Qu = quartz. Orbicular granite at Tafi Viego, 60 km west of Treuman, Argentina. With crossed nicols; enlargement 100 x.

Fig 572. Muscovite with K-feldspar. As the mica is in contact (or pushed) with a quartz, plastic mobilisation of the quartz results in the formation of a sheath partly surrounding the mica. K-f = K-feldspar, Qu = quartz, M = muscovite, Q-s = quartz sheath. Orbicular granite at Tafi Viego, 60 km west of Treuman, Argentina. With crossed nicols; enlargement 100 x.

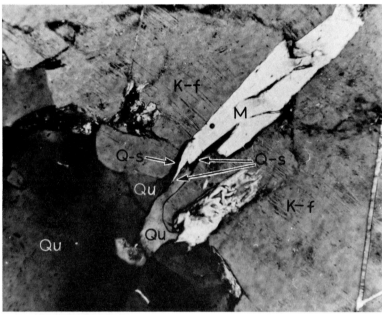

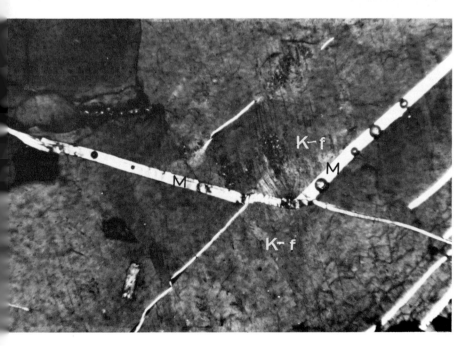

Fig. 573 and 574. Muscovite plastically mobilised and occupying micro-fissures in tectonically affected feldspar. The arrangement of the micro-fissures corresponds to the non-distortion planes of the theoretical ellipsoid. The muscovite is folded and creased as it is squeezed in a micro-fissure. K-f = K-feldspar, M = muscovite. Orbicular granite at Tafi Viego, 60 km west of Treuman, Argentina. With crossed nicols; enlargements 50 x, 100 x.

317

Fig. 574.

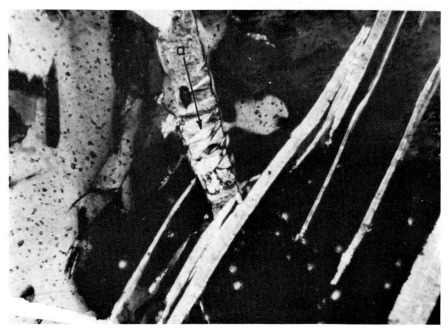

Fig. 575. Muscovite plastically mobilised and squeezed into micro-fissure. Folding and creasing of the muscovite has taken place as it is indicated by arrow "a". Orbicular granite at Tafi Viego, 60 km west of Treuman, Argentina. With crossed nicols; enlargement 100 x.

Fig. 576. Micro-fissures in K-feldspar following the non-distortion planes of theoretical strain ellipsoid. Both muscovite and quartz are mobilised in the micro-fissures. Due to its plastic flow the quartz partly sheaths the mica lamellae. K-f = K-feldspar, M = muscovite, q = quartz. Orbicular granite at Tafi Viego, 60 km west of Treuman, Argentina. With crossed nicols; enlargement 100 x.

318

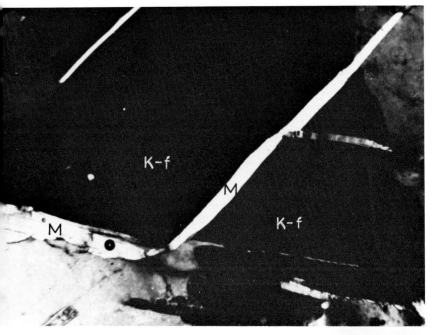

Fig. 577. Muscovite partly following the boundary of two differently orientated K-feldspars. Bending at a point and transversing the K-feldspar in the extinction position, it also sends a parallelly arranged branch occupying a tectonic micro-fissure. M = muscovite, K-f = K-feldspar (in extinction position). Orbicular granite at Tafi Viego, 60 km west of Treuman, Argentina. With crossed nicols; enlargement 100 x.

Fig. 578. Micro-fissures in K-feldspar occupied by muscovite. A small scale displacement of one of the muscovite lamellae is indicated by arrow "a". Orbicular granite at Tafi Viego, 60 km west of Treuman, Argentina. With crossed nicols; enlargement 100 x.

Fig. 579. Muscovite lamella following a zigzag fissure in K-feldspar. Fracturing and partial displacement of the muscovite has also taken place (see arrow "a"). Muscovite (white), K-f = K-feldspar. Orbicular granite at Tafi Viego, 60 km west of Treuman, Argentina. With crossed nicols; enlargement 100 x.

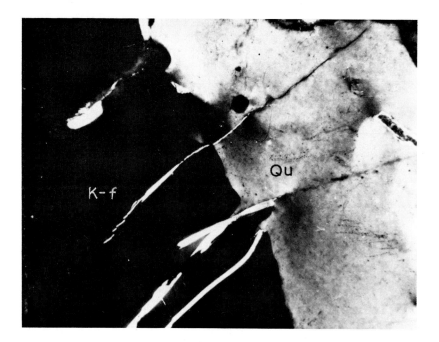

Fig. 580. Muscovite following a micro-fissure in the K-feldspar (extinction position) and partly extending into the micro-fissure's continuation in an adjacent quartz. Also mobilised quartz protuberance, plastically mobilised, extending between mica and K-feldspar. Muscovite (white lamellae), K-f = K-feldspar (in extinction position), Qu = quartz. Orbicular granite at Tafi Viego, 60 km west of Treuman, Argentina. With crossed nicols; enlargement 100 x.

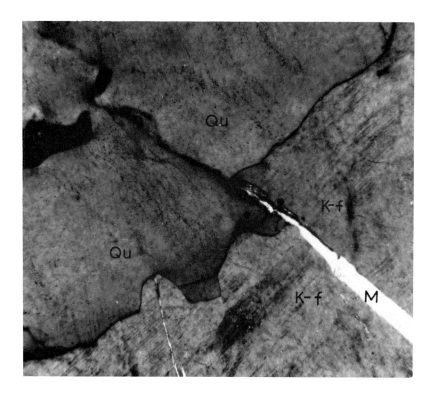

Fig. 581. K-feldspar with a micro-fissure occupied by tectonically mobilised muscovite; the fissure continues into an adjacent quartz; however, the micro-fissure progressively disappears in the quartz. Qu = quartz, K-f = K-feldspar, M = muscovite. Orbicular granite at Tafi Viego, 60 km west of Treuman, Argentina. With crossed nicols; enlargement 100 x.

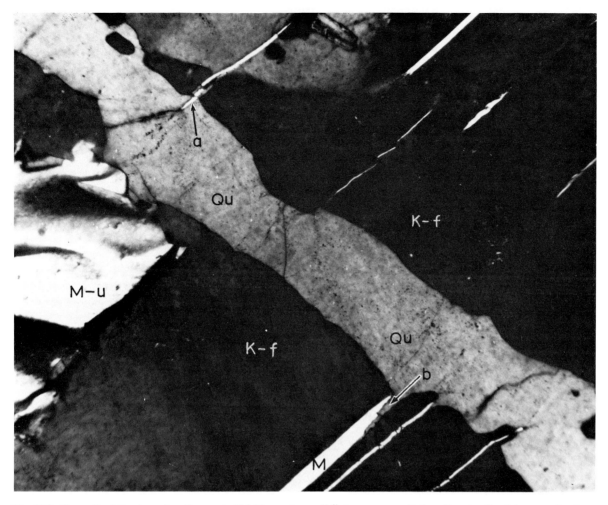

Fig. 582. Muscovite following micro-fissures in K-feldspar. Arrow "a" shows muscovite lamella extending into a quartz. Arrow shows plastically mobilised extension of the same quartz grain protruding between the K-feldspar and the mica, partly coating the muscovite. M = muscovite, Qu = quartz, K-f = K-feldspar, M-u = muscovite with undulating extinction. Orbicular granite at Tafi Viego, 60 km west of Treuman, Argentina. With crossed nicols; enlargement 100X.

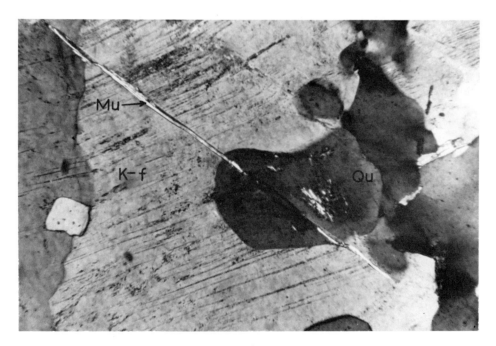

Fig. 583. A micro-fissure transversing both K-feldspar and quartz. Muscovite occupies the parts of the fissure transversing the feldspar. The part of the fissure transversing the quartz is almost free of muscovite. K-f = K-feldspar. Qu = quartz, Mu = muscovite. Orbicular granite at Tafi Viego, 60 km west of Treuman, Argentina. With crossed nicols; enlargement 100 x.

Fig. 584. Muscovite fragments (a and b), initially a single individual which has been fragmented. Fragment "b" has been pushed through the quartz (q). A shadow of anomalous extinction (q_1) shows the path of fragment "b" as it has been pushed tectonically through the quartz. The muscovite fragment "a" the shadow of the path in quartz (q_1) and fragment "b" of the muscovite are all in a continuous line. K-f = K-feldspar Orbicular granite at Tafi Viego, 60 km west of Treuman, Argentina. With crossed nicols; enlargement 100 x.

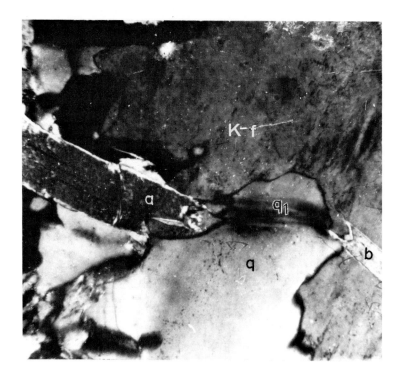

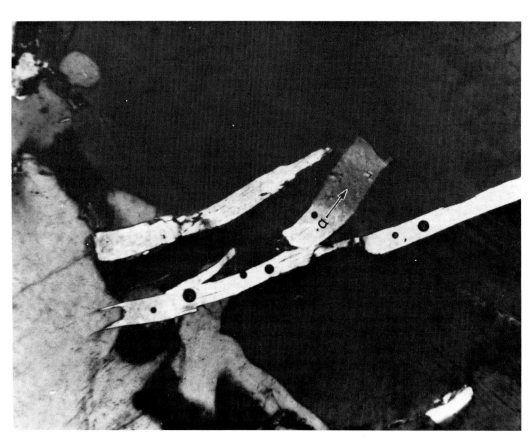

Fig. 585. Muscovite lamellae tectonically fractured and mobilised in K-feldspar fissures. Arrow "a" indicates muscovite with undulating extinction due to tectonic deformation. Orbicular granite at Tafi Viego, 60 km west of Treuman, Argentina. With crossed nicols; enlargement 100 x.

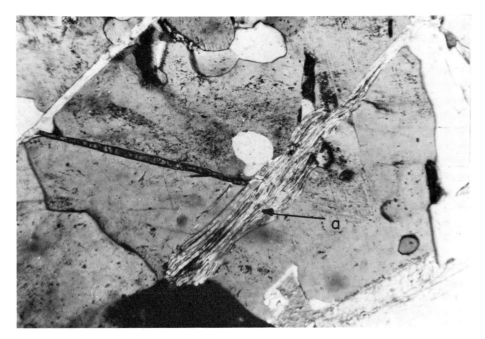

Fig. 586. Muscovite following micro-fissures in K-feldspar. Arrow "a" shows muscovite lamella "separating" in finer lamellae due to tectonic influence. Orbicular granite at Tafi Viego, 60 km west of Treuman, Argentina. With crossed nicols; enlargement 100 x.

Fig. 587. Plastically mobillised muscovite lamellae, with a mobilised branch following another micro-fissure (see arrow "a"). The muscovite locally separates into finer thin lamellae (see arrow "b"). Orbicular granite at Tafi Viego, 60 km west of Treuman, Argentina. With crossed nicols; enlargement 100 x.

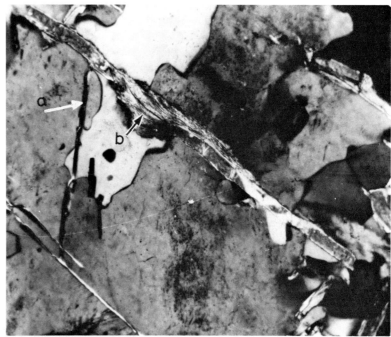

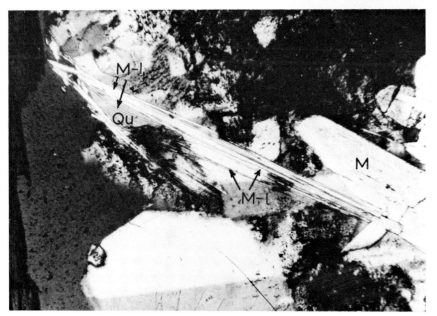

Fig. 588. Muscovite with muscovite lamellae separating from the main flake. M = muscovite, M-l = muscovite lamellae, Qu = quartz. Rapakivi granite, Wiborg, Finland. With crossed nicols; enlargement 100 x.

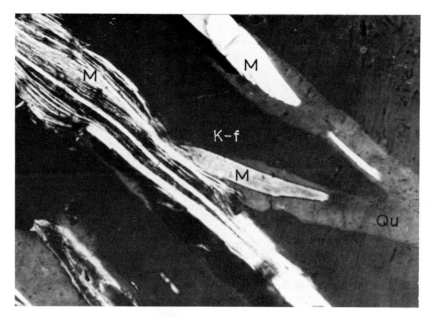

Fig. 589. Muscovite lamellae, and fine lamellae due to lamellae-separation in K-feldspar (extinction position), partly sheathed by mobilised quartz. M = muscovite, Qu = quartz, K-f = K-feldspar. Orbicular granite at Tafi Viego, 60 km west of Treuman, Argentina. With crossed nicols; enlargement 100 x.

Fig. 590. Quartz with extensions (see arrow "a") in K-feldspar. The quartz extensions are in continuation with the muscovite lamellae which follow micro-tectonic cracks in the orthoclase. The quartz shows a zone (shadow, arrow "b") of anomalous extinction, most probably due to tectonic influence. q = quartz, K-f = K-feldspar, white lamellae = muscovite. Orbicular granite at Tafi Viego, 60 km west of Treuman, Argentina. With crossed nicols; enlargement 100 x.

Fig. 591. K-feldspar with micro-fissures occupied by tectonically mobilised muscovite. Also quartz with protruding extensions partly occupying the micro-fissures. K-f = K-feldspar, Qu = quartz, M = muscovite. Orbicular granite at Tafi Viego, 60 km west of Treu-man, Argentina. With crossed nicols; enlargement 100 x.

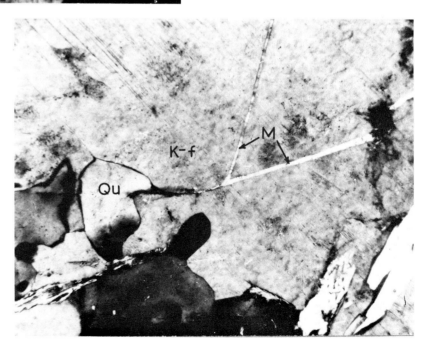

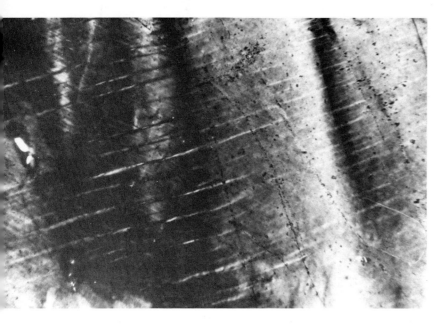

Fig. 592. Deformed plagioclase with wedge-shaped "undulation" anomalies in the extinction position. Wollaga Granite, Ethiopia. With crossed nicols; enlargement 100 x.

Fig. 593. Plagioclase showing a crystal bending (the polysynthetic twin lamellae are bent) due to permanent deformation. Ross Mull (biotite) Granite, Scotland. With crossed nicols; enlargement 100 x.

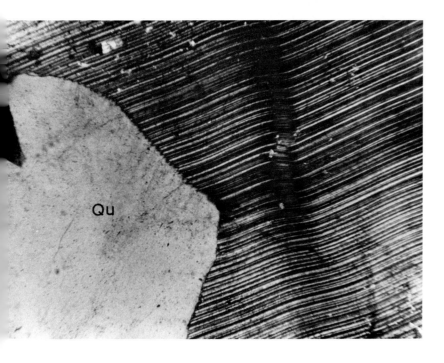

Fig. 594. Quartz in contact with plagioclase. Small quartz indentations protrude into the fine twinning of the plagioclase. Deformation (bending) of the plagioclase twinning has taken place. The deformation effects in the plagioclase seem to fade out from the centre of deformation outwards (the bending of the plagioclase lamellae tends to fade out). Qu = quartz. Pegmatite at Piona, Lake Como district, Italy. With crossed nicols; enlargement 100 x.

325

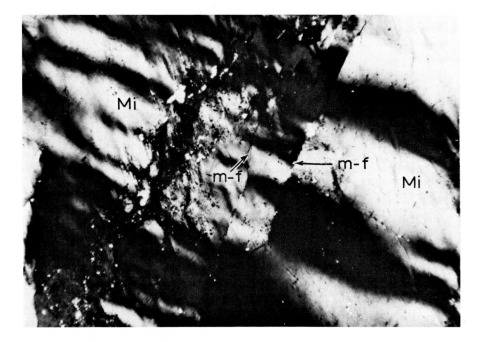

Fig. 595. Fractured microcline with micro-displacement of the microcline cross-twinning. Mi = microcline, m-f = micro-faults in the microcline. Iddefjord Granite, Norway. With crossed nicols; enlargement 100 x.

Fig. 596. Deformed plagioclase (bending of plagioclase lamellae) invaded and replaced by plastically mobilised quartz (showing undulating extinction). The plastic quartz has invaded the plagioclase along cracks and has replaced feldspar parts "delimited" by the plagioclase's twinning. Pl = plagioclase, Qu = quartz. Didessa Granite, Ethiopia. With crossed nicols; enlargement 100 x.

Fig. 597. Garnet tectonically fractured with muscovite and quartz squeezed plastically into cracks of the brittle garnet. Both fracturing and the plastic mobilisation occurred under the same tectonic movements. Garnet pegmatite at Carrara, Giggiga, Harrar, Ethiopia. With crossed nicols; enlargement 5 x.

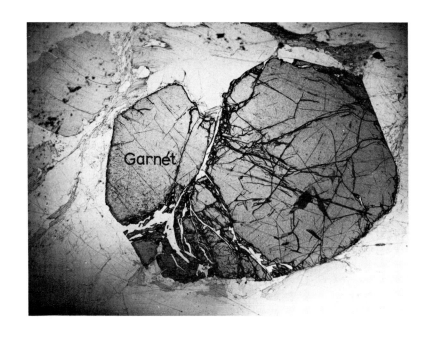

326

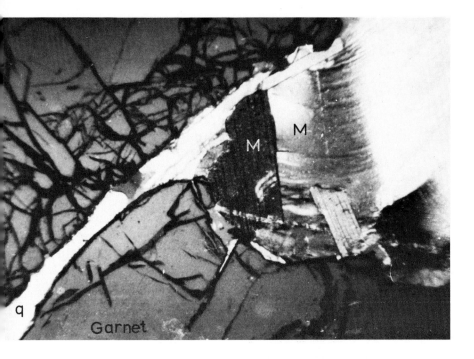

Fig. 598. (Detail of Fig. 597.) Shows muscovite and quartz squeezed plastically into the garnet. M = muscovite, q = quartz, black = garnet. With crossed nicols; enlargement 50 x.

Fig. 599. Tectonically produced augen structure of K-feldspar surrounded by recrystallised and plastically mobilised quartz. K-f = K-feldspar, Qu = recrystallised quartz. Naxos Granite, Greece. With crossed nicols; enlargement 100 x.

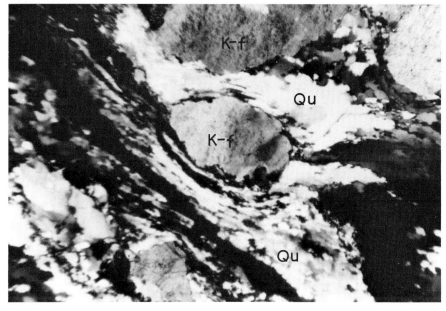

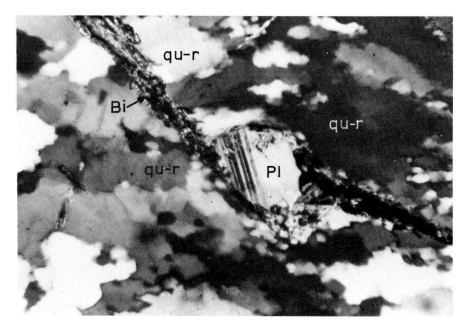

Fig. 600. Tectonically produced augen structure consisting of plagioclase partly surrounded by mobilised biotite in a background of recrystallised quartz. qu-r = recrystallised quartz, Bi = biotite (mobilised), Pl = plagioclase. Naxos Granite, Greece. With crossed nicols; enlargement 100 x.

Fig. 601. Granite with two intersecting mylonitised planes. Shattering of the quartz and mobilisation of the mica has occurred along the mobilisation zones. Naxos Granite, Greece. With crossed nicols; enlargement 10 x.

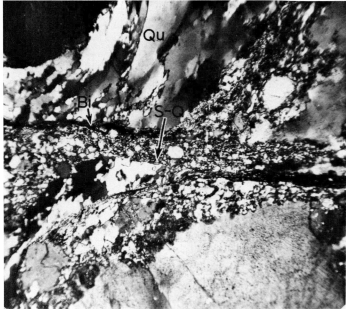

Fig. 602. (Detail of Fig. 601.) Recrystallised quartz and feldspar transversed by a plane of micro-mylonitisation (shattering of quartz and biotite mobilisation). Qu = quartz, S-Q = shattered quartz, Bi = mobilised biotite. With crossed nicols; enlargement 60 x.

Fig. 603. Quartz with undulating extinction fractured in the periphery. Chlorite has been mobilised in the quartz fractures. Qu = quartz, Ch = chlorite mobilised in the quartz cracks, Ca = calcite. Ondonock Granodiorite, West Ethiopia. With crossed nicols; enlargement 100 x.

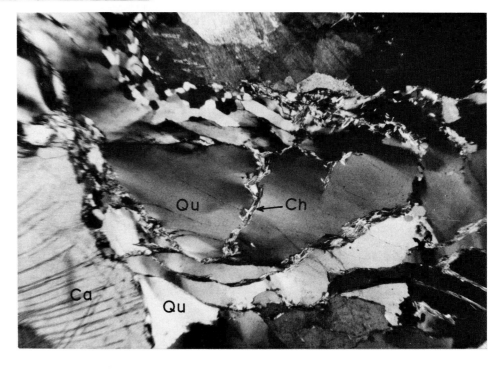

Fig. 604. General view of the tectonically affected Naxos Granite. Tectonically recrystallised and mobilised quartz (R-Q), in parts plastically squeezed between biotite and plagioclase. Often the mobilised and recrystallised quartz mass shows tectonically defined margins with the rest of the granitic components. Arrow "a" indicates tectonically defined margins of recrystallised quartz with the other granite components. Naxos Granite, Greece. With crossed nicols, enlargement 10 x.

Fig. 605. Tectonically deformed granite, with shearing planes marked by micro-displacements (see arrow). Naxos Granite, Greece. With crossed nicols; enlargement 60 x.

329

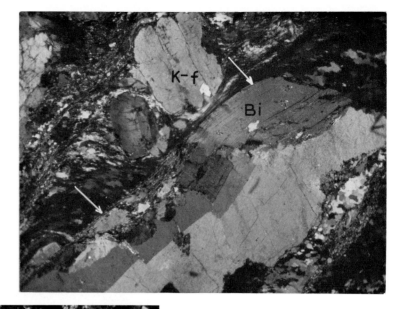

Fig. 606. Tectonically deformed granite, with a shearing plane partly following a biotite grain boundary (see arrow). Bi = biotite, K-f = K-feldspar. Naxos Granite, Greece. With crossed nicols; enlargement 60 x.

Fig. 607. Altered and sericitised plagioclases in K-feldspar megablast. Whereas both feldspars are affected the sericitisation is more marked in the plagioclases. Pl = plagioclases sericitised, K-f = K-feldspar megablast. Naxos Granite, Greece. With crossed nicols; enlargement 10 x.

Fig. 608. Plagioclase sericitised with the micaceous minerals orientated within the host feldspar. Pl = plagioclase, S = sericite, K-f = K-feldspar. Harrar Granite, Ethiopia. With crossed nicols; enlargement 100 x.

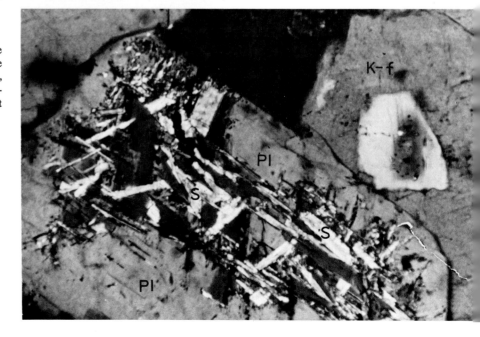

330

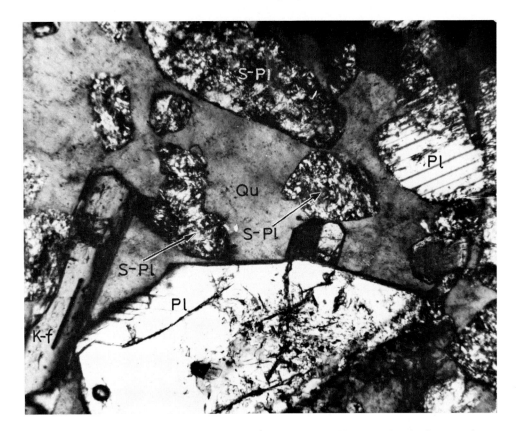

Fig. 609. Idiomorphic and sub-idiomorphic orthoclase and plagioclase enclosed in quartz. Despite the protective quartz the plagioclases show all gradations from unaltered to extremely sericitised grains. Qu = quartz, Pl = plagioclase, K-f = K-feldspar, S-Pl = sericitised plagioclase. Didessa Granite, Ethiopia. With crossed nicols; enlargement 100 x.

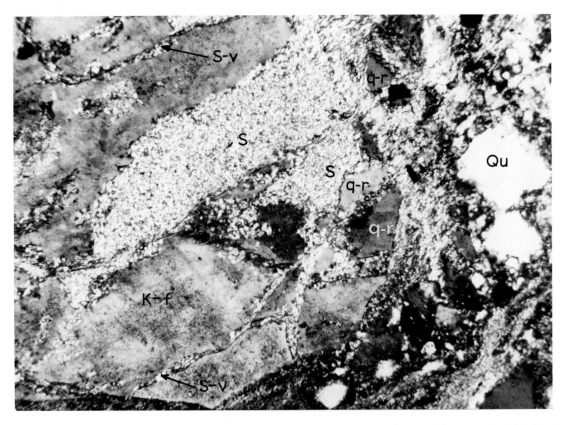

Fig. 610. Whereas the feldspar (orthoclase) is extensively sericitised quartz relics are left unaltered. "Vein-like" sericitisations are present in the orthoclase. S = sericite, q-r = quartz relics, S-v = sericitisation veins, Qu = quartz. Granite in Bernina region, Alps. With crossed nicols; enlargement 100 x.

Fig. 611. Microcline with perthites which show a preferential sericitization in comparison to the K-feldspar. S-Pe = sericitised perthite. Cap Carbonara Granite, Elba, Italy. With crossed nicols; enlargement 100 x.

Fig. 612. Altered plagioclase (sericitised) with preferential sericitisation of certain plagioclase twin lamellae. Pl = plagioclase, S = sericitised plagioclase twin lamellae. Riefenbachtal Granite, Brocken area, Harz, Germany. With crossed nicols; enlargement 100 x.

Fig. 613. Chloritised mass sending vein extensions which penetrate through quartz and feldspar. Ch = chloritised mass, Ch-v = veinlets of chloritised material, Qu = quartz, K-f = K-feldspar. Didessa Granite, Ethiopia. With crossed nicols; enlargement 100 x.

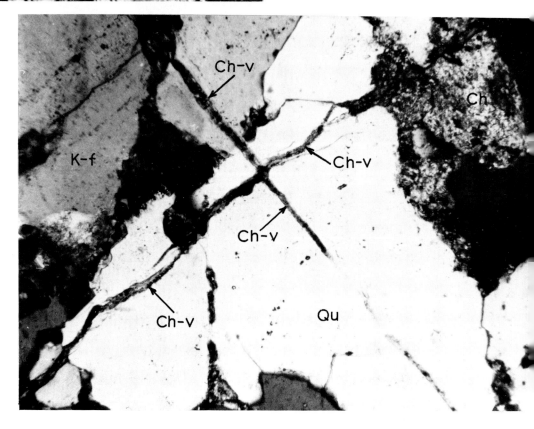

332

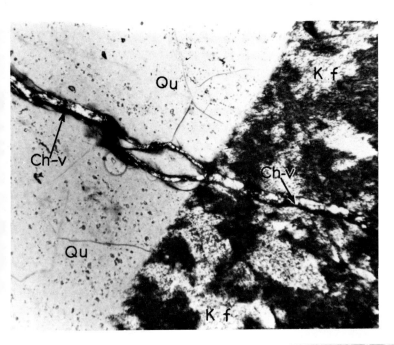

Fig. 614. Quartz in contact with perthitised K-feldspar. A chlorite veinlet transverses the quartz and the feldspar. Qu = quartz, K-f = perthitised K-feldspar, Ch-v = chloritic veinlet. Stön Granite, Kristiania area, Norway. With crossed nicols; enlargement 100 x.

Fig. 615. An intergranular cavity formed between idiomorphic and subidiomorphic quartz and feldspar, filled with secondary chlorite. K-f = K-feldspar, Qu = quartz, Ch = chlorite. Stön Granite, Kristiania area, Norway. With crossed nicols; enlargement 100 x.

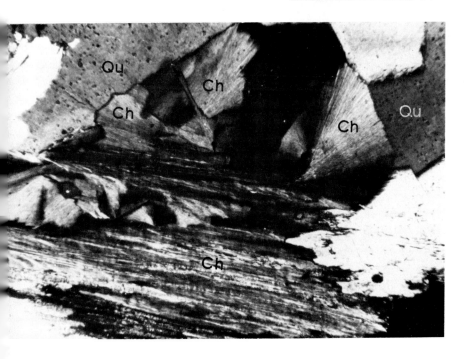

Fig. 616. Secondary chlorite filling the intergranular space of quartz grains. Ch = chlorite, Qu = quartz. Waldheim Granite, Saxony, Germany. With crossed nicols; enlargement 100 x.

333

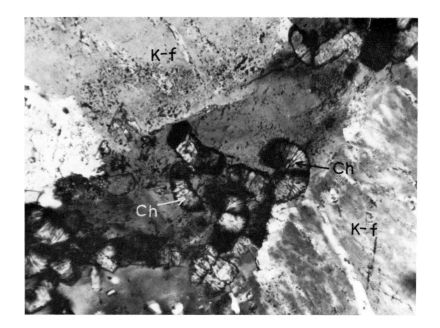

Fig. 617. Secondary chlorite in K-feldspar (perthitised). K-f = K-feldspar, Ch = chlorite. Granite at Mt. Blanc, Switzerland. With crossed nicols; enlargement 100 x.

Fig. 618. Secondary chlorite replacing biotite along cleavage. Ch = chlorite, Bi = biotite. Waldheim Granite, Saxony, Germany. With crossed nicols; enlargement 100 x.

Fig. 619. Chloritised biotite with quartz. Bi = biotite, Ch = chlorite, Qu = quartz. St. Genes Granite, Pyrenees, France. With crossed nicols; enlargement 100 x.

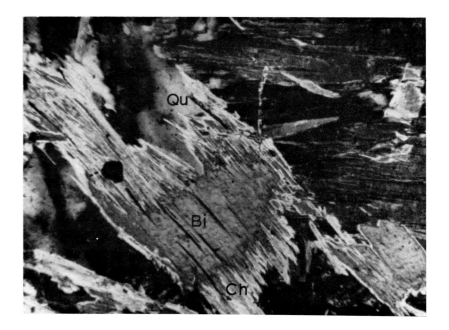

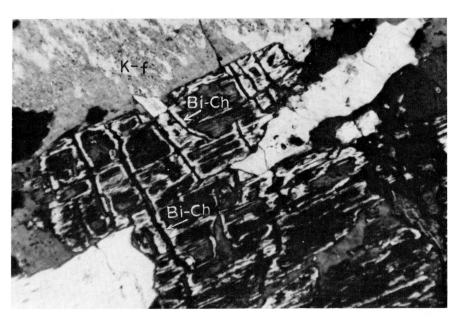

Fig. 620. "Cell-type" structure due to chloritisation of biotite along cracks and cleavage of the mica. K-f = K-feldspar perthitised, Bi-Ch = chloritised biotite. Hellewald Granite, Sewen, Vosges. With crossed nicols; enlargement 100 x.

Fig. 621. Biotite with chlorite replacements parallel to the mica's cleavage; a reaction border exists between the biotite and the chlorite. Bi = biotite, Ch = chlorite. Unterhof (mica) Syenite, Hausach, Schwarzwald (Black Forest), Germany. With crossed nicols; enlargement 100 x.

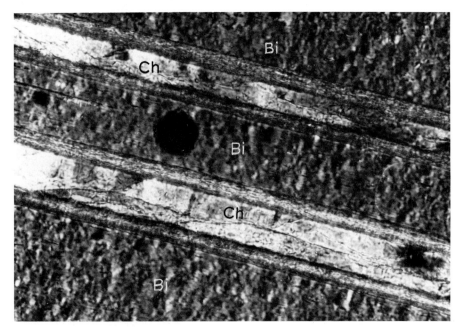

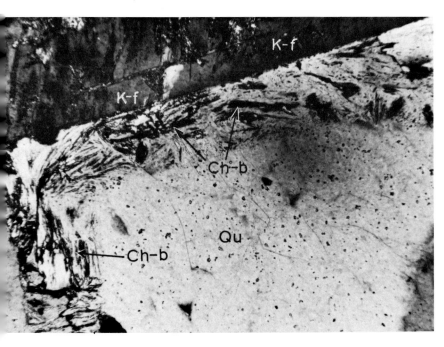

Fig. 622. Quartz in contact with K-feldspar. Chlorites or chloritised bodies are present in the marginal part of the quartz. Qu = quartz, K-f = K-feldspar. Ch-b = chlorites or chloritised bodies. Kåred (quartz) Syenite, Sweden. With crossed nicols; enlargement 100 x.

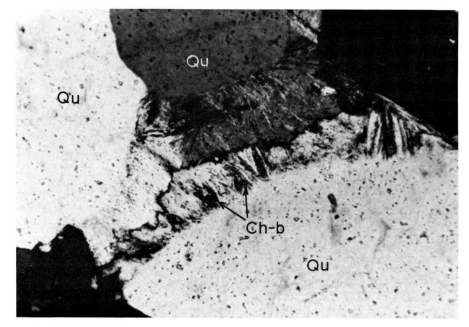

Fig. 623. Chlorite containing marginal parts of three quartz grains suggesting a common cause for the existence of chlorites or chloritised bodies in the three quartz individuals. Qu = quartz, Ch-b = chloritised bodies. Kåred (quartz) Syenite, Sweden. With crossed nicols; enlargement 100 x.

Fig. 624. Plagioclase with polysynthetic twinning with secondary biotite infiltrations with a tendency to concentrate along certain twin lamellae of the feldspar. Qu = quartz, Pl = plagioclase, biotite = white flakes. Hornblende-granite at Ilsetal, Brocken area, Harz, Germany. With crossed nicols; enlargement 100 x.

Fig. 625. Biotite with mobilised extensions into K-feldspar. Arrow "a" indicates linear infiltration of mobilised biotite along lines of greater penetrability within the feldspar. Bi = biotite, K-f = K-feldspar. Riefenbachtal Granite, Brocken area, Harz, Germany. With crossed nicols; enlargement 100 x.

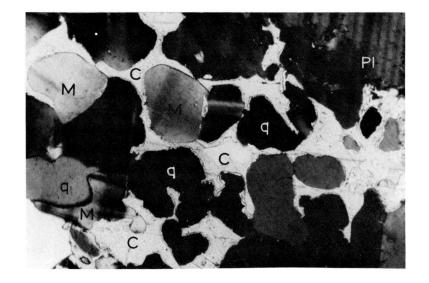

Fig. 626 and 627. Microcline, plagioclase, quartz corroded and extensively replaced by later calcite. M = microcline, Pl = plagioclase, q = quartz, C = calcite. Harrar Granite, Ethiopia. With crossed nicols; enlargement 100 x.

Fig. 627.

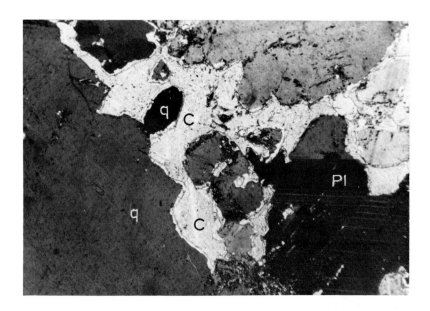

Fig. 628. Fan-shaped muscovite in quartz (the fan texture is the result of the radiating arrangement of the muscovite plates). M = muscovite, Qu = quartz. Kȧred (quartz) Syenite, Sweden. With crossed nicols; enlargement 100 x.

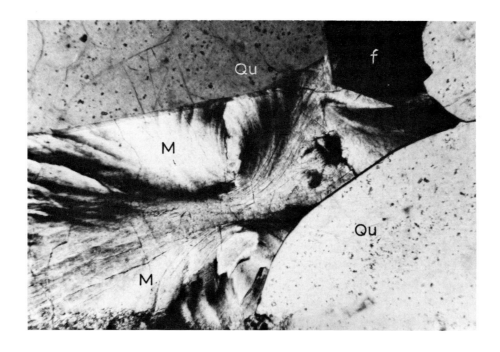

Fig. 629 and 630. (Different orientations.) Intergranular space delimited by quartz and an idiomorphic feldspar occupied by muscovite. The textural pattern of the muscovite depends on the arrangement and orientation of the muscovite "shells". M = muscovite, Qu = quartz, f = feldspar. Kåred (quartz) Syenite, Sweden. With crossed nicols; enlargement 100 x.

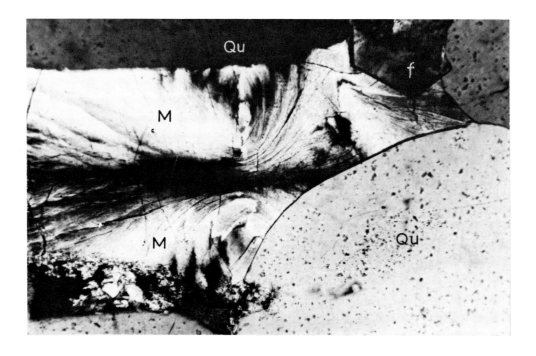

Fig. 631. Well-developed crystals of quartz with interzonal infiltrations of tourmaline. Qu = quartz, T = tourmaline. In quartz veins in Ondonock Granodiorite, West Ethiopia. Enlargement about 1½ x.

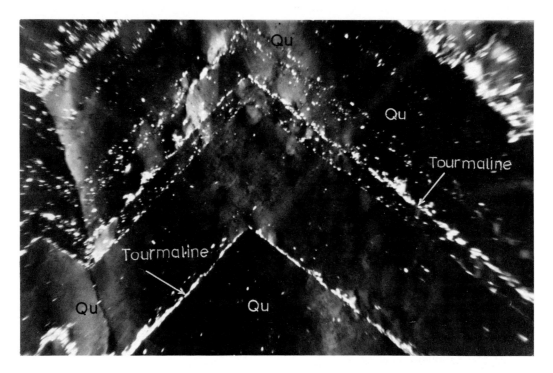

Fig. 632. Microscopic view of the zoned quartz with the interzonal infiltrations of tourmaline. The quartz shows undulating extinction due to straining. The tourmaline infiltrations transverse the boundaries of crystal grains. Qu = quartz, Tourmaline = white flakes. In quartz veins in Ondonock Granodiorite, West Ethiopia. With crossed nicols; enlargement 100 x.

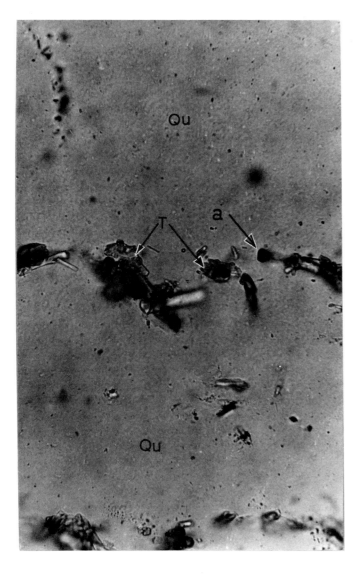

Fig. 633. Interzonal tourmaline, following directions of greater penetrability in the quartz host. Qu = quartz, T = tourmaline, arrow "a" indicates tourmaline section perpendicular to the three-fold symmetry axis. In quartz veins in Ondonock Granodiorite, West Ethiopia. With crossed nicols; enlargement 100 x.

340

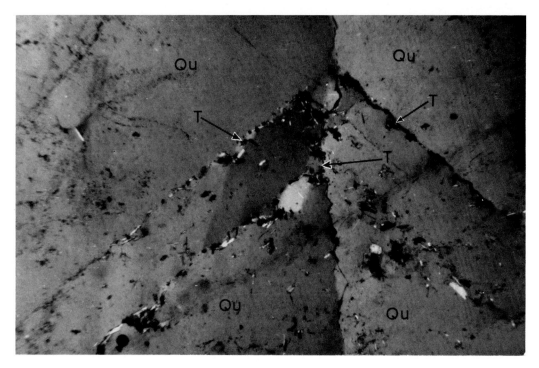

Fig. 634. Zoned quartz with interzonal infiltrations of tourmaline, also infiltration of tourmaline follows intergranular spaces. Qu = quartz, T = tourmaline as intergranular infiltrations. In quartz veins in Ondonock Granodiorite, West Ethiopia. With crossed nicols; enlargement 100 x.

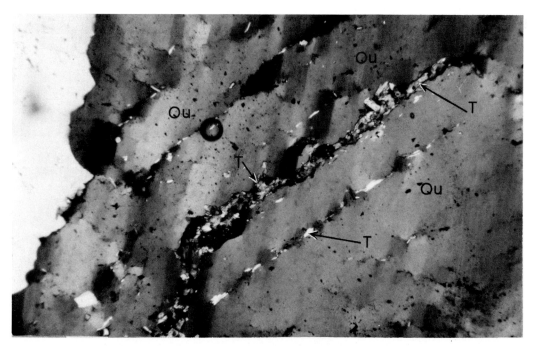

Fig. 635. Strained quartz (anomalies in the extinction position) infiltrated by metasomatic tourmaline (fine crystalline tourmaline mass) following directions of greater strain in the quartz. Qu = quartz, T = tourmaline. In quartz veins in Ondonock Granodiorite, West Ethiopia. With crossed nicols; enlargement 100 x.

Fig. 636. Part of a quartz vein, with cracks filled by later tourmaline metasomatic infiltrations. Chambe, Adolla, South Ethiopia. Handspecimen, about natural size.

Fig. 637. Tourmalinisation of quartz with partial replacement and infiltration along directions of greater penetrability of the SiO_2. T = tourmaline, Qu = quartz. In quartz veins in Ondonock Granodiorite, West Ethiopia. With crossed nicols; enlargement 100 x.

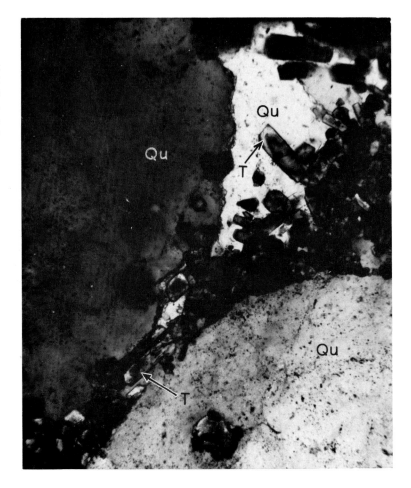

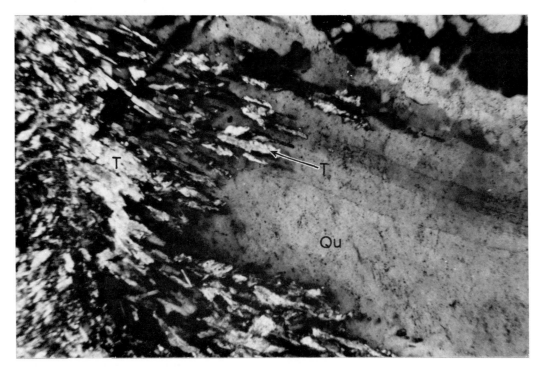

Fig. 638. Metasomatic tourmaline replacing quartz. The tourmaline infiltrations follow directions of greater penetrability in the quartz, as indicated by band of anomalous extinction. T = tourmaline, Qu = quartz. Chambe, Adolla, South Ethiopia. With crossed nicols; enlargement 100 x.

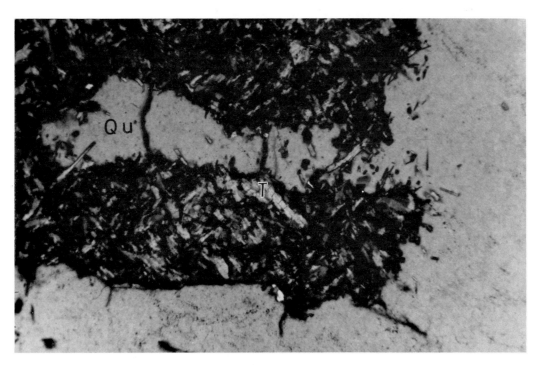

Fig. 639. Metasomatic tourmaline corroding and replacing quartz. Quartz relics are present in the metasomatic tourmaline microcrystalline mass. Qu = quartz, T = tourmaline. In quartz veins in Ondonock Granodiorite, West Ethiopia. With crossed nicols; enlargement 100 x.

Fig. 640. Tourmaline crystalloblast transversing the boundary of ankerite/prochlorite. An = ankerite, P = prochlorite, T = tourmaline. In quartz veins in Ondonock Granodiorite, West Ethiopia. With crossed nicols; enlargement 100 x.

Fig. 641. Tourmaline in the pegmatite perpendicular to the contact wall with the tourmaline containing gneiss of the country rock. T = tourmaline, G = gneissic country rock containing tourmaline. Piona, Lake Como district, Italy. The width of the pegmatite is about 1 m.

Fig. 642. Tourmaline in pegmatite, perpendicular to the contact of the gneissic country rocks which contain small tourmaline. Piona, Lake Como district, Italy. Natural size.

Fig. 643. Metasomatically formed aggregates of radiating tourmaline needles forming a "maltese cross". Luxillian Granite, Cornwall, England. With crossed nicols; enlargement 100 x.

Fig. 644. Crystalloblastic tourmaline needles, attaining a radiating character, with quartz and sericitised feldspars. Qu = quartz, s-f = sericitised feldspar, T = tourmaline. Luxillian Granite, Cornwall, England. With crossed nicols; enlargement 100 x.

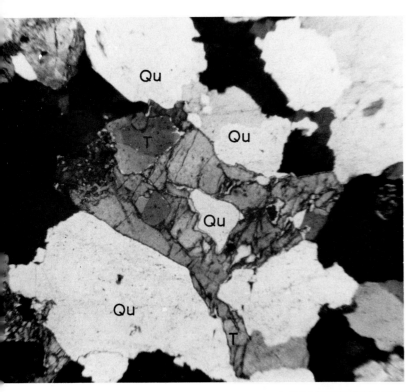

Fig. 645. Tourmaline enclosing quartz and extending intergranularly between the quartz grains. T = tourmaline, Qu = quartz. Pegmatite at Piona, Lake Como district, Italy. With crossed nicols; enlargement 100 x.

Fig. 646 and 647. Tourmaline enclosing biotite, zircons (with radioactive halo) and quartz infiltrations (protuberance of the external quartz grain). T = tourmaline, Zr = zircon, Bi = biotite, q = quartz. Elzach Granite, Schwarzwald (Black Forest), Germany. Fig. 647 with crossed nicols; enlargement 100 x.

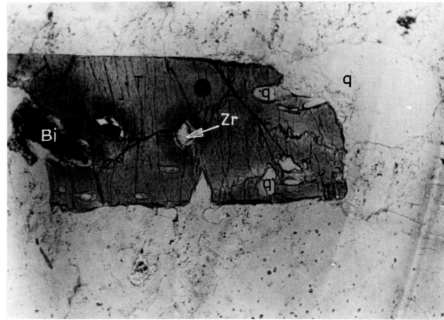

Fig. 647.

347

Fig. 648. Tourmaline with included quartz which is due to replacement. T = tourmaline, Q = quartz, m-q = myrmekitic-like quartz, K-f = K-feldspar. Elzach Granite, Schwarzwald (Black Forest), Germany. With crossed nicols; enlargement 100 x.

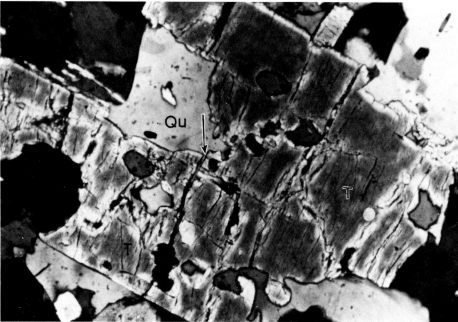

Fig. 649. Tourmaline invaded and replaced by quartz. Often the quartz invaded the tourmaline interleptonically along fine cracks (see arrow). T = tourmaline, Qu = quartz. Elzach Granite, Schwarzwald (Black Forest), Germany. With crossed nicols; enlargement 100 x.

Fig. 650. Tourmaline in contact with recrystallised quartz. A late generation quartz partly follows the recrystallised quartz/tourmaline margin and extends into a crack of the tourmaline. T = tourmaline, r-q = recrystallised quartz, y-q = young quartz extending into cracks of the tourmaline. Elzach Granite, Schwarzwald (Black Forest), Germany. Without crossed nicols; enlargement 100 x.

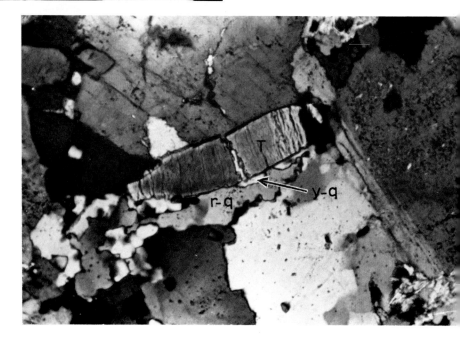

348

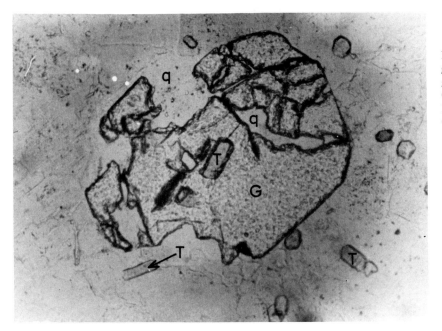

Fig. 651. Tourmaline crystal grains in a background of feldspar and quartz, also a blastic garnet with enclosed tourmaline and quartz. G = garnet, T = tourmaline, q = quartz. Elzach Granite, Schwarzwald (Black Forest), Germany. Enlargement 100 x.

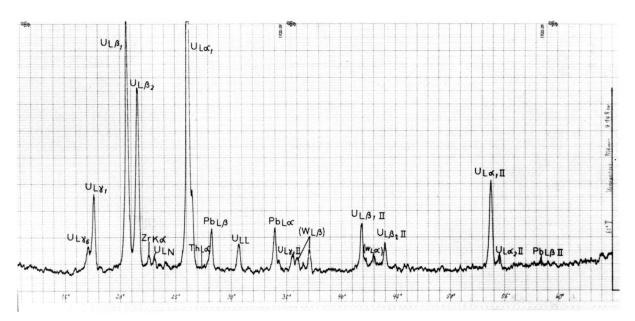

Fig. 652. X-ray fluorescence spectroanalysis of colloform pitchblende from Pribram, C.S.S.R.

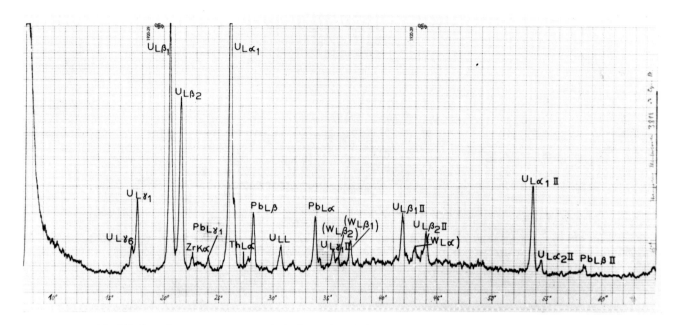

Fig. 653. X-ray fluorescence spectroanalysis of crystalline hydrothermal uraninite from Shinkolobwe, Katanga.

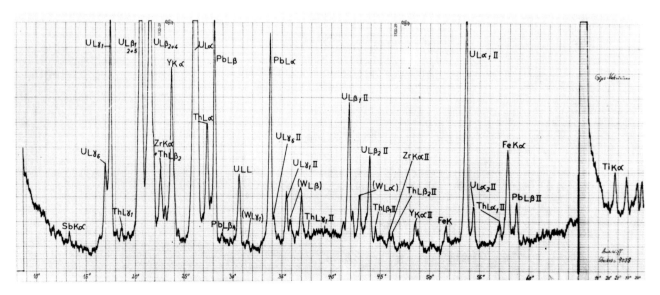

Fig. 654. X-ray fluorescence spectroanalysis of pegmatitic uraninite (well-formed cubes) from Stacebo, Wästergötland, Sweden.

350

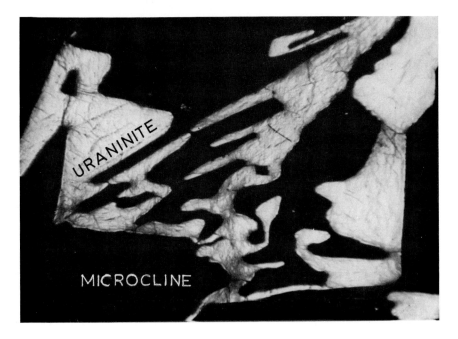

Fig. 655. Skeleton uraninite (crystalline) in intergrowth with microcline. Pegmatite at Ruggles Mine, U.S.A. Polished section; with one nicol. Oil immersion; enlargement 200 x.

Fig. 656. Zoned zircon (metamict malacon) surrounded by magnetite (M) and uraninite (Ura) which contain radioactive cracks radiating only in certain directions from the zircon margin. Faraday mine, Bancroft, Ontario. Canada. Polished section; oil immersion; with one nicol; enlargement approx. 250 x.

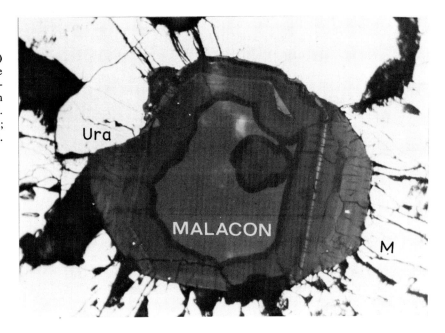

Fig. 657. Zoned zircon (malacon), enclosing pieces of uraninite (Ura) devoid of radioactive cracks. Faraday mine, Bancroft, Ontario, Canada. Polished section; with one nicol; oil immersion; enlargement approx. 250X.

351

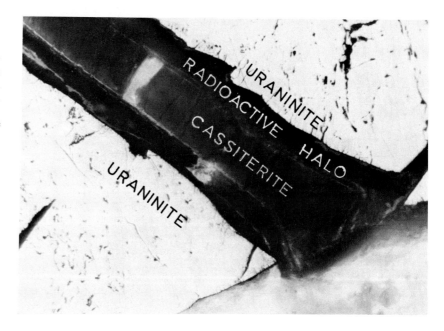

Fig. 658. Uraninite with cassiterite (pegmatitic occurrence). A strong radioactive halo marks the contact of the uraninite with the cassiterite, which is more recent. Ingersoll mine, Keystone, South Dakota, U.S.A. Polished section; oil immersion; with one nicol; enlargement approx. 250 x.

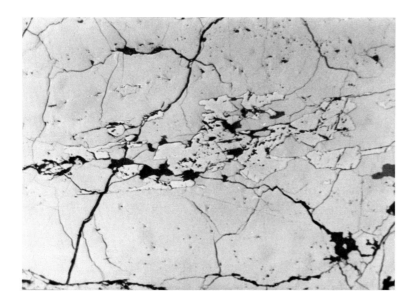

Fig. 659 A. Columbite including uraninite ex-solutions. Probably representing segregations of U along areas of weakness in the columbite. Hagendorf, Bavaria, Germany. Polished section; oil immersion; with one nicol; enlargement approx. 250 x.

Fig. 659 B. Columbite including uraninite with some well-developed crystal faces. Hagendorf, Bavaria, Germany. Polished section; oil immersion; with one nicol; enlargement approx. 250 x.

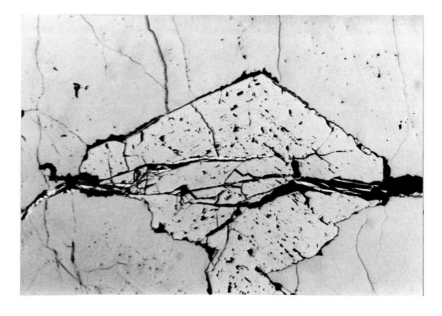

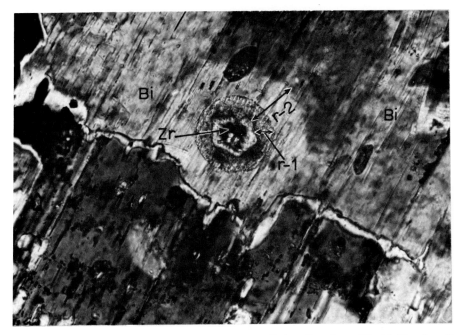

Fig. 660. Zircon in biotite. A double radioactive halo is produced due to radiation. Zr = zircon, Bi = biotite, r-1 = radius of first radioactive halo, r-2 = radius of second radioactive halo (ring). Kalbach (two-mica) Granite, Schenkenzell, Schwarzwald (Black Forest), Germany. With crossed nicols; enlargement 100 x.

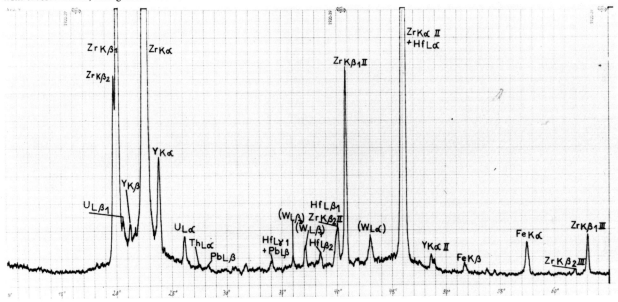

Fig. 661. X-ray fluorescence spectroanalysis of malacon from Hittero, Norway.

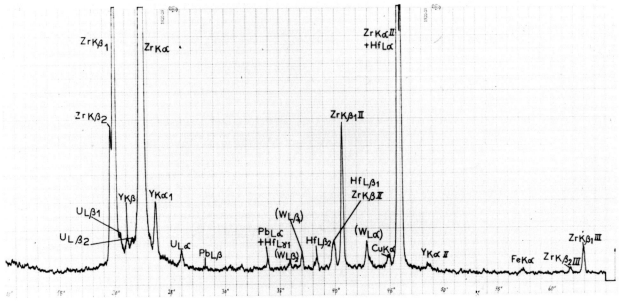

Fig. 662. X-ray fluorescence spectroanalysis of malacon from Takayama, Japan.

353

Fig. 663. Orthite (central part converted into metamictic aggregates), associated with biotite. Didessa Granite, Ethiopia. With crossed nicols; enlargement 100 x.

Fig. 664 A. Biotite with zircon surrounded by radioactive halos. Also ore granules (with radioactive halos) mobilised secondarily along cracks of the biotite. Harrar Granite, Ethiopia. Enlargement 100 x.

Fig. 664 B. Comparable to Fig. 653, in addition indicating a zircon with double radioactive halo. A radioactive halo caused by the radioactive ore granules is also shown. Harrar Granite, Ethiopia. Enlargement 200 x.

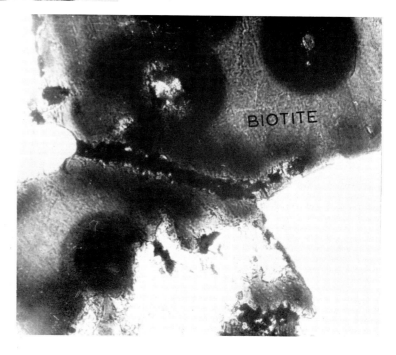

Fig. 665. Handspecimen showing a part of a phyllite xenolith with K-feldspar "double-inclusions". K-f = K-feldspar double inclusions in the phyllite xenolith. New Mt. Blanc tunnel; about natural size.

Fig. 666. Intrusive granitic vein in marble. No prominent metasomatic effects are produced in the marble as the granitic vein comes in contact with the calcareous rock. However, a metasomatic margin, due to epidote formation, is produced in the granite itself. Mt. Cadino, Alps.

355

Fig. 667. Intrusive apophysis of the Seriphos Granite which has caused an arching of the banded marbles into which it has intruded. Also metasomatic contacts of garnet–epidote are formed at the contact line of the granite with the metamorphosed calcareous rocks. G = granitic apophysis, M-C = metasomatic contact consisting mainly of epidote and garnet, M = arched banded marble. Halara, Seriphos, Greece.

Fig. 668. Intrusive granitic gang (vein-like form) into metamorphosed calcareous rocks, marble. Gneissic xenoliths are suspended in the granitic gang. G = granite, X = xenolith. M = marble, white circle is approx. 5 cm diameter. Mt. Mattoni, Val Fredda, South Adamello, Italy.

Fig. 669. Polymictic mylonite with an "augen" shaped body of plastically deformed gneiss-granite. G-g = gneiss-granite, p-myl = polymictic mylonite. Masino Bagni, Sondrio, Italy.

Fig. 670. A plastically deformed granite-gneissic body in a folded and mobilised gneissic background. g = gneiss, g-r = granite-gneiss. Masino Bagni, Sondrio, Italy.

357

Fig. 671. An isolated granitic body augen-form in banded metamorphosed calcareous rocks. G = granite body, m-c = metamorphosed calcareous rocks. Badilla region, Alps.

Fig. 672. Microcline, quartz, orthoclase rounded grains with later blastic quartz from an intrusive gang in gneiss. Kebra Mengist, Adolla, Ethiopia. With crossed nicols; enlargement 100 x.

Fig. 673. A calcareous fossiliferous limestone body entirely included in hornblende dolerite. The limestone was tectonically pushed into the dolerite. The contact of the limestone and dolerite is microbrecciated. The width of the limestone body is approx. 2–3 m. Katara, Greece.

Fig. 674. Leucocratic (K-feldspar rich) veins in the Adamello Granite. The leucocratic vein system, anastomosing and branching, is most probably due to hydrogenic solutions, indicating a type of metasomatic replacement. Relics of the granite are left in the leucocratic veins. r-g = relics of the granite in the leucocratic veins. Adamello Massif, Alps.

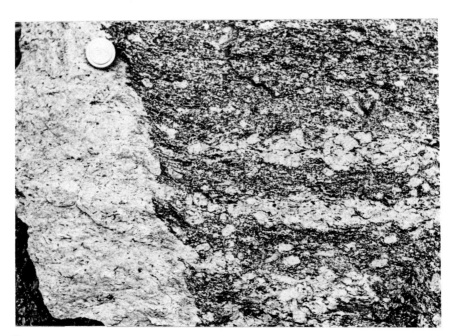

Fig. 675. A leucocratic "vein" mainly consisting of K-feldspars has sent extensions into the granite and caused K-feldspar megablastic growths. The extensions of the leucocratic vein and the K-feldspar blastesis in the granite have followed directions of greater penetrability. Bergeller Granite, Alps.

Fig. 676. An uninterrupted outcrop of the main vein. Kimmeria-Xanthe, Greece.

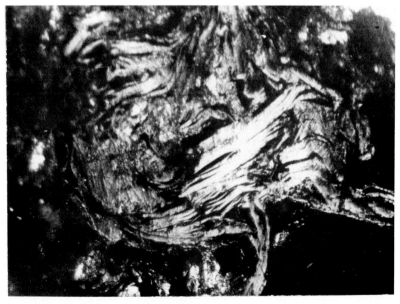

Fig. 677. Rich molybdenite in quartz. The molybdenite is tectonically bent and is exhibiting a twinning. Kimmeria-Xanthe, Greece. Polished section; oil immersion; with one nicol; enlargement 200 x.

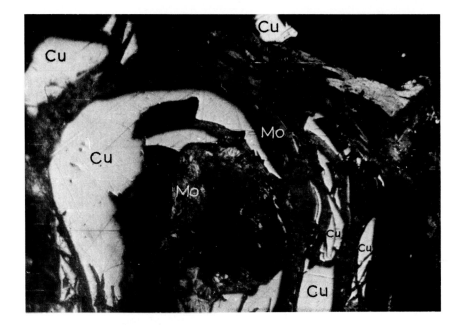

Fig. 678. Chalcopyrite (Cu) in a binding mass of molybdenite (Mo). Kimmeria-Xanthe, Greece. Polished section; oil immersion with one nicol; enlargement 200 x.

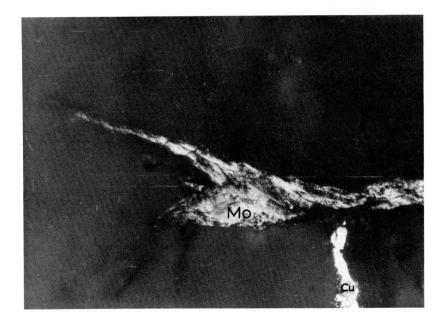

Fig. 679. Band of molybdenite (Mo) ending in the quartz vein. Chalcopyrite is also present (Cu). Kimmeria-Xanthe, Greeece. Polished section; oil immersion with one nicol; enlargement 200 x.

Fig. 680. Wolframite crystal grain (W) with a broad twin lamella surrounded by molybdenite (Mo). Chalcopyrite is also present (Cu). Kimmeria-Xanthe, Greece. Polished section; oil immersion with one nicol; enlargement 200 x.

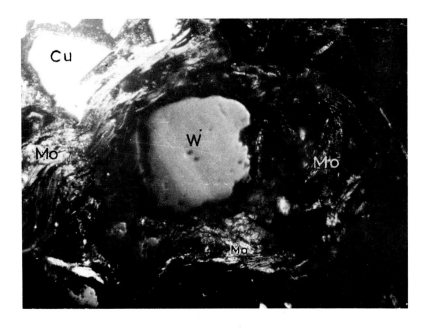

362

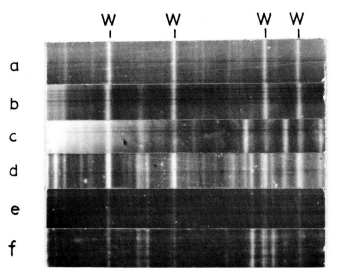

Fig. 681. Spectrographical analyses of the following samples: a) Scheelite from Saxony, Germany (standard sample for comparison). b) and c) Scheelite crystals separated under ultra violet light, SW (bluish—whitish, and yellowish) from the main magnetite skarn. d) and e) Scheelite crystals separated under ultra violet light, SW (bluish—whitish, and yellowish) from different parts of the main contact metasomatic body. f) Scheelite crystals separated under ultra violet light, SW (bluish—whitish, creamish, and creamish—yellowish) from the Quartz—Mo—W—Cu veins. SW = short-wave.

Fig. 682. General view of the main skarn body (containing scheelite) showing also the relationship of the skarn (S) to the granite (G) and to the marble (M). Kimmeria-Xanthe, Greece.

Fig. 683. Magnetite (M) with chalcopyrite impregnations (Cu). Maghemite (Mh) is also present as alteration of the magnetite. Kimmeria Skarn. Polished section; oil immersion; with one nicol; enlargement 200 x.

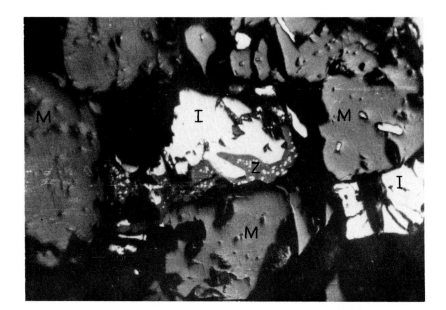

Fig. 684. General appearance of the magnetite ore of the main skarn body. Also sphalerite in intergrowth with the intermediate mineral. M = magnetite, I = intermediate mineral, Z = sphalerite. Polished section; oil immersion; with one nicol; enlargement 200 x.

Fig. 685. Spectrographic analysis showing the presence of strong Cu lines in the sample of the mineral intermediate in its optical appearance. A Cu-compound is also spectrochemically analysed. a = copper compound, b = intermediate mineral.

364

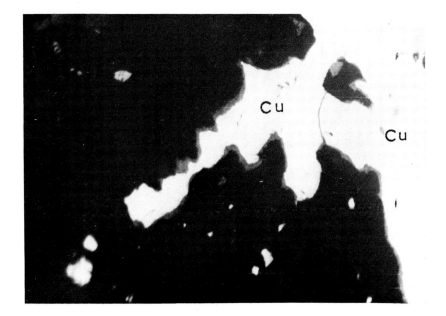

Fig. 686. Photomicrograph of chalcopyrite (Cu) with a margin of chalcocite.
Polished section; oil immersion; with one
nicol; enlargement 200 x.

Fig. 687. General appearance of the main contact metasomatic body (indicated by an interrupted
line). The length of the outcrop is over 700 m and the width about 20 m. Kimmeria-Xanthe,
Greece.

365

References

Adams, F. D., 1930. The transfusion of matter from one solid to another under the influence of heat – a new factor in the process of metamorphism. *Can. J. Res.*, 2: 153.

Albermann, K. B. and Anderson, J. S., 1950. The oxides of uranium. *J. Chem. Soc. Lond., Suppl.*, 2: 303–311.

Andersen, O., 1928. The genesis of some types of feldspar from granite pegmatites. *Nor. Geol. Tidsskr.*, 10: 116–205.

Andreatta, G., 1961. Metablastesen im kristallinen Sockel der Südalpen. *Neues Jahrb. Mineral., Abh.*, 96. 228–232.

Atomic Energy Commission U.S. (Frondel, C., Riska, D. and Frondel, J. W.), 1956. X-ray powder data for uranium and thorium minerals. *Geol. Surv. Bull.*, 1036-G: 91–153.

Augustithis, S. S., 1959/60. Über Blastese in Gesteinen unterschiedlicher Genese. (Migmatit, Granit, Metamorphit, (Smirgel,) Basalt). *Hamburger Beitr. Angew. Mineral., Kristallphys., Petrogen.*, 2: 40–68.

Augustithis, S. S., 1962a. Non-eutectic, graphic, micrographic and graphic-like "myrmekitic" structures and textures. *Beitr. Mineral. Petrogr.*, 8: 491–498.

Augustithis, S. S., 1962b. Researches of blastic process in granitic rocks and later graphic quartz in pegmatites (pegmatoides) from Ethiopia. *Nova Acta Leopoldina*, 156, 25: 5–17.

Augustithis, S. S., 1963. Oscillatory zoning of plagioclase-phenocrysts of the olivine basalt from Debra-Sina, Ethiopia. *Chem. Erde*, 23: 71–81.

Augustithis, S. S., 1964a. Quartz/feldspar micrographic (granophyric) intergrowths in volcanics and their comparison with graphic and granophyric structures and textures in granites and pegmatites. In: Augustithis (Editor), Festband Prof. F. K. Drescher-Kaden – Petrogen. Geochem., Spec. Bull., 1–14.

Augustithis, S. S., 1964b. Non-ex-solution perthites from pegmatoids of Yavello/Borona, southern Ethiopia. *Chem. Erde*, 23(4): 227–247.

Augustithis S. S., 1964c. On the phenomenology of phenocrysts (tecoblasts, zoned phenocrysts, holo-phenocrystalline rock types). In: S. S. Augustithis (Editor), Festband Prof. F. K. Drescher-Kaden – Petrogen. Geochem., Spec. Bull., 15–31.

Augustithis, S. S., 1964d. Geochemical and ore-microscopic studies of hydrothermal and pegmatitic primary uranium parageneses. *Nova Acta Leopoldina, Neue Folge*, 28(170): 1–233.

Augustithis S. S., 1965. On the phenomenology of plastic deformation of quartz and micas in some granites. *Tectonophysics*, 2(6): 455–473.

Augustithis S. S., 1966. Micrographic (granophyric) textures in quartzitic pebbles of the granitised conglomerate of Buri-Rashitcha, Ula-Ulo, Adolo district, southern Ethiopia. *Contrib. Mineral. Petrol.*, 13: 75–82.

Augustithis S. S., 1967a. The accessory minerals as relics of a pregranitic paragneissic phase. *Chem. Erde*, 26(1): 11–26.

Augustithis, S. S., 1967b. On the phenomenology and geochemistry of differential leaching and element agglutination processes. *Chem. Geol.*, 2: 311–329.

Augustithis, S. S., 1967c. On the textures and paragenesis of the gold-quartz-tourmaline veins of Ondonoc, western Ethiopia. *Mineral. Deposita (Berl.)*, 3: 48–55.

Augustithis, S. S., 1967d. Fossiliferous limestone bodies tectonically pushed in hornblende dolerities. *Chem. Erde*, 26(1): 27–42.

Augustithis, S. S. and Ottemann, J., 1966. On diffusion rings and sphaeroidal weathering. *Chem. Geol.*, 1: 201–209.

Backlund, H. G., 1936. Der Magma-aufstieg in Faltengebirgen. *Bull. Comm. Geol. Finl.*, 115: 324.

Backlund, H. G., 1938a. The Rapakivi puzzle, a reply. *Geol. Fören. Stockholm Förh.*, 60: 105.

Backlund, H. G., 1938b. Zur Granitisationstheorie; eine Verdeutlichung. *Geol. Fören. Stockholm Förh.*, 60: 177.

Backlund, H. G., 1938c. The problems of the Rapakivi granites. *J. Geol.*, 46: 339.

Backlund, H. G., 1946. The granitization problem. *Geol. Mag.*, 83:105.

Backlund, H. G., 1953. The granitization problem. *Estud. Geol., Inst. Invest. Geol. "Lucas Mallada" (Madrid)*, 9: 71.

Bader, H., 1961. Apatite und Zirkone als sedimentäre Relikte in Metablastitgneisen der Oberpfalz. *Neues Jahrb. Mineral., Monatsh.*, 1961: 169–179.

Bailey, S. W., Bell, R. A. and Peng, C. J., 1958. Plastic deformation of quartz in nature. *Bull. Geol. Soc. Am.*, 69: 1443–1466.

Barth, T. F. W., 1962a. Feldspar solid solutions. *Chem. Erde*, 22: 31–40.

Barth, T. F. W., 1962b. *Theoretical Petrology. A Textbook on the Origin and the Evolution of Rocks.* John Wiley, New York, N.Y, 2nd ed., 416 pp.

Barth, T. F. W. and Sørensen, H., 1961. Symposium on migmatite nomenclature, *Int. Geol. Congr., 21st, Copenhagen, 1960, Rep. Session, Norden*, 24: 54–78.

Beavis, C. F., 1964. Superposed folding in the Beechworth Contact aureole. *Proc. R. Soc. Victoria*, 77 (2): 265–272.

Becke, F., 1904. Über Mineralbestand und Struktur der kristallinischen Schiefer. *Compt. Rend. Congr. Géol. Int., 9me, Vienne, 1903:* 553.

Becke, F., 1908. Über Myrmekit. *Tschermaks Mineral. Petrogr. Mitt.*, 27: 377–390.

Becke, F., 1923. Zur Physiographie der Gemengteile der kristallinen Schiefer. *Akad. Wiss. Wien, Denkschr.*, 75:1.

Berman, E. R., 1955. Unit cell dimensions of uraninite. *Am. Mineral.*, 40: 925–927.

Berman, H., 1938. Experiments bearing on the orientation of quartz in deformed rocks. *Bull. Geol. Soc. Am.*, 49: 1723–1746.

Bowen, N. L., 1928. *The Evolution of the Igneous Rocks.* Princeton Univ. Press, Princeton, N. J., 334 pp.

Bowen, N. L., 1947. Magmas. *Bull. Geol. Soc. Am.*, 58: 263–279.

Bowen, N. L. and Tuttle, O. F., 1950. The system $NaAlSi_3O_8 - KAlSi_3O_8 - H_2O$. *J. Geol.*, 58: 489–511.

Breithaupt, A., 1839. Über regelmässige Verwachsungen von Kristallen zweier und dreier Mineralspezies. *Neues Jahrb. Mineral. Geol. Paläontol., Abh.*, 89.

Broegger, W. C., 1886. Die Minerale der Syenitpegmatite der südnorwegischen Augit und Nephelinsyenite. *Geol. Fören. Stockholm Förh.*, 5: 326.

Bugge, J. A. W., 1946. The geological importance of diffusion in the solid state. *Skr. Nor. Videnskap.-Akad., Oslo, I. Mat. Naturv. Kl.*, 13: 1–59.

Butler, J. R., Bowden, P. and Smith, A. Z., 1962. K/Rb ratios in the evolution of the younger granites of northern Nigeria. *Geochim. Cosmochim. Acta*, 26: 89–100.

Carey, S. W., 1962. Folding. *J. Alberta Soc. Petrol. Geol.*, 1962: 95–144.

Carman, J. H. and Tuttle, O. F., 1963. Experimental study bearing on the origin of myrmekite. *Geol. Soc. Am., Bull.*, 74: 29 A.

Chao, E. C. T., 1951. Granitization and basification by diffusion. *Nor. Geol. Tiddskr.*, 29: 84–107.

Christa, E., 1927. Über Regelungserscheinungen im Schriftgranit. *Verh. Phys. Med. Ges. Würzburg, Neue Folge*, 53: 000–000.

Christa, E., 1928. Über Myrmekit in zentralalpinen Gesteinen. *Neues Jahrb. Mineral Petrogr., Abh.*, 57A: 1185–1196.

Cloos, H., 1922. *Der Gebirgsbau Schlesiens*. Bornträger, Berlin.

Coppens, R., Durand, G. and Roubault, M. 1965. Etude de l'age des zircons par le rapport des plombs 207 et 206. Application a l'étude du granite de la Clarte-Ploumanac'h (Bretagne, France). *Sci. Terre*, 10(3/4): 291–302.

Cornelius, H. P., 1935, 1937. Zur Deutung gefüllter Feldspäte. *Schweiz. Mineral. Petrogr. Mitt.*, 15: 15–17; 17: 80.

Daly, R. A., 1917. Metamorphism and its phases. *Bull. Geol. Soc. Am.*, 28: 375.

Daly, R. A., 1949. Granite and metasomatism. *Am. J. Sci.*, 247: 753–778.

De Beaumont, E., 1847. Note sur les émanations volcaniques et métallifères. *Bull. Soc. Géol. France, 2me Sér.*, 4: 1259–1334.

Den Tex, E., 1965. Metamorphic lineages of orogenetic plutonism. *Geol. Mijnbouw*, 44: 105–132.

Derriks, J. J. and Oosterbosch, R., 1958. The Swambo and Kalongwe deposits compared to Shinkolobwe: contribution to the study of Katanga uranium. *U.N. Int. Conf., Geneva, 1958*, 2: 663–695.

De Sitter, L. U., 1956. *Structural Geology*. McGraw–Hill, New York, N.Y., 552 pp.

Dietrich, R. V., 1967. A geobarometer for certain migmatites. *Soc. Géol. Finl.*, 34: 3–9.

Dimroth, E., 1963. Untersuchungen zum Mechanismus von Blastesis und Syntexis in Phylliten und Hornfelsen des südwestlichen Fichtelgebirges. *Tschermaks Mineral. Petrogr. Mitt.*, 3(8): 361–402; 476–522.

Drescher-Kaden, F. K., 1926. Über granito-dioritische Mischgesteine des Friedeberger Intrusivmasse. *Neues Jahrb. Mineral., Abh.*, 54A: 243.

Drescher-Kaden, F. K., 1927. Über Mikroklinholoblasten mit Grundgewebseinschlüssen, Internregelung von Biotit und einige diesbezügliche genetische Erwägungen. *Sonderdr. Notizbl. Ver. Erdk. – Hess. Geol. Landesamt. Darmstadt*, 5(10): 246–269.

Drescher-Kaden, F. K., 1932. Über Quarzgefügeregelung im Dattelquarzit von Krummendorf. *Mineral. Petrogr. Mitt.*, 42(3/4): 217–263.

Drescher-Kaden, F. K., 1936. Über Assimilationsvorgänge, Migmatitbildungen und ihre Bedeutung bei der Entstehung der Magmen. *Chem. Erde*, 10: 271–310.

Drescher-Kaden, F. K., 1940. Beiträge zur Kenntnis der Migmatit- und Assimilationsbildungen sowie der synantetischen Reaktionsformen, 1. *Chem. Erde*, 12: 304–417.

Drescher-Kaden, F. K., 1942. Beiträge zur Kenntnis der Migmatit- und Assimilationsbildungen sowie der synantetischen Re-

aktionsformen, 2. Über die schriftgranitische Kristallisation und ihre Beziehung zur normalen Silikatmetasomatose granitischer Gesteine. *Chem. Erde*, 14: 157–238.

Drescher-Kaden, F. K., 1948. *Die Feldspat-Quarz-Reaktionsgefüge der Granite und Gneise, und ihre genetische Bedeutung*. Springer, Heidelberg, 259 pp.

Drescher-Kaden, F. K., 1954. Zur Darstellung des Regelungsgrades eines Gefüges. *Tschermaks Mineral. Petrogr. Mitt.*, 4(1/4): 159–177.

Drescher-Kaden, F. K., 1961a. Über Ultrametamorphismus und Granitgenese im Bergell und Adamello. *Ber. Geol. Ges. Berl.*, 6(1): 85–87.

Drescher-Kaden, F. K., 1961b. Zur Herkunft der dunklen Sphaeroide des Adamello Tonalits. *Naturwissenschaften*, 48(7): 217. (Sonderdr.)

Drescher-Kaden, F. K., 1961c. Transportvorgänge in Intergranularen. *Naturwissenschaften*, 48(7): 217–218.

Drescher-Kaden, F. K., 1961d. Olivin-Metasomatose in Carbonatgesteinen aus der Umrandung des Bergeller Granitmassivs (Oberengadin). *Naturwissenschaften*, 48 (8): 300

Drescher-Kaden, F. K., 1962. Versuche zur hydrothermal-Synthese (die Bedeutung der Intergranulare beim Kristallwachstum). *Ber. Geol. Ges. Berl. Sonderh.*, 1: 115–116.

Drescher-Kaden, F. K., 1969. *Granitprobleme*. Akademie-Verlag, Berlin, 586 pp.

Drescher-Kaden, F. K. and Böttcher, G., 1955. Erzwungene Ionenbewegungen einwertiger Metalle im Quartz. *Naturwissenschaften*, 42(11): 341–342.

Drescher-Kaden, F. K. and Heller, S. 1961. Reibungswärme als Energiequelle hydrothermaler Vorgänge. *Ber. Geol. Ges. Berl.*, 1 (6): 3–17.

Drescher-Kaden, F. K. and Stolz, M., 1929. Zur Tektonik und Genese des Bergeller Massivs. *Zbl. Mineral. Petrogr., Abh. A*, 1929: 239–251.

Dwight, A. E., 1960. Positions of thorium and uranium in the periodic table. *Nature (Lond.)*, 187: 505–506.

Emmons, R. C., 1964. Granites by recrystallization. *Am. J. Sci.*, 262: 561–591.

Engel, A. E. and Engel, C. G., 1960. Progressive metamorphism and granitization of the major paragneiss, northwest Adirondack Mountains, New York, 2. *Bull. Geol. Soc. Am.*, 71: 1–57.

Erdmannsdörffer, O. H., 1912. Die Einschlüsse des Brockengranits. *Jahrb. Preuss. Geol. Landesamtes*, 32(2): 341.

Erdmannsdörffer, O. H., 1924. *Grundlagen der Petrographie*. Ferdinand Enke, Stuttgart, 321 pp.

Erdmannsdörffer, O. H., 1936. Neuere Arbeiten über Metamorphismus und seine Grenzgebiete. *Fortschr. Mineral. Kristallogr. Petrogr.*, 20: 143.

Erdmannsdörffer, O. H., 1939. Die Rolle der Anatexis. *Sitzungsber. Heidelb. Akad. Wiss., Math. Naturw. Kl.*, 7: 72 pp.

Erdmannsdörffer, O. H., 1941a. Beiträge zur Petrographie des Odenwaldes, 1. Schollen und Mischgesteine im Schriesheimer Granit. *Sitzungsber. Heidelb. Akad. Wiss., Math. Naturw. Kl., Abh.*, 1: 3.

Erdmannsdörffer, O. H., 1941b. Myrmekit und Albitkornbildung in magmatischen und metamorphen Gesteinen. *Zbl. Mineral. Petrogr., Abt. A.*, 1941: 41.

Erdmannsdörffer, O. H., 1943. Hydrothermale Zwischenstufen im Kristallisationsablauf von Tiefengesteinen. *Chem. Erde*, 15: 283.

Erdmannsdörffer, O. H., 1946. Über Intergranularsymplektite und ihre Bedeutung. *Nachr. Akad. Wiss. Göttingen, Math. Phys. Kl.*, 1946.

Erdmannsdörffer, O. H., 1948. Aus dem Grenzgebiet magmatisch-metamorph. *Z. Dtsch. Geol. Ges.*, 100: 204–212.

Erdmannsdörffer, O. H., 1950. Die Rolle der Endoblastese in Granit. *Fortschr. Mineral.*, 28: 22–25.

Erhart, M. H., 1963. Sur le cycle de la silice hydratée dans la biosphère. *Compt. Rend.*, 256: 3731–3734.

Eskola, P., 1922a. On contact phenomena between gneiss and limestone in western Massachusetts. *J. Geol.*, 30: 265–294.

Eskola, P., 1922b. The mineral facies of rocks. *Nor. Geol. Tidsskr.*, 6: 143.

Eskola, P., 1928. On rapakivi rocks from the bottom of the Gulf of Bothnia. *Fennia*, 50(27): 1–29.

Eskola, P., 1932a. On the origin of granitic magmas. *Mineral. Petrogr., Mitt.*, 42: 455–481.

Eskola, P., 1932b. On the principles of metamorphic differentiation. *Compt. Rend. Soc. Géol. Finl.*, 5: 68–77.

Eskola, P., 1933. On the differential anatexis of rocks. *Compt. Rend. Soc. Géol. Finl.*, 7: 12–25.

Eskola, P., 1934. A note on diffusion and reactions in solids. *Compt. Rend. Géol. Finl.*, 8: 144.

Eskola, P., 1948. The nature of metasomatism in the processes of granitization. *Int. Geol. Congr., 18th, London, 1948, Rept.*, 3: 1–9.

Eskola, P., 1955. About the granite problem and some masters of the study of granite. *Compt. Rend. Soc. Géol. Finl.*, 28: 117–130.

Exner, Ch., 1951. Mikroklinporphyroblasten mit helizitischen Einschlusszügen bei Bad Gastein. *Tschermaks Mineral. Petrogr. Mitt.*, 2(3): 355–374.

Ferguson, R. B., Traill, R. J. and Taylor, W. H., 1958. The crystal structures of low-temperature and high-temperature albites. *Acta Crystallogr.*, 11(5): 332–348.

Fersman, A. E., 1915. Die Schriftstruktur der Pegmatite und die Ursachen ihrer Entstehung. *Isw. Akad. Wiss.*, 12: 1211.

Filatova, L. I., 1964. Porphyroblastic plagioclase gneisses in the Precambrian of central Kasakhstan. *Kristallinikum*, 2: 39–60.

Fonteilles, M., 1962. Contribution a·l'étude des skarns de Kamioka, préfecture de Gifu, Japon. *J. Fac. Sci. Univ. Tokyo*, 14(1): 152–177.

Fourmarier, P., 1959. Le granite et les déformations mineures des roches (schistosite, microplissement, etc.). *Mém. Acad. R. Belg.*, 31: 5–101.

Fourmarier, P. and Anthonioz, P. M., 1963. Remarques au sujet des schistes cristallins et des migmatites de la vallée de la Gartempe (Basse Marche, France). *Bull. Acad. R. Belg. 5e Sér.*, 49: 760–768.

Fyfe, W. S., Turner, F. J. and Verhoogen, J., 1958. Metamorphic reactions and metamorphic facies. *Geol. Soc. Am., Mem.*, 73: 259 pp.

Gansser, A. and Gyr, Th., 1964. Über Xenolithschwärme aus dem Bergeller Massiv und Probleme der Intrusion. *Eclogae Geol. Helv.*, 57: 577–598.

Gavelin, S., 1960. On the relations between kinetometamorphism and metasomatism in granitization. *Geol. Fören. Stockholm Förh.*, 82: 230–269.

Geijer, P., 1912. Basische Schlierengebilde in einigen nordschwedischen Syeniten. *Geol. Fören. Stockholm Förh.*, 34: 197–201.

Geijer, P., 1916. On the intrusion mechanism of the Archean granites of central Sweden. *Bull. Geol. Inst. Univ. Uppsala*, 15:47.

Gerlach, H. and Heller, S., 1966. Über künstliche Flüssigkeitseinschlüsse in Steinsalzkristallen. *Ber. Dtsch. Ges. Geol. Wiss.*, 11(2): 195–214.

Golding, H. G. and Conolly, J. R., 1962. Stylolites iw volcanic rocks. *J. Sediment. Petrol.*

Goldschmidt, V. M., 1911. Die Kontaktmetamorphose im Kris-

tianiagebiet. *Videnskapsselsk. Skr., 1, Mat, Naturv. Kl., Kristiania*, 1: 226 pp.

Goldschmidt, V. M., 1920. Über die Injektionsgneise des Stavangergebietes. *Videnskapsselsk. Skr., 1, Mat. Naturv. Kl., Kristiania*, 10: 142 pp.

Goldschmidt, V. M., 1922. Über die metasomatischen Processe in Silikatgesteinen. *Naturwissenschaften*, 1922: 1–8.

Goldschmidt, V. M., 1954. *Geochemistry*. Clarendon Press, Oxford, 288 pp.

Goldsmith, J. R., 1952. Diffusion in plagioclase feldspars. *J. Geol.*, 60: 288–291.

Goodspeed, G. E., 1948a. Origin of granites. *Geol. Soc. Am., Mem.*, 28: 55–78.

Goodspeed, G. E., 1948b. Xenoliths and skialiths. *Am. J. Sci.*, 246: 515–525.

Graton, L. C., 1940. Nature of the ore-forming fluid. *Econ. Geol.*, 35: 205.

Green, A. H., 1882. *Physical Geology*.

Gruner, J. W., 1951–52 ,Ne data of syntheses of uranium minerals. *U.S. Atomic Energy Comm., Ann. Rep.*, 1951–1952, R.M.O. 983.

Grigoriev, D. P. and Luschnikov, V. G., 1962. Die Kristallisation von Quartz auf Pegmatit und Granit. *Ber. Geol. Ges. Berl.*, 7(4): 519–532.

Grubenmann, U., 1910. *Die Kristallinen Schiefer*. Bornträger, Berlin, 2nd ed., 298 pp.

Grubenmann, U and Niggli, P., 1924. *Die Gesteinsmetamorphose*. Bornträger, Berlin, 538 pp.

Guitard, G., 1963. Sur l'importance de l'orthogneiss derivant du métamorphisme d'anciens granites parmi les gneiss oeilles du Canigou (Pyrenées orientales). *Compt. Rend. Soc. Géol. France*, 4: 130.

Guyot, W. and Paulitsch, P., 1967. Die Quarzmaxima am Röntgen-Universaldrehtisch. *Naturwissenschaften*, 54(4): 88.

Gyr, T. and Gansser, A., 1964. Über Xenolithschwärme aus dem Bergeller Massiv und Probleme der Intrusion. *Eclogae Geol. Helv.*, 57: 577–598.

Harder, H. and Flehmig, W., 1967. Bildung von Quarz aus verdünnten Lösungen bei niedrigen Temperaturen. *Naturwissenschaften*, 54(6): 140.

Harker, A., 1909. *The Natural History of Igneous Rocks*.

Harker, A., 1932 (1950). *Metamorphism*. Methuen, London, pp. 362.

Härme, M., 1958. Examples of the granitization of plutonic rocks. *Bull. Comm. Géol. Finl.*, 30: 45–64.

Härme, M., 1959. Examples of the granitization of gneisses. *Bull. Comm. Géol. Finl.*, 184: 41–58.

Härme, M., 1962. An example of anatexis. *Bull. Comm. Géol. Finl.*, 204: 113–125.

Härme, M., 1965. On the potassium migmatites of southern Finland. *Bull. Comm. Géol. Finl.*, 212: 1–43.

Härme, M., 1966. Experimental anatexis and genesis of migmatites: a reply. *Beitr. Mineral. Petrogr.*, 12: 13–14.

Harry, W. T., 1951. The migmatites and feldspar-porphyroblast rock of Glen Dessarry, Inverness-shire. *Q. J. Geol. Soc. Lond.*, 107: 137–158.

Harvey, R. D., 1931. The geometrical pattern of contacts in determinative paragenesis. *Econ. Geol.*, 26: 764.

Heritsch, H., Paulitsch, P. and Höller, H., 1962. Über Schriftgranitquarze. 8(1): 152–165. (Sonderdr.)

Hills, H. S., 1953. *Outlines of Structural Geology*. Methuen, London, 182 pp.

Hintze, C., 1904. *Handbuch der Mineralogie, 1/2.*   1347 pp.

Hirota, S., 1952. Some considerations of the mode of formation of certain "granitoid migmatites" of Hidaka metamorphic zone, Hokkaido. *J. Geol. Soc. Japan*, 58: 163–164.

Hoenes, D., 1940. Magmatische Tätigkeit, Metamorphose und Migmatitbildung im Grundgebirge des südwestlichen Schwarzwaldes. *Neues Jahrb. Mineral. Petrogr., Abt. A*, 76: 153–256.

Hoenes, D., 1948. Petrogenese im Grundgebirge des Südschwarzwaldes. *Heidelb. Beitr. Mineral. Petrogr.*, 1(2/3): 121–202.

Högbom, A. G., 1899. Über einige Mineralverwachsungen. *Bull. Geol. Inst. Univ. Uppsala*, 3: 314.

Holmes, A., 1936. Transfusion of quartz xenoliths in alkali basic and ultrabasic lavas of southwest Uganda. *Mineral. Mag.*, 24: 408–421.

Holmes, A., 1945. Natural history of granite. *Nature*, 155: 412.

Holmes, A., 1964. *Principles of Physical Geology*. 1288 pp.

Holmes, A. and Reynolds, D. L., 1947. A front of metasomatic metamorphism in the Dalradian of Co. Donegal. *Compt. Rend. Soc. Géol. Finl.*, 20: 25–65.

Holmquist, P. J., 1901. Om Rapakiwistruktur og granitstruktur. *Geol. Fören. Stockholm Förh.*, 23: 150.

Hoppe, G., 1957. Das Erscheinungsbild der akzessorischen Zirkone des Lausitzer Granodiorits von Wiesa. *Geologie*, 6: 289–305.

Hoppe, G., 1962a. Petrogenetisch auswertbare morphologische Erscheinungen an akzessorischen Zirkonen. *Neues Jahrb. Mineral., Abh.*, 98: 35–50.

Hoppe, G., 1962b. Die akzessorischen Zirkone aus Gesteinen des Bergeller und des Adamello-Massivs. *Chem. Erde*, 22: 245–263.

Hoppe, G., 1962c. Die Formen des akzessorischen Apatits. *Ber. Geol. Ges. D.D.R.*, 7(2): 233–235.

Hoppe, G., 1963. Die Verwertbarkeit morphologischer Erscheinungen an akzessorischen Zirkonen zu petrographischen Auswertungen. *Abh. Dtsch. Akad. Wiss. Berl., Kl. Bergbau Hüttenw. Montangeol.*, 1: 1–130.

Hoppe, G., 1964. Morphologische Untersuchungen als Beiträge zu einigen Zirkon-Altersbestimmungen. *Neues Jahrb. Mineral., Abh.*, 102: 89–106.

Hoppe, G., 1966. Zirkone aus Granuliten. *Ber. Dtsch. Ges. Geol. Wiss., Beil. Mineral., Lagerstättenf.*, 11(1): 47–81.

Hutton, J. 1788. *Theory of the Earth*. R. Soc. Edinburgh, Edinburgh.

Hutton, J., 1795. *The Theory of the Earth*. R. Soc. Edinburgh, Edinburgh.

Issamuchamedow, I. M., 1961. Die Rolle der Assimilation in der Petrogenese. *Geologie*, 3: 133–150.

Johansen, A., 1923. Zur Kinematik der eutektischen Kristallisation. *Sitzungsber. Preuss. Akad. Wiss. Berl.*, 1923: 208.

Jones, K. A., 1961. Origin of albite porphyroblasts in rocks of the Ben More-Am Binnein area, western Perthshire, Scotland. *Geol. Mag.*, 98: 41–55.

Jost, W., 1937. *Diffusion und Chemische Reaktion von Festen Stoffen*. Dresden, Leipzig.

Kennedy, G. W., 1944. The hydrothermal solubility of silica. *Econ. Geol.*, 39: 25–36.

Kidd, D. F. and Haycock, M. H., 1935. Mineralogy of the ores of Great Bear Lake. *Bull. Geol. Soc. Am.*, 46: 879–960.

King, B. C., 1965. The nature and origin of migmatites: metasomatism or anatexis. in: W. S. Pitcher and G. W. Flinn (Editors), *Controls of Metamorphism, 11*. Oliver and Boyd, Edinburgh-London, pp. 219–234.

Kizaki, K., 1953. On the gneisses and migmatites of the central Hidaka metamorphic zone. *J. Geol. Soc. Japan*, 59: 203–215.

Koch, W., 1939. Metatexis und Metablastesis in Migmatiten des nordwestlichen Thüringer Waldes. *Mineral. Petrogr. Mitt.*, 51: 1–101.

Köhler, A., 1948. Erscheinungen an Feldspäten in ihrer Bedeutung für die Klärung der Gesteinsgenesis. *Tschermaks Mineral. Petrogr. Mitt., 3. Folge*, 1(1): 51–67.

Kranck, E. H. and Oja, R. V., 1960. Experimental studies of anatexis. *Int. Geol. Congr., 21st, Copenhagen, 1960, Rep. Session Norden*, 14: 16–29.

Kraus, G., 1963. Das Apatit-Zirkon-Gefüge in den Wirtmineralen Hornblende und Biotit effusiver und "granitischer" Gesteine. *Tschermaks Mineral. Petrogr. Mitt., 3. Folge*, 8: 335–360.

Kropotkin, P. N., 1940. On the origin of granites. *Sovjet Geol.*, 9: 32–43 (in Russian).

Kushiro, I., Nakamura, Y. and Akimoto, S. 1970. Fractional crystallization of some lunar mafic magmas and generation of granitic liquid.

Lacroix, A., 1898/99. Le granite des Pyrénées et ses phénomènes de contact. *Bull. Serv. Carte Géol. France*, 10(64): 241–308.

Langerfeldt, H., 1961. Über Syenitbildung durch Palingenese und Kalifeldspat-Metablastesis im mittleren Schwarzwald. *Jahrb. Geol. Landesamt Baden-Württemb.*; 5: 19–51.

Laves, F., 1951. A revised orientation of microcline and its geometrical relation to albite and cryptoperthites. *J. Geol.*, 59: 510–511.

Laves, F. and Soldatos, K., 1963. Die Albit-Mikroklin-Orientierungs-Beziehungen in Mikroklinperthiten und deren genetische Deutung. *Z. Kristallogr.*, 118(1/2): 69–102.

Lemmlejn, G. G., 1929. Der Prozess des Ausheilens von Rissen in Kristallen und die Umwandlung der Hohlformen in sekundäre Einschlüsse. *Dokl. Akad. Nauk. S.S.S.R.*, 78.

Leutwein, F., 1957. Alter und paragenetische Stellung der Pechblende erzgebirgischer Lagerstätten: *Mitt. Mineral. Inst. Bergakad. Freiburg*, 75: 797–805.

Levicki, O. D., 1955. On the question of the importance of colloidal solutions during the deposition of ores. Basic problems in science. On magmatogenic ore-deposits. *Izv. Akad. Nauk. S.S.S.R.*, 1955: 312–334 (in Russian).

Lewinson-Lessing, F., 1933. Über die Raumbildung grosser flacher Intrusivlager. *Tschermaks Mineral. Petrogr. Mitt.*, 43: 271–282.

Lyell, C., 1830. *Principles of Geology, 1*. John Murray, London, 511 pp.

Lyell, C., 1833. *Principles of Geology, 2*. John Murray, London, 35d ed., 655 pp.

Lyell, C., 1838. *Elements of Geology*. John. Murray, London.

Lyell, C., 1875. *Principles of Geology, 3*. John Murray, London, 12th ed., 652 pp.

MacGregor, M. and Wilson, G., 1939. On granitization and associated processes. *Geol. Mag.*, 76: 193.

Machatschki, F., 1953. *Spezielle Mineralogie auf geochemischer Grundlage*. Springer, Vienna, 378 pp.

Mackenzie, W. S. and Smith, J. V., 1955. The alkali feldspars, 1. Orthoclase-microperthites. *Am. Mineral.*, 40: 707–732.

Mäkinen, E., 1913. Die Granitpegmatite von Tamela in Finnland und ihre Mineralien. *Bull. Comm. Géol. Finl.*, 35: 28.

Marmo, V., 1956. On the emplacement of granites. *Am. J. Sci.*, 254: 479–492.

Marmo, V., 1958. The problem of late-kinematic granites. *Schweiz. Mineral. Petrogr. Mitt.*, 38: 19–42.

Marmo, V., 1968. On the granite problem. *Earth Sci. Rev.*, 3: 7–29.

Marmo, V., 1971. *Granite Petrology and the Granite Problem*. Elsevier, Amsterdam, 244 pp.

Mayo, E. B., 1941. Deformation in the interval Mt. Lyell–Mt. Whitney, California. *Bull. Geol. Soc. Am.*, 52: 1001.

Means, W. D., 1963. Comments on dynamic interpretation of faulting. *N.Z. J. Geol. Geophys.*, 8(5): 757–768.

Mehnert, K. R., 1940. Über Plagioklas-Metablastesis im mittleren Schwarzwald. *Neues Jahrb. Mineral., Monatsh.,* 1940: 47–65.

Mehnert, K. R., 1959. Der gegenwärtige Stand des Granitproblems. *Fortschr. Mineral.,* 37: 117–206.

Mehnert, K. R., 1962. Zur Systematik der Migmatite. *Kristallinikum,* 1: 95–110.

Mehnert, K. R., 1968. *Migmatites.* Elsevier Amsterdam, 393 pp.

Michel-Levy, A., 1874. Structure microscopique der roches acides anciennes. Granite porphyroïde de Vire. *Bull. Soc. Géol. France,* 3: 201.

Michot, P., 1961. Struktur der Mesoperthite. *Neues Jahrb. Mineral., Abh.,* 96: 213–216; 227.

Milch, L. and Riegner, F., 1910. Über basische Konkretionen und verwandte Konstitutions-facies im Granit von Striegau. *Neues Jahrb. Mineral. Petrogr.,* 29: 359–405.

Misch, P., 1949a. Metasomatic granitization of batholithic dimensions. *Am. J. Sci.,* 247: 209–245.

Misch, P., 1949b. Static granitization in Slieku area, northwestern Yunnan, China. *Am. J. Sci.,* 247: 372–406.

Misch, P., 1949c. Relationship of synkinematic and static granitization. *Am. J. Sci.,* 247: 673–705.

Moorhouse, W. W., 1956. The paragenesis of the accessory minerals. *Econ. Geol.,* 51: 248–262.

Mosebach, R., 1955. Neue Ergebnisse auf dem Gebiet der Hydrothermalen Forschung *Chem. Z.,* 79(17)

Mügge, O., 1903. Die regelmässigen Verwachsungen von Mineralen verschiedener Art. *Neues Jahrb. Mineral.,* 16: 391.

Mügge, O., 1917. Weiterwachsen von Orthoklas im Ackerboden. *Zbl. Mineral.,* 1917: 121–123.

Mügge, O., 1921. Über Quarz als geologisches Thermometer und die Bedeutung des Zusammensetzungsfläche von Zwillingen. *Zbl. Mineral.,* 1921: 609.

Neuerburg, G. J., 1957. Origin of porphyroblasts. *Bull. Geol. Soc. Am.,* 68: 653–654.

Nickel, E., 1953. Zur Perthitbildung durch Plagioklasresorption bei Kalifeldspatblastese. *Neues Jahrb. Mineral. Petrogr., Monatsh.,* 1953: 246–264.

Niggli, P., 1942. Das Problem der Granitbildung. *Schweiz. Mineral. Petrogr. Mitt.,* 22(1): 1–84.

Niggli, P. and Beger, P. J., 1923. *Gesteinen und Mineral-provinzen.* Bornträger, Berlin, 574 pp.

Noble, J. A., 1952. Evaluation of criteria for the forcible intrusion of magma. *J. Geol.,* 60: 34–57.

Nockolds, S. R., 1947. The granitic cotectic curve. *Geol. Mag.,* 84: 19–28.

Nordenskjöld, J., 1910. Der Pegmatit von Itterby. *Bull. Geol. Inst. Univ. Uppsala,* 9: 203.

Oen, J. S., 1968. Magnesium-metasomatism in basic hornfelses near Farminhão, Viseu district (northern Portugal). *Chem. Geol.,* 3: 249–279.

Oftedahl, I., 1964. On the occurrence and distribution of boron in pegmatite. *Norsk. Geol. Tidsskr.,* 44(2): 217–225.

Palm, Q. A., 1960. Wet and dry regional metamorphism. *Geol. Mijnbouw,* 22: 244–252.

Paraskevopoulos, G. M., 1953. Beitrag zur Kenntnis der Feldspäte der Tessiner Pegmatite. *Tschermaks. Mineral. Petrogr. Mitt., 3. Folge,* 3(3): 191–271.

Paulitsch, P., 1966. Die optische Quarzundulation aus verschiedenen Paragenesen am Röntgen-Universaldrehtisch kristallographisch definiert. *Jahrb. Geol. Landesamt.,* 8: 7–11.

Paulitsch, P. and Ambs, H., 1963. Undulation in Quarzgeröllen. *Mineral. Petrog. Mitt.,* 8(4): 579–590.

Perrin, R., 1954. Granitization, metamorphism and volcanism. *Am. J. Sci.,* 252: 449–465.

Perrin, R., 1956. Granite again. *Am. J. Sci.,* 254: 1–18.

Perrin, R. and Roubault, M., 1937. Les reactions a l'état solide et la géologie. *Bull. Serv. Carte Géol. Algérie, 5me Sér., Petrogr.,* 4:1–168.

Perrin, R. and Roubault, M., 1939. Le granite et les reactions a l'état solide. *Bull. Serv. Carte Géol. Algérie, 5me Sér.,* 4: 1.

Perrin, R. and Roubault, M., 1949. On the granite problem. *J. Geol.,* 57: 357–379.

Pieruccini, R., 1955. Eaux juveniles ou eaux fossiles? Une nouvelle hypothèse sur l'origine des eaux thermales et sur les causes de leur thermalisme en relation avec les recentes théories sur l'orogénèse géosynclinale. *Rev. Pathol. Gen. Comparee,* 665: 283–293.

Pieruccini, R., 1960. Il ruolo geochimico dell'energia fossile in relazione al problema della genesi del granito. *Sicilia-Messina.*

Pieruccini, R., 1961. Su di un particolare processo pseudomorfico: la transformazione dell'augite in termini plagioclasici. *Sicilia-Messina.,* 0: 3–26.

Pieruccini, R., 1962. Einige in der Theorie und Praxis gewonnene geochemische Erkenntnisse über das Verhalten des Wassers bei der metamorphitischen Umwandlung von vulkanischen Tuffen und Sedimentgesteinen. *Ber. Geol. Ges. D.D.R. Erfurt, Sonderh.,* 1: 117–144.

Poldervaart, A., 1955, 1956. Zircon in rocks, 1. Sedimentary rocks; 2. Igneous rocks. *Am. J. Sci.,* 253: 433–461; 254: 521–554.

Popoff, B., 1928. Mikroskopische Studien am Rapakiwi. *Fennia.,* 50: 1–43.

Quirke, T. T., 1927. Killarney gneisses and migmatites. *Bull. Geol. Soc. Am.,* 38: 753–766.

Raguin, E., 1949. Aspects de la formation de granite. *Jaarb. Mijnbouwk. Ver. Delft,* 1948/49.

Raguin, E., 1957. *Géologie du Granite.* Masson, Paris, 275 pp.

Raguin, E., 1965. *Geology of Granite.* Interscience, New York, N.Y., 312 pp.

Ramberg, H., 1952. *The Origin of Metamorphic and Metasomatic Rocks.* Univ. Chicago Press, Chicago, Ill., 317 pp.

Ramberg, H., 1962. Intergranular precipitation of albite formed by unmixing at alkali feldspar. *Neues Jahrb. Mineral., Abh.,* 98 (1): 14–34.

Ramdohr, P., 1958. Weitere Untersuchungen über radioaktive Höfe und andere radioaktive Einwirkungen auf natürliche Mineralien. *Abh. Dtsch. Akad. Wiss. Berlin, Kl. Chem. Geol. Biol.,* 4: 1–9.

Ramdohr, P., 1960. *Die Erzmineralien und ihre Verwachsungen.* Akad. Verlag, Berlin

Ramdohr, P. and Strunz, H., 1967. *Lehrbuch der Mineralogie.* Ferdinand Enke, Stuttgart, 820 pp.

Ramsauer, H., 1941. *Achsenverteilungsanalysen an Quarztektoniten.* Inst. Mineral. Petrogr., Innsbruck.

Read, H. H., 1943/44. Meditations on granite. *Proc. Geol. Assoc.,* 54: 64–85; 55: 45–93.

Read, H. H., 1948. Granites and granites. *Geol. Soc. Am., Mem.,* 28: 1–19.

Read, H. H., 1951. Metamorphism and granitization. In: *Alex.du Toit Memorial Lectures, 2 – Trans. Geol. Soc. S.Africa.,* 54: 1–17.

Read, H. H., 1957. *The Granite Controversy.,* Murby, London, 430 pp.

Reinhard, M., 1935. Über Gesteinsmetamorphose in den Alpen. (Auszug aus einem Vortrag in der Mijnbouwk. Ver. Delft), 39 pp.

Reinhard, M., 1943. Über die Entstehung des Granits. *Basler Universitätsreden,* 16: 1–38.

Remy, H., 1955/57. *Lehrbuch der anorganischen Chemie,* 1, 2. Leipzig; 1, 9. Aufl., 1957; 2, 8. Aufl., 1955.

Reynolds, D. L., 1943. Granitization of hornfelsed sediments in the Newry granodiorite of Goraghwood Quarry, Co. Armagh. Ibid. 48, sect. B, 231.

Reynolds, D. L., 1946. The sequence of geochemical changes leading to granitization. Q. J. Geol. Soc. Lond., 102: 389–446.

Reynolds, D. L., 1947a. The association of basic "fronts" with granitization. Sci. Pogr., 35(138): 205–236.

Reynolds, D. L., 1947b. A front of metasomatic metamorphism in the Dalradian of Co.Donegal. Compt. Rend. Soc. Géol. Finl., 20: 25–65.

Reynolds, D. L., 1947c. On the relationship between "fronts" of regional metamorphism and "fronts" of granitization. Geol. Mag., 84: 106–109.

Reynolds, D. L., 1947d. The granite controversy. Geol. Mag., 84: 209–223.

Robertson, F., 1959. Perthite formed by reorganization of albite from plagioclase during potash feldspar metasomatism. Am. Mineral., 44: 603–619.

Robinson, S. C. and Sabina, A. P., 1955. Uraninite and thorianite from Ontario and Quebec. Am. Mineral., 40: 624–633.

Rose, G., 1837. Reise nach dem Ural. 1,445.

Rosenbusch, H., 1877. Die Steiger-Schiefer und ihre Kontaktzone an den Graniten von Barr-Andlau und Hohwald. Abh. Geol. Spezialkarte Elsass-Lothringen, Strassburg., 1: 80–393.

Rosenbusch, H., 1901. Elemente der Gesteinslehre. Schweitzerbart, Stuttgart, 565 pp.

Rosenbusch, O. and Mügge, E., 1927. Mikroskopische Psysiographie der petrographisch wichtigen Mineralien, 1, 2, Schweizerbart, Freiburg, 814 pp.

Rösler, H. J., 1953. Zur Frage der Hybridität von Graniten. 2. Freib. Forschungsh., C, 35: 0 pp.

Roubault, M., 1962. Sur les porphyroblastes de feldspaths. Quelques remarques sur leur signification pétrogénetique. Norsk. Geol. Tidsskr., 42(2): 514–532.

Sabersky, P., 1891. Mineralogisch-petrographische Untersuchung argentinischer Pegmatite usw. Neues Jahrb. Mineral., Geol. Paläontol., 7: 394.

Salomon-Calvi, W., 1891. Über einige Einschlüsse metamorpher Gesteine im Tonalit. Neues Jahrb. Mineral., Geol. Paläontol., 7: 471–487.

Salomon-Calvi, W., 1908/10. Die Adamellogruppe. Abh. Geol. Reichsanst. Wien., 21(1): 1–433; 21(2): 435–603.

Sander B., 1930. Gefügekunde der Gesteine. Springer, Vienna, 352 pp.

Sander, B., 1948/50. Einführung in die Gefügekunde der geologischen Körper, 1,2. Springer, Wien-Innsbruck, 1: 215 pp; 2: 409 pp.

Sarma, S. R. and Raja, N., 1958. Some observations on the myrmekite structures in Hyderabad granites. Q. J. Geol., Mining Metal. Soc. India, 30(4): 215–220.

Sarma, S. R. and Raja, N., 1959. On myrmekite. Q. J. Geol. Mining Metal. Soc. India 31(2).

Savolahti, A., 1962. The rapakivi problem and the rules of idiomorphism in minerals. Compt. Rend. Soc. Géol. Finl., 34: 33–111.

Savolahti, A., 1963. Regeln der Kristallisation, der idiomorphen und der idioblastischen Reihenfolge und ihre Anwendbarkeit in der Petrologie. Geologie, 12: 556–567.

Schädel, J., 1961. Untersuchungen zur Bildungsfolge der Mineralien in den Drusen der Granite von Striegau (Schlesien). (Strzegom NRP.) Nova Acta Leopoldina, Neue Folge, 135: 1–32.

Schaller, W. T., 1927. Mineral replacement in pegmatites. Am. Mineral., 12: 59–63.

Scheerer, T., 1847. Discussion sur la nature plutonique du granite et des silicates cristallins qui s'y rallient. Bull. Soc. Géol. France, 2me Sér.,4: 468.

Scheumann, K. H., 1936. Zur Nomenklatur migmatitischer und verwandter Gesteine. Tschermaks Mineral. Petrogr. Mitt., 48: 297–302.

Scheumann, K. H., 1937. Metatexis und Metablastesis. Tschermaks Mineral. Petrogr. Mitt., 48: 402–412.

Scheumann, K. H., 1962. Über die Entstehung migmatitischer Gneise. Neues Jahrb. Mineral., Monatsch., 5: 106–108. 106–108.

Schloemer, H., 1962. Hydrothermal-synthetische gemeinsame Kristallisation von Orthoklas und Quarz (Untersuchungen im System $K_2O-Al_2O_3-SiO_2-H_2O$). Radex-Rundscht., 3: 133–173.

Schmidt, W., 1934. Tektonik und Verformungslehre. Bornträger, Berlin.

Scholtz, D. L., 1946. On the younger Precambrian granite plutons of the Cape Province. Proc. Geol. Soc. S. Africa, 49(35).

Sederholm, J. J., 1907. On granite and gneiss. Bull. Comm. Géol. Finl., 23: 1–110.

Sederholm, J. J., 1910. Die regionale Umschmelzung (Anatexis) erläutert an typischen Beispielen. Compt. Rend. Int. Geol. Congr., 11 me, Stockholm, 1910: 573–586.

Sederholm, J. J., 1913a. On regional granitization (or anatexis). Compt. Rend. Int. Geol. Congr., Canada, 12: 319–324.

Sederholm, J. J., 1913b. Die Entstehung der migmatitischen Gesteine. Geol. Rundsch., 4: 174–185.

Sederholm, J. J., 1913c. Über die Entstehung der migmatischer Gesteine. Geol. Rundsch., 4: 174–185.

Sederholm, J. J., 1916. On synantetic minerals and related phenomena. Bull. Comm. Géol. Finl., 48: 1–148.

Sederholm, J. J., 1923. On migmatites and associated Precambrian rocks of south-western Finland, 2. Bull. Comm. Géol. Finl., 58.

Sederholm, J. J., 1926. On migmatites and associated Pre-Cambrian rocks of south-western Finland, 3. Bull. Comm. Géol. Finl., 107.

Sederholm, J. J., 1928. On orbicular granites, spotted and nodular granites and on the rapakiwi texture. Bull. Comm. Géol. Finl., 83.

Sederholm, J. J., 1932. On the geology of Fennoskandia, with special reference to the Precambrian. Bull. Comm. Géol. Finl., 98.

Sederholm, J. J., 1934. On migmatites and associated Pre-Cambrian rocks, 3. Bull. Comm. Géol. Finl., 107: 1–68.

Sederholm, J. J., 1967. Selected Works, Granites and Migmatites. Oliver and Boyd, Edinburgh–London, 608 pp.

Seim, E., 1963. Petrologische Untersuchungen an kontaktmetasomatischen Gesteinen am Ostrand des Brockenmassivs. Z. Geol., 37 (Beiheft): 66 pp.

Shelley, D., 1963. On myrmekite. Am. Mineral., 49: 41–52.

Shelley, D., 1970. The origin of myrmekitic intergrowths and a comparison with rod-eutectics in metals. Mineral. Mag., 37(290): 674–681.

Simpson, D. R., 1962. Graphic granite from the Ramona pegmatic district, California. Am. Mineral., 47: 1123–1138.

Smekal, A., 1938. Über die Molekularvorgänge an der Elastizitätsgrenze. Phys. Z., 39: 229–230.

Smithson, S. B., 1965. Oriented plagioclase grains in K-feldspar porphyroblasts. Contrib. Geol., 4: 63–68.

Smulikowski, K., 1948. On the anatectic differentiation in granitic areas. Int. Geol. Congr., 18th, London, 1948, Rep., 131–138.

Spencer, E., 1937. Potash-soda-feldspars, thermal stability. *Mineral. Mag.*, 24: 453–494.

Steuhl, H. H., 1962. Die experimentelle Metamorphose und Anatexis eines Parabiotitgneises aus dem Schwarzwald. *Chem. Erde.*, 21: 413–449.

Stewart, D. B., 1959. Rapakivi granite from eastern Penobscot Bay, Maine. *Petrologia Mineralogia*, Sec. XIA: 293–320

Stone, M. and Austin, G. C., 1961. The metasomatic origin of the potash feldspar megacrysts in the granites of southwestern England. *J. Geol.*, 69: 464–472.

Strunz, H., 1961. Epitaxie von Uraninit auf Columbit. *Aufschluss*, 4: 81–84.

Termier, P., 1912. Sur la génèse des terrains cristallophylliens. *Compt. Rend. Congr. Géol. Int., 11me, Stockholm*, 1910: 587.

Termier, H. and Termier G., 1970. Sur une roche cristalline renfermant une écaille d'échinoderme (Massif du Tichka, Haut Atlas occidental, Maroc). *Compt. Rend. Acad. Sci.*, 270: 1092–1095.

Tilley, C. E., 1924. The facies classification of metamorphic rocks. *Geol. Mag.*, 61: 167.

Tilton, G. R., Davis, G. L., Hart, S. R., Aldrich, L. T., Steiger, R. H. and Gast, P. W., 1964. The microcline–orthoclase transition within a contact aureole. *Ann. Rep. Geophys. Lab.*, 1964: 253–256.

Tishkin, A. I., Tananayeva, G. D., Gladishev, I. V., Melnikov, I. A., Polikarpova, V. A. and Tsibulskaya, M. S., 1958. Paragenetic associations of hydrothermal uranium minerals in uranium deposits of the Soviet Union. *U.N. Int. Conf.*, 2: 445–465.

Tuttle, O. F., 1955. The origin of granite. *Sci. Am.*, 194: 77–82.

Tuttle, O. F. and Bowen, N. L., 1958. Origin of granite in the light of experimental studies in the system $NaAlSi_3O_8$ –$KAlSi_3O_8$–SiO_2–H_2O. *Geol. Soc. Am., Mem., 74*: 1–153.

Tyrell, G. W., 1955. Distribution of igneous rocks in space and time. *Bull. Geol. Soc. Am.*, 66: 405–426.

Vallerant, F., 1902. Über die Gruppierungen von Kristallen verschiedener Art. *Compt. Rend.*, 135.

Virlet (d'Aoust), 1847. Observations sur le métamorphisme normal et la probabilité de la non-existence de véritables roches primitives à la surface du globe. *Compt. Rend.*, 498.

Vogt, J. H. L., 1931. Die Genesis der Granite, physicochemisch gedeutet. *Z. Geol. Ges.*, 83: 193–214.

Von Eckermann, H., 1937. The genesis of the rapakivi granites. *Nature (Lond.)*, 59: 503.

Von Eckerman, H., 1938. The rapakivi facts, an answer to a reply. *Nature (Lond.)*, 60: 113.

Von Gaertner, H. R., 1951. Über die Alkaliquelle der Granitisierung. *Z. Dtsch. Geol. Ges.*, 103: 7–8.

Von Platen, H., 1965. Experimental anatexis and genesis of migmatites. In: W. S. Pitcher and G. W. Flinn (Editors), *Controls of Metamorphism, 10*. Oliver and Boyd, Edinburgh-London, pp. 203–218.

Von Rath, G., 1870. Geognostisch-mineralogische Fragmente aus Italien, 3. *Z. Dtsch. Geol. Ges.*, 22: 659.

Wahl, W., 1929. Eutectics and the crystallisation of the igneous rocks. *Compt. Rend. Soc. Géol. Finl.*, 2.

Walenta, K. and Pantzartzis, P., 1969. Die Molybdänglanz–Lagerstätte von Kimmeria bei Xanthi in Nordgriechenland. *Erzmetall*, 22(6): 272–278.

Wahlstrom, E. E., 1939a. Graphic granite. *Am. Mineral.*, 24(11): 681.

Wahlstrom, E. E., 1939b. Graphic granite. *Am. Mineral.*, 42: 859–888.

Walker, T. L., 1932, 1933. Plagioclase in graphic granite. *Univ. Toronto Studies Geol. Serv.*, 32: 11.

Walton, M., 1955. The emplacement of "granite". *Am. J. Sci.*, 253: 1–18.

Walton, M., 1960. Granite problems. The exploration of physical and chemical processes leads to a reorientation of our thinking. *Science*, 131: 635–645.

Wasserstein, B., 1954. Ages of uraninites by a new method. *Nature* (Lond.), 174: 1004–1005.

Wegmann, C. E., 1931. Übersicht über die Geologie des Felsgrundes im Küstengebiete zwischen Helsingfors und Onas. *Bull. Comm. Géol. Finl.*, 89: 1–65.

Wegmann, C. E., 1935a. Über einige Fragen der Tiefentektonik. *Geol. Rundsch.*, 26: 449.

Wegmann, C. E., 1935b. Zur Deutung der Migmatite. *Geol. Rundsch.*, 26: 307.

Wegmann, C. E. and Kranck, E. H., 1931. Beiträge zur Kenntnis der Svecofenniden in Finnland, 1, 2. *Bull. Géol. Finl.* 89.

Weibel, M. and Locher, Th., 1964. Die Kontaktgesteine im Albigna- und Fornostollen (Nördliches Bergeller Massiv). *Schweiz. Mineral. Petrogr. Mitt.*, 44: 157–185.

Weill, D. F. and Fyfe, W. S., 1964. The solubility of quartz in H_2O in the range 1,000–4,000 bars and 400–550°C. *Geochim. Cosmochim. Acta*, 28: 1243–1255.

Weill, D. F., McCallum, I. S., Bottinga, Y., Drake, M. J. and McKay, G. A., 1970a. Mineralogy and petrology of some Apollo 11 igneous rocks. *Apollo 11, Lunar Sci. Conf., Houston, Texas.*

Weill, D., McCallum, S., Drake, M., McKay, G. and Bottinga, Y., 1970b. Petrology of fine-grained lava from Mare Tranquillitatis. *Apollo 11, Lunar Sci. Conf., Houston, Texas.*

Wenden, H. E., 1957. Ionic diffusion and the properties of quartz, 1. The direct current resistivity. *Am. Mineral*, 42: 859–888.

Wenk, E., 1962. Das reaktivierte Grundgebirge der Zentralalpen. 52: 754–755.

Wimmenauer, W., 1963. Einschlüsse im Albtalgranit (Südschwarzwald) und ihre Bedeutung für dessen Vorgeschichte. *Neues Jahrb. Mineral, Monatsch.* 6–17.

Winkler, H. G. F., 1961. On coexisting feldspars and their temperature of crystallization. Cursillos Conf. Inst. "Lucas Mallada". 8: 9–13.

Winkler, H. G. F., 1965. *Die Genese der Metamorphen Gesteine.* Berlin–Heidelberg, 218 pp.

Winkler, H. G. F., 1967. *Petrogenesis of Metamorphic Rocks.* Springer, Berlin, 2. Aufl. 218 pp.

Winkler, H. G. F. and Von Platen, H., 1957, 1960, 1961. Experimentelle Gesteinsmetamorphose. *Geochim. Cosmochim. Acta*, 13: 42–69; 15: 91–112; 18: 294–316; 24: 48–69; 24: 250–259.

Woitschach, G., 1881. Die Granitgebirge von Königshain in der Oberlausitz. *Abhandl. Naturforsch. Ges. Görlitz*, 17.

Wyatt, M., 1954. Zircons as provenance indicators. *Am. Mineral.*, 39: 983–990.

Wyllie, P. J., Cox, K. G. and Biggar, G. M., 1962. The habit of apatite in synthetic systems and igneous rocks. *J. Petrol.*, 3: 238–243.

Yoder, H. S., 1955. Role of water in metamorphism. ("The crust of the earth".) *Geol. Soc. Am., Spec. Paper*, 62: 505–524.

Yoder, H. S., Stewart, D. B. and Smith, J. R., 1957. Ternary feldspars. *Ann. Rep. Geophys. Lab., Carnegie Inst.*, 56: 206–214.

Zeschke, G., 1964. Mineralfundstellen in Griechenland. *Aufschluss*, 15: 205–208.

References Index

Subject Index

Transfusion, 3
Transmutation, 16
Type, 87

Ultragranitisation, 87
Ultrametamorphic origin, 2
Ultrametamorphism, 3

Vectorial property, 13
Vein perthites, 42
Visco-elastic, 86
Visco-elastic body, 64
Viscosity, 86

Xenoblastic, 13
Xenocrysts, 40
Xenoliths, 16
Xenomorphic, 13, 23

Wegsamkeit (penetrability), 51